A History of the Oklahoma State University College of Education

CENTENNIAL HISTORIES SERIES

Centennial Histories Series

Committee

W. David Baird
LeRoy H. Fischer
B. Curtis Hamm
Harry Heath
Beulah Hirschlein
Vernon Parcher

Murl Rogers
J. L. Sanderson
Warren Shull
Milton Usry
Odell Walker
Eric I. Williams

Robert B. Kamm, Director
Carolyn Hanneman, Editor
Carol Hiner, Associate Editor

CENTENNIAL
1890 • 1990

A History of the Oklahoma State University College of Education

by Thomas A. Karman, Ph.D.

OKLAHOMA STATE UNIVERSITY / Stillwater

Published by Oklahoma State University
Centennial Histories Series, Stillwater, Oklahoma 74078

Library of Congress Cataloging-in-Publication Data

Karman, Thomas A.
    A history of the Oklahoma State University College of Education / by Thomas
A. Karman.
        p.   cm.—(Centennial histories series)
    Bibliography: p.
    Includes index.
    ISBN 0-914956-37-X :
    1. Oklahoma State University. College of Education—History.
I. Title.   II. Series.
LB2167.05K37   1989
370'.7'30976634—dc20

Contents

Foreword   vii

Preface   ix

1 And Then There Was None   3

2 And Then There Was One   19

3 Consolidating Gains, Confronting Challenges   43

4 On the Springboard   67

5 Building on a Firm Foundation   107

6 Seeking and Achieving Quality   133

7 Toward the Centennial Year   159

   Appendices   201

      1 Deans of the College of Education   201

      2 Faculty of the College of Education   201

      3 College of Education Scholarships   223

      4 Distinguished Alumni of the College of Education 231

      5 Kappa Delta Pi   236

      6 Education Student Council   265

   Bibliography   277

   Index   281

Foreword

The role of Oklahoma State University as an *educational* institution has been clearly understood since its founding as Oklahoma A. and M. College. Yet, the establishment of a separate discipline and a supporting academic division for the purposes of enhancing the teaching efforts of faculty and the learning experiences of students was slow in becoming reality on the campus. Although there was, from the institution's earliest days, a willingness on the parts of a few to share their educational "know how" with colleagues (largely on an overload basis), it was not until the second half of the first century of OSU's existence that a comprehensive program of educational instruction came into being. Now, at the end of its first century, OSU boasts a College of Education with state, regional, national, and international reputation for the preparation of educators. Indeed, with its Department of Aviation and Space Education, it can also be said that the college enjoys a reputation in space!

The Centennial Histories Committee was fortunate in securing Dr. Thomas A. Karman, professor and head of the Department of Educational Administration and Higher Education at OSU, to write *A History of the Oklahoma State University College of Education*. An historian and an educator, he has been able to combine appreciations, understandings, and competency in relation to both in the writing of this volume. The thoroughness of his research is especially noteworthy, as is his obvious understanding of the educational process in the preparation of teachers, counselors, and administrators at all levels.

Working closely with authors of Centennial Histories volumes are

Carolyn Hanneman, editor since March 1, 1988, and Carol Hiner, associate editor since March 21, 1988. Both bring excellent prior experience to their positions; both have an excellent vision of what the Centennial Histories Project should be, and both are deeply committed to the production of a high quality series of books. Early in the project, Judy Buchholz served ably as editor. Following her, Ann Carlson served as editor for some three and one-half years and contributed greatly to the project.

Appreciation is expressed to Mr. Dale Ross, the executive director of the Centennial Coordinating Office, who provides enthusiastic support for the Centennial Histories Project. His predecessor, as coordinator of OSU's overall centennial observance, Dr. Richard Poole, conceived the idea originally of a Centennial Histories Project, and special appreciation is expressed to him. Dr. John Campbell, OSU's president since August of 1988, generously supports the project, as did his predecessor, President Emeritus L. L. Boger. Dr. Ralph Hamilton, director of Public Information Services; Gerald Eby, head of University Publications Services; Edward Pharr, manager of University Printing Services; Heather Lloyd, librarian in Special Collections and Archives; and their respective staffs have assisted generously. Also, Dick Gilpin's dust jacket art adds much to the series.

Appreciation is also expressed to Dean Emeritus Donald Robinson, who served as dean of the College of Education during the preparation of this volume, and to his successor, Dean Kenneth King. Both were most helpful and supportive at all times.

Robert B. Kamm, Director
Centennial Histories Project
President Emeritus
Oklahoma State University

June 1989

Preface

When I was asked by Dean Donald W. Robinson to undertake writing a history of the College of Education at Oklahoma State University, I accepted the task with no small measure of fear and trepidation. Having read more than a few institutional histories, I had found many—if not most—to be catalogs of dead events. However, once into the available historical material, I found that the School and later the College of Education had and has life, vitality, drive and purpose—all the result of the dynamic people who made the institution what it is today.

The college, though, has never been an entity in a vacuum, for it has always lived within the eddies and swirls of Oklahoma Agricultural and Mechanical College, Oklahoma State University, the city of Stillwater, the state of Oklahoma, and the nation, let alone in the midst of the world of professional education at all levels. For that reason, attention has been paid to the broader context in which the college lived, whenever that was appropriate.

It would be a lie to claim that this book is the result of a single person's efforts, for without the help of countless individuals, the tale would not have been told. I would like to acknowledge the students, both graduate and undergraduate, who labored long for me in the library—Ronald Beeson, Jimmy Turner, Mike Xu, Linda Zou. I am indebted to Julia Crow for developing the material on the beginning of the Council on Teacher Education and for helping with the interviews. I would like to thank the staff in Special Collections in the Edmon Low Library for the support, camaraderie, and encouragement they supplied over many, many months—Heather Lloyd, Greg Hines, David Peters, and, above all, Kathleen Bledsoe.

In order to give me blocks of time for organizing, thinking, and writing, Gerald Bass in the Department of Educational Administration and Higher Education uncomplainingly took over most of the administration of the department for the fall of 1987 and did a great job. Likewise, I want to thank Lynn Arney, who picked up a class I usually teach in Tulsa in the fall. I would like to express appreciation to William Segall of the Department of Curriculum and Instruction in Education who helped conceptualize the effort during the early stages prior to his taking a sabbatical.

I am also grateful to Dean Robinson, who provided great moral support, who arranged for released time, and who did not even raise his voice—let alone fire me—when he learned I had interviewed him for two hours with a defective tape recorder and had to redo it.

Many of the insights into the history of the college were provided by people who lived through it and shared their experiences with me in interviews: alumni, including Bill Hindman, Marjorie Orloski, Benn Palmer, Gladys Skinner, Rose Mary Tompkins Duncan, Dorothea Hodges, Florence Ellen Conger Lowe, Anita Kezer Morton, and Kathryn Tompkins McCollom; faculty, including Harry Brobst, Richard Jungers, Haskell Pruett, Russell Babb, Della Farmer Thomas, and John Tate; and administrators, including Raymond Girod, Donald Robinson, and Helmer Sorenson.

Appreciation is also extended to all of the people who comprise the highly competent staff of the Centennial Histories Project: to Robert B. Kamm, the director of the project, president emeritus of Oklahoma State University, and prized colleague and friend; to Ann Carlson, who was serving as editor when work began on this volume; to the current editors Carolyn Hanneman and Carol Hiner; and to graphic designer Gayle Hiner.

In writing a work of any size, the author can develop a myopia regarding organization and emphasis, and I am grateful to the people who read the text in draft form and offered very valuable insights—Dr. Kamm, Idella Lohmann, Betty Abercrombie, Dr. Sorenson, Ralph Brann, Thomas Smith, and Kenneth King.

Special thanks go to Betty Rutledge, who put up with me throughout the project, who keyboarded interviews and text, and who doggedly made sure all the endnotes were in the right order. If her cheery smile, quick laugh, and highly professional skills had not been here, the work would have been a real burden. Thanks also go to Sherril Mitchell and Brenda Brown who compiled the student lists and index, respectively.

Finally, I would like to dedicate this book to the people who made it possible and who hold the future in their hands—the educators of

Oklahoma.

Despite the mountain of assistance from those I have named and from others, this study has many faults. For all errors of commission and omission, I alone am responsible.

Thomas A. Karman
Professor and Head
Educational Administration and
Higher Education

June 1989

A History of the Oklahoma State University College of Education

1 And Then There Was None

Corporations are not necessarily soulless; and of all corporations universities are the most likely to have, if not souls, at least personalities. Perhaps the reason is that universities are, after all, largely shaped by presidents and professors. Presidents and professors, especially if they are good ones, are fairly certain to be men of distinctive, not to say eccentric, minds and temperaments. A professor, as the German saying has it, is a man who thinks otherwise.

Cornell University: Founders and the Founding by Carl Becker

Oklahoma is a state filled with contrasts. It has a highly varied geography, ranging from the green and heavily wooded southeast, through the rolling prairie of the center of the state, to the high and relatively dry mesas of the northwest and the Panhandle. Claiming the longest shoreline of any state in the nation, Oklahoma also sports a desert. Dotted with tiny towns, it also has the metropolitan and cosmopolitan centers of Oklahoma City and Tulsa. Known for cattle, wheat, and oil, it now strives to develop tourism and high-tech industry more fully. Oklahoma also has a highly developed and highly coordinated state system of higher education. The flagship of that system is Oklahoma State University.

After a century, the university has a student body of 20,000 plus; has campuses in Oklahoma City, Okmulgee, and Tulsa, in addition to Stillwater; is a major power delivering course work especially in education and business at the thriving University Center at Tulsa; and is a member of the Big Eight Athletic Conference. The sprawling, beautifully landscaped Stillwater campus encompasses 519 acres on which approximately 80 buildings stand. Sprawling from the east at Knoblock and University (previously called College) to the west past Hester, Washington, and Monroe Streets, the main campus has facilities beyond Western Road. The southern limit of the campus is edged by Campus Corner, "The Strip," and rows of fraternity and sorority houses. On the northeast corner of the campus is the recently refurbished Gallagher-Iba Arena and the Allie P. Reynolds Stadium. Nestled between these sites of athletic prowess is the sturdy Bennett Complex. To the northwest is a vast expanse of married student housing apartments, an extensive physical plant warehouse, and the internationally known fire service publications and training facilities. Of course, OSU conducts research and instruction at many sites on the west side of Stillwater and has facilities and land scattered throughout Oklahoma.

OSU is the home of eight self-standing colleges, one of which is the College of Education, the focal point of this book. Each college is headed by a dean. With the exception of the Graduate College, each one is organized by academic departments and offers comprehensive curricula that lead to degrees at both the undergraduate and the graduate levels. Going beyond resident instruction, each college has highly developed programs of research, both pure and applied, and public service or extension.

This university, which had small beginnings, is not only a place of education, research, and service, it is in itself a small city. In student housing, OSU has a hotel/motel/condominium operation that private rental owners would envy; it has a food service that would rival many major franchises—5,718 meals bought, served, and usually eaten each day. This was a far cry from 1913, when Oklahoma A. and M. College hooted that the dorm bunch boosted the local economy because they consumed $50 worth of food daily. In addition to counseling services, the university has a security force to keep the peace and a foundation to help fund scholarships. There is also a placement service to assist graduates in securing jobs. This mini-city has a president, four vice presidents, deans and associate deans, as well as organized advisory councils representing faculty, staff, and students.

Slightly over a century ago, the land which was to become Oklahoma was still virgin territory, regarded as unsuitable for habitation by the civilized white man. In fact, the region was designated as Indian Territory. The territory became the home of the Five Civilized Tribes after they were forcibly removed from the southeastern part of the United States and marched to the area. Following the Civil War, these Indians relinquished much of their land to the federal government which, in turn, used the land on which to settle various Plains Indian tribes. While the Indians had been required to relocate to Indian Territory against their will, the area nonetheless became increasingly attractive to white men as they viewed a gradually dwindling frontier.

Although barred by federal law from entering and settling the Unassigned Lands which had been assigned to no tribe, aggressive frontiersmen were not prone to worry much about such technicalities. The Boomers slipped across the border and staked out homesteads, only to be forced out again periodically by federal troops. One of the areas that was highly attractive to these pioneers was in present north-central Oklahoma on the banks of Stillwater Creek, so called because when other streams dried up, it continued to run.

While the Boomers and troops did their dance of acquisition and eviction over and over again, pressure built to open the Unassigned Lands to the white man. It was simply a matter of time before the federal government consented to the first of a series of famous land runs that saw the area flooded with new and eager settlers. On April 22, 1889, the Unassigned Lands was opened to homesteaders. Communities were born literally overnight, although they were little more than collections of tents.

In 1890, the federal government passed the Organic Act which created Oklahoma Territory (the six counties of the Unassigned Lands and the Panhandle) and provided for a territorial government. Almost as quickly as the land itself was staked out and claimed, communities—such as they were—attempted to stake out claims that would help assure the success of the community itself. For example, Guthrie laid claim to be the territorial capital while Kingfisher fought to be selected as the site for the penitentiary. The leaders of Stillwater were at first unsure which agency of government they wanted. Fourteen Republicans, eight

In January 1890, Stillwater was a collection of ramshackle, clapboard buildings in the middle of the prairie. Indeed, the village exhibited few characteristics of permanence. Yet, the community was fortunate to have townspeople who could "see" into the future. With civic pride, political savvy, and a willingness to continue despite the odds, the people of Stillwater sought and won a prized plum—the agricultural and mechanical college.

Democrats, and four People's Party Alliance (Populists) members were elected to the house of representatives. The council had seven Republicans, five Democrats, and one Populist member. Of the five Populist members of the legislature, four were from Payne County. At the opening of the first legislative assembly on August 28, 1890, the Republican majority split along townsite lines and was not able to organize leadership. In the council, the nearly equal representation made organization impossible. As a result, the Populist members dominated both houses, even though a minority. After spirited debate, it was eventually agreed that the county would forget about seeking the capital and opt instead for the agricultural and mechanical college. After a brief battle against Perkins as the site for the college, Stillwater was victorious, but only if the city's leaders could raise money and acquire land. Interestingly, while Guthrie became the territorial capital, it eventually lost as the site of the state capital to Oklahoma City. Also, McAlester ultimately won the penitentiary.

The city fathers of Stillwater had no small task to accomplish, for the legislature required eighty acres of land and $10,000 before it would finalize placing the college in Stillwater. The citizens rallied to the cause. Several went together to deed a total of 200 acres for the purpose of establishing a college, thereby exceeding the legislature's requirement for real estate by two and a half times. But land in Oklahoma was far more plentiful than money. To raise the required funds, ten bonds for $1,000 each were sold at a discount, which meant the cash available was less than the amount stipulated by the political leaders. Not to be daunted, Stillwater's citizens came up with cash to make up the difference, proceeded

Robert Barker was installed as the first president of Oklahoma Agricultural and Mechanical College when the institution was struggling not only to survive but also to establish an agricultural and mechanical program along with the supporting liberal arts. During his tenure, formal programs in education were not regarded as being within the sphere of the college's mission.

to notify the powers in Guthrie, and got the school—officially named "The Agricultural and Mechanical College of the Territory of Oklahoma."

Although any public college or university of necessity is tied to a greater or lesser degree to the politics of the state in which it is located, Oklahoma A. and M. College was essentially a political pawn at least until it had a president appointed who was himself so strong politically that governors hesitated to interfere. In 1890, no such buffer was in place. Consequently, there were strong and obvious ties from the governor's office and the legislature to the college's board of trustees and from the board to the college itself. The legislation which established the college stipulated that the board would consist of five people appointed by the governor with the advice and consent of the legislature. In addition, the governor was to serve as a sixth member ex officio. In the event that an Oklahoma Board of Agriculture were created, that agency would be granted the right to forward the names of two people to serve on the college board, and those people were to be appointed automatically by the governor.[1]

In 1890, Governor George Steele nominated Robert Barker (a forty-two-year-old farmer from Logan County), J. P. Lane (a thirty-eight-year-old minister from Cleveland County), Arthur Daniels (speaker of the house of representatives from Canadian County), and John Wimberly (a twenty-four-year-old farmer from Kingfisher County). All four were members of the legislature; Barker and Lane were Republicans while Daniels was a Populist, and Wimberly was a Democrat. The fifth seat was filled by Amos Ewing, a Republican railroad employee from Kingfisher County. Ironically, only Speaker Daniels failed to be confirmed by the legislature.

Having tied the board to the legislature, the next step was to link the board with the college. This was accomplished when Barker, Ewing, and Lane met in a Guthrie hotel in June of 1891 and elected Barker as the first president and secretary of the college and Ewing as the first treasurer.

The faculty of 1891 was small. Under the circumstances, President Barker taught moral and mental science. He was joined by James C. Neal as professor of natural science, Alexander C. Magruder as professor of agriculture and horticulture, Lewis J. Darnell as tactician and commandant, and Edward F. Clark as professor of English literature and mathematics. Although other faculty were added as resources allowed, and although Professor Clark also served as the principal of the preparatory school, faculty oriented toward the field of education as a profession were obvious in their absence.

It was clear that the original mission of the college was to educate the sons and daughters of the citizens of the territory to be useful mem-

When Oklahoma Agricultural and Mechanical College opened its doors to students, the college owned no door of its own and had to launch classes downtown in the Congregational Church. Over time, the ties between the college and the religious community were maintained, and once the School of Education was added to the college, a healthy program in Christian education was a part of that school.

bers of an agrarian society. In fact, the enabling legislation specified: "The design of the institution is to afford practical instruction in agriculture and the natural sciences connected therewith, and also the sciences which bear directly upon all industrial arts and pursuits. The course of instruction shall embrace the English language and literature, mathematics, civil engineering, agricultural chemistry, animal and vegetable anatomy and physiology, the veterinary arts, entomology, geology and such other natural sciences as may be prescribed; political, rural, and household economy, horticulture, moral philosophy, history, bookkeeping and especially the application of science and the mechanical arts to practical agricultural in the field."[2]

Although there appears to be no logical reason for listing the courses in the order in which they appeared, the statement began and ended with an emphasis on agriculture, as was appropriate for an agricultural and mechanical college. From the list one can foresee the beginnings of what would eventually develop into the Colleges of Agriculture, Arts and Sciences, Business, Engineering, Home Economics, and Veterinary Medicine. These are the current undergraduate and professional colleges, with the exception of the College of Education.

Having land but no buildings, classes were first taught in local churches with very few students and even fewer faculty. At the time of the golden anniversary of the Oklahoma A. and M. College, Frank D. Northup, editor of the *Stillwater Gazette*, reflected on the first days: "No buildings for the purpose, classes were held in downtown churches, not the structures of the time this is written, but flimsy, unpainted affairs, siding nailed to studding, no inside sheeting, plastering, or naturally papering. In winter they were uncomfortable, heated by a wood-burning stove near the center. In summer the winds sifted dust over students, seats, and books with indiscriminate regularity. Outside sanitation, inside discomfort, dust, the muddy streets, a few board sidewalks limited to the fronts of buildings caused no unhappiness. So, I beg you this night, feel no pity for those pioneer students, their instructors or the citizens of the community. They were enjoying privileges far in excess of the less fortunate who were unable to 'go to college,' and the faculty members had jobs paying as high as $100 monthly—a princely sum in those days.''[3]

To be sure, there was a college complete with a board, a president, a faculty, and a student body, but there was no *campus*, only a vacant plot of barren land northwest of the infant city. That made the college supporters very nervous, for they were fully aware that if political forces in the legislature shifted, the college could be relocated.[4] It was of critical importance to create a tangible campus. That was finally accomplished in 1893 when the first permanent building at Oklahoma A. and M. College—ultimately called Old Central—began to rise in all of its glory out of the treeless prairie.

Initially the building was to be located approximately where the Edmon Low Library stands and that would have lent a sense of geographic reality to the building's name. Knowing that the college would

OSU AGRICULTURAL INFORMATION

Although there was never any doubt that Oklahoma would have its agricultural and mechanical college, its location in Stillwater was not secure until Central—now Old Central—rose majestically from the virgin prairie.

never fill up all of that space, and feeling that students should not be required to walk any farther than necessary from their boarding houses in town, it was decided to place the college building as close to town as was possible but to leave the name unchanged. Somehow, "Old Central" has a more solid and collegiate ring to it than does "Old Southeast Corner." By the standards of today, it is a small building, but it was adequate for the needs of the college and meant that the discussion regarding the relocation of the college began to wane.

Starting a college only a year and a half after the territory opened up proved to be no small challenge, for all aspects of a civilized society were being developed simultaneously. The initial enrollment at Oklahoma A. and M. College was tiny, partly because higher education was an option exercised by a very small percentage of the total American population prior to World War II, partly because the population base in Oklahoma was small, and partly because the college sat at the apex of an educational "system" that for the most part did not exist. It was perfectly clear that, in order to survive, the college would not only need to offer collegiate work—limited though that was in both scope and depth—but would also need to do something to help assure that there would be a supply of students adequately prepared to benefit from higher education.

One obvious step to alleviate the problem was to establish a sub-collegiate division or preparatory school. This was by no means a novel step since colleges throughout the nation had such units either to provide a full secondary education program or to enable high school graduates to strengthen weak areas of preparation and hence to qualify for admission into higher education. In fact, when the Oklahoma A. and M. College enrolled its first crop of students, all were in the preparatory department. In 1893, the college formally presented a proposal to the board of regents which requested permission to establish the preparatory department. Subsequently, Harry E. Thompson was assigned the responsibility for developing and teaching those subjects which he believed to be necessary.[5]

By the following year, the preparatory school had proven to be so popular that Ella E. Hunter of Tarkio, Missouri, joined the staff. In her early twenties, Miss Hunter added to the cultural life of the rugged community by providing frequent piano recitals. During her brief, two-year tenure, Miss Hunter worked with the juniors while Mr. Thompson instructed the senior class in an educational program that was essentially like the common schools of the day. According to the *1893-94 College Catalog*, the collegiate population consisted of forty-one freshmen and twenty-five sophomores while the preparatory department enrolled sixty-six, which equalled the higher education students in numbers.[6]

While Mr. Thompson and Miss Hunter toiled with the pre-college

10

Oklahoma Agricultural and Mechanical College's first faculty included Harry E. Thompson (*third from left*) and Ella E. Hunter. While the professional training of teachers for Oklahoma had been assigned to the various normal schools in the state, the preparatory school—for which Thompson and Hunter were responsible— was an essential part of the Stillwater operation and, without a doubt, provided the base which enabled the college to survive during the difficult early years.

crowd, the Oklahoma A. and M. College tried to publicize itself realistically and honestly. In New York, Cornell University, a land-grant institution backed with the millions of dollars provided by Ezra Cornell, could boast of its ability to work with "Any student, Any Study"—a comprehensive program. The Stillwater institution was willing to go halfway with Cornell by serving any student. But for the curriculum: "The College provides at present, one course, known as the Agriculture course. In comparison with other courses in other colleges and universities, it would be best described as a general scientific course. It will be noted that special prominence is given to natural and economic science, and that the college has special facilities for instruction in these lines. Agricultural and horticultural studies are so closely allied with these that they form a valuable amplification of the training in the natural sciences, while at the same time the natural science form the proper basis for agricultural investigation. The object is then, first, to give a broad education, a thorough training, and a practical mental discipline."[7]

For decades, the preparatory department at Oklahoma A. and M. College had enrollments that overwhelmed those in the collegiate program, and it is debatable whether the college would have survived those early years without the foundation provided by having secondary students on campus. To illustrate the meager resources of the collegiate section of the college, one need only consider two statements printed in the catalog announcing the 1896-97 academic year. The cover of the catalog blazed forth with zeal and vigor:

FOUNDED BY THE TERRITORY—ENDOWED BY THE NATION

To give instruction in Agriculture, the Mechanical Arts, the English Language, and the various branches of Mathematical, Physical, Natural and Economic Science, with special reference to their application to the industries of life.

TUITION FREE—NO INCIDENTAL EXPENSES

Open to Both Sexes. [8]

But after assuring the reader that the college had a four-year curriculum reflecting the intent of the legislation which created it and that the program culminated in the degree of bachelor of science, the catalog noted: "As yet it has been impractical to provide for systematic instruction in the Mechanical arts."[9] While the college had existed for several years by that time, Oklahoma A. and M. was in actuality Oklahoma A. and P.—agriculture and preparatory. But the important point is that it continued.

By 1897-98, Oklahoma A. and M. had a full range of college classes and an enrollment totaling ninety-four: forty-two freshmen, seven sophomores, seven juniors, eight seniors, four postgraduates, and twenty-six special students. But by that same time, preparatory enrollment had zoomed to 125 students, giving it nearly 60 percent of the students in Stillwater.

Writing at the time of the college's fiftieth anniversary in 1941, Thompson reflected that "the brochures we taught were mostly those of the common school, including reading, spelling, writing, U.S. history, geography, arithmetic, singing, public speaking or reading. We tend in talks and lectures to teach morals and manners and respect for law and order. It was a two-year course for some. Quite a number took this training for teaching."[10]

Apparently many of the students did not complete the entire course of study, but that phenomenon was not at all unusual, especially in rural areas. Although most of the American citizens valued education and

Even after World War I, when the college was a viable institution in its own right, the preparatory—or secondary—school still flourished, partly as a way of remedying weaknesses in Oklahoma's public high schools. Included in this photograph is DeWitt Hunt (*second row, second from left*), a member of the faculty for forty years. First associated with the School of Engineering as head of the Department of Shops and later the Department of Industrial Engineering, he reaffiliated with the School of Education when industrial arts education left engineering for education.

saw it as a means of upward social and economic mobility for their children, to be able to afford it and to be able to continue with the farm without the aid of the young scholars were other matters. It was quite regular for students to attend either a common school or a college for a term, only to disappear from the campus until such time as finances and other circumstances would allow them to resume their studies. While the concept of the so-called "stop-out" gained great popularity with the rapid growth of the community/junior college movement during the 1960s, it was alive, well, and functioning during the late nineteenth and the early twentieth centuries.

For example, Jessie Thatcher Bost—for whom Thatcher Hall was named—was the first coed to graduate from Oklahoma A. and M. She was a classmate of Gertrude Diem Martin. Miss Diem came to Stillwater with her family in a covered wagon pulled by mules, taught in the Stillwater public schools in 1892-93, was able to attend college in 1893-94, dropped out in 1894, and became the first teacher in the Cleveland, Oklahoma, schools. In 1970, at the age of ninety-seven, she returned to Stillwater and wondered if a building would have been named in her honor if only she had stayed to graduate.[11]

During the 1890s, it was not uncommon for students to attend college for a term only to drop out until finances or other circumstances allowed them to resume their studies. For example, Jessie Thatcher and Gertrude Diem were classmates in 1892; Miss Thatcher became the first woman graduate of Oklahoma A. and M. in 1897, while Miss Diem dropped out to teach. In this early photo of campus personalities, Miss Thatcher is on the back row at the left while Miss Diem is on the front row at the right.

Thompson's statement also suggests that people used Oklahoma A. and M.'s preparatory department as a means to prepare not only for a collegiate education but for a teaching career. In the mid-nineteenth century, Horace Mann, then the superintendent of public instruction for the commonwealth of Massachusetts, had argued zealously for creating normal schools for the professional training of educators. In a fully developed state such as Massachusetts that idea made a great deal of sense. Even in thinly developed Oklahoma, the legislature had stipulated that the city of Edmond was to be the seat of Oklahoma's normal school, but it was also understood that formal, professional training to become an educator in the common schools—although desirable—was not essential. In a territory in which the one-room schoolhouse would dominate for many decades, it was taken for granted that older pupils could and should tutor younger pupils and that common school graduates could be bona fide teachers.

Although Oklahoma A. and M. College clearly did not regard a formal program of teacher education or a school of education to be a part of its mission—after all, Edmond had been awarded the normal school— it did not necessarily follow that graduates stayed out of that field. By 1908, Oklahoma A. and M. had graduated a total of 171 students. In a directory of alumni, 34 were listed as being educators.[12] It seemed a little ironic that nearly one in five of the alumni served as professionals in an area not recognized within the official structure of the college. Most of these graduates served as teachers or principals in small Oklahoma towns, but Mamie G. Houston was employed in Monmouth, Oregon, while Hattie I. Oschman was on the opposite side of the continent in Brooklyn, New York. Others had moved successfully into positions in other colleges.

Charles L. Kezer, a graduate of the class of 1901, had already risen to the position of superintendent of city schools for Stillwater by 1908. After receiving his B.S. at Oklahoma A. and M., Mr. Kezer proceeded to earn a life diploma from Oklahoma Central Normal, an A.B. from the University of Kansas, and an M.A. from Iowa State College. In 1919, he was employed by the Oklahoma A. and M. College as principal of the secondary school and as supervisor of practice teaching. When he retired in 1944, he was professor of secondary education and director of certification. Professor Kezer's penchant for giving true/false examinations naturally earned him the moniker of ''Professor True-False.''[13]

For the first decade and a half, the Oklahoma A. and M. College was not officially in the business of preparing people to enter the teaching profession, even though that career was selected by many graduates. However, Oklahoma A. and M. throughout its history has been especially successful at recognizing a need to be met and developing programs to address it. Finally, in 1905-06, the college for the first time

The Engineering Building (located south of present Gundersen Hall) was a part of the original quadrangle at Oklahoma Agricultural and Mechanical College. Over the years, the building was used as the annex to the library and eventually housed part of the College of Education. The building's second floor was removed after it was condemned in 1937. The structure was eventually razed.

referred to teachers as people to be taught rather than as alumni. In a section of that year's catalog which provided detailed information about the agriculture program offered by the college, a part entitled "Spring Term Course for Teachers in Natural Studies, Agriculture, and the Common Branches" noted: "To meet the rapidly growing demand for the teaching of nature study and agriculture in the public, and particularly in the rural schools, this course in those branches, together with review work in the common school studies, has been established. The expert instructors and the extensive equipment of the College in these lines assure the utmost benefit that the student can receive in so short a time. The Burkett, Stevens, and Hill text, 'Agriculture for Business', [sic] is used and lectures are given on such subjects as Garden Plots for Schools, Beautifying the School Grounds, Bacteriology in the School, Hygienic Conditions of School Life, Oklahoma Soils Studies, Stock Feeding, Care and Management of Live Stock, Milk and its Products, Improvement of Farm Crops, etc. In the common branches advanced instruction is given in arithmetic, grammar, composition, geography, American history, physiology, civics, physics, and bookkeeping."[14]

It was very logical for Oklahoma A. and M. College to take steps toward working with educators. Oklahoma was largely an agricultural state, and the public school teachers—especially in the rural areas— had a responsibility to instruct their pupils in agriculture. Only a handful of Oklahoma's people went on to higher education in those years, and if those on farms and ranches did not receive formal instruction while in high school, they would probably get no scientific training. Because the college specialized in teaching agriculture, there was no reason its faculty could not adapt their courses to meet the particular needs of teachers in the common schools, thereby both preparing faculty to do a better and more up-to-date job as well as enriching the learning available to students. Still, this first, tentative move to enter the field of formal education was in itself incomplete, for the program was predicated on the assumption that the students who enrolled would already be trained in how to teach. It was to emphasize specific content, thus assisting the teacher with what should be taught and ignoring teaching strategies. Pedagogy was as yet not formally recognized at Oklahoma A. and M. College even with its preparatory department and its special programs for common school teachers.

During the early years, the Oklahoma A. and M. College endured only against great odds. Who would have wagered that a handful of educators ensconced in a tiny, isolated town twenty miles from the nearest railroad could have succeeded? From the railroad station at Mulhall, Orlando, or Perry to Stillwater was a slow journey of several hours over dirt roads by horse and buggy or wagon or foot. That trip could be tiring at best, and in at least one case it was fatal.[15]

It would have been folly to attempt any educational scheme on a grander scale. The college leaders played to their strength, and that was agriculture. A more comprehensive program was an object to be sought, a goal to be reached. Gradually enrollments crept upward, and that, in turn, enabled the college to employ additional faculty who were able to enhance the curriculum. By 1906, the total student enrollment reached the heady figure of 587, and outside pressures were about to cause the college to add another formally recognized course of study—education.

Endnotes

1. Robert A. Martin, compiler, *Statutes of Oklahoma, 1890* (Guthrie, OK: State Capital Printing Company, 1891), p. 83. Henry G. Bennett was the first president to have a substantial tenure. He was largely responsible for insulating the college to a certain extent from the ebb and flow of politics by campaigning for the constitutional amendment which established the coordinating board—the Oklahoma State Regents for Higher Education—in 1941.

2. Martin, compiler, *Statutes of Oklahoma, 1890*, p. 84.

3. Record Book Committee, compiler, "Selections from the Record Book of the Oklahoma Agricultural and Mechanical College, 1891-1941. Compiled on the Occasion of the Fiftieth Anniversary of the Founding of the College." vol. 1, p. 50, Special Collections, Edmon Low Library, Oklahoma State University, Stillwater, Oklahoma.

4. George L. Holter, "When the School Was Young," *Oklahoma A. and M. College Magazine*, vol. 1, no. 3 (November 1929), p. 12.

5. Thompson eventually left both the college and the field of education. On July 19, 1925, he was awarded his Ph.D. degree from Carver Chiropractic College and established himself in private practice in McPherson, Kansas. He frequently returned to the college, maintained a regular correspondence with historian Dr. B. B. Chapman, and was honored in 1949 as the last surviving member of that pioneering faculty. "Last of the First A. and M. Faculty," *Oklahoma A. and M. College Magazine*, vol. 21, no. 4 (December 1949), p. 11.
   As with many other administrative units which comprised Oklahoma A. and M. College/Oklahoma State University, names evolved with time, and frequently two or more names were used concurrently. Consequently, what began as the preparatory department was referred to as the preparatory school, the sub-freshman department, and the secondary school or department.

6. *Stillwater NewsPress*, 14 January 1963, p. 4; *Annual Catalog, Oklahoma A. and M. College, 1893-1894*, p. 5.

7. *Annual Catalog, Oklahoma A. and M. College, 1894-1895*, p. 30.

8. *Annual Catalog, Oklahoma A. and M. College, 1896-1897*, p. i.

9. *Annual Catalog, Oklahoma A. and M. College, 1896-1897*, p. 5.

10. Record Book Committee, compiler, vol. 1, pg. 64.

11. Mrs. Martin died on January 17, 1975, one day short of her one hundred and first birthday. Contrary to the commonly accepted lore regarding the early days of Oklahoma A. and M. which says that James Homer Adams was the first to enroll, she and her brother—Dr. W. Banks Diem (who became a chiropodist in Cleveland, Oklahoma)—said that Banks was the first one. Whatever the facts, upon graduation he left education for real estate and later oil leasing. Oklahoma A. and M. College *Daily O'Collegian*, 1 February 1950, p. 8, 26 March 1957, p. 1; "Last of First Class Visits Campus," *Oklahoma State Alumnus Magazine*, vol. 11, no. 6 (June-July 1970), p. 21; "100 Year-Old Former Student Dies," *Oklahoma State University Outreach*, vol. 16, no. 3 (March 1975), p. 31; "Loyal Alumnus Dead; His Reports Gave Account of A&M Opening," *Oklahoma A. and M. College Magazine*, vol. 21, no. 8 (April 1950), p. 22.

12. *Annual Catalog, Oklahoma A. and M. College, 1908-1909*, pp. 137-41.

13. Author interview with Bill Hindman, Marjorie Orloski, Benn Palmer, and Gladys Skinner, 1 July 1986, Centennial Histories Oral Interview Collection, Special Collections, Edmon Low Library. Professor Kezer's daughter, Irene, was the first child of an Oklahoma A. and M. alumnus to earn a degree from Oklahoma A. and M. College, when she graduated on May 21, 1923. See Oklahoma A. and M. College *Orange and Black*, 10 May 1923, p. 1.

14. *Annual Catalog, Oklahoma A. and M. College, 1905-1906*, pp. 22-23.

15. Philip Reed Rulon, *Oklahoma State University—Since 1890* (Stillwater: Oklahoma State University Press, 1975), p. 29.

2 And Then There Was One

In 1907, Oklahoma entered the union as the forty-sixth state. That entailed—among other things—drafting a state constitution and writing legislation that would have a profound effect on the emerging Oklahoma A. and M. College in Stillwater. During the first decade after statehood, the college took the initial steps toward its original mission by admitting the formal study of education. At first, education was under the existing aegis of the School of Science and Literature. A separate School of Education complete with its own dean and equal in rank with the older academic units was created shortly thereafter.

A year before statehood, the college had a well-established agricultural program, and the agricultural faculty had accepted the responsibility of working with common school teachers to enable them to introduce agriculture as a subject in those schools. Such instruction for teachers was given not necessarily because it was supported by the state's school administrators or because it was encouraged by visionary boards of education which believed the state's economic foundation should be grounded in the produce of the farms and ranches. Rather, it was mandated by the state itself. Having established the "Spring Term Course for Teachers" in 1905, the Oklahoma A. and M. College added the teachers' correspondence course in agriculture the following year. In reality, this was not like a course today, for it was presented as a highly structured two-year program. Each year was comprised of nine months of study divided into three terms, following the academic calendar used on the campus. Each subject was essentially identical with work done on campus with the exception of the practical work in laboratories and fields.

This program was significant for a couple of reasons. First, it was an innovation to take education to where the people were, rather than requiring them to journey to the campus for instruction. That is the standard land-grant mission of outreach and service to the working people of the state. In keeping with the college's philosophy of service and accessibility, it was stressed that students (up to 300) could enroll at any time and could take either all of the course or only those parts that were desired. The only costs involved were for postage and texts, and even those expenses were reduced "by the fact that the principal is usually able to sell the texts at two-thirds of the original price." Second, it was a program designed to save at least the positions and incomes of the teachers in Oklahoma, many of whom listed Oklahoma A. and M. as their alma mater. In announcing the teacher correspondence course in agriculture, the college gave teachers reason to take serious notice of the offering: "It has been established in order to enable them [that is, the common school teachers] to introduce agriculture into their schools even before required to do so by law, as well as to enable them to pass an examination in agriculture when it is required as provided for in the pending Constitution."[1]

If the faculty in Stillwater were aware that changes were pending

1915 REDSKIN

The home of the dean and faculty of the School of Education for decades, Morrill Hall was begun in 1906 after Angelo Scott got the U.S. Congress to waive the prohibition against raising additional public buildings in the territory. In 1914, as World War I was about to break out in Europe, flames engulfed the structure. Even though Acting President L. L. Lewis himself led the charge to save Morrill, drought—a constant problem—dictated that there was no water to stop even what was initially a small fire. Both Dr. Lewis and Dean of Education John Bowers were relocated in the Engineering Building.

regarding the preparation and qualifications of public school teachers, the State Department of Education was no doubt even more cognizant of the way the winds of reform were blowing. In October of 1908, John W. Wilkinson, the assistant superintendent of education, wrote to the college and urged that a special course be added to the curriculum which would be "not less than a year's work in pedagogical lines, including history of education, philosophy of education, and school management."[2] Wilkinson's suggestion was reinforced by State Superintendent E. D. Cameron, who personally appeared before the Oklahoma State Board of Agriculture, which was by then the college's governing body, and urged the introduction of a special course for teachers.

The college and the leaders in the State Department of Education had accurately forecast the direction that the political leaders of the state would take in regard to education, for the new state constitution stated simply: "The Legislators shall provide for the teaching of the elements of agriculture, horticulture, stock feeding, and domestic science in the common schools of the State."[3]

In addition, the 1908 statutes stated: "After July 1, 1909, no persons shall teach and no certificate shall be granted to an applicant to teach, in the public schools receiving aid from this State, who has not passed a satisfactory examination in the elements of agriculture and allied branches mentioned in this act."[4] This had sweeping implications for all people already engaged in the teaching profession and all who aspired to such a career. Regardless of what teachers had studied in their college years or what subjects they were responsible for teaching in the common schools, all would be tested in agriculture. If they did not pass that examination, then they would not teach in the new state of Oklahoma. In light of this development, the correspondence course offered by the Oklahoma A. and M. College was no doubt an option appreciated by many of the state's teachers who had not proceeded through an agricultural program already.

Next, the legislature moved to ensure both that the agricultural sciences would be taught in the public schools and that they would be taught in a modern and correct fashion, doing so by assigning special obligations to the Oklahoma A. and M. College in Stillwater. "The Agricultural and Mechanical College shall be the technical head of the agricultural, industrial, and allied science system of education, and its president, professors, and employees shall lend such assistance in carrying out the objects, aims, and purposes of the State Constitution requiring the teaching of agriculture and the allied practical subjects as shall not conflict with the immediate duties incumbent on them in said institution."[5]

Through that section of the law, broad and rather vague duties were placed on the college. But the legislature could be far more specific, and it was. The next section stated:

"Chair of agriculture—There is hereby created a chair of Agriculture for schools, who shall be a member of the faculty of the Agricultural and Mechanical College, whose duties shall be to direct and advise in all matters relating to the teaching of agriculture and the allied subjects in the common schools, under the supervision of the president of the Agricultural and Mechanical College, and he shall be paid from the funds of the Agricultural and Mechanical College. He shall visit the schools, the teachers' institutions, the summer normal schools, the State normal schools, advise with the teachers and officers concerned and plan such means of co-operation in the improvement of methods, appliances, the use of seeds, plants, and trees as may from time to time be necessary, and shall prepare, print, and distribute such leaflets and other literature as may be helpful to teachers and pupils concerning or engaged in teaching industrial, practical, and scientific subjects on technical and practical agriculture and its allied branches."

Oklahoma's first legislators had an interesting concept of education, agriculture, and the Oklahoma A. and M. College. In the *General Statutes of Oklahoma—1908*, chapter one dealt with administration and set forth the necessary structure of state government. The second chapter— from which the above quotations were drawn—dealt with agriculture which clearly suggests the high priority assigned by the legislature to that industry. Within that chapter are the sections dealing with the Oklahoma A. and M. College. While other chapters in the statutes pertained to other higher education institutions individually, such as the University of Oklahoma and even the tiny preparatory school at Tonkawa (later Northern Oklahoma College), the Oklahoma A. and M. College did not merit a separate chapter. It was subsumed under agriculture, which strongly suggests that the legislators regarded the college partly as an educational institution but more importantly as an integral part of the state's leading industry.

The college, in general, and the chairman of agriculture for schools, in particular, were given a special relationship to the state's public schools. Although the law made it perfectly clear that the state stipulated duties, it did not obligate itself for funding the operation. Combining the outreach functions associated with the extension program with the development and dissemination of information associated with the experiment station was a substantial undertaking. When the legislators thought about Stillwater and education, they largely restricted their focus to agricultural education, for no reference was made regarding persons who were trained as professional educators.[6]

Fortunately for the state of Oklahoma and for its citizens, thinking was not equally constrained at the Oklahoma A. and M. College. In 1908, the college had survived for nearly two decades. That year, J. H. Con-

Angelo Scott was brought to Stillwater as a member of the faculty and was almost immediately catapulted into the presidency. Largely responsible for completing the initial campus building program, he was unable to survive the winds of political change which swept Oklahoma with the advent of statehood. After assuring a smooth transition for his successor, Scott moved to Oklahoma City and built a career as a civic leader. He maintained warm ties to the college and frequently returned to participate in public events.

nell replaced Angelo C. Scott, thus becoming the sixth president of the institution. The fact that the college got a new president the year after the state entered the union should not be regarded as a mere coincidence. During territorial days, the federal government was dominated by Republican administrations, and every president of every institution of higher learning in Oklahoma was also a member of the Grand Old Party. With statehood, though, came statewide elections which swept the Democrats into power. Needless to say, every college president was quickly succeeded by a Democrat acceptable to the leadership in Guthrie.

An attorney by profession, President Scott was brought to Stillwater to teach English and almost overnight was called by the board to accept the presidency. None of his four predecessors had stayed at the helm for more than a few years. George E. Morrow, Scott's immediate predecessor, served the longest from 1895 to 1899. Edmond D. Murdaugh survived only from January 18 until June 30 of 1895. President Scott served from 1899 until 1908 and was largely responsible for developing the college's old quad on what is the southeastern portion of today's campus. In order to secure badly needed classroom and administrative space and to anchor the north end of the quad, President Scott secured special legislation in Washington to construct Morrill Hall. After the first statewide election, he realized his presidency was doomed, but he still behaved responsibly by asking the board of regents to accept his resignation effective at the end of the fiscal year rather than immediately. The board agreed, and President Scott "put his house in order" and helped ease the transition to new leadership under Connell. After leaving Stillwater, he became a very prominent citizen of Oklahoma City and frequently visited the college for public celebrations, apparently harboring no ill will for the political factors which led to his demise as an academic leader.[7]

Under President Scott's leadership, the essential structure of the undergraduate college took full shape. The college still did not have administrative subdivisions such as formal departments or schools, but it did have recognized courses of study in agriculture, engineering, domestic arts and science, science and literature, teachers' normal, and business training. These paralleled six of the current undergraduate colleges. By all measures, the Oklahoma A. and M. College was booming. Forty-five professors and their assistants worked in eight brick and stone buildings.

In addition to Old Central, the college had added the rambling, Gothic-style Library (later called the Biology Building and eventually Williams Hall, named after Benjamin Franklin Williams), the Chemistry Building, the College Barn, Morrill Hall, the Engineering Building, the Dairy Building, the Shop Building, and the Gymnasium. While the

When most of the Oklahoma Agricultural and Mechanical College students took room and board in town, they approached the campus from the southeast. Shown in this photo are (*left to right*) the Chemistry Building, the Engineering Building (behind the flag pole), the power plant, Central, Morrill, and the Biology Building (later the Library and still later Williams Hall).

campus had expanded to the point where it had major physical facilities, it was devoid of any sense of architectural unity—it was a collection of towers and turrets, Roman columns, and brick boxes. Of those first buildings, Old Central and Morrill Hall have survived to see the Centennial, the former as a museum of Oklahoma higher education operated by the Oklahoma Historical Society and the latter as a still-functioning academic building. The other buildings no longer exist. In 1908, the college was on the move. Three other buildings were under construction, the student body numbered a very respectable 1,352, and education was finally admitted as a collegiate-grade field. Even though the catalog noted that the position of professor of pedagogy had not yet been filled, it had indeed been established.[8]

In order to attend the college, students had to be at least fourteen years of age and had to take an entrance examination. In a state in which the one-room schoolhouse was the rule, the preparation must have varied widely. Thus, the college had no sure way of ascertaining the extent of prior learning except by administering its own examination. In 1904-05, "applicants for admission to the freshman class must pass an examination in . . . [English and mathematics], and in higher arithmetic, algebra to quadratic equations, physiology, physical geography, and general history. Students from high schools who have satisfactorily completed the ninth grade may be admitted on trial without examination. Graduates of approved high schools may be admitted to the sophomore class, on their diplomas without examination."[9] In 1908, the examinations were scheduled for September 7 and 8. Students were encouraged to arrive in Stillwater at nine o'clock "or as soon thereafter as possible," which suggested that the college administration was tolerant of the fact that travel into Stillwater was still a challenge and that a time of arrival could be estimated with no great certainty.

While the college was in the process of constructing a "boy's" dormitory that would have bathrooms, all necessary facilities, steam heat, and electric lights, that structure would not be available for use until 1910. At that time, residents would be charged $3 per month—payable in advance. In the meantime, students lived off-campus with Stillwater families or in boarding houses. If one took room and board with a private family, the cost ranged between $3 and $4 a week, but a furnished room—without board—could be obtained for $2 to $2.50 per month if it were shared by two people. In addition to keeping body and soul together and having a roof over his or her head, the student also faced college fees. Unlike 1896, there was an incidental fee of $1.50 per term, and text books might be even as high as $5 a term. If one enrolled for stenography or typewriting, a $2 typewriter fee was assessed, and the unlucky sophomores were required to deposit $2 each term to cover any breakage that might occur in the chemistry lab. All in all, it was esti-

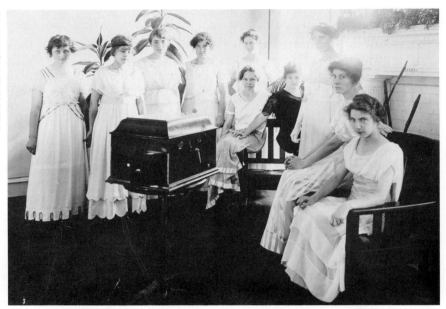

For many Oklahomans living in the early decades of statehood, life was rough as they strug-
gled to create a new existence on the prairie. In contrast to the more than Spartan rigors of
home on the farm or ranch, women residing in the Women's Building must have felt they were
in a palace with running water, plaster walls, wooden floors, electricity, and steam heat.

mated that a student could spend nine months studying at Oklahoma
A. and M. College for between $136 and $172. After all, there was still
no charge for tuition.[10]

Even without a professor of pedagogy on the campus, the college
in 1908 had clearly adopted the preparation of teachers as one of its pro-
fessed purposes and had put in place a system for organizing education
that would prevail until the present. While some courses of study were
assigned exclusively to specific segments of the faculty, such as agriculture and engineering, education was handled in a decentralized fashion and was claimed by three separate areas. Agriculture was to equip
young men to be expert, scientific, and practical farmers, but it also prepared them "as teachers." Domestic science and arts hoped to groom
young women for homemaking and government service, but it also saw
that it had a legitimate right "to prepare teachers" as well. In its turn,
the purpose of the teachers' normal training was "to educate and train
young men and women to become expert teachers of high professional
standing, having first a broad foundation consisting of the common
branches and the natural sciences."[11] At least teachers' normal training
did not have its students stereotyped by sex.

Centennial Histories Series

This educational hydra was no doubt not the result of systematic thinking and effective planning, but rather the legacy of tradition. From the very beginning of the college, the faculty in agriculture and domestic science and arts, and to a more limited degree science and literature, had offered de facto teacher education programs. While these faculties emphasized content rather than pedagogy, they did have an historic claim to being teacher educators, and especially the first two were both political heavyweights in an agricultural and mechanical college. Yet, in light of the charge given to the college by the assistant superintendent of education, the existing programs in both agriculture and domestic science and arts had to be augmented. Those programs stressed academic content, and Wilkinson had specifically noted history and philosophy of education and school management. Those were areas that neither of the existing programs treated. To respond to the suggestions from the department of education, pedagogy was added as an element within the School of Science and Literature while the role of agriculture and domestic science in the preparation of teachers was neither challenged nor abridged.

Having established a professor of pedagogy in the 1908-09 academic year, President Connell moved to staff that position the following year by appointing John H. Bowers. Holding a bachelor of arts and a bachelor of laws from the University of West Virginia, Professor Bowers received the master of arts and doctorate degrees from Illinois Wesleyan University. He also continued graduate work at Ohio Wesleyan University and the University of Chicago. Like so many others who entered the teaching profession in the late nineteenth and early twentieth centuries, Professor Bowers began his career in an ungraded county school. Having his degree in hand, he advanced quickly through the ranks, serving as high school principal and city superintendent before linking up with higher education. Prior to joining the Oklahoma A. and M. faculty, he served as principal of a preparatory school and as professor in a state normal school. Clearly, he had the prior experiences that suited him well to assume responsibilities in Stillwater.[12]

Having lived in Chicago, Professor Bowers must have wondered about Stillwater and its robust student population from the farms and ranches of Oklahoma. Until a couple of years before he appeared on the local scene, it was typical for the freshman and sophomore classes to pit themselves against each other in serious battle. In the dead of night, one class or the other would put its class colors at the top of a tall tree west of Old Central and stand guard until dawn when "boys" of the other class would spot the colors and attack. On those days, all students gladly cut classes either to watch or to engage in the melee, in which fists and clubs were regarded as the most harmless of weapons. C. E. Sanborn, a professor in the Department of Entomology, recalled that one

While American colleges still had fairly small enrollments, loyalty to one's class trailed only that of loyalty to one's fraternity and school, especially among freshmen and sophomores. At Oklahoma Agricultural and Mechanical College, a challenge for a tug-of-war across a college pond would pit adversaries in intense battle. Indeed, if no one got wet, combatants and witnesses were equally disappointed.

student was literally disemboweled by a shot through the stomach. Brass knuckles were popular on both sides, and their use resulted in broken noses, cuts, bruises, and cracked ribs. It was not unusual for the young men to have their clothes shredded and torn completely off in many cases as they tried to scale the tree.

One year into his administration, President Connell believed enough was enough and moved to ban the riot and replace it with a far safer tug-of-war. Local lore always assigns the site of such contests to Theta Pond, but in the 1910s that pond was a watering hole for the college livestock and less than sanitary, to say the least. Instead, the boys used ponds northwest of the campus or Willow Pond, which was situated between where the Student Union and Classroom Building now stand. Initially, all males in the classes participated, but when the number grew unwieldy, each class selected a team of champions.[13]

There was an institutional tradition, though, which did not involve class conflict but was instead designed to serve the serious-minded student. The preparatory school played a special role in the early years of the college, which ensured the life of the institution. To a somewhat lesser extent, the same can be said about the summer school, which brought large numbers of people to Stillwater for credit and non-credit work. Many of the offerings, in line with the major mission of a land-grant college, were oriented toward farm life, but just as many were focused on Oklahoma's schools and teachers, and that had a two-way

Centennial Histories Series

benefit. Every additional enrollment helped secure the fledgling Department of Pedagogy, and every class, institute, or workshop offered helped to enhance the expertise of people working in the public schools, always by increasing skills and frequently by moving a practicing educator toward a college degree. It was impossible for many teachers working without the degree to attend Oklahoma A. and M. except during the vacation months in the summer.

The first summer session for teachers was organized in 1908 by Charles Evans. A native of Salem, Kentucky, he was a neighbor of Lee Cruce, who became Oklahoma's second governor after statehood. Cruce encouraged Evans to migrate to the new state. He accepted the position of superintendent of schools at Ardmore, having held the same position in Salem. His accomplishments in Ardmore attracted the attention of President Connell, who brought him to Stillwater. In 1911, he left the Oklahoma A. and M. campus to accept the presidency of Central State College in Edmond. Five years later he became the president of Kendall College in Tulsa, where he was largely responsible for launching the building program that would transform Kendall College into the University of Tulsa.[14]

T. M. Jeffords was clearly associated with the School of Agriculture but played a vital role in helping establish professional education as an integral part of Oklahoma Agricultural and Mechanical College. He was convinced that Oklahoma's agricultural economy would make maximum progress only if the college prepared common school teachers who could teach modern agricultural techniques. These students could then influence their fathers to try new and improved methods of farming.

In 1910, Oklahoma A. and M. College's T. M. Jeffords, professor of agriculture for schools, was especially critical of summer institutes offered in the counties, saying they mindlessly followed the outlines issued by the state and allowed teachers to take too much work. Because prospective teachers had to pass an examination in each subject area to be taught, it often meant that some tried seven to nine subjects, thus getting the merest smattering of each. He called for reform: "A Teachers' Institute should be a place of inspiration, a source of new ideas, of new and better ideals. There should be time for reflection, conference, round table features, assimilation. Methods of teaching should be discussed and exemplified. Because of the dreaded examination, and because neither the County Superintendent nor instructor has any voice in preparing the questions, the 'cramming' proceeds." Yet, he noted some institutes were brave enough to break away from the standard model and to adapt the work to the needs of schools and teachers. He believed that Oklahoma A. and M. was progressing well in the offering of a summer program. In 1908, all teachers had had to take the examinations to be certified, and it was a high-pressure situation. But in 1909 and 1910, a larger percentage took work even though they did not need to be certified, and "this suggests that teachers welcome proper professional training and that mere certificate getting becomes of secondary importance."[15]

Likewise, L. F. Stewart, who served as county agent for Hughes County and who wrote for *New Education*, lauded the work at Oklahoma A. and M., noting that the 1910 enrollment was up by 25 percent at Stillwater but that other institutes had lost ground. He said: "The class of work done by the students is spoken of in the highest terms by all of the professionals. The earnestness of the students did not diminish, but rather increased, from the time the summer term opened until the last day of recitation work. There was a kindly sympathy and spirit of fellowship existing between the students and the professors that made the work a great pleasure to the latter, and a benefit to the former. And we believe that this is as it should be; certainly the professors of this institution are not on a pedestal to be looked up to with wonder, or worshipped afar off by the students."[16] Surely, the land of red clay and heat had been transformed into the academic Eden of milk, honey, and camaraderie! Mr. Stewart's words, perhaps, should be taken with a grain of salt at least, for the college used the *New Education* as a way to attract students to Stillwater and no doubt allowed him to "gild the lily" a little. On the other hand, the gild cannot be applied if a real lily does not exist.

It would appear that Jefford's criticism regarding faculty having no input to the teacher certificate examination had an impact and was shared by others. In 1912, the process was changed so that credit earned

Oklahoma's early educational system had some obvious gaps, and Oklahoma Agricultural and Mechanical College moved as best it could to fill the breach. The summer institute was a good way to add college-level depth to partially prepared professionals. Even though Stillwater was by state law a racially segregated campus for the first half of the twentieth century, such racial barriers were permeable when it came to institutes and extension work, as may be seen by the inclusion of three black teachers.

at the college in required courses would be accepted in lieu of the examination in that subject. The college tried to offer as many required courses as possible during the regular semesters, but it guaranteed to offer all such courses during the summer, playing to a major block of its summer clientele.[17]

Mr. Stewart had gloated in 1910 that the summer program at Oklahoma A. and M. was growing while rival programs were fading. But six years later, the shoe was on the other foot. Using the *Orange and Black* as his mouthpiece, Paul Hoggard, who was vice president of the sophomore class and enrolled in the School of Education, bemoaned the fact that the summer normal at the college had only 600 students in attendance while the six institutions that were classified only as normal schools managed to attract almost 1,000 each. How could this happen when Oklahoma A. and M. had more and better equipment than all the normal schools combined and when the program was backed by a faculty second to none? Professor Bowers and Charles W. Briles, associate professor of education and social science at Oklahoma A. and M. and the former president of East Central State Normal, laid the blame on the fact that, although the instruction was excellent, the school did not augment classwork with a summer lecture series as did the normal schools. Furthermore, the competing normal schools did not rely only on their own resources. Instead, they assessed a $2 entrance fee on each student and used the income to finance lectures by leading national educationalists and sociologists. Hoggard believed if such a fee were required in Stillwater, then the college could move ahead aggressively, not to transform the place into a normal school but to provide the best preparation possible to the people responsible for molding the destiny of the youth of Oklahoma—the secondary school teachers.[18]

The next year this strategy was successful. Oklahoma A. and M. was authorized by the legislature and the state attorney general to collect a fee to support a series of summer lectures. This was to be a regular and highly publicized part of the summer offerings and would continue for decades. By the summer of 1922, the lecture series had reached its stride, with daily presentations at 9:00 A.M.[19]

By the summer of 1919, two other features were added that were also to become standard components. The demand for the preparation of primary teachers had reached the point where Oklahoma A. and M. was willing to hire a special teacher to conduct courses such as Methods and Materials of Primary Teaching, Primary Music, Lesson Planning, Plays and Games, and Handwork and Nature Study—quite an ambitious set of offerings, to be sure. Thus, the permanent faculty was augmented not only by "visiting firemen," luminaries with national reputations who were to add luster to the program, but also by practicing educators invited to the campus because they had perfected special skills "in the trenches." The second feature was the creation of a primary room in which the special teacher would be able to demonstrate abilities within an actual classroom setting while the summer students observed the techniques and the interaction between teacher and pupils.[20]

While 1909 may be regarded as a breakthrough or as a benchmark in the development of professional education at Oklahoma A. and M., the significance of the advance should be kept in perspective, for pedagogy was far from being recognized as a major academic element within the college. At that point, there was simply what was called a "chair of pedagogy" which was housed administratively within the School of Science and Literature, with Bowers recognized as professor of history as well as pedagogy. Following the already established tradition of a decentralized approach to the preparation of teachers, the program was divided into three separate elements, only one of which was involved with education. This was the block of "professional subjects" consisting of courses such as pedagogy, psychology, the history of education, and methods and management. The other elements were the "common branches," such as arithmetic, English, music, algebra, and the sciences—all of which would be taught by faculty other than professional educators—and the "industrial" subjects, such as woodworking, stock judging, soils, and domestic science. When all three areas were completed and combined, it was maintained that the program "built for the education and training of the strong, well-balanced teacher."[21]

Within this early structure, Professor Bowers was required to operate initially as a "one-man band." For example, during his first academic year of three terms, he was responsible for teaching the History of Education, Theory and Practice of Teaching, School Management, Special Methods, Philosophy of Education, and Psychology.[22] In other years, he would complete his portion of the teacher education program by offering the other professional courses. In some respects, by accepting his position in Stillwater, Dr. Bowers' career had gone full circle, for he was once again in a sort of one-room schoolhouse, albeit now on a collegiate level.

Even though Professor Bowers carried a heavy load on campus, he—along with those who later succeeded him as head of the professional education unit at Oklahoma A. and M.—realized he had additional duties that could not be ignored. Chief among these was his responsibility to ferret out weaknesses in the educational system of the state and to provide leadership that would address those problems. He was a champion of rural education, being convinced that improving the education available to children on Oklahoma's ranches and farms would automatically improve the quality of rural life, and that in turn would have a beneficial impact on the climate of the entire state since it was so overwhelmingly rural. He believed that the farm children should have the same advantages educationally as those who lived in cities, for he was sure that the future of not only rural life but of the nation would be determined by people being raised in rural areas. He argued that people ought not need to move to town to acquire an adequate education, which was a common practice in his day, for that would break the link between the child and his or her rural environment. Still, he was a realist who recognized that the urban schools were of comparatively superior quality, which made them highly attractive to farm parents who were concerned about their children's education and saw schooling as the means of social and economic upward mobility.[23]

Having recognized the problem, Dr. Bowers moved ahead to propose ways of solving it by making recommendations that have been ringing in Oklahoma's educational and political circles ever since. One part of the solution was economic. In Dean Bowers' judgment, rural people simply did not spend enough money to provide adequate support for their schools. They surely did not tax themselves at the same rate as people in the cities did. Yet, he was also cognizant of the fact that most of the wealth of the state was in the urban areas, and to create a more equitable educational system, he proposed a state tax which would be used to supplement the local base for the schools—today referred to as "equalization."[24]

Another aspect of the problem was sheer size. Obviously, a tiny school with a small enrollment would be able to offer only an anemic academic program. To Professor Bowers, the solution was the consolidation of country schools, which would create a larger school with more teachers and fewer students in each class. If available resources were concentrated in a consolidated plant, he was sure the school could be as beautiful, comfortable, and convenient as the best home, with good grounds and a school garden. He was adamant, however, in his emphasis that even a consolidated school with a broader curriculum had an obligation to prepare its charges for the *rural* life and was never to imitate the programs of the city schools. In the consolidated high school, students would learn about the most modern agricultural techniques, for, after all, the teachers would be following the leadership provided by the Oklahoma A. and M. College. They, in turn, could carry the ideas to the farms and ranches, where their conservative fathers might be convinced to try the new ways.

Dr. Bowers noted: "The consolidated high school will keep intact the country home, educate the child within the environment in which he is growing up, and make him the intellectual equal of his city cousin. Better schools mean more money for schools, higher rates of school taxes,

1916 REDSKIN

John Hugh Bowers joined the School of Science and Literature as a faculty member responsible for pedagogy. Although Bowers was designated as dean of the School of Education in 1913, professional education had established only a tiny beachhead. In 1919, he left Stillwater to accept a faculty position in Kansas.

better standards of training for teachers, more mature teachers, more experienced teachers, a larger number of teachers and a smaller number of pupils for each teacher, greater appreciation for the school, longer terms, consolidation and better supervision. And all of these things call for more money for public schools.''[25] Clearly, he was concerned about matters that are still on the agenda of educational leaders decades later.

This champion of rural education continued to be active on campus and to develop the educational program. By 1913, it was decided that education was a professional field that did not fit easily with the other disciplines included in the School of Science and Literature. That year, the School of Education was recognized as a separate administrative unit within the Oklahoma A. and M. College.[26]

One year after Professor Bowers was elevated to his deanship, World War I broke out in Europe. Although the college would be heavily involved with the war effort during World War II, in the Great War little changed in Stillwater. In fact, by reading the *Orange and Black*, the school paper, it would have seemed that no major war was in progress save for two features—letters written to the paper by Oklahoma A. and M. students in the trenches in France and the fact that the college "boys" were then referred to as "men."

President James W. Cantwell was prepared to have the college serve as a training site for 400 men and was willing to vacate the two dormitories and send the students packing into town to be housed once again by the people of Stillwater. The contract failed to materialize since there was no mention of the military arriving on the campus and since the students continued to reside in the dormitories. It seemed that Washington was concerned that the city and college had an inadequate and unreliable supply of water. That would be a correct assessment of the local water situation for years to come.[27]

The college did offer a special summer program for teachers under the direction of Sgt. Major Michael McDonald, who was in charge of the Reserve Officer Training Corps program. This was in response to a state board of education mandate that all teachers in the rural schools, high schools, state normal schools, the University of Oklahoma, the state training school, and the Oklahoma State School for Dependent or Orphan Children were to teach students eight years or older military training at least one period each day.[28]

While Dean Bowers was willing to leave such military training to Sgt. Major McDonald, he moved ahead personally to draft a statement of purpose which would recognize that the School of Education was established on a par with even the premier Schools of Agriculture and Engineering. The statement, printed in the college yearbook, proclaimed:

"The purpose of the school of education at the Oklahoma A&M College is to more effectively utilize in the service of the state the excellent opportunities which the college offers. The School of Education organizes courses of study for teachers by selecting suitable subjects already offered in the other schools of the college, and supplementing such special and professional subjects as may be needed to give symetry [sic] to a teacher preparation. The girls of the School of Education get their Domestic Science Arts under efficient specialists in the School of Home Economics. The boys in the School of Education have the best possible opportunities to learn Agriculture in the School of Agriculture. The student in the School of Education takes those studies which are the standard requirements for a teacher's certificate and upon graduation is awarded both a B.S. degree and a permanent state certificate.

"Along with these regular requirements the student in this school has a rather wide and a very useful range of elective studies which permit him to get work under many good strong teachers in the college. The Oklahoma A&M College is a good place to train teachers, teachers of all the more useful academic and collegiate subjects, and especially teachers of agriculture and home economics. It is a good place to train teachers because it is broad in its ideals and combines all worthy phases of education; vocational, cultural, social, disciplinary and moral. It is a good place for the rural teachers, because it offers the work he needs and sympathy with rural life. Some excellent teachers of experience who have already attained notable success have come to the School of Education to supplement their earlier training and increase their power of service.

"The worth of the School of Education is best attested by its graduates, and they have proved their worth by their success in many difficult and honorable positions as teachers and as school executives."[29]

This quotation, appearing in the 1916 college yearbook, seems almost like an advertisement to recruit new students rather than something that would evoke nostalgic memories of a graduate as he or she leafed through the publication years later. Yet, this type of statement was not out of place or unusual for this period in the history of the Oklahoma A. and M. College. All of the institution's publications, whether intended for students, alumni, or the general public, carried messages designed to "sell" the college and its programs.

Dean Bowers not only tried to reach people off campus through publications but also brought people to campus who might be able to encourage students to make teaching their career. Most colleges during this era had a required chapel, and Oklahoma A. and M. was no exception. Capitalizing on that captive audience, Dr. Bowers initiated the idea of inviting leading educators to address the assembled students as a body, letting them know what the educational field was all about and serving as role models for prospective educators. When he got a leader to Stillwater, the dean took full advantage of his visitor. For example, when

The second Engineering Building (now Gundersen Hall) was erected on the original quad and is an example of the uncoordinated architecture of the pre-Henry G. Bennett days. Over the years, the doors were changed, the windows were replaced, the interior was gutted, and engineering vacated in favor of education. It has always remained in instructional use and is currently the third oldest building still used for such purposes, following Morrill Hall and the Bartlett Center for the Studio Arts (formerly the Women's Building and still later Gardiner Hall).

Thomas Scott, the superintendent of Guthrie, was brought to campus, he spoke first at chapel, then to the Educational Society, and, finally, in the evening, returned for an informal meeting with students and faculty.[30]

Through his work on and off the campus, Dean Bowers proved to be both effective and popular, no doubt in large measure because he was sincerely concerned about students and education. He was so popular, in fact, that the *1917 Redskin* was dedicated to him:

"To Dr. John H. Bowers, dean of the School of Education, is dedicated the 1917 Redskin. . . . Dr. W. L. Carlyle and Dean Ruth Michaels were the other candidates. The selection was made in appreciation of the work Dr. Bowers has done for the College and for the members of the 1917 class. It is known that he is always ready to assist the students whenever opportunity affords, and several times he has loaned needy students money entirely upon their honor. Over twenty members of the senior class will graduate under him, and nearly every member has taken work in his department.

"Dr. Bowers . . . entered upon his duties in the Aggie School, as professor of education and history, and dean of the Summer School and teachers normal division. During the eight years that he has had charge of their work the teachers normal division has grown from a two-year course and a few students to the present School of Education with a hundred students and two professors. . . .

"He has proved a successful school supervisor, and has been offered many such positions. . . . Since at A&M he has been elected to positions in South Carolina and Mississippi similar to the one held here and at higher salaries. As a speaker he is in great demand. Nearly every week he is called out to address teachers county and district associations, and frequently he is called upon for aid in rallies for school improvement in various high schools. Appreciation for such work is very well summarized in the following quotation from a city superintendent: 'I have heard you speak on the improvement of schools so effectively that I would like you to come over and help us' . . . .

"Through the arrangements of friends he is able to respond to 15 or 20 [commencements] each year. Throughout the time he has been here he has carried the work of two men, but he has never been too busy to lend aid and encouragement to needy students. Dr. Bowers is known by every student for his position on moral and social problems, and in appreciation of such a character is the Redskin dedicated."[31]

While it is true that the program expanded under Dean Bowers, for obvious reasons, the curriculum offered during the early years was initially very restricted—after all, Dean Bowers was at first the sole educator on the college staff, and how many areas could a single person handle? "Education" first appeared in the catalog for 1911, which was midway between the appointment of Dr. Bowers and the creation of a self-standing School of Education. It consisted of six courses: Methods and Management, Theory and Practice of Teaching, School Supervision, History of Education, Psychology, and Philosophy of Education. In addition, it was noted that the School of Agriculture offered Agricultural Pedagogy in the summer institute and that the School of Domestic Science included "methods of teaching and arrangement of courses of study in handwork" in the domestic arts course.[32]

In 1914-15, when Professor Bowers was still the only faculty member, the curriculum surged forward to a total of seventeen courses—an unbelievably huge number of preparations for any mere mortal to handle. Some were clearly related to education, such as Applied Psychology, High School Teaching, High School Administration and Rural Education; others, however, were very broad, such as Ethics, Logic, Principles of Sociology, the Duties of American Citizenship, Social Welfare, Political Method, Government-Local, and Government-Federal. It can only be surmised why the second listing was assigned to the School of Education rather than to the School of Science and Literature. Whatever the reasons, and it might easily have been because of the man involved rather than because of the school itself, all of the courses listed for education were taught at the upper division level, and that phenomenon has prevailed throughout the history of the School/College of Education.[33]

The educational program at Oklahoma A. and M. College was given something of a boost with the passage of the federal Smith-Hughes Act, which provided funding for vocational education in the secondary schools. The *1917-18 College Catalog* was used as a recruiting device and indicated that the course in general agriculture for teachers qualified graduates to be vocational teachers and that "already a demand for trained teachers is noted which, it seems, cannot be met unless more students prepare to teach these subjects." The catalog noted that students in the School of Agriculture who took thirteen hours from the School of Education would be able to teach vocational subjects in schools receiving Smith-Hughes money.[34]

By the fall of 1918, the program within the School of Education had expanded to a total of twenty-nine courses. They ranged from freshman classes through graduate, although nearly 70 percent of the work was still assigned to the undergraduate, upper-division years. Furthermore, the curriculum was now organized into four areas—educational psychology, educational administration, educational methods, and educational philosophy, with the last being a hodgepodge of philosophy, foundations, sociology, and rural education.[35]

Obviously, a curricular program of that magnitude could not be offered by a single faculty member, no matter how dedicated and even

Putting her professional reputation on the line, a woman demonstrates state of the art teaching skills, while a group of teachers observes. Such demonstration programs usually were offered during the summer and could be led either by Stillwater faculty or by noted educators brought to campus for the expressed purpose of augmenting the regular faculty. This photo was probably taken in Morrill Hall. What educator would not jump at the chance to work with a ratio of one teacher to twelve pupils!

if subjects were rotated over several years. The situation was compounded further by the fact that enrollments were not meager. Approximately 40 percent of Oklahoma A. and M.'s students took education, which many regarded as service courses since they were not majoring in education.[36] Dr. Bowers clearly needed assistance, and he finally got a staff to go along with his deanship. It consisted of Samuel A. Maroney, the principal of the sub-freshman department, and Fred McCarrel, who was shared with the School of Agriculture.

In the final analysis, neither student recognition through the dedication of the Redskin nor administrative support through the addition of faculty proved adequate to keep Dean Bowers at the helm of the new School of Education. In the fall of 1919, he cleared out his office in the Engineering Building, packed up his family, and left Stillwater to assume duties on the faculty of the Kansas State Normal School (now Pittsburg State).[37] For a dean to move to another college as a faculty member might be regarded as career reversal today. But, in 1919, Oklahoma Agricultural and Mechanical College and Kansas State Normal were not that dissimilar, and the latter institution had the distinct advantage to Dr. Bowers of having the training of teachers and educational administrators as its chief mission.

Still, Dr. Bowers must have left Stillwater with a sense of pride, for the school had made some real progress. After all, professional education had been thrust upon Oklahoma A. and M. largely by agricultural interest groups in the state. It had initially been accommodated only as a chair within science and literature, where the occupant was responsible for history as well as pedagogy. From that small beginning, Dr. Bowers developed an academic program which had remarkable breadth, assisted with the birth of a school with a separate administrative identity, and acquired a small staff. In 1908, there was no School of Education; in 1919 there was one. It would be up to new leadership to nurture what Dean Bowers had started.

Endnotes

1. *Annual Catalog, Oklahoma A. and M. College, 1906-1907,* pp. 31-32.

2. *Annual Catalog, Oklahoma A. and M. College, 1908-1909,* p. 15.

3. This legislation requiring instruction in agriculture in the high schools of the state was championed mightily by John Fields, who was responsible for the Agricultural Experiment Station in Stillwater. After supervising careful research and after publishing the results, Fields was frustrated because the farmers of the day steadfastly refused to make use of the material. If he could get the public school teachers to get current students used to studying agriculture and learning of the latest scientific advances, he believed there was an excellent chance that they would continue that habit once they themselves were farming, thus creating a new generation of enlightened and scientific farmers. To implement this provision of the constitution, the solons addressed both teachers and the Oklahoma A. and M. College in regular legislation. First, instead of leaving existing colleges with separate boards of control, it was stipulated that the Oklahoma State Board of Agriculture would serve as the board of regents for all of the agricultural and mechanical colleges, and that included Oklahoma A. and M. as well as several two-year agricultural colleges located across the state. *General Statutes of Oklahoma—1908. A Compilation of all the Laws of a General Nature including the Session Laws of 1907* (Kansas City, MO: Pipes-Reed Book Company, 1908), p. 128.

4. *General Statutes of Oklahoma—1908,* p. 224.

5. *General Statutes of Oklahoma—1908,* p. 225.

6. *General Statutes of Oklahoma—1908,* p. 225. Although the language of the statute specifically called for a "chairman of agriculture for schools," Oklahoma A. and M. College was apparently not complex enough at that point to create such a department or division. Instead, the institution responded by establishing a position called "Professor of Agriculture for Schools."

7. Angelo C. Scott, *The Story of an Administration of the Oklahoma Agricultural and Mechanical College* [Stillwater: Oklahoma Agricultural and Mechanical College, 1942], pp. 1-19.

8. Author interview with Bill Hindman, Marjorie Orloski, Benn Palmer, and Gladys Skinner, 1 July 1986, Centennial Histories Oral Interview Collection, Special Collections, Edmon Low Library, Oklahoma State University, Stillwater, Oklahoma. Gladys Skinner, a graduate of the class of 1936, stated in the interview: "I want to tell you about a professor I had in literature, Benjamin Franklin Williams. He was a bearded gentleman, real sophisticated-looking guy. An excellent professor. He said since he was named Benjamin Franklin he thought he should write a proverb. He wrote, 'Virtue has no news value.'" *Annual Catalog, Oklahoma A. and M. College, 1908-1909,* p. 12.

9. *Annual Catalog, Oklahoma A. and M. College, 1904-1905,* p. 21.

10. *Annual Catalog, Oklahoma A. and M. College, 1908-1909,* pp. 34-36.

11. *Annual Catalog, Oklahoma A. and M. College, 1908-1909,* pp. 17-18.

12. Oklahoma A. and M. College *New Education,* 15 January 1910, p. 1.

13. Jack Ray, "Is A. & M. Tradition Bound?" *Oklahoma A. and M. College Magazine,* vol. 10, no. 8, (May 1939) p. 3.

14. Oklahoma State University *Daily O'Collegian,* 1 May 1959, pp. 1, 6.

15. *New Education,* 1 September 1910, pp. 1, 4.

16. *New Education,* 15 July 1910, p. 2.

17. *Annual Catalog, Oklahoma A. and M. College, 1912-1913,* p. 106.

18. Oklahoma A. and M. College *Orange and Black,* 2 December 1916, p. 2.

19. *Orange and Black,* 20 June 1917, p. 1; *Annual Catalog, Oklahoma A. and M. College, 1921-1922,* p. 281.

20. *Oklahoma A. and M. College Summer Bulletin, 1919,* pp. 11-12.

21. *Annual Catalog, Oklahoma A. and M. College, 1908-1909,* pp. 49-51.

22. *New Education,* 15 December 1909, p. 3.

23. *New Education,* 1 July 1911, p. 4.
24. *New Education,* 1 July 1911, p. 4.
25. *New Education,* 1 July 1911, p. 4.
26. *1937 Redskin,* p. 30, Oklahoma A. and M. College Yearbook.
27. *Orange and Black,* 19 April 1918, p. 1.
28. *Orange and Black,* 25 May 1918, p. 1.
29. *1916 Redskin,* p. 56.
30. *Orange and Black,* 17 February 1917, p. 1.
31. *Orange and Black,* 13 January 1917, p. 1.
32. *Annual Catalog, Oklahoma A. and M. College, 1911,* p. 5.
33. *Annual Catalog, Oklahoma A. and M. College, 1914-1915,* pp. 103-105.
34. *Annual Catalog, Oklahoma A. and M. College, 1917-1918,* pp. 27-28.
35. *Annual Catalog, Oklahoma A. and M. College, 1919-1920,* pp. 136-139.
36. *Daily O'Collegian,* 14 May 1929, p. 1.
37. *Orange and Black,* 17 September 1919, p. 1.

3 Consolidating Gains, Confronting Challenges

The roots of the fledgling School of Education were not yet deep-set, and whether the enterprise would flourish or wither depended heavily on a new leader. Clearly, John Bowers had done yeoman service on behalf of education during his tenure as dean. On the surface, at least, signs were positive. World War I had ended, and, in spite of postwar recession, the nation was about to embark on the heady Roaring Twenties. Yet, gnawing at Oklahoma were the first bites of the Dust Bowl, which would flow inexorably into the black days of the wholly unexpected Wall Street crash. Anticipating, hoping for boom, the new leader would also have to deal with bust.

The man selected to succeed Dr. Bowers as dean was Herbert Patterson. Born in Chilmark, Massachusetts, on February 17, 1887, he was the son of the Reverend and Mrs. John Nelson Patterson. After graduating from Wesleyan University in Middletown, Connecticut, with his B.A. degree and membership in Phi Beta Kappa in 1908, he stayed on to earn his M.A. from the same institution in 1911. He served briefly as a high school teacher in both Massachusetts and Pennsylvania, but he decided to return to school to pursue the Ph.D. The doctorate was awarded by Yale University in 1913. He then moved to Mitchell, South Dakota, where he served as dean of the College of Liberal Arts at Dakota Wesleyan University and introduced innovations such as extension classes for the Mitchell public school teachers, practice teaching, and the summer school.[1]

Dr. Patterson was neat to the point of fastidiousness and had an owlish aura of scholarship. Yet, beneath that somewhat cold exterior, students who knew him found a person who was approachable, patient,

Herbert Patterson, the second dean of the School of Education, served until 1937 and worked systematically to build a more dynamic body of faculty and scholars and to establish the school firmly in Stillwater. In 1937, he was appointed as dean of administration, a post which he occupied until he retired in 1952.

and caring. To his friends, he was simply "Pat." Shortly after arriving in Stillwater, he set forth a statement that was to characterize his attitude both as dean of the School of Education and later as dean of administration: "The qualities prized in the teacher should be stressed to the students. Regular, punctual attendance and regularity in work counts for more than brilliancy."[2]

Almost at once Dean Patterson moved to create a service that was internally associated with and vital to the operation of the School of Education, even though it was not always administratively housed in the school. This was the placement service, which helped thousands of education alumni secure their initial appointments and facilitated later moves up the ladder as careers advanced. But there were some earlier steps on which Dr. Patterson no doubt built. The initial effort at placement and follow-up occurred in the fall of 1916, when C. W. Briles, an associate professor of education and social science, conducted a survey to see if graduates were in positions for which they were suited. If they were not so placed, "the School of Education will put forth every effort to place such graduates in positions where their talents may be used to advantage." He also planned to contact Oklahoma school officials to find out "what vacancies will be open next year, so that the School of Education may place the teachers who expect to go out from this institution this year to the very best possible advantage."[3]

Throughout the 1910s, the college catalog stated flatly that Oklahoma Agricultural and Mechanical College people got jobs. In the 1919-20 catalog, however, the process by which this occurred was formalized by the new education dean and was heralded as a "free service . . . available for teachers, prospective teachers, superintendents and school boards. Blanks for this purpose are found in the secretary's office, Morrill Hall."[4]

By the mid-twenties, the placement bureau was "swinging along" in good shape and was still operating out of the dean's office. Of forty-seven graduates in 1926, thirty-two were teaching, nine were "living at home," and two were pursuing graduate degrees. Only four—or 8.5 percent of the graduates—were working outside of education. In addition, Dean Patterson reported receiving 286 requests for teachers during the previous year, which was roughly six times larger than his supply of graduates. The salary range offered that year was $720-$3,000 for high school teachers and $675-$1,350 for elementary teachers.[5]

During the summer of 1929, the bureau was reorganized. It is probably no coincidence that this occurred not long after the arrival of Henry G. Bennett in Stillwater. At that time, A. O. Martin, class of 1920, was appointed to a college-wide post which combined the secretary of the Former Students Association with the director of the Placement Bureau. The new office, which was located on the second floor of Old Central, was assigned a dual purpose: to place former students and graduates in good jobs; and to cement alumni and former students to the college. It had the added advantage of collapsing two existing positions into one, which made good sense since the college was in the jaws of the Great Depression. Putting the Former Students Association together with what was predominantly a teacher placement service speaks silently to the weight that educators had among the alumni. As late as 1954, Gerald T. Stubbs, Oklahoma A. and M.'s director of public school services, estimated that fully 30 percent of Oklahoma A. and M.'s graduates were teaching and said that all seven of the schools were represented in that figure. Even veterinary medicine graduated a small number of people who taught at the college level.[6]

But in 1919, when Dean Patterson arrived in Stillwater, the newest academic unit had yet to be recognized as a major force with which to be reckoned. That, however, did not prevent the new dean from moving ahead aggressively. Ensconced in his office in the Old Engineering Building only four months, Dean Patterson stated that the school ought to get a new home. Less than two weeks later, he upped the ante by claiming that the school was due no less than an entire building dedicated to its work. This seemed like an odd request since the faculty was not especially large. Still, bravado must have been appropriate, for in his second year in the deanship Dr. Patterson announced that the school had grown so much "that President J. W. Cantwell has decided to locate the school in separate quarters. Plans have been made and the work will start immediately toward the remodeling of the Old Chemistry Building for the educational headquarters." It might have been an old building, and it might have been compromised in design, but it was to be his; and he envisioned one floor with offices, lecture rooms, and laboratories, and another floor with large classrooms and an experimental laboratory for psychology. The dean would be away from the engineers and would have his office next to a reading room and the school library—a perfect setting for a quiet scholar. With refurbished faculty offices in sight, Dr. Patterson sought to fill them. Charles L. Kezer was brought in as principal of the secondary school, supervisor of practice teaching, and acting head of the history department. Fred McCarrel continued as assistant professor of education; and, in 1922 Solomon L. Reed, formerly of Gustavus Adolphus College, was added as professor of education, which brought the staff of the school to four. In a pinch, the school could seek the assistance of Samuel A. Maroney, who was professor of history but also was involved with the secondary school. Finally, in terms of programs, the dean incorporated student teaching into the junior and senior years, following the model he had used in South Dakota.[7]

For some reason, rather than settling down comfortably in the Old Chemistry Building, the school in fact became quite peripatetic, sort of an academic vagabond. There is no evidence that education actually occupied the Old Chemistry Building, but in the fall of 1921 the school was vacating the Vocational Building in favor of space in the basement of the new library, which was located west of Old Central and south of the Engineering Building. Five years later, once the administration

In this pre-1930 aerial photograph, the old quad seems relatively secure on the southeast corner of the campus. During the years after World World I, many buildings sprang up to the west and north of the original campus including a new administration building, a gymnasium, a library, and residence halls. Although campus architects and planners discussed removal of Old Central and some other alterations to the quad, it would be several years before major changes would occur.

Centennial Histories Series

of the college moved out of Morrill Hall and into nearly-completed Whitehurst Hall, education was shifted to four rooms in Morrill Hall, sharing space with foreign languages, the School of Commerce, physics, and the correspondence school.[8]

The new dean was after more than space, though. He was concerned with image. In 1921, he stated that the school had a two-fold purpose: "First, to prepare superintendents, principals, supervisors and teachers for the public schools of Oklahoma; second, to enlarge the appreciation of the importance of the American public school system in the advancement of civilization."[9] On a wider front, he was concerned about the image of the college as a whole and argued in public that the institution ought to be called Oklahoma State College of Agricultural and Mechanical Arts, even though he admitted that Oklahoma Agricultural and Mechanical College had worked quite well with the legislature and public for thirty years. He forwarded several reasons for suggesting the change: "State College" would connote the breadth of the curriculum, while "A. and M." suggested only two programs; the term "A. and M." had no meaning to many people and had to be explained; "A. and M." sounded totally masculine, so women came to the college only in spite of the name; and "State College" would distinguish Stillwater from the district agricultural schools, which were secondary schools. Although Dr. Patterson's proposal apparently was ignored by the administration and the legislature, it was embraced by the editors of the student paper and garnered a page one spread.[10] Until Bradford Knapp assumed the presidency in 1923, the paper consistently referred to Oklahoma State College, but then the petit revolution was ended with Oklahoma A. and M. back in the ascendancy for another thirty plus years.

A second major attempt to adopt the name of Oklahoma State College took place in the spring of 1940 and was again strongly backed by the editors of the O'Collegian. The matter was put to a vote, but only about a quarter of the student body chose to participate, which suggests the editors had failed to make it a burning issue. By a majority of 11 (801 to 790), the electorate supported Oklahoma A. and M. College for the name of the institution. It was said the women were strongly pro-change but were defeated by the largely Aggie males.[11]

It would appear that Dean Patterson liked to change more than names, and he was also something of a joiner. Under Dean Bowers, an Education Society was created. In October of 1919, Patterson called a meeting of all the students of the school for the purpose of organizing "the whole school into a society," and he had already met with the senior class to elect officers. "The purpose of the society is to furnish a means whereby students and professors of the school may become better acquainted, may make their school more of a force in the college, and may help themselves to better positions when they have finished. It is also a plan of

Although every dean of the School of Education encouraged the formation of a student organization, such groups appeared and then faded away until recently. This 1911 photograph shows the Educational Society, which predated the school by two years. Unlike later such associations, it was heavily weighted toward the masculine side, which mirrored the college's concern that graduates be involved with educating future generations of farmers and ranchers. Members included G. D. Shallenberger, science and literature; Allen J. Moore, science and literature; C. E. Wilson, science and literature; H. C. DeMumbrun; O. C. Griggs; M. B. McKay, general science; A. C. Brodell, teachers' normal; E. E. Harnden, teachers' normal; F. R. Hennigh; J. C. McIntyre, civil engineering; Edna Newton; W. N. Wright, teachers' normal; and C. H. Roberts, agriculture.

this society to get in touch with the alumni of its school and do some publicity work through them.''[12]

Perhaps this indicated something about Dean Patterson's ''take charge'' personality, for he surely did not leave anything to chance since he had both the officers in place and the purposes articulated before he bothered to involve the student body as a whole. In a later issue of the *Orange and Black*, students who had not attended the meeting were admonished: ''If you were not there, you are a slacker.''[13] Remember, this was the man who prized ''regular, punctual attendance.'' Still, he did have professional interests in the matter and saw the society as a place where students, professors, and teachers could interact positively and thus opened the organization to any teacher of education in the college and to any Stillwater public school teacher who wished to join.

The *1919-20 Catalog* said that the Education Society held frequent meetings to discuss practical problems relating to teaching as a vocation, to develop friendship among its members, and to emphasize the importance of technical teacher training. Three years later, the college proudly announced that it was offering eight cash prizes, and two of these were available through Kappa Delta Pi, the education honorary—$15 to the sophomore and $10 to the freshman in the School of Education with the highest average in scholarship.[14] Kappa Delta Pi originated at the University of Illinois in 1910 and was established at Oklahoma A. and M. in 1921.

While a dean might be able to will an organization into being and stipulate a set of purposes, he or she cannot force it to flourish no matter how well intended. That was the fate of the Education Society. It met irregularly, never became a force in the college, and eventually died.

Still, education students and faculty did interact informally from time to time. For example, in 1925, the masculine side of the School of Education received some campus notoriety through participation on a school football team. After the education gridiron heroes fell to the team fielded by the School of Science and Literature in a 20-7 battle, it faded away. In the early 1930s, Kathryn Long worked with Kappa Delta Pi and the Stillwater teachers to sponsor a Christmas party in Swim's Hall. The following fall, Dorothy Caldwell, Guy Lackey, and Gordon Mott organized a steak fry in behalf of Kappa Delta Pi. The picnic must have been a success, as a similar party was repeated in the fall of 1933 at Ripley Bluffs. Kappa Delta Pi provided food and transportation for over a hundred people.[15]

It was apparent that the faculty actively supported Kappa Delta Pi, not only with moral support but with time and advice. For example, in the fall of 1933, upper division students served in leadership roles, with Beverly Queal (senior) as president, Arthur Ackenbom (senior) as pledge captain, Ruth Patterson (junior) as recording secretary, and Inez McSpadden Andrews (senior) as corresponding secretary. Reinforcing the students were not only faculty but senior faculty at that: Professor Lackey was vice president, Professor Reed was counselor, and C. L. Kezer was secretary.[16]

Although Dr. Patterson did not succeed in creating a new group, he was able to utilize an existing organization. In 1917, the Ancient and Beneficent Order of the Red Red Rose was created in Durant in order to "bind the teaching profession into a clear feeling of brotherly love," with the organization financially supported by a "wealthy old school teacher" who was unknown to people outside the fraternity. While the Red Red Rose was to a large extent more social than professional, membership did put Dean Patterson in touch with school people of influence. For example, the Oklahoma A. and M. chapter boasted over fifty members, one of whom was President Cantwell, who happened to be initiated at the same time Dean Patterson was.[17]

Dean Patterson may have had cause to be cool toward President Cantwell, though, for during that presidency the fortunes of the preparatory school fell on hard times. With the college established fully as a collegiate grade institution and with the spread of public education in Oklahoma's towns and villages, the president was convinced that the

Students in education had a penchant for out-of-town outings, and frequently faculty and students with vehicles assembled in front of Morrill Hall and the Women's Building to give a lift to colleagues lacking their own transportation. This group is preparing the School of Education's entry in a 1917 parade.

preparatory school was no longer necessary either to keep the college afloat or to fill an educational gap that was closing. When President Cantwell arrived in Stillwater in 1915, the preparatory students still outnumbered the college people, but during his tenure the college enrollment doubled even though those were the years of World War I. Because there were twice as many college students as there were preparatory students, the president adopted the policy of gradually phasing the school out, one year at a time. When he left office in 1921, the first two years had been eliminated, and the third year was scheduled for the chopping block.

Oklahoma A. and M.'s eighth president, James B. Eskridge, had different ideas. He moved quickly to reinstate the secondary school and to bring it up to the standards of accredited high schools in the state.[18]

In the spring of 1925, the preparatory school experienced a "good news/bad news" situation. On the positive side, for the first time in the history of the school, there was a graduation for the twenty-five people who finished the program, complete with a banquet at Trinity Methodist Church followed by an address by the tenth president, Bradford Knapp.[19] On the negative side, five months later the same president who had graced the graduation ceremonies stated: "Likewise, it should be understood that we are turning away all secondary students that we possibly can. For example, a year ago this fall, we had 113 students in the secondary school, where this fall we have only 57."[20] Still, in spite of this second presidential assault, the school continued. It was renamed the training high school in the fall of 1925 and was permitted to admit up to 100 students who had academic backgrounds equal to a completed eighth grade education.[21] When this noble educational unit finally died, after enabling thousands of pupils to complete high school, after preparing almost as many to meet college entrance requirements, and after guaranteeing the viability of Oklahoma A. and M. College for decades, it was not afforded the dignity of a public funeral. There was no formal farewell; after the 1928-29 academic year, it simply vanished.

Even though Dean Patterson was unable to spark a sustained student organization and was unable to prevent the demise of the secondary school, he was more successful in introducing an innovation in the area of vocational counseling. During World War I, the area of testing and counseling—trying to match individual talents with tasks that needed to be done—had come into its own. It was logical to adapt that procedure to civilian use after the war. Working with H. I. Jones, head of the Department of Chemistry, Dean Patterson developed an extensive questionnaire, called "The Individual Analysis Blank." It dealt with personal history, ambitions and interests, work preferences, work record, vocational choice, personal qualities, and general vocational questions. Volunteering their time, Dean Patterson and Professor Jones went over the form with the student in a personal interview and tried to fit the student to the right educational program.[22] While such counseling was done on an informal, ad hoc basis in the 1920s, the concept was a viable one. As time went on, the program was greatly expanded and was finally formalized as the Bureau of Tests and Measurements.

Dean Patterson had administrative duties that went beyond the School of Education. He, as well as a string of his successors, also served as the director of the summer school. This was a logical combination since so much of the summer session pertained to education. For example, in 1925, education accounted for 42 percent, the preparatory school for 19 percent, home economics for 13 percent, science and literature for 11 percent, commerce and agriculture for 6 percent each, and engineering for 2 percent of the summer enrollments. Together, education and the preparatory school had 61 percent of the summer students.[23]

The dean did not restrict himself to education, though, and he was willing to make the college facilities available for worthy causes and special projects. One such effort was attempted in 1925 when R. L. Spalburg, the superintendent of the United States Indian Field Service in the Midwest, was seeking a site to teach 100 Indian teachers drawn from Nebraska, Kansas, and Oklahoma. The purpose of the special offering was to focus attention on school hygiene and to develop a program of health education for Indian schools. Spalburg, who directed the participants to enroll, said he selected Oklahoma A. and M. College "because of the variety of courses offered, because of the willingness to give the courses needed in health education, and because of the small expense involved in sending them to the Aggie school." Indeed, there was substantial variety, for the summer roster included 235 courses in 44 different fields of study.[24]

In that same year, the demonstration school was firmly established under the leadership of Kathryn Long, who was a long-lived and dedicated member of the faculty of the School of Education. Although demonstration teaching had been an instructional technique employed virtually from the first year, it was now used in cooperation with the Stillwater School Board and was mutually beneficial: 200 Stillwater school children from grades one through eight attended summer school five days a week, from eight o'clock until noon for the grand fee of one dollar; and Mrs. Long could coordinate her four regular teachers, who taught two grades each, could organize special teaching demonstrations, and could provide her college students with opportunities to observe, practice teach, and help supervise the playground. Eventually, the program expanded to include all grades and was moved off campus into Jefferson Elementary, the junior high school, and the senior high school in town to take advantage of more natural school settings.[25]

Four years later, in 1929, Dean Patterson added the final segment of the summer session. In 1916, Oklahoma A. and M.'s summer offerings were found wanting because of the lack of a high-powered lecture series. The normal schools had such series, and Oklahoma A. and M. simply "stole a page out of their books." The dean realized the college was foregoing opportunities by not utilizing the month of August, because Oklahoma A. and M. students were taking up to nine credits in Stillwater during the regular summer session and then migrating to other schools for August classes. Capitalizing on the successful records of others, Dean Patterson added a four-week August intersession which afforded students the opportunity to earn an additional four credits.[26] It was a mutually beneficial arrangement. The school teachers earned additional credits without the hassle of relocating in August, while the college faculty were given another opportunity to augment their meager salaries.

The enrollment of the School of Education gradually increased during Dean Patterson's administration. This same trend was taking place in the college as a whole, but at a different rate. When Dr. Patterson arrived in 1919, the school had only 57 students and was the smallest of all the academic units. After eight years, he was supervising 386 students and led the largest of the schools. Yet, in at least one respect, nothing had changed since the days of Dean Bowers—education was still a huge service operation. While Dr. Bowers had estimated that 40 percent of the students in the Oklahoma A. and M. College took some education courses, Dean Patterson upped that figure to 50 percent. He attributed the greater than average growth of the school to the demand for better trained teachers, to greater recognition of the teaching profession as a vocation, to the cooperation of other collegiate departments, and to the dedication of his corps of instructors.[27]

But quantity is not always the criterion one wants to use, especially in a collegiate setting. To check quality, Dean Patterson gave intelligence

Midway through the Roaring Twenties, the School of Education had acquired a faculty of far greater size and diversity than when Dean Patterson arrived in 1919. When the Great Depression hit, a core of faculty stayed with the school until well after World War II. While obviously dedicated, this did leave future deans with an aging and heavily overworked faculty. Some of the faculty include left to right (*front row*) H. E. Harrington, K. M. Long, Elizabeth C. Miller, Dean Herbert Patterson, Eula Oleta Jack, Mabel Davis Holt, and Allen S. Davis; and (*back row*) Marlin Ray Chauncey, Benjamin C. Dyess, Walter H. Echols, Guy A. Lackey, Bee Chrystal, Solomon L. Reed, James R. Campbell, and William R. Baker.

tests to the 137 freshmen who were enrolled in his orientation class. He found that 28 students were superior—having an I.Q. range of 109 to 119—while four others were very superior, scoring from 120 to 139. It would seem that an academic dean would be pleased to announce that nearly a quarter of his freshman students were at least superior and stop there. Not Dean Patterson. He trotted out his standard admonition—bright students should not depend on intellectual brilliance; weaker students should study more than average; success in college, as in life, does not depend entirely upon intellectual ability; hard work is necessary.[28]

Dean Patterson was a man who had interests in a variety of areas and held several positions of responsibility. For example, in 1931, at the twentieth annual meeting of the Oklahoma Academy of Science, he was elected president of the organization, thereby ending his four-year stint as secretary-treasurer. In that same year, he was elected to chair the Section for College Professors of Education of the Central Division of the Oklahoma Education Association. A few years earlier, he was Oklahoma's representative at the American Association for the Advancement of Science in Nashville. While he was in Nashville, he was the Oklahoma delegate at the national convention of Phi Kappa Phi. Dean Patterson had a keen interest in science and sometimes a flair for the sensational. In 1928, he invited the Oklahoma Academy of Science to meet in Stillwater and arranged to have a demonstration of television. It was believed this was the first scientific group in Oklahoma to see television, and the set—the only one in the state and one of only a dozen in the entire West—was owned by a Mr. Wilson and brought from Tulsa to Stillwater for the occasion. In December of 1935, he was appointed as a consultant to the National Education Association's (NEA) educational policies commission in Washington. He was to help prepare long-range plans for the improvement of the nation's schools. It was stressed that the purpose of the commission was to provide leadership and service to American educators; it was not intended to bring about standardization and uniformity.[29]

In spite of the progress made under Dean Patterson, it cannot be denied that times were tough, too. Henry G. Bennett, who succeeded President Knapp in 1928, holds the distinction of being the first president of Oklahoma A. and M. College who held that office for an extended period of time. But he also had to face the fact that the position was difficult because Oklahoma was already in the grips of the Dust Bowl when he assumed the office—doing so without a formal inauguration in order to economize. In his second year, a critical situation became desperate because of the stock market crash on Wall Street and the ensuing Great Depression.

Many might say that Henry G. Bennett was president of Oklahoma Agricultural and Mechanical College during the worst of times, for he worked surrounded by the disaster of the Depression, the havoc of World War II, and the dislocation of the post-war years. Yet in the midst of darkness and problems, he saw light and opportunity. He laid a foundation upon which a significant university would be built, nurtured elements that would be integral parts of the School of Education, and gave his life trying to achieve democracy and security for a war-weary world.

Dr. Bennett was aware that the college would survive only if students had enough money to stay in school, and he moved to enlarge the student employment program that had existed since the college was founded. He had the Oklahoma A. and M. College cabinet shop—using student labor—build twenty looms which eventually employed fifty students. The Tiger Tavern, formerly called the College Cafeteria, shifted almost totally to student labor, employing fifteen students. In addition, the college supported a broom factory, a ceramics plant to produce mostly flower pots, and a shop to produce all-wool hooked rugs. Of course, the college farms continued to use students. All in all, these efforts offered employment for between 185 and 220 students, who earned between 25 and 50 cents an hour.[30]

The students of Aggieland, however, did not rely completely on the college administration to raise money to keep body and soul together. By the fall of 1931, both the *O'Collegian* and the Young Men's Christian Association were operating as labor bureaus and getting students odd jobs in town. Three students formed the Car Washers Association and would wash a car and dust the inside for a dollar. Soon other groups organized to wash windows, mow lawns, and do other work.[31]

In spite of his many skills as an administrator, Dr. Bennett was unable to provide total protection to the faculty, either in salary or employment. In 1931, the faculty feared a salary cut of 7.5 percent. The Oklahoma State Board of Agriculture, the administrative governing body for the college, however, managed to keep the damage at 3 percent by removing twenty-eight faculty from the payroll. President Bennett assured the remaining faculty that no salary reduction would be made if a person were supporting a family and earning an annual salary of $2,100 or less. When the list of people taken off the payroll was published, it included Mabel D. Holt, assistant professor of education whose leave of absence to attend the University of Southern California was extended for an additional year; an unnamed instructor in education who was also on leave; and Raymond G. Campbell, assistant professor of education.[32] All in all, Dean Patterson's staff got off quite lightly because only one person who had actually been working on the campus the previous year lost his job.

In light of the crash in the private sector, serving the public schools seemed to the students to have a degree of security to it. Educators might be paid "dirt poor" salaries, but at least they usually got paid, even though their pay might be in scrip. The college proclaimed that the class of 1933 was the largest in the history of Oklahoma A. and M. College. An examination of the graduation list revealed that the largest portion was in education and that some of those graduates moved into exceptionally good positions. For example, John E. Holcomb got his M.S. and was elected president of Northeastern Oklahoma Junior College at Miami.

Jack Van Bebber, an Olympic champion wrestler, was employed as a coach at Texas Tech University. After earning the M.S., Henry V. Witt was hired as a faculty member at Northwestern State Teachers College, while Mildren Randels joined the faculty at Northeastern State Teachers College, also with a master's in hand. Fred P. Drake was superintendent of Okeene; James D. Dunlap became the school administrator at Morris; and John W. Ruter served as county superintendent in Rogers County—each with a master's degree.[33]

That record of accomplishment in teacher placement continued as the nation bottomed out of the Depression and began the painfully slow process of economic recovery in 1936. That year, Dean Patterson was pleased to report to the alumni that only four of the ninety-five graduates were without jobs—for an amazingly low unemployment rate of 5 percent. Dr. Patterson, who was concerned that the preponderance of women in the public school faculties was "making the boys sissified," was pleased that the percentage of men in his programs was gradually rising, moving from 20 percent in 1931-32 to 36 percent in 1935-36.[34]

Even though employment in education was relatively secure, the faculty in the college were still nervous because there was one area that could be easily sliced away and would relieve a significant amount of the financial pressure—cut the summer session. After all, the state budget in 1933 was down 30 percent from two years ago. Dr. Bennett said not to worry, but his people were still deeply concerned. The Oklahoma A. and M. College president was as good as his word. The legislature included $38,000 for the 1933 and 1934 summer sessions, and the president said that amount would be sufficient. At the same time, W. B. Bizzell, president of the University of Oklahoma, had his request for $36,000 denied. He responded by saying the university's summer program would continue—the faculty would simply have to carry on without pay. In 1933, Dean Patterson's twenty-sixth Oklahoma A. and M. College's summer session served in excess of 1,100 students, with 208 enrolled in the School of Education.[35]

Having the summer session might have been a battle won, but at the same time it appeared that the war to keep the School of Education might be lost. Governor William H. "Alfalfa Bill" Murray struck with an executive order: "Much duplication of educational work in the several higher institutions is indulged in, creating small classes with large salaried teachers of such classes at great cost to the taxpayers. It therefore becomes necessary to eliminate such duplication, and thereby the excess expenses upon the people. Now, therefore, I, William H. Murray, the governor of the State of Oklahoma, do hereby order the president of the University and the Agricultural and Mechanical College; and the regents of the two said institutions to effectuate that result, beginning with the fiscal year, July 1, 1933, by provided: First: The elimination of 'education

During March of 1933, Governor William H. "Alfalfa Bill" Murray issued an executive order to ban work in education at Oklahoma A. and M. College. Although this gubernatorial move to economize shook the school badly, the threat soon passed, allowing the school to continue moving ahead through both the Depression and World War II years. Governor Murray speaks to an Armistice Day crowd during the early 1930s.

classes' or normal school work, from both the University and A&M College, leaving such 'education work' to be performed only by the six normal schools, or teachers colleges of the state. Second: It is also ordered that all engineering be transferred from the University at Norman, Oklahoma, to the state A&M College at Stillwater, Oklahoma. Third: That all pre-medical and pre-law education taught at A&M College be transferred to the University. Fourth: That all classes in geology be transferred from the Agricultural and Mechanical College to the University; and that all classes of pathology be transferred from the University to the A&M College, together with all classes in home economics. And that after July 1, no money shall be expended for such purposes; and the president of the University and the president of A&M College, together with the members of the board of regents and the board of agriculture are hereby directed to take notice and to effectuate rules, orders, and regulations in conformity to and with this order."[36]

Two days after the order was made public, the board of agriculture stated only that Dr. Bennett's contract would be renewed for the next fiscal year. Because the presidents were always hired on a year-to-year basis, that was not an unusual announcement. It said nothing about the governor's action. On his part, Governor Murray appointed a nine-member committee, including three representatives from Oklahoma A. and M. College and one representative from the university, to work out the details of implementing his plan. Presidents Bennett and Bizzell were excluded.[37]

A week later, the committee generally supported Governor Murray, saying that all undergraduate classes in professional education should be taught at the state teachers colleges but that Oklahoma A. and M. College should have a graduate program for the professional training of teachers in agriculture, home economics, and vocational education. After all, the state constitution had specifically assigned that obligation to the Oklahoma A. and M. College. Furthermore, the committee recommended that all engineering and related areas should be taught in Still-water, save for petroleum engineering and geological engineering; that all geological work should be assigned to the university except for soil geology; that all home economics work should be restricted to Oklahoma A. and M. College; and that all pre-law, pre-medicine, and pre-pharmacy should be given to the University of Oklahoma. In addition, it recommended that students should have to pay for individual work in art and music and that all extension work should be ended, save for agriculture and home economics.[38]

In the fall of 1933, Dean Patterson announced that the courses in elementary education were being discontinued because of the action of the committee, although steps were taken to ensure that juniors and seniors currently enrolled would be able to complete the requirements for graduation in elementary education. None of the freshman and sophomore courses were offered.[39]

All of this excitement and activity on behalf of reforming, streamlining, and economizing the higher education system in Oklahoma gradually faded away. There is no evidence that either the president of Oklahoma A. and M. or of the University of Oklahoma directly challenged the governor's directive, although Bennett earlier had said he would visit with the governor about the plan. It appears that the order was largely ignored and that the attention of the political leaders of the state shifted to other matters. In early 1935, for example, Dean Patterson was again using the *Oklahoma A. and M. College Magazine*, the alumni magazine, specifically to recruit educators to enroll in the "full range of courses" that would be offered in the summer session.[40]

It was not only the School of Education at the Oklahoma A. and M. College that was being adversely affected by the ravages of the Great Depression. Everyone suffered, even the relatively secure public schools. For example, in Stillwater—which was classified as a "group four" school, one of 158 in Oklahoma having more than 1,000 students—the teaching load for faculty had increased by 30 percent between 1929 and

1933. Both men and women had salary reductions of 27 percent and 15 percent respectively. In 1929, 62 faculty taught 1,621 children; in 1933, 53 faculty taught 1,812 pupils. The average annual man's salary slipped from $1,631 to $1,195 while the woman's fell from $971 to $821. The cost of education per pupil fell from $60.13 to $37.53. Ford C. Harper, who was with the Oklahoma State Chamber of Commerce, was shocked and said: "How many politicians have had their work increased substantially while taking salary cuts of 20 percent or more?"[41]

In spite of being buffeted between the Scylla of depression economics and the Charybdis of Oklahoma politics, the school was able to do remarkably well, even though it was a struggle. By 1936, it had eleven faculty on board, and the course offerings had blossomed to a total of eighty-one, organized by topic. Twenty-one courses, the largest curricular unit, were collected under educational administration, which included the usual administrative courses plus a miscellany such as Counseling and Guidance for Girls (taught by Dean of Women Julia Stout), Adult Education, Junior College, and School Statistics. There was an unusual degree of specificity revealed by the courses. For exam-

Julia Stout and Clarence McElroy, dean of women and dean of men respectively, were forces with whom to be reckoned by all Oklahoma A. and M. students. College students from time out of mind have felt duty-bound to beat the system, and deans of such students have been equally energetic to overlook a lot in order to apply rules with reason. Dean Stout taught courses in educational administration including Counseling and Guidance for Girls. The dormitory west of Murray Hall was named for Dean Stout on her retirement. Over the years, Dean "Mac" served in a multitude of administrative positions. His name is memorialized on one of Stillwater's major thoroughfares north of the campus.

ple, separate supervision courses were available for rural schools, elementary schools, secondary schools, and village and consolidated schools. Likewise, there were administrative courses for rural schools, for secondary schools, and for public schools in Oklahoma.

The second largest curricular division was elementary education, which also served as the home for work in Visual Education, Educational Measurements, Management and School Law, Rural School Management, and Maladjusted School Children. Elementary education had a total of nineteen classes. The third curricular category was psychology, with fifteen courses, all of which would be assigned to such a current listing. The fourth, with thirteen classes, was secondary education, and—like psychology—it included only courses that were related quite closely to that education field. The last two curricular areas were relatively small. Philosophy had only seven classes, and some of those, such as Educational Sociology and Comparative Education, were fairly far afield from philosophy. Furthermore, all of these classes were taught by one faculty member—W. H. Echols—except for Materials and Methods of Character Education, which was handled by Guy Lackey, and Comparative Education, which was taught by J. C. Muerman. Last, and least in regard to the scope of offerings, was religious education with six courses, all of which were available for college credit but taught by Stillwater ministers rather than by college faculty.[42]

It would be misleading to leave the impression that education was broadening and strengthening only on the Oklahoma A. and M. campus, for that was occurring throughout the profession as a whole as Oklahoma continued to develop. Virtually from the time Oklahoma was opened as a territory, professional educators were concerned that people with substandard qualifications were turned loose in the schools of the state. In the spring of 1930 the state was able to take steps to strengthen its educational requirements. Previously, one could receive a two-year state elementary certificate after completing only thirty hours of collegiate level work. This explained in part why many people took the freshman year, grabbed the certificate, taught for a couple of years, and then returned to college for further study.

The requirement was increased to at least forty hours, with twenty-six prescribed: six in English; four in natural science; six in social science, mathematics or language; two in agriculture; and eight in education, including two hours of practice teaching. At the same time, the state high school certificate required ninety collegiate hours, instead of the previous sixty, and included eight hours of education, with two in practice teaching.[43] Finally, a life certificate would now be granted to one who completed the four-year program in elementary education and who earned the bachelor of science degree. Formerly, life certificates were available only for high school teachers, but by 1930 especially the larger Oklahoma towns were demanding that grade school teachers also have completed undergraduate collegiate degrees. It was only fair that graduates with comparable training should have comparable certificates.

In 1931, the requirements were made even stiffer. Dean Patterson proclaimed that such advances were made possible because of the surplus of available teachers in the public schools, which was caused largely by the advent of the Depression. This was only one of several peaks and valleys of teacher supply. Most professional fields have salary linked to the size of the pool of available personnel. When the pool is small, salaries offered are high, and when the pool is large, salaries will fall. But in education, salaries always seemed to stay in a depressed state regardless of the number of people entering the field. The variable was standards for certification—when the field was glutted, standards were increased since public school employers could be more selective; in times of scarcity, especially during war years, standards were simply dropped until enough people "qualified" to meet the need.

In 1931, it was decided that a person would have to be twenty years old, instead of nineteen, to be certified as a teacher. Dr. Patterson believed that this change would result in most of his students completing the college degree before applying for a teaching certificate and entering the field. If a person went to school each year until age twenty, he or she would be so close to obtaining the undergraduate degree that it would usually not make sense to drop out short of getting the sheepskin. With these changes, the dean forecast that within a few years all elementary teachers would have a B.S. while high school teachers would have the M.S. Indeed, education was advancing as a profession, and this was in the depths of the Great Depression.[44]

Since quite a few of the school's graduates were leaving Stillwater with the M.S. in hand to accept leadership positions, Dean Patterson's forecast was made in light of the fact that Oklahoma A. and M. was beginning to approach graduate study more systematically. Although Oklahoma Agricultural and Mechanical College was created strictly as an undergraduate college, it was only a matter of time before the idea of advanced graduate work reared its head. Oddly enough, this initiative did not come from the scholars on the faculty but from a chemistry assistant who was working with the Agricultural Experiment Station. On September 28, 1910, R. O. Baird petitioned the faculty to conduct research for graduate credit. This left the faculty in a quandary as they were not sure they had the legal right to award postbaccalaureate credit. Their response was to form a committee to study the matter, and the eventual recommendation was to accommodate Baird's request. He was awarded his degree in 1912. Two years later, the postgraduate committee was established on a standing basis, with both John Bowers and Carl Gundersen as members. Still, graduate work was not encouraged, and no financial help was requested from the legislature to support it. In fact, "faculty members regarded it [that is, graduate education] with disdain, . . . [and] students who desired to do research and advanced work almost forced themselves into the various departments."[45] In 1915, the faculty finally authorized the M.S. as a regular degree.

With these expanded offerings, it was possible for the school to announce that it was now able to offer the degree of master of science in education, which would be awarded to students who fulfilled all degree requirements and who provided evidence of at least nine months of successful teaching. No certificate accompanied this academic achievement because during this time students were granted a state life high school certificate upon completing the bachelor of science program.[46]

Students in education, though, were a little slow to take advantage of the new graduate degree, for it was not until 1925 that the first master's in education was awarded. Considering that most graduate students in education took work only in the summer, a lapse of several years to complete the program is not unreasonable. The student who earned the first master's degree was A. O. Martin, who wrote a thesis entitled "A Survey of Silent Reading in Eighteen Oklahoma Schools." Unfortunately,

Getting jobs was always of critical importance to Oklahoma A. and M. College students, many of whom entered education either as a permanent or temporary career. Likewise, keeping track of former students and alumni was of vital importance to the college. Both tasks were ably discharged by A. O. Martin, who was a graduate of the college and the first person to earn a master's degree in education.

Centennial Histories Series

the thesis itself does not reveal which faculty member supervised the research.

In the fall of 1929, President Bennett appointed Daniel C. McIntosh as dean of the newly formed Graduate School and established a new graduate committee with one representative from each school, appointed by the president. Solomon L. Reed represented the School of Education. By 1930, there was a separate catalog for the Graduate School, and the following year the M.A. was added to the M.S. At that time, the School of Education had fourteen courses for graduate students only plus another sixteen for either advanced undergraduate or graduate students.[47]

Since his installation in 1919, Dr. Patterson had confronted an endless series of opportunities and challenges, all of which would be wearing for any college administrator. After seventeen years of service, it was time for him to have a change of pace. He requested and was awarded a sabbatical leave, which was to begin right after the end of the 1936 summer session. He planned to drive to the University of California at Berkeley, visiting many universities en route to see especially what their summer programs were like since he still served as the director of the summer session. During the spring semester, he planned to study at the University of California at Los Angeles, after which he was to resume his responsibilities in Stillwater on June 1, 1937. While he was away, it was expected that Professor Reed would be acting dean of the school.[48]

It would appear that the request for leave was both logical and appropriate, if for no other reason than his length of service as dean, but something seems unusual about it. Typically, each spring the college published the list of sabbatical leaves awarded for the following fiscal year. But Dr. Patterson's sabbatical was announced later in July. Was that because of a clerical oversight? Or was the request made late and suddenly? The record is mute on the matter. Second, and even more unusual, while Dean Patterson was away, President Bennett replaced him not with an acting dean but with a dean—Napoleon Conger.

Two different explanations have been suggested for this chain of events. Harry Brobst, who joined the school a few years after Dean Conger took over, offered a rather harsh one. According to Dr. Brobst, President Bennett told Dr. Patterson it was time to take a vacation. "He hadn't been out of Stillwater a day before Bennett appointed . . . Conger as dean. Then, when Patterson came back, he had no job! . . . Finally, Bennett made a job for him. He called him dean of administration."[49] Another possibility has been forwarded by Florence Ellen Conger Lowe, the new dean's daughter. She said that when her father left the Oklahoma A. and M. College's personnel department in 1931 to take a position in the State Department of Education, Dr. Patterson had been told by President Bennett that Dr. Conger would be appointed to the deanship in five years. Thus, Dean Patterson was given time to adjust to the idea. In reality, it would have been out of character for Dr. Bennett to act on the spur of the moment, while a five-year plan fits his personality and leadership style perfectly. In addition, creating a new position would not be unusual, for President Bennett did not fire people. If they failed to perform, he would typically keep them on the payroll but assign their duties to others.[50]

For whatever reason, Dr. Patterson moved out of Morrill Hall and into the first floor of Whitehurst as dean of administration, which was a strange title since his duties were actually those of registrar and director of admissions. According to Raymond Girod, who as a student in the 1940s worked with Dr. Patterson and who later succeeded him as registrar of Oklahoma A. and M. College/Oklahoma State University, the dean "was very, very precise. He would keep records as if the neatness was all-important, rather than the use of those records. I remember when students would come to the counter to look at their permanent record, he would slide it under a glass so they would not get their fingerprints on the record. Of course, he also did not want them to have an opportunity to change that record . . . . But he protected the permanent record as if it were all-important—very neat, pretty."[51]

Apparently, Dean Patterson manifested two personalities. While dean of the School of Education, he was involved, forward-looking, and described as a "really . . . nice man."[52] But then a different side emerged when he was shifted to Whitehurst. There is no record of a formal complaint being made by Dr. Patterson, but he may have been bitter about his reassignment. This bitterness may have fueled different behavior. During the World War II era, however, he seemed to have settled into his new role. He changed recordkeeping from an alphabetical to a numerical system, making it vastly easier to locate the appropriate transcript, and he purchased a photostat machine so that copies could be made instantly. His office was regarded as "efficient, speedy, and courteous."[53]

In 1952, after thirty-three years of service at Oklahoma A. and M., he decided to retire, at age sixty-five, so that he and Mrs. Patterson could travel. But he planned on staying usually in Stillwater to enjoy the pleasures of golf, fishing, and chess. His retirement was effective as of June 1, 1952. He apparently experienced another identity crisis like the one when he was replaced as dean of the School of Education. He enjoyed retirement only seventeen months, for on November 1, 1953, he was installed as the dean of Piedmont College in Demerest, Georgia. After retiring from Piedmont College, Dean and Mrs. Patterson relocated in Florida and California. Following the death of his wife in 1969, he moved to Memphis, Tennessee, to be near his son, John. He managed to maintain daily two-mile walks until shortly before he died at the age of eighty-two.[54]

In the final analysis it can be said that Dean Patterson, while called

"Pat" by friends, certainly did not stand pat when it came to the School of Education. Upon occasion he did show flair, but more often he operated as a quiet, purposeful force who worked to consolidate the base laid by Dean Bowers by adding staff, courses, and facilities. While he personally was engaged in national organizations and associations, his main thrust was to secure the school against all challenges, be they academic, economic, or political, and to advance the standards of the profession. In light of the environment of his day, he saw fit to focus largely on Stillwater, which was appropriate. By so doing, he was able to position the fledgling school so that it could—under his successors—move to yet another higher level.

Endnotes

1. Oklahoma A. and M. College *Orange and Black,* 10 September 1919, p. 1; Oklahoma A. and M. College *Daily O'Collegian,* 14 May 1929, p. 1.

2. *Orange and Black,* 26 February 1920, p. 1.

3. *Orange and Black,* 20 November 1916, p. 3.

4. *Annual Catalog, Oklahoma A and M. College Catalog, 1919-1920,* p. 141.

5. Oklahoma A. and M. College *O'Collegian,* 6 October 1926, p. 3, 15 October 1926, p. 4.

6. *Daily O'Collegian,* 25 June 1929, p. 1, 11 November 1954, p. 3.

7. *Orange and Black,* 12 July 1920, p. 1.

8. *Orange and Black,* 15 September 1921, p. 1.

9. *Annual Catalog, Oklahoma A. and M. College, 1921-1922,* p. 234.

10. *Orange and Black,* 8 December 1921, p. 1.

11. *Daily O'Collegian,* 7 March 1940, p. 1.

12. *Orange and Black,* 22 October 1919, p. 1.

13. *Orange and Black,* 12 November 1919, p. 3.

14. *Annual Catalog, Oklahoma A. and M. College, 1919-1920,* p. 130; *Orange and Black,* 21 December 1922, p. 1.

15. *O'Collegian,* 3 November 1925, p. 1; *Daily O'Collegian,* 5 December 1931, p. 1, 20 October 1932, p. 1, 25 October 1933, p. 1.

16. *Daily O'Collegian,* 19 November 1933, p. 1.

17. *Orange and Black,* 2 July 1920, p. 1, 4 February 1920, p. 1.

18. "College Has Greatest Growth Under Cantwell," *A. and M. Boomer,* vol. 1, no. 7 (April 1921), p. 9; "Reinstate Secondary Schools; Enterprise Ticket Compulsory," *A. and M. Boomer,* vol. 1, no. 9 (July-August 1921), p. 4.

19. *O'Collegian,* 29 April 1925, p. 3.

20. *O'Collegian,* 15 September 1925, p. 1.

21. *Annual Catalog, Oklahoma A. and M. College, 1925-1926,* p. 287; *Annual Catalog, Oklahoma A. and M. College, 1927-1928,* p. 45.

22. *Orange and Black,* 16 February 1922, p. 4.

23. *O'Collegian,* 7 June 1925, p. 1.

24. *O'Collegian,* 2 May 1925, p. 1.

25. *O'Collegian,* 2 May 1925, p. 1; *Daily O'Collegian,* 27 May 1931, p. 1.

26. *Daily O'Collegian,* 14 February 1929, p. 1.

27. *Daily O'Collegian,* 19 November 1927, p. 1.

28. *Daily O'Collegian,* 19 November 1927, p. 1.

29. "School and Faculty News," *Oklahoma A. and M. College Magazine,* vol. 3, no. 3 (December 1931), p. 9; *Daily O'Collegian,* 19 October 1928, p. 1, 25 November 1928, p. 1, 29 February 1936, p. 1.

30. "Student Industries Are Enlarged," *Oklahoma A. and M. College Magazine,* vol. 1, no. 10 (July 1930), p. 7.

31. *Daily O'Collegian,* 3 October 1931, p. 1.

32. *Daily O'Collegian,* 2 June 1931, p. 1, 13 June 1931, pp. 1, 3.

33. "1933 Class Largest in History," *Oklahoma A. and M. College Magazine,* vol. 5, no. 2 (November 1933), p. 4.

34. Author interview with Harry K. Brobst, 31 July 1986, Centennial Histories Oral Interview Collection, Special Collections, Edmon Low Library, Oklahoma State University, Stillwater, Oklahoma; "Education Graduates Employed," *Oklahoma A. and M. College Magazine,* vol. 7, no. 5 (February 1936), p. 6.

35. *Daily O'Collegian,* 19 April 1933, p. 1, 9 June 1933, p. 1.

36. *Daily O'Collegian,* 14 March 1933, p. 1.

37. *Daily O'Collegian,* 16 March 1933, p. 1.

38. *Daily O'Collegian,* 23 March 1933, p. 1.

39. *Daily O'Collegian,* 7 September 1933, p. 1.

40. "Summer Session Attractions," *Oklahoma A. and M. College Magazine,* vol. 6, no. 8 (May 1935), p. 6.

41. *Daily O'Collegian,* 14 February 1934, p. 1.

42. *Annual Catalog, Oklahoma A. and M. College, 1936-1937,* pp. 235-236, 239-240, 286-289.

43. *Daily O'Collegian,* 9 April 1930, p. 6.

44. *Daily O'Collegian,* 19 September 1931, p. 4.

45. Wendell Hagood, "The Graduate School Grows," *Oklahoma A. and M. College Magazine,* vol. 1, no. 7 (March 1930), p. 11. The current home of the College of Education was named for Carl Gundersen, a longtime mathematics professor at Oklahoma A. and M. College.

46. *Annual Catalog, Oklahoma A. and M. College, 1919-1920,* p. 131.

47. Hagood, p. 11; *Oklahoma A. and M. Graduate School Catalog, 1931-1932,* p. 48.

48. *Daily O'Collegian,* 17 July 1936, p. 1.

49. Brobst interview.

50. Author interview with Florence Ellen Conger Lowe, Rose Mary Tompkins Duncan, Dorothea Hodges, and Kathryn Tompkins McCollom, 14 April 1987, Centennial Histories Oral Interview Collection.

51. Author interview with Raymond Girod, 7 July 1986, Centennial Histories Oral Interview Collection.

52. Author interview with Bill Hindman, Marjorie Orloski, Benn Palmer, and Gladys Skinner, 1 July 1986, Centennial Histories Oral Interview Collection.

53. 'Your Credit is Safe With Him!" *Oklahoma A. and M. College Magazine,* vol. 19, no. 2 (November 1947), pp. 10-11.

54. *Daily O'Collegian,* 3 June 1952, pp. 1, 10, 3 October 1953, p. 1; John A. Patterson to Thomas A. Karman, 28 March 1989, Special Collections, Edmon Low Library.

4 On the Springboard

Institutions are not themselves living, breathing entities. They are created by people and draw any life they have from those people. As the people change, so does the institution, and that surely was the case at Oklahoma A. and M. College by the mid-1930s. Earlier, the college had been subject to the vagaries of the frontier and of a political structure which saw no reason why power wielders should not seat and unseat college personnel at will. While the School of Education had largely been exempted from such political intervention, college presidents had not always enjoyed the same degree of isolation from Oklahoma City.

That changed drastically with the appointment of Henry Bennett as president, for he became the first person to occupy the presidency for an extended period and was himself powerful enough politically to keep state officials at bay, usually. Furthermore, Dr. Bennett was a man of substantial vision whose dreams saw Oklahoma A. and M. College as a vastly larger and more influential organization than it was when he assumed leadership during the rocky days of dust and depression. Finally, the president was through and through a schoolman with strong emotional ties to the profession and personal ties to the professionals.

The first two deans of the School of Education had been brought in from the outside to lead the organization, but for the third, the school was to be led by a known commodity—Napoleon Conger. According to the official record, he graduated from Cumberland University with an LL.D. degree in 1911 and earned his B.S. degree from the University of Ohio in 1917. He then moved on to take both his M.A. and Ph.D. degrees from Columbia University, receiving the last degree in 1929.[1] According to his daughter, the future dean "had been ordained as a minister, though I do not think he ever had a church—or wanted one . . . . Although he was admitted to the bar in Tennessee, . . . I believe he practiced law for only a short time. I really think that he was not only trying to 'find himself' but even more to satisfy a very deep craving to learn and master different fields of study. Ultimately, of course, he found his real interest to be in education—specifically in educational administration. He was superintendent of schools in Warren, Ohio, when he met my mother; and he was on the faculty of Sue Bennett College in London, Kentucky, before he moved to Southeastern Normal School (as it was then) in Durant. There, he was principal of the Lab School (called a Training School in those days) and I believe taught courses in educational administration."[2]

Although named Napoleon, he never used it, preferring to sign simply "N." That feeling was evidently shared by the woman he married, for she decided he looked like a John and called him Jack. Others followed suit. Students, however, conjured up yet another image by describing him as "Lincolnesque," with brown-gray eyes peering from beneath bushy brows and showing the soft humaness of a man with a shock of black hair beginning to go gray.[3]

It was not sheer happenstance that Dr. Conger landed in Stillwater

1936 REDSKIN

Napoleon Conger was the only dean of the School of Education who served the institution prior to assuming the deanship and also maintained an active role in the school after relinquishing the office. Inheriting problems associated with the late years of the Depression, he fought to keep education from sinking into mediocrity during World War II and from being swamped by rapid postwar expansion. During his tenure, the school evolved from focusing largely on local situations and began making its influence felt more strongly across the state.

one year after Dr. Bennett assumed the presidency of Oklahoma Agricultural and Mechanical College. A "tried and true friend" of the Bennetts, Dr. Conger was a member of that inner circle of friends and colleagues whom Dr. Bennett worked with in one capacity or another while he served public and later higher education in southeastern Oklahoma. He brought a number of professional colleagues from Durant, including Roy Tompkins, Joseph C. Ireland, Schiller Scroggs, and James H. Zant. Dr. Conger's daughter remarked, "I now, but not then, realize that there were people who did not think all Dr. Bennett did was glorious and wonderful, as we did."[4] In fact, some believed the president's professional colleagues were really "cronies" and referred to them as the "Durant Gang."[5]

In 1929, though, Dr. Conger was not hired as dean since Herbert Patterson still occupied that position. Instead, he was brought in as the director of the newly established personnel department, which in spite of its name was a unit of the college that dealt more with the students than with the paid employees. The department was to help guide the student into a vocation for which he or she was best adapted and to establish a more intimate liaison between the student and the faculty, which was becoming more difficult to do because of the increasing size of Oklahoma A. and M. College.[6]

Dr. Conger was not fated to stay long as director of personnel at the Oklahoma A. and M. College. After two years, he was appointed state director of teacher training in Oklahoma and left Stillwater for Oklahoma City, where he stayed until he returned as dean of the School of Education. During his sojourn in the state's capital, he did his job and took full advantage of opportunities to make friends throughout the state. Dr. Conger exercised considerable influence in education in the state and was also willing to become involved in the politics of the day. He became very good friends with many state politicians including Governor (later U.S. Senator) Robert S. Kerr.[7]

Dr. Conger was deeply concerned about the future of the nation. In his personal papers, he frequently wrote about and discussed the advent of totalitarianism in Russia, Germany, and Italy, using them as examples of what America should not become. When a plan for economic recovery for the South was being considered in the late 1930s, he responded cautiously that regulation would work if basic freedoms were preserved, and those freedoms were directly related to the schools. "So long as the schools are free to teach and respond to the wishes of the community that supports them as they are today, we have nothing to fear; but the moment they cease to have this freedom, we will most certainly be in danger of losing what is vastly more essential to our happiness in the long run, namely, a maximum degree of personal freedom and our traditional way of life . . . . Democracy is a 'way of life'; it

Marlin R. Chauncey joined the School of Education in 1923 and spent the next three decades serving the college and the interests of Oklahoma education. Like so many of his colleagues within the school, he earned graduate degrees from Columbia University. He worked diligently, kept a fairly low profile, and gradually acquired a great deal of informal power within the school.

involves freedom to change, freedom to limit its own freedom, if it desires. If economic planning can be introduced in the South in a democratic way, and maintained in harmony with democratic princi-ples, the schools could be counted on to perform their part in making such plans work successfully.''[8]

Although the school's curriculum had been grouped by subject area for quite a while, by the late 1930s Dean Conger assigned what were essentially contact people with each area. Guy Lackey was listed with elementary education, and he was to give special attention to the rural schools, which fit well with his dean's concerns for that educational sector. Secondary education was the domain of M. R. Chauncey, a profes-sor of education since 1923. Professor Chauncey trained both teachers and supervisors for the junior and senior high schools. A. S. Davis was tied to religious education; S. L. Reed was associated with psychology as well as philosophy; and the dean himself was responsible for educa-tional administration. It is quite possible that Dr. Conger hoped this organization would engender a healthy sense of competition among the groupings as they vied for resources and recognition. It should be stressed, though, that these were not like today's several academic departments; they were interest groups. Thus, for example, Professor Lackey was listed with elementary education, yet he was also able to flow into the psychology faculty group when that suited his interests.

From a curricular point of view, though, the School of Education was far from "clear." Psychology and philosophy, normally housed administratively in a college of arts and sciences, were under education largely for historical rather than academic reasons. Such courses as educational psychology and the philosophy of education stayed within the school for decades before being relocated. If found in a state college at all, religion courses would be listed with humanities in arts and sciences. Religious studies started as a Christian education program to prepare people for Sunday school work. Gradually other courses more closely tied to religion than education were added. While such courses carried college credit, local clergy taught them on a voluntary basis, usually on Wednesday night, thus recognizing separation of church and state.

There should not be undue emphasis placed on the existence of departments in the school, as there were no departmental heads or chairmen. For some time after World War II, the functional organization of the school was simply elementary education and secondary education, although the school did have two people who were at least quasi-administrators. Dr. Reed was identified as director of educational psychology (even though psychology and philosophy were grouped as a single department), and Kathryn Long was director of the elementary demonstration school. Although departmental heads eventually emerged in the administrative structure, they were accompanied by unofficial administrators known as ''coordinators'' of various academic programs. This approach to governing the school was apparently logical initially, but it became awkward as the Department of Education gradually developed into an umbrella department. Still, it survived until 1973.

The School of Education was characterized as being principally upper-division. Its official policy was to discourage students from taking any professional courses prior to their junior year. This was to be an abiding policy of the school and later of the college, based on the belief that the future teacher ought to complete his or her general education prior to engaging in professional studies. Such a decision was sound from an educational point of view, but it did make it more difficult for the school to establish strong ties with its lower-division students and may at least partially explain why student organizations within the school were so anemic for so long.

The school laid out clearly what would be required if the student were to be qualified to receive a certificate to teach, reflecting the state's standards. Essentially, there were four expectations: that the person be at least twenty years old; that he or she provide evidence of having graduated from an approved high school or have had equivalent training; that the collegiate work was from an accredited institution with grades as high as the average required for graduation; and that ''applicants shall present evidence that they are in sound physical health and of good moral character.''[9] If the person satisfied those requirements, one of two certificates could be acquired. A one-year certificate could be granted

In the late 1930s, a deadly school conflagration in Texas and an explosion in Whitehurst's base-ment changed the face of the Oklahoma A. and M. campus. The college abandoned the con-demned English and History building, which was regularly used by education students, and moved classes to tents north of Morrill. Given Oklahoma springs, the storms blew the tents down, which was also the fate of the much larger 4-H Club Round-up tent. Quietly deploring the situa-tion, President Bennett gracefully pried an appropriation out of the legislature to restore the English and History Building, to add the fourth floor and peaked roof to Whitehurst, and to con-struct the 4-H Club and Student Activity Building, dubbed Gallagher Hall.

after completing seventy-six semester hours of college work for elemen-tary education or ninety hours for secondary education. It was not yet necessary to be a college graduate to teach in the public schools. How-ever, if one were the owner of either a B.A. or a B.S. degree, then a life certificate could be granted for either elementary or secondary schools.

Teaching was no picnic in those days. Marjorie Orloski, a graduate of the class of 1936, recalled: "I got a little school in Mooreland so I could live with my sister and brother-in-law, [the vocational-agriculture teacher]. Seventy-five dollars a month, fourth grade, in a condemned building. The dust storms would come up, and the whole building would shake . . . . I was scared to death. The next year I took an apart-ment and made eighty-five a month. I sent most of that money home to give to my younger brother and two sisters so they could continue their schooling."[10] During the Depression, it was typical for relatives to share lodging, food, money, and other resources and to sacrifice individual and personal interests in order to meet priorities of the larger group.

To Ms. Orloski, beginning a career in education during the Depres-sion might have been regarded as an adventure and a challenge, but to those in the twilight of their careers, the sunset held frustration and bit-terness. A. R. Hickam who had represented Ginn and Company for twenty-two years wrote the following to C. L. Kezer, a professor of edu-cation:

"This new age is one of excesses, of determination to live beyond honestly earned means. Just as well try to keep a moth from flying into a candle as to persuade these modern younger operators from running into debt. There is a lack of reliability and dependability which makes the transaction of any kind of legitimate business hazardous for any conservative man. It was my conclusion that I did not bring about these terrible conditions which are equally as bad as war and that it should not be my lot to adjust or solve them.

"Moreover we seem to have reached a condition in which the schools and colleges have found a way to run their schools without the purchase of newly published books. No one ever dreamed that there were enough dilapidated textbooks to supply the institutions for a period of years. It is odd that the sale of cosmetics, tobacco, tooth paste, and picture show tickets has actually increased since 1929 and yet during the same time the sale of standard textbooks has fallen off more than 50 percent. The Pepsodent Company alone sold more products last year than did all the standard publishers of school books combined . . . .

"'I have given the best there was in me to an effort to present the best books from the Ginn list entirely upon their merits and to cooperate in every way possible with school people in every endeavor to improve the educational situation, but I came to the conclusion that the stampede could not be checked and I came to the deliberate conclusion that I wanted to leave the job to the younger generation which seems to think present methods and procedure are the wise course.'"[11]

Dean Conger could, no doubt, sympathize with the bookseller lacking a market and with the greenhorn teaching in a condemned building buffeted by Oklahoma's famous dust storms. One of his ongoing early concerns was the challenge provided to education in the rural areas of the state. Even though he had served as director of teacher training for the state and understood the pressing needs in all types of schools, he was acutely aware that two-thirds of Oklahomans were from rural areas and that 4,816 school districts existed with 5,340 schools. Of those schools, 4,558—or 85 percent—had four rooms at most. In the elementary schools, rarely was a teacher responsible for only one grade, and it was not unusual for the "school marm" to teach all eight grades. Under those circumstances, it might be safe to assume that the average rural educator must have been grateful that Oklahoma had not yet adopted the kindergarten, for that would simply have added to an already "weighty" load. At the high school level, 62 percent of the schools—or 536 out of 864—had fewer than 100 students, which made it difficult to offer a comprehensive curriculum.

Dr. Conger was especially concerned about the formidable tasks faced by the elementary teacher. "She is expected to teach as many as eight grades in many instances, prepare the pupils in the upper grades for the county or state test in order that they may be admitted to high school, and in addition she must perform the duties of janitor, health officer, and business manager.''[12] He was also aware that urban superintendents, who had more resources, preferred to hire experienced teachers, which meant that the inexperienced and untested young teacher typically began her career in a rural school with a minimum of equipment and little if any supervision or assistance. Dean Conger felt a special responsibility to do what could be done to improve on these conditions. After all, his school was in an agricultural and mechanical college that was closely tied to the farm and village.

Furthermore, he did not stop with the teacher in the trenches, for he realized that the administrators in rural areas, whether principals, superintendents, or county superintendents, also faced problems that were very real. While the teacher attended to all facets of instruction, the administrator was likewise a one-person office acting as business manager, director of personnel, public relations officer, athletic director, and whatever else that needed to be done. To provide succor to both teacher and administrator, the School of Education developed a series of courses on rural education beginning with the 1937 summer session.[13] This was an especially appropriate way to deal with the issues since practicing teachers and administrators typically went back to college

1920 REDSKIN

Charles L. Kezer, a 1901 graduate of Oklahoma A. and M. College, returned to the School of Education in 1918 after a successful school career. He was especially concerned about and a champion for the preparatory school, which he served as principal. Although the preparatory school helped the college survive in the early decades, it fell victim to the Depression in the early 1930s. Professor Kezer retired in 1945.

during the summer, and having been confronted directly with many of the problems noted by Dr. Conger, they would be anxious to find solutions.

After a hiatus of one year, the special summer program was back in place in 1939 and was targeted especially for county superintendents. These educational officials stood for election every other year, and many who were successful in the contests were unfamiliar with the work which the office required—hence the need to provide a nuts-and-bolts crash course in administration. Although service to the profession was important, Dr. Conger gave the program an even broader focus by making the administrators, diagnosticians. He had acquired a Keystone Telebinocular, which was used to test school children for visual handicaps, and a Western Electric 4B Audiometer, which tested for auditory deficiencies. The dean had already had his staff test all of the school children in Payne County, but he obviously did not have the resources to take on the entire state. But if he could train the superintendents to use the equipment, he could loan them the machines, and the administrators could give the examinations while making their regular inspection visits to the dependent schools. Finally, the summer program also touched on guidance, health, dramatics, music, and adult educational programs.[14] Dr. Conger hoped to convince the superintendents that they could make their educational programs more comprehensive even in rural areas and with limited resources.

In 1940, Dean Conger added a novel twist to the summer program by establishing a new type of workshop. The school had been underway for a third of a century by that time, and the offerings had been designed and delivered by the faculty, augmented by visiting lecturers. Dean Conger changed that in part by designating a special suite of rooms for a workshop in which teachers and administrators would deal with actual problems they faced in their schools, trying to devise practical solutions under the guidance of college faculty serving as consultants. The format worked best when a district superintendent sent a team to the workshop. These independent group investigations were then augmented with some common readings and some lectures which were designed to bind all of the groups into a single unit.[15]

This format was identical in virtually every detail with that utilized in the 1960s by the Danforth Foundation when it launched its summer liberal arts workshops in Colorado Springs, Colorado. Danforth invited liberal arts colleges to identify their own problems and to select a team of faculty and administrators to work on them. It brought together all of the teams at Colorado Springs, where the participants could ponder and reflect in an environment away from home and daily duties, and it augmented the teams' own resources with nationally-recognized leaders who lectured and served as consultants. The comparison is strik-

A long-time, dedicated member of the faculty of the School of Education, Kathryn Long was instrumental in the development of the elementary demonstration school. Although more and more men were seeking careers in education, this picture shows an overwhelming preponderance of women attending a conference for the observation of teaching in elementary schools.

ing and leads one to wonder whether somebody in the Danforth Foundation had come across a yellowed copy of a 1940 *O'Collegian*! The only differences between the programs was that Oklahoma A. and M's went all summer, while Danforth's stopped after two and a half weeks; also, Danforth paid teams to attend, while Oklahoma A. and M. charged a dollar per credit hour up to a maximum of six.

In 1941, the summer workshop was modified slightly under the direction of Dr. Chauncey. The operation worked out of the recreation room of Willard Hall. There was to be no group work, and a Balanced Life Committee was added to try to unify the people in the workshop by harmonizing their professional and social lives. Each Thursday evening at 6:30, a square dance was held in Willard.[16]

The School of Education did not always expect teachers and administrators to come to Stillwater for professional development. As a land-grant college, Oklahoma A. and M. was heavily involved with extension from its very inception. The School of Agriculture led the way with some highly creative ideas, such as demonstration trains that rattled over Oklahoma's rails and literally took a piece of Oklahoma A. and M. to the public. Arriving at tiny Oklahoma railheads, the trains must have generated nearly as much excitement as the appearance of a traveling circus. In 1922, when James Eskridge was president of Oklahoma A. and

M., correspondence study was added to the college's offerings. By 1925, a program of extension teaching in education and psychology was approved. Three years later, Educational Extension, including the School of Correspondence, was established, which was a central office rather than a part of the School of Education.

The evolution of the extension program is a good example of natural initiative followed by an effort to coordinate. Gradually, the Schools of Engineering and Science and Literature as well as the Department of Agricultural Education began to get involved in off-campus work. This meant that a single community might be contacted by Cooperative Extension (that is, agriculture and home economics) plus at least three of the other schools, which led to no little confusion. Consequently Bennett created the Division of College Extension under the leadership of people such as Roy Tompkins and Gerald T. Stubbs and stipulated that the division would be responsible for coordinating all aspects of extension work except for agriculture and home economics, which stayed with Cooperative Extension. Almost all of the non-Cooperative Extension work was related to the public schools in those years. Because President Bennett had his doctorate in school administration and had years of experience with the common schools before moving to college presidencies, it was only natural that he would feel Oklahoma A. and M. College had an obligation to help the elementary and secondary schools.

In the fall of 1941, the cooperative relationship between the School of Education and Educational Extension was fully developed and operating smoothly. Dean Conger and his staff were actively involved in efforts to help the state's schools adapt their educational materials to meet the problems of the day in a better way. He recognized that not all training needed to take place on a college campus and that some instruction was often better received if offered in the local setting, for then the material could be tailored exactly to fit a specific school or district.

To help with that effort, he added two people to his staff. Frank Fuller was brought from Yale University to take charge of the in-service program for non-rural secondary teachers. One of his major interests was to work with the schools using the evaluation criteria of the North Central Association and to see that the schools either retain or acquire accreditation from that regional body. Fuller started working with the schools in Elk City, Sapulpa, Sand Springs, and some of the smaller systems in Bryan County. The second person added to the faculty was Meredith Darlington. He came to Stillwater from the University of Nebraska and accepted the task of developing appropriate in-service training programs for the rural teachers. Working with county superintendents of schools, Darlington was making an impact on schools in

Delaware, Okfuskee, Osage, and Kay counties, with the work being supported financially by the American County Life Association.

Assisting both Fuller and Darlington, who were obviously new to the Oklahoma scene, was J. C. Muerman, a seasoned veteran of the School of Education. Because Dr. Muerman was both well known and well respected in the state's educational circles, this arrangement, without a doubt, assisted in having the newcomers accepted by Oklahoma school people. Professor Muerman was heavily involved at that time in the field of visual education and demonstrated how visual aids could add dynamism and effectiveness to what might otherwise be a dry presentation that would fail to capture the imagination and interest of the pupils. Visual aids could drastically broaden the horizons of school children who often had not been able to travel more than a few miles from the farm and who frequently saw nothing more cosmopolitan than the county seat—if they got that far.[17]

The extension program continued and expanded as World War II raged in Europe and Asia. "Just as it is important for the Chief of Staff of the armies to visit front lines of battle to see the problem to be faced, so it is important for instructors in teacher education to participate in actual experiences on the front lines of education" to feel the pulse of the American public school system and keep pace with the problems confronting it.[18] The attention given to extension grew to the point where Dean Conger appointed an in-service committee that represented most academic areas and was used to augment the skills of the two faculty assigned to work with the schools. It was found that extension was really a two-way street—not only could the college staff stimulate, guide, and enrich the classroom teachers, but the teachers could introduce the professors to problems and findings that made a definite contribution to the campus classes. That symbiotic relationship, which began so nat-

1936 REDSKIN

Known throughout Oklahoma as one of the most capable rural supervisors, J. C. Muerman was a strong advocate of visual education. Through his educational films, slide shows, and talks, Dr. Muerman was the "toast" of many civic groups because of his presentations.

urally between Oklahoma A. and M. and the teaching professionals in the 1940s, was eventually mandated across the entire state through education reform legislation passed nearly forty years later.[19]

In the fall of 1945, Gerald T. Stubbs headed the Department of Public School Service. By that time, he already had thirty years of experience in education, including service as a rural school teacher, an elementary teacher, and a principal. For the previous sixteen years, he had been superintendent of the Durant schools, a position which enabled him to establish close ties to President Bennett before he moved to Stillwater. Director Stubbs vigorously publicized his program, stating that it had six purposes: upon invitation, furnish advice to counsel in all school areas with school administrators; plan programs of teacher training improvement; with school administrators, develop school evaluation programs in order to reorganize and improve programs; with teachers and administrators, plan to bring any Oklahoma A. and M. agency services that could help the local schools, its personnel, and its community; establish and maintain wholesome relations between Oklahoma A. and M. and the public schools by helping the college render all services needed; and cooperate in the educational planning and leadership being provided through the professional organizations in Oklahoma and the nation. Although the School of Education was willing to assist professional colleagues in the field in all of these areas, the bulk of the help requested was in regard to the school physical plant. This, of course, also had implications for the academic programming that would take place within the facility.[20]

The tone of Director Stubbs' message deserves attention. Oklahoma Agricultural and Mechanical College was not there as a big brother to lead the benighted school men and women to a better day. Rather, the college would work with the administrators and the teachers, and jointly they would make progress. The approach was effective, for almost immediately Barnsdall and Pawhuska requested that the college make comprehensive school surveys, while Shawnee sought advice regarding the construction of a new senior high school building.

Educational travel, an unusual and highly successful facet of educational extension, was the brainchild of J. Conner Fitzgerald, a man with wide experience in continuing education. He had experimented with educational travel before joining the staff of Oklahoma Agricultural and Mechanical College. When he served as superintendent of the Hillside Consolidated School near Cushing, he and his wife enjoyed traveling and realized that most of the children in the school were very poor and had no similar opportunities. He worked with the children, and by May of 1937 each had managed to save $5. With $90, eighteen school children, three women teachers, and the bus driver, Mr. Fitzgerald headed for the Carlsbad Caverns in New Mexico, going via the school bus and camping on the way. Having seen the Caverns, they still had $60 in their pooled treasury, and they voted to continue to El Paso and Juarez before returning to Oklahoma through Fort Worth. Once back in Cushing, Fitzgerald returned $1.71 to each of his pupils.[21] That initiated a series of annual trips, and Fitzgerald encouraged the pupils to save 50 cents each month to ensure they would have the necessary $5 at the end of the school year. These tours put Hillside on the map. Soon people from outside the district were asking to send their children along, but Fitzgerald took only his own pupils.

Once he joined Oklahoma Agricultural and Mechanical College in the late 1940s, Fitzgerald continued to conduct such educational tours, now taking teachers rather than grade school children and chartering Greyhound busses instead of using a yellow school bus. He led groups to the nation's capital, to New England, to the Great Lakes, to the Pacific Northwest, to the South Pacific islands, to Europe, to Canada, and to many other spots. Yet, he was still interested in staying within a strict budget. It was no longer only $5, but for less than $215 per person he could take a group to Canada for more than three weeks—and they no longer were expected to sleep à la belle étoiles and to cook their own food.[22]

Extension was not the only feature that grew and changed within the school. As early as the fall of 1941, just before World War II was about to wash over the nation, the educational faculty at the Oklahoma A. and M. College made a change in the way they handled student teaching. The School of Education had had arrangements for early observation experiences and student teaching since the arrival of Dean Patterson in 1919. At first, students were placed usually in the college's preparatory school, but by 1924, student teachers went to the public schools of Stillwater. Eventually, student teachers went to areas some distance from Stillwater. Until 1941, though, it was inconvenient to be placed very far from the campus because the seniors took regular college classes for part of the day and then moved into the public schools to do their practice teaching for the rest of the day.

As early as 1930, Richard E. Hyde, who took over high school apprentice teaching from Charles Kezer, was able to place twenty seniors and graduate students in the Cushing schools. The Cushing Board of Education invited Oklahoma A. and M. College to continue using their facilities even though it recognized the transportation and coordination problems. In 1941, the pattern of concurrent class work and student teaching was changed so that the students could spend the first nine weeks of the semester in class studying the theory of education and then could put theory to practice for the last nine weeks in the schools. Thus, the "block system" was embraced at the college—the first teacher-training institution in the state to adopt this procedure.[23]

Professors in the School of Education each for over thirty years, S. L. Reed (*left*) and Guy A. Lackey (*right*) made notable contributions to education. Dr. Reed, a psychology and philosophy professor, was known for his research and experimentation. Dr. Lackey served in many capacities in the school including efforts to develop closer student-faculty ties.

This new approach to apprentice teaching gave added flexibility. For example, Dean Conger's daughter convinced her father that she should "have a real practice teaching period over in Tulsa." Although she did not recall doing much actual teaching, she was impressed with the Spanish teacher's disciplinary techniques—boys were whacked on the head with a long stick, while girls were tapped on the shoulder. Indeed, she recalled "the students were very respectful as long as their regular teacher was in the room. They were holy terrors if he were out!"[24] One suspects that the war waged between pupils and practice teachers has raged ever since practice teaching was implemented, for pupils seem to regard student teacher taunting as nearly a God-given right.

But there were rewards as well as challenges in student teaching. Ware Marsden, head of the Department of Education and director of student teaching, and Guy Lackey, a professor who had served the school since 1925, agreed that graduates of the program consistently stated that practice teaching was the outstanding feature of their program. Dr. Marsden was also convinced that the benefits were mutual since supervising a student teacher made the cooperating teacher better. A letter sent to him by a cooperating teacher reinforced his observation: "May I say, also, that I think having worked with Miss 'X' and evaluating my work in her eyes has made me a better teacher. I have tried in my own inexperienced way (this was my first time to work with a student teacher) to guide her into seeing a relationship between theory and practice."[25]

Furthermore, Professor Marsden believed involving public school faculty was beneficial to education as a whole. "Public school teachers who are willing to share their skills and techniques with the student teachers are likewise making teaching a true profession," for success in preparing teachers "depends upon the willingness of the members of the teaching profession to work together. Just as a devoted doctor gives regular time to clinics, to the training of interns, to volunteer service for community health, so must teachers be willing to give of their time and energy for the betterment of the greatest of all professions, teaching."[26]

While Dean Conger was concerned with the quality of education, he was also a very democratic person who regarded education not only as a way to enhance one economically and socially but also as a way to create a better society. He wrote: "The primary purpose of education is not to develop the genius, but to lift the general level of intelligence of the masses. It is, in my judgment, far more important to lift the general educational level of the masses from the eighth to the ninth grade than it is to lift a few from the ninth grade to a college degree."[27] If interaction among professions was a good idea, Dean Conger—always the democrat—earlier had applied that concept to professions and pre-professions in his quest to establish closer student-faculty ties. That was his original assignment at Oklahoma A. and M. back in 1928. He developed various programs and events to encourage student participation. In 1940, the dean tried to establish an annual Education Day. The Schools of Agriculture and Engineering had been fairly well-organized rivals virtually since the college was founded. In fact, Engineering Week was celebrated each spring around St. Patrick's Day because he is the patron saint of engineers.[28] On that day, the O'Collegian was dedicated to the engineers and even printed on green paper.

Dr. Conger appointed a faculty committee consisting of Guy Lackey, Vera Jones, and Melvin Rigg to spearhead the activity, which never aspired to anything quite as elaborate as Engineering Week. They did, however, recommend a day of activities for April 24, at which time students in the School of Education were excused from all classes. The festivities began with a 1:30 convocation in the College Auditorium located east of Gundersen and north of Williams Hall (now the site of the Concert Hall of the Seretean Center for the Performing Arts). L. N. Perkins led the group in singing, and President Bennett gave a short address. After that, the students and faculty were transported to Yost Lake for an afternoon of play. While the songs and the president's speech may have been uplifting, one must conclude that they were brief since the convocation was over, the drive to the lake made, and a treasure hunt completed, all before the students and faculty were called at 3:00 to horseshoes, click golf, croquet, golf, softball, volleyball, and kickball, followed at 5:30 with swimming, boat races, and boat tipping contests. Finally after the picnic supper, Martha Shirley Welch was crowned as the 1940 "Streamline Schoolmarm." Tickets for the day's activities were

50 cents apiece—date or stag.[29]

In 1940, the dean also moved to initiate an Education Student Council, something he had believed had been needed for at least a decade. He realized that some of the 500 plus students in education took much of their work within the school, but he was also aware that other "students have very little in common as their major courses are found in every school on campus." He hoped the council would be a way to unite the students. The council was unique on the campus because the candidates were nominated by a joint student-faculty committee on which the students had a majority of the votes. In other schools, it was typical for the student council members to be appointed by the dean. The arrangement in the School of Education is another reflection of the dean's values, for he was both highly supportive of a democratic structure and strongly encouraged student-faculty interaction. The officers of the 1941 council were Florence Ellen Conger, president; Carol Colvin, vice presi-

Due to its demographics, the School of Education was less affected by World War II than some of the predominantly male disciplines. The faculty, nevertheless, pledged total support to the all-out campus effort for victory. The 1942 faculty included (*first row*) Wylma Black, Anna Stringfield, Dean N. Conger, Vera Jones, and Kathryn M. Long; (*second row*) J. C. Muerman, Melvin C. Rigg, W. H. Echols, C. L. Kezer, Ben C. Dyess, Frank Fuller, and O. K. Campbell; (*third row*) Haskell Pruett, Eleroy L. Stromberg, Guy A. Lackey, Clarence M. Pruitt, M. W. Darlington, Eli C. Foster, and M. R. Chauncey.

dent; and Rose Mary Tompkins, secretary-treasurer.[30]

Once it got organized, the ten-member council and its two faculty advisors were responsible for activities such as sponsoring the annual Education Day, selecting the senior man and senior woman who would receive a plaque for making the greatest contributions to the School of Education and for having the most professional promise as teachers, and advising the dean on matters related to student affairs.[31] It would appear that the new council was still not of major importance, though, for when asked in 1987 whether there was a School of Education Student Council, Dean Conger's daughter replied: "There must have been. I must have been on it, according to the yearbook, but I don't think we did anything."[32] The Education Student Council faded by the mid-1940s.

When Dr. Conger left the State Department of Education for Stillwater, he must have been optimistic that the time was right to move the School of Education at Oklahoma A. and M. College ahead with progressive change. To be sure, some preconditions had to be satisfied, including a stronger and more vigorous faculty, a brighter and more eager student body, more adequate non-human resourses, and stability. But the school had faired well against great economic and political odds, and the worst of the Great Depression was already behind him. As the state of the state brightened, he hoped to be able to advance the state of the school. What he was not to have, though, was stability. War loomed in Europe and Asia, and that brought havoc to Oklahoma education.

Because of their demographics, the Oklahoma A. and M. College School of Education and the School of Home Economics were no doubt less affected by the war than particularly agriculture, business, and engineering, where enrollments consisted almost totally of draft-age males. But the campus as a whole became a whirlwind of change and creative adaptation early in World War II.

It must have been patently clear to nearly everyone inside or outside higher education that a major war would quickly knock the underpinnings out from under the colleges and universities. After all, higher education at that time was skewed strongly toward the men. To make matters worse, these young men—usually between the ages of eighteen and twenty-two—made perfect recruits for the military. Few schools reacted as well as the Oklahoma A. and M. College in taking action to remain viable. Dr. Bennett, immediately after the bombing of Pearl Harbor, all but literally gave the campus to the federal government, pledging that Oklahoma A. and M. was prepared to do anything and everything necessary and possible to help with the war effort.

President Bennett made his position absolutely clear in a letter which was published in the *1942-43 College Catalog*: "True to its traditions and its chartered objectives, Oklahoma A. and M. College has converted its major emphasis to war. A pioneer in the training of U.S. Navy men in Radar, as well as men and women for industry in Defense Training Courses, A. and M. has added the training of WAVES, Army Aircrew men, Army Specialized Training of Engineers, and the processing of STAR troops. These are but the war activities of the college that are connected directly with the armed services. In addition to them, the traditional basic R.O.T.C. instruction is maintained.

"The civilian program of A. and M. College goes on as usual, diminished so far as numbers are concerned but in no way reduced in extent, standards, or seriousness. We urge that young men and women give thought to the fact that unless they are participating in necessary war industry, even a year of college work now will equip them better for the future and will shorten by that much the time required for professional or technical specialization after the war.

"It is the wish of every official of the College, whether of the administration or the faculty, to make Oklahoma A. and M. synonymous with service. If there is any question that we can help answer, write or call."[33]

As the young students enlisted or were drafted into the service, the fraternity houses in Stillwater soon were vacant. The college administration relocated the women into the empty fraternity houses. Stripped of their Greek letters, these houses were redesignated as Victory Halls, each with its own number. As soon as the dormitories were vacated, they were refilled with military personnel who were to be given specialized training in, for example, the use of radar or with civilians who were preparing to serve in the war industries. All of these programs were

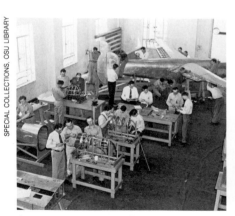 

One of the hallmarks of Oklahoma A. and M. College/Oklahoma State University has been its ability to respond effectively to needs. In World War II, that included educating civilian and uniformed personnel to staff the war industries as well as the battlefields. Oklahoma A. and M. was more than equal to the challenge. This effort served the nation, sustained the college when the bulk of the student body vanished from the campus, and profoundly changed the atmosphere at the college.

remarkable because of the speed with which they were developed. Because of the quantity of trained people it produced, probably the most outstanding program was designed to provide aircraft manufacturers with metal workers. That program, based on the short course model used so effectively in the college's summer and interim sessions, soon was operating with three shifts, twenty-four hours a day. Initially, it was designed as a twelve-week program suited for men with previous experience, but it was redesigned to take men who were raw recruits. At the end of the war, about 75 percent of the trainees were women.[34]

Almost overnight, the WAVES moved into Willard, Murray, and North Murray Halls; the Navy took over Cordell; and the Air Force used Hanner, Thatcher, and the College Courts, which were barracks situated on West Sixth Street.[35] Students were not the only ones relocated. For example, Gundersen Hall was emptied of architecture, mathematics, and physics so that it could be converted to training the WAVES, the Air Crew, and the Army Specialized Training Unit (ASTU).

Under the circumstances, Stillwater and its Oklahoma A. and M. campus became a sea of uniforms, and those uniforms were worn not primarily by people from Oklahoma but from all over the nation. The place became far more cosmopolitan, far less isolated than it had been before. Surely not a few of these young men and women preparing to fight Naziism must have walked by a tree planted on the southwest corner of College (now University) and Monroe, in front of the Sigma Chi house. That oak was given by Adolph Hitler to an Oklahoma A. and M. College student who had won a gold medal in wrestling at the 1936 Berlin Olympics. Frank Lewis, who won the medal and the oak, belonged to Sigma Chi and had the tree planted in front of the house. It was amazing that the tree managed to survive World War II and Stillwater's strong military establishment. Well after the war, some Sigma Chi members said they had protected the tree carefully to prevent other fraternities from cutting it down. Their memories may have done a little to romanticize the situation, however, for during the war the fraternities had been suspended, leaving no Sigma Chi's to defend or other fraternities to attack. A more plausible explanation is offered by women who were attending Oklahoma A. and M. during the war years—they simply did not realize that the tree was a gift from Hitler.[36]

Even in the best of times, travel was always a challenge for people trying to reach or leave Stillwater, and the war did not make it easier. For years, paving ended at the city limits except for Perkins Road, which had been hard surfaced since 1930 all the way—all nine miles—to Perkins Corner at Route 33. Once there, a traveler could hitchhike—the preferred mode of travel for students on a tight budget—or catch a bus to either Tulsa or Oklahoma City, going via Drumright to the former or via Guthrie to the latter. Route 51, let alone Interstate 35, was only a dream

1950 REDSKIN

Oklahoma's frontier heritage engendered a spirit of individualism, but the flip side of that was a high level of cooperation or mutual dependence, exemplified by hitchhiking, which was a way of life for Oklahoma A. and M. College students well into the 1950s. It was a science—look like you would be an interesting passenger, state your destination, let them know you were from Aggie-land, and pray the driver didn't cheer for Big Red.

for the future. It could easily take four hours to reach Tulsa, partly because the top speed was about thirty-five miles per hour and partly because the bus was unloaded at Drumright so it could get up the hill. The people had to walk. Bus drivers cheerfully discriminated. WAVES boarded first, followed by sailors, soldiers, and finally civilians—if there were space available.[37]

Travel in town was perhaps a little more reliable. Because there were probably fewer than two dozen private cars on the campus, there was no need for parking regulations. In fact, since very few of today's lots had been put in—there was one off Morrill Avenue as it circled White-hurst Hall—the campus had a lot more green space. There was only one traffic rule: a man could not stop his car to pick up a girl on campus. Usually students got from the college to downtown on shanks' mare,

College life is at least made up in part of what goes on off the college campus. Student hang-outs come and go at a rapid pace, but two which were popular for years were Swim's, at the corner of Knoblock and Elm, and Peck's, at the corner of Knoblock and College.

but taxies were available. It was not surprising for five or six couples to cram into one cab. As long as they all boarded and exited together, the total cost for the trip was ten cents.[38]

World War II was also a period for experimentation with the regular college students. It was decided that if war training could be greatly accelerated, much the same could be done with the college crowd. In 1943, the president's office announced that there would be no Easter vacation and that the summer session could be either a complete third semester of sixteen weeks or two eight-week sessions, with the schools and departments deciding which format they would follow. The goal was to enable students to finish their academic training as fast as possi- ble, no doubt hoping they could get done before being called up by Uncle Sam. While this was a highly efficient operation, it may be questioned whether it was very effective. Being ''in harness'' for forty-eight weeks out of the year just about ''did in'' both the students and the faculty. No doubt many exhausted scholars breathed a sigh of relief when the Oklahoma State Regents for Higher Education restored the older and more civilized system.[39]

Although Oklahoma A. and M. College was deeply involved in the war effort, each of its schools did not contribute equally. The School of Education was minimally concerned with preparing people for combat given the nature of its offerings, but the school faced a battle of a different sort. The crisis Dean Conger tried to manage was related more closely to events taking place off the campus. Public school teachers and administrators were leaving education in droves, either to serve in the military or to accept assignments in the war plants. Unlike teaching, the factory jobs were not white collar and professional. These jobs, nevertheless, were not only a lot more lucrative, but they were also seen as making direct contributions to the war effort. Because of this exodus, the staffing situation in Oklahoma education was described as "acute." In response, the State Department of Education unofficially moved to attract more people into the field by lowering standards and granting a one-year certificate after the person completed forty semester hours of college work, which reduced the minimum preparatory program by one full year.[40]

From the Oklahoma A. and M. College, two different responses were made to those steps to dilute the quality of preparation for teaching in the common schools. A. O. Martin, who served the college both as the secretary of the Former Students Association and as the head of the Placement Bureau, expressed considerable concern. Although his office was swamped with requests for teachers, he was hard pressed to find a person who would even listen to him talk about a position that paid between $100-$2,000 less than others available.[41]

Dean Conger, usually the quiet diplomat and realist, proposed more practical ways to deal with the crisis. He urged that former teachers should be encouraged to return to the classroom after updating their skills at any qualified institution in the state. Second, he assigned Vera Jones and Guy Lackey to meet on Saturday mornings to counsel with people who believed they would qualify as teachers with a little "brushing up."[42] In 1943, Oklahoma probably reached a new low point in terms of what was required before a person was allowed to teach in the state's public school classrooms.

Still, Oklahoma, like other states in the nation, really had no option but to allow less than fully qualified people to supervise the education of the state's children during World War II. Had that not been permitted, the children would have had to teach each other. But the State Department of Education was aware that it had the power to make a bad situation somewhat better. In 1944, it required people who were teaching with substandard qualifications to enroll in a two-week course that was designed to accomplish four purposes: master the accepted system of keeping attendance records; learn the methods of sending reports to the county superintendent; introduce the state course of study; and introduce the state-adopted textbooks. In Stillwater, this program was under the direction of Professor Jones, who offered two sessions for two hours of credit for a fee of $5.[43] While admittedly some training is better than no preparation at all, it is obvious that these two-week wonders surely were no masters of pedagogy. It is also amazing, with time so limited and with so much that ought to have been addressed, that priority was given to record keeping and record transmission.

The dean of the School of Education at Oklahoma A. and M. was not opposed, however, to taking advantage of the critical shortages to lay the groundwork that would lead the profession to a higher plain. He was especially pointed when he called on boards of education to recognize that a new day was dawning. "The old type country school board member who frowns upon the woman teacher wearing fine hosiery, who thinks it is his business where the girl who teaches has her hair curled, and who positively can not stand to see her act normal, soon may find himself complaining to the winds," said Dean Conger. Modern education did not need teachers who felt obliged to teach that the earth was flat because some narrow-minded board member thought that way. Educators would be foolish to stay in the profession if it were odius to them since they now had many new job openings in other

Veteran's Village popped up in Stillwater almost as fast as the tent cities had when Oklahoma was opened with the original land runs. The vast influx of seasoned citizens had implications for both the city and the college. City fathers de-annexed the Village, because if residents voted as a bloc, it might swing local elections. The campus quickly found that the veterans, even though classified as freshmen, were not apt to take a lot of "guff" from anyone.

professions. The dean stressed: "This does not mean, necessarily, that all teachers are faced with hatchet-faced morons for school board members, but on the other hand it does mean that tomorrow's teacher is going to demand her rights and get them." Finally, he emphasized that a tenure law was required to take away the "dictatorial power from school boards" and to put teachers on a common sense footing if there were to be enough teachers to staff the state's public schools.[44] Personally, Dr. Conger favored democratic, liberal principles and apparently believed the time was right to state a case for progress.

Eventually World War II came to an end, and Oklahoma A. and M. College, like many other institutions of higher education, became a sort of "organized madhouse." Beginning in the fall of 1945 and moving to full-speed frenzy the following spring, the massive demobilization released millions of men and women from the service. The Servicemen's Readjustment Act of 1944—the famous G.I. Bill—encouraged the new civilians to avoid the dislocated job market in favor of the college campus. It was a heady time for Stillwater. Single and married people flooded in. Veteran's Village sprang up as a complete town "with its own government, commissary, bus, mail, telephone and other services; sidewalks and roadways; nursery for children; gardening plots and canning facilities; and recreational ground." "Temporary" frame buildings and Quonset huts were scattered all over to take care of the new students.[45]

In the fall of 1945, with partial demobilization taking place, Dean of Administration Herbert Patterson reported that 53 percent of the total student body was classified as freshman. By the following spring, H. Vance Posey, administrator for veteran's affairs, expected the veterans to outnumber the old Aggies by 3 to 1.[46] These new students were quite a different breed from those who had walked the college acres prior to the war. Dean Conger, who had anticipated this change before the war ended, noted: "When the war is over, there will probably be the greatest influx of students to colleges we have ever had. Many of these students will be battle scarred veterans. They will be old men, in many ways, though only twenty. They will be anything but gullible."[47]

Dean Conger was right. For example, freshmen who were veterans took umbrage at the idea of wearing a beanie and obeying a sophomore several years younger and usually vastly less experienced. Merchants were accorded no kinder treatment. In 1946, the dry cleaners in Stillwater colluded to raise their rates, and the vets helped launch the "Aggie Baggie"' campaign, which resulted in the cleaners being "taken to the cleaners." They folded. Toward the end of the huge veteran enrollment period, the Stillwater Restaurant Association increased the cost of a cup of coffee from a nickle to a dime. On the day that this was announced, a *Stillwater NewsPress* reporter said, during the typical coffee break hour,

Following World War II, a "different" student body swarmed to the Oklahoma A. and M. campus. Older, more mature veterans packed the classrooms. Still, there was a need to forget the bad times of the war years—to look toward the future. Campus traditions which had waned during the early 1940s reappeared. Indeed, what well-dressed freshman dared to be without a beanie!

"you could have shot a cannonball down the aisle of most downtown cafes and the only thing you could have hit was that pot with the ten cent coffee." The next day, coffee cost a nickle.[48]

There were some college-related costs that the veterans could not and did not attempt to contain. This involved tuition. Oklahoma A. and M. College had free tuition when it opened its doors to students in 1891. By the Depression years, that policy had altered as certain fees were assessed for specific items such as the infirmary, the library, laboratories, entertainment, and student publications, but it was rare for any single fee to exceed $5 for a semester. In 1932, the most expensive item was private piano lessons at $20 for the entire semester. In that year, it was estimated a student could attend college for a full year and spend between $250-$300 for room, board, books, supplies, and fees.[49]

In 1947, all of that changed. According to the G.I. Bill, the federal government pledged to pay by far the lion's share of college expenses incurred as veterans took advantage of higher education. Yet, obviously nothing could be collected if there were no charges. In short, the state was spending money to maintain its higher education system, but the federal government would bear a lot of those costs if the state law were changed. This was the case when the twenty-first session of the Oklahoma Legislature adopted House Bill 161. On June 27, 1947, the Oklahoma State Regents for Higher Education approved a fee schedule calling for $4 per credit hour, with a minimum of $20 and a maximum of $40 for in-state students. At the same time, the schedule was adjusted upward to $10 per credit hour, with a minimum of $50 and a maximum of $120 for out-of-state students.[50] While the change had little impact on the ex-military people, since money flowed from Washington through them and into the college coffers, it can be assumed that many of the women who were enrolled in the School of Education and who were usually ineligible for military benefits felt a real financial jolt with this change of policy.

The heady postwar years of Oklahoma A. and M. College were not shared with the School of Education. Education in Oklahoma was still in trouble in both pre-service and in-service training of teachers. That put Dean Conger's hopes of making significant progress in jeopardy. In the first three months of 1946, the Placement Bureau had received some 300 notices of teaching vacancies, which was far beyond the agency's ability to fill. Two factors further complicated the situation. First, nationally colleges of education had enrollments that were only half as large as they were in 1941. Second, although ex-military personnel were gradually flowing back to other professions, that was not the case for education. It appeared that former educators either were taking advantage of the G.I. Bill to prepare for a different career or were sticking with the jobs they had taken during the war.[51]

Dean Conger joined the effort to increase enrollments once again by turning to the alumni magazine and using that publication to "sell" the college and its programs. The dean declared that the shortage of qualified educators would not end automatically. Because he believed at least 60,000 substandard teachers with war emergency certificates needed to be replaced across the nation, he called on all Oklahoma A. and M. graduates, regardless of their school, to encourage more people to enter education. Using an argument that educators found useful before and after the war, Dr. Conger stated that poorly prepared public school teachers would produce poorly prepared students for college. He was also eager to point out that, although teachers had been paid tragically meager salaries in the past, the legislature had recently been more generous. Hence, young men and women entering education could do so "with full assurance of a reasonable living, certain employment, and an opportunity to serve the nation in a vital way."[52]

Although Dean Conger's appeal was sincere and appropriate, it was not effective. As the profession lowered standards during the war to fill teaching vacancies, now in the late 1940s, the School of Education let standards slide to fill the classroom. Admissions standards were somewhat wanting throughout the college, but they were even lower in education. Because athletes who were dismissed from other schools could always be admitted to the School of Education, it became known as the "School of Athletes."[53]

Dean Conger was aware of the inadequacy of students in all of Oklahoma A. and M.'s schools—not only in education—and was further concerned that the college was not living up to its moral obligation to provide special services to meet the needs of those students. Instead of allowing students to flounder and drift on their own, Dr. Conger proposed to President Bennett that Oklahoma A. and M. College follow the lead of the University of Minnesota by creating an "all-university college" in which all freshmen would enroll for at least a year. During that year, much emphasis would be placed on orientation to the college and its academic programs, on academic evaluation to identify the field that would be right for the student, on addressing areas of weakness in the student, and on developing a tailor-made program, if such were needed to meet the student's special needs. The dean concluded: "These recommendations are made with the firm belief that if adopted, [they] would enable A&M to more nearly carry out the spirit that created the Land-Grant Colleges and to meet the moral obligation we have to our students."[54]

Although no response from Dr. Bennett was found, many of Dr. Conger's suggestions were instituted by the 1970s and 1980s when a large proportion of high school graduates attempted college regardless of their preparation. Freshman Programs and Services was established to guide the undecided student into the right area. The Career Assistance and Learning Laboratory or CALL Center served any student who sought advice or who wanted to strengthen weak areas. The bachelor of university studies was a degree option for those who needed a unique academic plan to prepare them for an unusual career. Indeed, Dean Conger was a forward-looking man.[55]

Simply because an academic unit admits some marginally qualified students, it does not follow that all of the students could be so described. Rose Mary Tompkins Duncan believed her education at Oklahoma A. and M. College gave her a "good start." Florence Ellen Conger Lowe, the dean's daughter, was even more expansive: "Well, when I went to Yale University it was a time when there were not so very many people in graduate school who were not from one of the Ivy League schools. In one of my classes, I learned that every one was from a school I considered better than my little backwater school. But, I soon found that I could hold my own with any of them. If that is any kind of a criterion, yes, I had a good start. I had *learned* how to study.''[56]

Dr. Conger had an added problem concerning the demographics of the faculty. Mrs. Lowe said that "one of the interesting things about the faculty we had is that most of the faculty were not young, and they had been inherited. When my father came, they were already on the faculty, and you simply did not fire people or move them up and out. The first new faculty member I can remember was Eleroy Stromberg, the first unattached male under the age of sixty!" Although some of the faculty were superannuated, given the salaries that were paid, few could plan for retirement. Things were made even more difficult when postwar inflation took off. Burn-out took its toll.[57]

In short, Dean Conger had his work cut out for him. To his credit, it must be stated that he was able to make progress, even against great odds. Gradually he was able to bring in new faculty after the war. Harry Brobst, one of the first new professors, had done his doctoral studies in Philadelphia. Indeed, he suffered culture shock when he arrived in Stillwater, which boasted only two paved roads out of town. Actually, Dr. Brobst really wanted to take a job with a South American oil company based in Caracas, but the person who would conduct the inter-

The director of the Bureau of Tests and Measurements since 1946, Harry Brobst served Oklahoma A. and M. College for nearly thirty years. Through his efforts, the bureau and the Department of Public School Service offered testing services to schools around the state in addition to vast testing services to on-campus departments. Dr. Brobst (*seated*) operates an IBM grading machine while Jim Reynolds, assistant editor of the *Daily O'Collegian*, looks on.

view would not arrive before Christmas, and Brobst needed a job. He decided to accept Dean Conger's offer of a teaching position in Stillwater for a semester or two. Professor Brobst, however, stayed nearly thirty years and continued living in Stillwater even after he retired.

With younger and more vigorous faculty, Dean Conger could have expectations of increased student performance. By the time he left the deanship, the school was moving in the right direction. This feeling of gradual advancement was reflected by Dr. Brobst several years after he retired. ''I would say that the College of Education, which I have known over the years, has made a real contribution to the state programs. We've had some excellent students come through here. I've always felt that the attitude, as a whole, of the people, was positive and directed toward trying to improve what we had, what we were doing. That's one thing I've always liked about Oklahomans; they seem not to hesitate to try things, and try to sort of look ahead with an optimistic eye . . . work toward achieving goals, rather than just sitting around despairing. I think the College of Education can feel pretty good. There's no human organization that doesn't have some problems and drawbacks. We just don't live in a world where everything works perfectly. In the long run, you measure achievement in terms of what's been accomplished over a period of time. There have been many, many, dedicated people in this program.''[58]

Even though Dean Conger and his colleagues faced challenges and problems during the Depression and World War II, it can also be said that they experienced real accomplishments during those years. In February 1939, Dean Daniel McIntosh of the Graduate School had announced that work toward the doctor of education (Ed.D.) degree would begin the next summer. He also noted that, following a well-established practice at Oklahoma Agricultural and Mechanical College, the regular summer staff would be augmented by outstanding lecturers from other institutions throughout the nation. Course work was to emphasize school administration and vocational education, which then included agricultural education, commercial education, and engineering and trade and industrial education.[59] The first Ed.D. degrees were awarded on July 31, 1942, to two men from Tulsa. Earl Charles Denney entitled his dissertation ''An Evaluation of the Placement Plans for First Year Entrants in the Tulsa Public Schools'' while Oliver J. Swan conducted ''A Study of Parents' Opinions Regarding Certain Aspects of Public Elementary Education in Tulsa, Oklahoma.'' Both studies were directed by Professor Chauncey with Professor Reed serving as a committee member and with Professor Lackey signing as departmental head. Drs. Conger and McIntosh signed as dean of the School of Education and the Graduate School, respectively.

In July of 1948, the School of Education accomplished yet another first when Edith Ricks Lindly became the first woman to earn an Ed.D. degree from Oklahoma A. and M. College. She was a native of Yale and taught in the public schools as a health educator after receiving her B.A. in 1931 from Oklahoma Agricultural and Mechanical College. She utilized her summers to launch a program of graduate study and got her M.S. in 1939. After earning a second master's degree in public health from the University of Michigan, she moved to California where she accepted a position as a public health administrator at Fresno State College rather than staying with the public schools. Each summer, she returned to Stillwater until she finally completed all of the requirements for the degree. Her dissertation was entitled "Survey of School Health Coordinators" and was directed by Professor Lackey, with Margaret Hampel and Vera Jones as members.[60]

The doctor of philosophy (Ph.D.) degree appeared first in the 1947-48 *Catalog*, which stated that that degree was offered by animal nutrition, animal breeding, chemical engineering, and zoology and wildlife conservation. The first Ph.D. was awarded to James S. Dinning on May 31, 1948, and he focused on animal nutrition, physiology, and biochemistry.[61]

Another advance which was closely associated with the School of Education involved the formal evaluation of students which Dean Conger had included in his recommendation regarding the "all-university college." Oklahoma A. and M. College was heavily involved with testing, virtually from the day the college was established. Such duties were generally assigned to faculty attached to the Department of Psychology because they were professionally equipped to administer and interpret the forms. The penchant for testing was not confined to college students and psychology professors. As early as 1936, education students who worked with Benjamin Dyess were developing tests that were used in contests among rural school children in the elementary grades.[62] Tests were developed for reading, arithmetic, history and geography, penmanship, civics, language, and health. No doubt, it was believed these contests would help motivate the children to higher levels of scholarship.

The ongoing testing functions were brought formally together under the Bureau of Tests and Measurements, first under E. L. Stromberg, and later under Dr. Brobst. While the bureau did provide many services to the entire college/university, it should be said that it was virtually always attached to the School/College of Education, which was usually responsible for the salaries of the staff. With office space in Morrill Hall, Professor Brobst and his few assistants were charged with testing, scoring the tests, providing statistical services to the college and its administrative units, and validating test items developed by faculty. If that were not enough, the bureau also counseled freshman and transfer students, worked with the physically handicapped, referred students to agencies for socialization counseling, helped rehabilitate emotionally maladjusted students, and supplied educational and vocational services as needed. Professor Brobst oversaw this massive undertaking in addition to teaching![63]

The bureau was located close to G. T. Stubbs' office, and as director of public school service, he was responsible for maintaining good relations with the state high schools. Director Stubbs was especially interested in getting the school administrators to use aptitude measures, and when he learned that Dr. Brobst had such an instrument, a natural alliance developed between the two men. Operating on a fiscal shoestring, they ordered the tests from the Psychological Corporation and started marketing the service to the schools. Partly because a real need existed and partly because the service was unique in the state, Dr. Brobst emphasized, "I'm telling you, that caught on."

Success gradually strengthened the fiscal health of the bureau, to the point that it was approaching self-sufficiency when Dean Conger retired. Once, when Dr. Brobst needed some funding, he recalled that "Stubbs went to Bennett and told him what the problem was . . . . Bennett said, 'You tell that guy, Brobst, to order what he needs and just order it against my account. I have an account of my own, and I can buy and spend it any way I want.' So, all my test materials for about six months were purchased on Bennett's private account."[64] One factor that helped lead to financial independence was a contract which the bureau landed with the Veterans Administration. This was a large program in which the bureau was paid to evaluate many veterans who were sent to Stillwater for that expressed purpose. By the end of the 1940s, the bureau moved out of Morrill Hall and was relocated on the first floor of Old Central, sharing space with philosophy and psychology.

In 1948, after serving thirteen years as dean of the School of Education, Dr. Conger decided to retire to emeritus status. It appeared that the college would again choose a known individual. Wilson Little, who had served Oklahoma A. and M. College as an associate professor of education during the 1944-45 academic year, was selected. While he was with the college, he helped the Oklahoma City superintendent develop instructional and curricular programs. Although born in Arkansas, Dr. Little regarded Denton, Texas, as home and had earned his doctorate at the University of Texas at Austin.[65]

Although Oklahoma A. and M. College had several presidents whose tenure could be measured in terms of days, deans of the School of Education had far greater staying power—with the exception of Dean Little. A reporter who interviewed Dr. Little for the *O'Collegian* was favorably impressed, saying, "He greets you with a hearty handclasp and is modest in manner. He looks you 'right in the eye' while speaking in a sincere and deliberate manner." He also said the new dean liked

Deans of the School/College of
Education typically enjoyed long
tenure. Wilson Little, however,
only served from 1948-51.

to fish for trout and bass and to read historical novels, contemporary
American authors, and major nineteenth century poets.[66]

Although Dr. Little was known for his expertise in educational
administration, he really never "clicked" with the administration and
the faculty. Perhaps, Dr. Little was placed in an unfair situation in that
Dr. Conger remained on campus as an "advisory dean." Because the
dean emeritus was readily available, faculty often took their problems
to him. Thus, Dr. Little was at a disadvantage. It may be that both the
dean and the faculty behaved inappropriately toward each other, but
regardless of who was at fault, the designated leader and the people he
hoped to lead did not get along. By 1951, Dean Little had relinquished
his duties.[67] Dr. and Mrs. Little retired to Florida where the former dean
died in 1965.

Even though Dean Little had problems dealing with people, he was
able to focus on what functions the school should embrace and developed four statements. As expected, teacher education was ranked first.
The school was to provide basic professional training for those preparing to teach at all levels, from the primary school through the college
level and with work available for both undergraduate and graduate students. The second function was the training of administrators and supervisory personnel. This work was offered only at the graduate level and
was designed for a wide range of positions—superintendents of schools,
assistant superintendents in charge of business management, person-

nel, directors of junior colleges, elementary or secondary school principals, supervisors and coordinators of instruction, and counseling and guidance professionals. The third function was professional service, which had grown greatly in stature under Dean Conger. The School of Education was prepared to provide professional services such as working with school systems to develop in-service training for teaching, supervisory, and administrative personnel, consultative services, and assistance to school superintendents with special and comprehensive educational studies. In the final statement, the school pledged itself to what was called "cooperative services," whereby it would offer service courses in philosophy, photography, psychology, and religious education to the other schools at Oklahoma A. and M. College.[68]

Clearly, the School of Education had "bought into" two of the major thrusts of a land-grant institution—instruction and service—but the third area of research was ignored almost totally. The school should not be judged too harshly for that omission, though, for faculty and administrators who know of that era from personal experience are unanimous that, given the heavy on-campus teaching loads and the grueling demands made by extension, few had either the time or the energy to accept obligations for conducting research.

Even though Dean Little had problems relating to the staff he had inherited, he was still willing to say that the school would offer a very comprehensive educational program to its students and broad services to professional colleagues in the field. In regard to the former, he had course work in place that would support the claim of being comprehensive. In terms of curricular groupings, education boasted one freshman course, one sophomore course, ten junior courses, twenty senior courses, thirty at the master's level, and eighteen at the doctoral level. For philosophy, there were two freshman, no sophomore, eight junior, five senior, and three master's courses. Photography offered one sophomore and three junior courses, while psychology had four sophomore, five junior, nine senior, and eleven master's courses. Finally, religious studies had two freshman, two sophomore, five junior, and two senior courses.

Ninety-one percent of the work was at the upper-division or graduate-level, with 44 percent at the graduate-level. To support this academic enterprise, an adequate staff was required. Education listed a faculty of twenty-two people, including both Dean Emeritus Conger and Dean Little, who each taught one course. In addition, people taught in education whose major responsibilities were in other administrative units. For example, Julia Stout, who was the dean of women, and J. Conner Fitzgerald, who was engaged at the college-level with Educational Extension and the Audio-Visual Center, both taught. The other faculty groups in the school were somewhat smaller. While psychology had a staff of four plus a professor of sociology who taught Social Psychology, phi-

Dr. and Mrs. Haskell Pruett were well known for party photographs. Over the years, Dr. Pruett took, developed, printed, and catalogued thousands of photos. He estimates that the negatives would stretch from his home in west Stillwater north to the Twelve-Mile Corner at Highways 177 and 64.

losophy had four on the faculty. Religious education—in keeping with the long-standing policy of the School of Education—listed several Stillwater clergymen who volunteered their services plus the directors of the Young Men's Christian Association and the Young Women's Christian Association. The Ys were still powerful organizations which operated actively on the campus and utilized college facilities, specifically the building which housed the dean of men and the dean of women. Finally, the photography program was a one-man show under the leadership of Haskell Pruett.[69]

"Doc" Pruett rivaled the deans themselves in regard to published reports in the college's papers and magazines. A product of George Peabody College for Teachers, Dr. Pruett later received an M.S. from the University of Oklahoma. He was unusual partly because of the various areas in which he studied, for his B.S. was in agricultural education, his M.S. was in industrial arts and physical-chemical sciences, his M.A. was in educational administration, and his Ph.D. was in social sciences.[70] Coming to Oklahoma A. and M. College in 1936 as special instructor of visual education and business manager, the following year he was made chairman of the Department of Audio-Visual Aids and Photography, with the rank of associate professor of education, positions which he retained until 1950.

Photography was not his first professional love, though, for he had a national reputation in the fields of school building construction, school finance, and educational administration. In addition to serving a stint with the State Department of Education, he was the superintendent of Greer County who consolidated the schools, taught at both Peabody and the University of Arkansas, for nine years was a special consultant to the United States Bureau of Education on school plant problems, and was one of a dozen educators called to Washington, D.C., in 1934 by the Commissioner of Education to help formulate federal policies regarding financing public education. It was clear that "Doc" brought a great deal of talent and experience to the Stillwater campus. He was also a man of "firsts": Oklahoma's first state rural school supervisor; Oklahoma's first director of school transportation, a vital program if the state were to consolidate the small rural schools; and the first director of schoolhouse planning.[71]

"Doc" was especially loved for his extracurricular activities. In 1939, a couple of Kappa Delta sorority women followed him into his office in Morrill Hall and asked if he would be available to take pictures at their dance the following Saturday. This first dance of the year was a costume dance called the Coed Prom, which was for women only. He decided he would accommodate them and arrived carrying his 35-mm camera and wearing a large, black, beaverskin top hat since it was a costume dance. The hat was originally his uncle's and had been given to him years before by his mother. It was destined to become his extracurricular trademark. Working over the weekend, he managed to develop and print the photos by Monday and sold them for fifteen cents apiece. His price stayed the same for over a quarter of a century, but his efficiency increased to the point where he would have his handiwork displayed by Sunday evening. The "Party Pic" concept had been introduced to America. His record was covering thirteen dances in a single weekend, and he estimated he attended a total of more than 25,000 dances, which was another record. Another first was achieved two weeks after the Coed Prom. When asked to cover the Sigma Phi Epsilon dance, again in his black top hat, he used a bicycle built for two as a prop; no props had ever been used before. Over the years, Dr. Pruett collected literally tens of thousands of negatives, which he catalogued and kept in his basement. In one year alone, he sold 20,000 photos through the College Book Store, which he said made some money for the Student Union but not for him.[72]

There was no great rush to move to fill the deanship again following Dr. Little's departure. For about a year, the School of Education was governed by a troika consisting of Professors Chauncey, Stubbs, and Morris Wallace.

By the time Dean Conger had retired in 1948, the School of Education had changed markedly. Given his knowledge of education, his professional association with the education decisionmakers in the state, his collegial ties to education in the field, and his close personal ties with the president of the college, he was secure enough that he could speak out against the inadequacies of the system and in favor of desired changes. The voice of the dean of the School of Education in Stillwater was being heard at least throughout the state.

Although Dr. Conger never had either a large staff or a lavish budget, he husbanded those resources so that the instructional program developed at the undergraduate and especially the graduate level. Furthermore, he was willing to send the denizens of the school across Oklahoma to assist local people. In the latter effort, he willingly used personnel associated with college extension and public school services. These three units—education, extension, and public school services— worked together so closely over the years that it is often impossible to tell where one stopped and the others started when it came to providing service to the field. Consequently, under Dean Conger's leadership, the school broadened and strengthened the instructional base inherited from earlier eras and expanded into the second area of the college's mission—extension. This did not result in the solid tripod of instruction, extension, and research since the last was far from robust, but it can be said that it was present in an embryonic form since graduate degrees were in place and would eventually lead to greater scholarly investigation.

As early as 1938, E. L. Stromberg had stated Dean Conger's goal was to start "the school of education . . . on its way to the place where it will no longer be known as one of several schools of education in Oklahoma, but as the school of education in Oklahoma."[73] While it would be grandiose to say Dr. Conger had achieved that, it cannot be denied that he was the springboard that could be used to catapult the school into that status.

To be sure, the base laid by Dr. Conger was momentarily shaken with the advent of his successor, but the school was strong enough to survive that trauma, which was real at the time but hardly more than a hiccup in historical retrospect. With Dr. Little's deanship fading away and with the immediate situation handled by the emergence of the troika, what the school needed was a dean who could spur it on to the next evolutionary stage.

Endnotes

1. *1938 Redskin*, p. 26, Oklahoma A. and M. College Yearbook; Oklahoma A. and M. College *Daily O'Collegian*, 2 November 1929, p. 2.

2. Florence Ellen Lowe to Thomas A. Karman, 20 September 1987, Special Collections, Edmon Low Library, Oklahoma State University, Stillwater, Oklahoma. Mrs. Lowe graduated from Oklahoma A. and M. College, completed her graduate education at Yale University, and in 1987 was still active in the field of education, serving Southern Connecticut State University as professor of philosophy, a discipline that was housed in her father's school while he was dean.

3. *1940 Redskin*, p. 139; Author interview with Florence Ellen Conger Lowe, Rose Mary Tompkins Duncan, Dorothea Hodges, and Kathryn Tompkins McCollom, 14 April 1987, Centennial Histories Oral Interview Collection, Special Collections, Edmon Low Library.

4. Lowe, Duncan, Hodges, and McCollom interview.

5. Author interview with Harry Brobst, 31 July 1986, Centennial Histories Oral Interview Collection.

6. *Daily O'Collegian*, 22 September 1929, p. 1.

7. Brobst interview.

8. N. Conger, "Economic Planning In The South In Light of Philosophy and Education," transcript of address to the Oklahoma Academy of Science, 2 December 1938, pp. 2, 9, N. Conger Collection, Special Collections, Edmon Low Library.

9. *Annual Catalog, Oklahoma A. and M. College, 1936-1937*, p. 95.

10. Author interview with Bill Hindman, Marjorie Orloski, Benn Palmer, and Gladys Skinner, 1 July 1986, Centennial Histories Oral Interview Collection.

11. A. R. Hickam to C. L. Kezer, 19 March 1934, C. L. Kezer Collection, Special Collections, Edmon Low Library.

12. N. Conger, "A&M Accepts Rural Challenge," *Oklahoma A. and M. College Magazine*, vol. 8, no. 5 (February 1937), p. 9.

13. Conger, "A&M Accepts Rural Challenge," p. 3.

14. *Daily O'Collegian*, 10 February 1939, p. 1.

15. *Daily O'Collegian*, 14 May 1940, p. 1.

16. *Daily O'Collegian*, 18 July 1941, p. 1.

17. "Faculty Changes," *Oklahoma A. and M. College Magazine*, vol. 8, no. 1 (October 1936), p. 10; "News About the Faculty," *Oklahoma A. and M. College Magazine*, vol. 12, no. 6 (March 1941), p. 7. For more information on the history of extension at Oklahoma A. and M. College/Oklahoma State University, see Robert C. Fite, *A. History of Oklahoma State University Extension and Outreach*, another volume in the Centennial Histories Series.

18. "In-Service Education at A. and M.," *Oklahoma A. and M. College Magazine*, vol. 16, no. 7 (February 1944), p. 13.

19. "New Department Serves Schools," *Oklahoma A. and M. College Magazine*, vol. 18, no. 5 (February 1946), p. 4.

20. "New Department Serves Schools, p. 4.

21. Oklahoma City *Daily Oklahoman*, 21 May 1939, p. 1D.

22. "Eyes, Ears, Wheels and Wings," *Oklahoma A. and M. College Magazine*, vol. 26, no. 1 (September 1954), p. 12; *Daily O'Collegian*, 5 June 1953, p. 3.

23. *Daily O'Collegian*, 26 September 1941, p. 1, 21 May 1958, p. 7.

24. Lowe, Duncan, Hodges, and McCollom interview.

25. *Daily O'Collegian*, 21 May 1958, p. 7.

26. *Daily O'Collegian*, 21 May 1958, p. 7.

27. N. Conger, "School Children Do Not Vote," 13 February 1940, p. 5, N. Conger Collection.

28. Author telephone interview with Bennett Basore, December 1987.

29. *Daily O'Collegian*, 24 April 1940, p. 1.

30. *Daily O'Collegian*, 18 May 1940, p. 1.

31. *Annual Catalog, Oklahoma A. and M. College, 1943-1944*, p. 72.

32. Lowe, Duncan, Hodges, and McCollom interview.

33. *Annual Catalog, Oklahoma A. and M. College, 1942-1943*, p. iii.

34. H. P. Adams, "War Training Programs at A&M," *Oklahoma A. and M. College Magazine*, vol. 17, no. 8 (May 1945), p. 5.

35. Author interview with John Tate, 22 March 1986, Centennial Histories Oral Interview Collection.

36. "Hitler's Oak Tree," *Oklahoma State University Outreach*, vol. 19, no. 2 (March-April 1978), p. 23; Lowe, Duncan, Hodges, and McCollom interview.

37. Tate interview.

38. Author interview with Raymond Girod, 7 July 1986, Centennial Histories Oral Interview Collection.

39. *Daily O'Collegian*, 24 March 1943, p. 1, 30 June 1943, p. 1.

40. *Daily O'Collegian*, 15 September 1942, p. 1, 19 September 1942, p. 1.

41. *Daily O'Collegian*, 6 October 1942, p. 1.

42. *Daily O'Collegian*, 15 September 1942, p. 1, 19 September 1942, p. 1.

43. *Daily O'Collegian*, 3 May 1944, p. 1.

44. *Daily O'Collegian*, 31 December 1942, p. 1.

45. *Daily O'Collegian*, 30 November 1945, p. 1.

46. *Daily O'Collegian*, 30 November 1945, p. 1.

47. N. Conger, "Looking Ahead Educationally in Oklahoma," undated, p. 7, N. Conger Collection.

48. *Daily O'Collegian*, 19 January 1951, p. 8.

49. *Annual Catalog, Oklahoma A. and M. College, 1932-33*, p. 23.

50. *Oklahoma A. and M. College Bulletin—Revision of Catalog Issue for 1946-47*, p. 1.

51. *Daily O'Collegian*, 13 April 1946, p. 3.

52. N. Conger, "The Teacher Shortage," *Oklahoma A. and M. College Magazine*, vol. 18, no. 5 (February 1946), p. 3.

53. Girod interview.

54. N. Conger, "A Proposed New School for A&M College," no date, N. Conger Collection.

55. To develop a bachelor of university studies degree, a student needed to have a valid set of academic goals that could be met only by integrating professional elements from at least two colleges—for example, turf management and business for a person who wanted to prepare for a career in country club management. After meeting mandated requirements in English, history, and political science, a student could proceed with any program approved by the colleges involved and the vice president for academic affairs and research.

56. Lowe, Duncan, Hodges, and Tompkins interview.

57. Lowe, Duncan, Hodges, and Tompkins interview.

58. Brobst interview.

59. *Daily O'Collegian*, 10 February 1939, p. 1.

60. *Daily O'Collegian*, 23 July 1948, p. 1; Geneva Holcomb Wise, "Do You Remember When . . . ?" *Oklahoma A. and M. College Magazine*, vol. 27, no. 9 (May 1956), p. 13.

61. *Daily O'Collegian*, 1 May 1948, p. 1.

62. *Daily O'Collegian*, 28 April 1936, p. 1.

63. *Daily O'Collegian*, 24 September 1946, p. 1.

64. Brobst interview.

65. *Daily O'Collegian*, 17 September 1948, p. 1.

66. *Daily O'Collegian*, 5 October 1948, p. 1.

67. Brobst interview; Author interview with Helmer Sorenson, 25 June 1986, Centennial Histories Oral Interview Collection; Girod interview; Lowe, Duncan, Hodges, and McCollom interview.

68. *Annual Catalog, Oklahoma State University, 1948-1949*, p. 134.

69. *Annual Catalog, Oklahoma State University, 1948-1949*, pp. 378-379, 389-392.

70. *Daily Oklahoman Orbit*, 27 August 1961, pp. 14-15.

71. "Staff and Faculty Changes," *Oklahoma A. and M. College Magazine*, vol. 7, no. 1 (October 1935), p. 3.

72. *Daily O'Collegian*, 4 November 1982, p. 12; B. B. Chapman, "Photographs for Posterity," *Oklahoma A. and M. College Magazine*, vol. 22, no. 8 (April 1951), p. 12.

73. E. L. Stromberg, "Progress in Education," *Oklahoma A. and M. College Magazine*, vol. 9, no. 5 (February 1938), p. 3.

5 Building on a Firm Foundation

By the time J. Andrew Holley was asked to assume leadership of the School of Education in 1951, it already had a history stretching back half a century. For the first two deans, John Hugh Bowers and Herbert Patterson, the primary task had been to embed professional education as an integral part of the Oklahoma Agricultural and Mechanical College. For Dean Bowers, that meant securing a separate and recognized identity for the school. For Dean Patterson, that meant suffering growing pains while acquiring the resources to meet the demand for an educational program that clearly was always popular even if not deemed to be high priority by everyone. After all, under Dr. Patterson, the School of Education was attacked by a governor who wanted to strip education from the Oklahoma A. and M. College and restrict it to the original emphases on agriculture, engineering, and home economics. When survival is the issue, one tends to keep his or her eyes on the home front.

Napoleon Conger had the distinct advantage of being a school leader recognized throughout the state and a person with close ties to the president's office. This position gave a large measure to the school as well as to the dean, and it led to an era when development of instructional programs in Stillwater was paralleled by increased growth of influence throughout the state. It would fall to new leadership to consolidate gains made by Dean Conger and to build a school of education with greater balance, for both Oklahoma A. and M. College and its School of Education were moving quickly away from being institutional neophytes.

Born in Yale, Mississippi, Dean Holley came from a family of educators. His father and uncle, G. A. and J. T., respectively, founded Oakland Normal Institute near Fulton, Missouri, in 1877. Holley moved from

J. Andrew Holley served as dean of the College of Education from 1951-64. During his years as dean, Dr. Holley strived for higher standards and a more elevated professional status for educators at all levels.

Missouri to Stigler, Oklahoma, in 1902 with his family, but he went out-of-state for his collegiate education. He earned his bachelor's degree in 1923 in economics and pre-law from the University of Colorado. He later went to Columbia University where he majored in administration and supervision of secondary education and earned a master's degree and a diploma as a high school principal in 1928. It was nearly twenty years later when he returned to Columbia to obtain his Ed.D., in 1947. While at Columbia University he had a General Education Board Scholarship for 1927-28, was a Columbia Fellow in 1932-33, and was an Associate in Educational Administration for 1946-47.[1]

Dean Holley launched his educational career at the age of seventeen when he was granted a county teaching certificate and went to teach at San Bois, which he described as a "diminutive rural community in Haskell county in eastern Oklahoma" and as a "one horse" village. There, he served as janitor, teacher, principal, and superintendent. Later, he moved to a grade school at Luther. From 1926 until 1940 he served in the State Department of Education in various capacities such as assistant state high school inspector, chief state high school inspector, and director of curriculum. During those years he became involved with the

North Central Association and gradually assumed positions of leadership as a member of and later chair of the Commission on Secondary Schools, as a member of the Committee on Cooperation in Research, as chair of the Committee on High School and College Relations, and as vice president of the Executive Committee.

He left the State Department of Education in 1940 and joined Oklahoma A. and M. College as head of the Department of Business Education, but two years later he enlisted in the Navy. He was instrumental in contracting with colleges and universities for training programs for future officers. He served as the assistant district director of training for the Eighth Naval District in New Orleans, the assistant director of training for the Fourth Naval District in Philadelphia, and as the commanding officer of the V-12 units at the University of Louisville. He ended his naval career as a lieutenant commander and continued to be active in the Naval Reserves. It is a little ironic that Dr. Holley came from a college that was heavily involved with military training programs in World War II, yet his own military service did not get farther west than Kentucky.[2]

After the war ended, Dr. Holley returned to his position in the Division of Commerce until Henry Bennett selected him to lead the School of Education in 1951. During those years, Dr. Holley stayed in Morrill Hall, which was shared by commerce and education. While his immediate environment might have been tranquil, this was the age of great postwar expansion at Oklahoma A. and M. College. The lawn north of his building sprouted little grass but instead grew a "patch" of temporary Quonset huts and frame buildings to take care of the huge influx of students. A block and a half to the west (which today is the beautiful lawns and gardens south of the Edmon Low Library) was either a sea of mud or a cloud of dust as the Library, the Student Union, and the Classroom Building were constructed.

Like Dr. Conger before him, Dean Holley was concerned that the schools recognize their responsibility to prepare students both academically and morally. Like his predecessor, he used the alumni publications as a way to reach a larger audience. Having been in the deanship only a little over a year, he identified what he regarded as two critical issues in education. First, he asked, "Can the schools and colleges develop young people who are morally honest and socially responsible? . . . Is it possible to develop a higher level of morality and social responsibility in the schools than exists in the community at large?" To the dean, there was clear evidence of "moral boredom," but he believed it was not fair to lay the blame primarily on the schools, because to do so would ignore the steady flow of influences from the home and community. He asked what the proper role of the schools was in teaching character. He called for the schools, homes, churches, and courts

While graduation exercises were still held in the College Auditorium, features of the immediate area shifted. The upper photo shows (*left to right*) the library, the library annex with its second story, and Gundersen, with its old wooden windows. Two decades later, the second story of the library annex is gone, showing the top of the new Student Union. Also, foliage has sprouted and lamp posts have been replaced.

Centennial Histories Series

to work together to "develop young people with high moral and intellectual standards, attitudes, and practices."[3]

Dean Holley then considered the academic aspects of education. He said, "Can acceptable standards in reading, spelling, oral and written expression, and number work be attained under the conditions of mass education?" This was a matter of real concern because the hoard of post-war baby-boom youth was starting to swamp the elementary schools by 1952. He noted that the schools now served "masses of children," where formerly they worked only with "the few select ones." Setting the stage for support for greater resources, Dr. Holley said: "Lower standards of attainment is the price we pay for the low-cost mass education. We have the resources and we have the techniques for doing a much better job of teaching the fundamentals to all the children of all the people. The question is: Are we willing to pay the price required for better programs of instruction?"[4]

Interestingly, concerns often stay the same through the ages. The citizens of Socrates' Athens were worried about the moral corruption of its youth, to the point where Socrates was put to death. If the dean of education were fretting about "moral boredom" in the fall of 1952 as Dwight D. Eisenhower was about to take over the Presidency, one can only wonder what he would have thought of either the advent of the Age of Aquarius in the late 1960s and early 1970s or the collapse of the traditional family in the 1980s. Also, Dean Holley wrote before the Scholastic Aptitude Test scores started their steep plunge in the late 1950s and before onerous grade inflation at all levels of education sent grade point averages soaring. If Dr. Holley felt the academic and social house of his day was in a state of disarray, his successors would realize that the situation could get worse.[5]

In the fall of 1951, under the leadership of Dean Holley, efforts were made to revive the Education Student Council. The organization was referred to as "new to the campus" in spite of its activities in the preceding decade. The rebirth of this student organization was a little complicated. On October 31, 1951, the Future Teachers of America chapter chose the representatives who would be responsible for coordinating the activities of the three major educational organizations on campus— Kappa Delta Pi, the Association of Childhood Education International, and the Future Teachers of America. The first slate of officers included Walter Ethridge as president, Dean Miller as vice president, Arlene McElroy as secretary, Mary Ann Weimer as treasurer, George Williams as song leader, Grace Stephens as historian, Jim Murry as parliamentarian, and Joan Maneval as publicity chairman.

Although this sounded like a very well-organized group, for some reason a second planning committee—the Student Organization Committee—took over. Under the leadership of Jack Byrom, this com-

In the early 1950s, what had evolved into the central quad of the campus was still littered with construction debris and cluttered with temporary structures. While sadly lacking the eventual Williamsburg-like charming landscaping, it still offered significant oases of air-conditioned pleasure in the Library, Classroom Building, and Student Union for the summer scholars.

mittee was to create a student council that would promote the interests of the education student body, bring unity and enthusiasm to the School of Education, help with Senior Career Day and freshman orientation, conduct education evaluations, work on teacher-evaluation projects, select people for *Who's Who*, and plan convocation and homecoming activities. This committee was comprised of a totally different group of students—Ruth Trendle, Nelda Baker, Bernard Lafevre, Marilyn Laird, Ann Davidson, Mac Bulger, Susie Askew, Sue Snell, and Sue-Nell Wimer—and faculty—Byrom, Eli Foster, Raymond Young, Evert Little, and Myrtle Schwartz. It was finally decided that the council would consist of fourteen students, two from each class plus two each from the Future Teachers of America, American Childhood Education International, and Kappa Delta Pi. The School of Education representative to the Student Senate was to be an ex officio member.[6]

This time the student organization held. By 1953, the school elected its first education queen and managed a full Education Week. Since that time, the Education Student Council has continued to operate as the body within the school/college, planning special events such as the Honors and Awards Banquet (the successor of the Education Day festivities) and providing advice to the dean as it was needed.

Although heavily involved with education at the state and national level, Dr. Holley is also credited with work on the international front. This work, however, was not the first international involvement by the education faculty. In 1901, J. C. Muerman, who would later be a long-time professor of education at Oklahoma A. and M., went to the Philippines. By the time he left the islands, he was the high commissioner of education and was second in stature only to William Howard Taft, the governor general. In 1940, the Stillwater Chamber of Commerce appointed Dr. Muerman as "Ambassador of Goodwill." He was sent to Java, the Philippines, and Borneo. W. V. Phelan, who was the dean of the School of Education at the University of Oklahoma from 1912 to 1926 and who was appointed professor of education at Oklahoma A. and M. College in 1931, was invited to help reorganize the University of Chung Chou in Kaifeng, China, along American lines in 1923.[7]

In the 1950s, Oklahoma A. and M. College was deeply committed to assisting Ethiopia develop as a modern country. While the largest part of Oklahoma A. and M.'s effort was related directly to agricultural education at the collegiate level, it was clear that an effective program in higher education had to be supported by at least an adequate program at the elementary and secondary levels. Recognized as an excellent curriculum man, Dr. Holley was dispatched in early 1955 for five weeks to consult about language projects and to survey the problems in developing and improving both the elementary and secondary school programs in Ethiopia. He was also to explore how Oklahoma A. and M. College specifically might be able to aid Ethiopian education.[8]

Once he arrived in Ethiopia, he believed as though he were centuries removed from the modern world, although he acknowledged that the educational task faced by the Point Four people was in good hands. "The secret of our success in Ethiopia lies in the fact that we have sent some of our best people. They are fine technicians, sincere in their desire to help the Ethiopians and have a fine sense of diplomacy—good representatives of America and of A&M." But in remote areas as yet untouched by Point Four, he found education was in the hands of priests who used a chanting method of teaching and who limited their instruction to the Amharic alphabet and the catechism of the Coptic Christian Church. It was easy for him to conclude that one of the greatest needs was to establish schools to teach the fundamentals, the rudiments of academic learning plus sanitation, agriculture, and other courses. Dean Holley suggested a two-pronged attack: first, he recommended a plan for establishing modern elementary and secondary schools in all of the provinces of the empire to advance academic programs; second, he suggested that trade schools be added to the educational system to prepare people for skilled and semi-skilled work.[9]

Since the Ethiopian project focused especially on agricultural development, the School of Education was not usually directly involved on the site. The exceptions were Dean Holley's trip and the five-year tour of duty provided by Lloyd Wiggins as a vocational instructor, after which Wiggins joined the faculty of the School of Occupational and Adult Education. Still, the Jimma Agricultural Technical School was a school, and nearly all of the staff was recruited and selected by the School of Education, including Evert T. Little, who temporarily left his position as an assistant educational psychology professor in Stillwater to serve as director at Jimma.

A year after his sojourn to Africa, Dean Holley lauded the work of his school. In addition to pre-service instruction, the School of Education was significantly involved with field service and worked with the director of school services to help survey school building needs (which were massive as public school enrollments bulged). The school also

Although the School of Education was not usually directly involved on the site in Ethiopia, faculty including J. Andrew Holley, Lloyd Wiggins, and Evert Little all offered expertise in the African nation. Shown examining coffee beans are Robert Loomis, instructor of biological science; Hugh Rouk, instructor of agronomy and director of coffee research; William Moran, Jr.; Ambassador Joe Simonson; Marc Gordon, director of Technical Cooperation Administration Operations in Ethiopia; Dr. Little, director of the Jimma Agricultural Technical School; Dick Turner; Luther H. Brannon, president of Imperial College; C. L. Angerer, dean of the Ethiopian College of Agriculture; and Herbie Birk.

worked with the Bureau of Tests and Measurements to help test the school children and then to prepare the teachers and counselors to interpret the test results properly. Living up to its duty to the profession, the school also provided in-service educational programs tailored to the developmental needs of particular schools or school systems; offered workshops, conferences, and clinics to improve reading instruction; and worked with school administrators to improve overall educational leadership. Finally, for the past three years, a professor of secondary education had been released part-time to work with the Oklahoma Curriculum Improvement Commission. Clearly, the school was advancing on several fronts; it was a force to be reckoned with in the state. But Holley also made sure that people realized how successful the school was *in spite* of the fact that it faced pressing needs.

He proceeded to list nine areas where action had to be taken. Not only did the curriculum and teaching for both resident and extension instruction need to be improved, the school had to get and especially retain qualified staff. To accomplish this, salaries and working conditions had to be addressed. The school needed to secure adequate laboratory facilities for the observation and demonstration of good teaching techniques. Laboratories servicing psychology, art education, the reading clinic, photography, and meteorology lacked space and suitable equipment. It was vital that additional office space be obtained for the staff and graduate students, plus space that could be used for conferences. The dean hoped to develop and improve graduate programs for teachers, school counselors, school psychologists, and college teachers and administrators. Improving services offered to public and private schools and colleges in Oklahoma was also a critical need, as was strengthening the certification programs for elementary and secondary school teachers and administrators. Finally, there was a need to improve guidance and counseling services and to develop methods for screening candidates for student teaching and for certification.[10]

In the report, Dean Holley made excellent use of the "good news/bad news" technique by praising the real accomplishments of his faculty and staff yet simultaneously suggesting that infinitely better service could be provided to the state if only genuine needs were met. Indeed, it was almost a case of putting the 4-H Club motto into action: "To Make the Best Better." While the dean's appeal may have been artful, it was not simply self-serving, for education as a whole was facing a crisis that grew more serious the further away it got from World War II. For every 72 students served by the schools in 1945, there were 100 in 1956; that number would grow to 121 by 1960 and 136 by 1965. Dr. Holley expected a 71 percent enrollment increase between 1954 and 1969, which meant schools of education would need to prepare three new teachers for every two currently enrolled. The need for staff was even more acute at the college and university level, for enrollments there were growing relatively faster than in the elementary and secondary schools as first-generation college students greatly taxed available higher education facilities.[11]

On a bright or positive side, the dean was pleased to report in 1956 that undergraduate enrollments in the School of Education had increased by 40 percent (to 600 students) over the previous three years, which suggested that education as a profession was once again gaining in popularity. An increased supply of prospective students enabled the school to establish higher standards for admission to teacher education. A student had to demonstrate above-average scholarship in order to be admitted to his or her student teaching courses. It also meant that the faculty could enhance the rigor of the curriculum.[12]

The demographic problem, however, would not go away in spite of what educators did. In 1959, Dean Holley was predicting that enrollments would increase during the next decade from 80-120 percent in post-secondary education, from 40-60 percent in secondary schools, and 30 percent in elementary school. Schools of education had increased their productivity, but they were not keeping up with the need. As a result, he estimated there were at least 80,000 public school teachers who had substandard or emergency credentials, and the number of marginally prepared college and university teachers was substantial.

Once again, Dr. Holley assigned major blame for the situation on the twin evils of low salaries and unsatisfactory working conditions, which in combination successfully kept many competent people out of the field and caused other qualified educators to leave teaching. He suggested it would be appropriate to provide substantial salary increases for effective teaching. Doubling the salary would be fitting since it would recognize the importance of the services rendered by the teaching profession. He also repeated his call for society to provide adequate libraries, teaching and research facilities (including modern buildings and equipment) suitable for a modern educational program, and more adequate and stable sources of financial support for the whole educational enterprise.

While Dean Holley appealed for additional resources to elevate the quality of the programs, he realized that "educators have long recognized that increased support often follows, not precedes, respect and confidence earned through more efficient and effective services rendered by educational institutions." He assured the public that that was already happening, for in spite of stunted resources, standards were being raised, the curriculum was being updated, content was being evaluated for relevance and meaning, and teaching and evaluation methods were being scrutinized.[13]

While the School of Education was moving ahead well programatically, it was suffering in terms of administrative organization. Dean Hol-

John Tate (*left*) and Cary L. Hill, both faculty members in industrial arts education, served the College of Education for over thirty years and twenty years, respectively. Dr. Tate received his undergraduate degree from Oklahoma A. and M. in 1945 and was a contributor to the famous "Record Book" compiled by B. B. Chapman's history class on the occasion of the golden anniversary of the college.

ley served both as dean and departmental head of all the school's units. Although the school was not large, it was big enough that it could not be administered by a single person. Recognizing his need for assistance, especially in the area of finance and budget, Dr. Holley called Helmer Sorenson into his office and shared a letter with him that was drafted to President Willham asking that Dr. Sorenson be named as vice dean of the school. Professor Sorenson had no advance notice of the move. He hesitated to accept until he was assured that key faculty such as Drs. Chauncey and James Richardson had been consulted and supported the idea. Knowing that, Dr. Sorenson accepted the vice deanship, although he readily admitted that he did a great deal of work that would be delegated to a departmental head once that system was put in place.[14]

College enrollments, which would grow to a flood once Lyndon Johnson's "Great Society" was launched, were already beginning to surge by the mid-1950s and were affecting access to higher education. Universities could not produce college faculty fast enough to satisfy the demand. The problem was compounded for many of the smaller colleges which could not justify hiring a separate professor for each special field. Often graduates in the "hard sciences" such as physics and chemistry were assigned classes that took them well beyond their highly focused Ph.D. programs. These alumni, usually of arts and sciences programs, communicated back to the campus that they were only rarely able to incorporate their area of specialization in their classes but were frequently expected to assume responsibility for teaching subjects which were ignored in their doctoral program. Instead of the rigorous, highly focused, and research-oriented Ph.D. programs, they believed their university preparation would have stood them in better stead if they had been allowed to study in several related areas instead of in one sub-specialty.

In response to that situation, Vice Dean Sorenson worked with education faculty such as Dr. Richardson to open conversations with Schiller Scroggs, dean of the College of Arts and Sciences. They developed multidisciplinary, intercollegiate doctoral programs in which candidates engaged in course work in several related areas. In addition to studying in fields that the person would teach, there was also a block of courses in higher education which gave the future college professor a background in the historical development and organization of American higher education, the principles of curriculum development and instruction adapted to the collegiate level, and a perspective on issues facing higher education. It was especially unusual for people going into college teaching to have either knowledge of the art of teaching or of the nature of the enterprise they would be serving.

The Ed.D. in college teaching, as the program was known, proved

In the mid-1950s, universities could not produce faculty fast enough to satisfy the demand. Also, many educators realized the value of a multi-disciplinary, intercollegiate doctoral program. Through the efforts of various faculty and college administrators, including James Richardson, a program for the Ed.D. in college teaching soon became very popular.

to be very popular across campus. Over the years, the faculty in higher education cooperated with departments ranging from accounting to zoology, with the bulk of the cooperating departments housed administratively in the School/College of Arts and Sciences. In some cases, graduate students had the option of selecting between a highly focused research Ph.D. in a discipline and the teaching-oriented Ed.D. through the same department plus higher education. In other cases, departments without a self-standing doctoral program were able to operate on that level through higher education.

The advent of the Ed.D. in college teaching really added an interesting twist to graduate education within the world of teacher education at Stillwater. From its inception, it was heralded as a cooperative program. It quickly brought the other Ed.D. programs under an umbrella. After all, students in agriculture, home economics, and business who were pursuing advanced graduate work were almost universally planning for a career in an institution of higher learning. Consequently, it was only logical that their programs should be wedded to the higher education programs on campus.

As a result, the degree programs were coordinated, with the admissions committee, chaired by Dr. Sorenson, reviewing all Ed.D. applicants. All plans of study reflected the higher education core program so all candidates had at least some common elements when they sat for the qualifying examination. In order to guard against the college teaching program becoming a second-class citizen, all applicants were checked to ensure that they met the admissions and exit criteria.

While the summer problem-solving workshops initiated under Dean Conger could have served as the model for the widely publicized Danforth Foundation liberal arts workshop, Oklahoma A. and M.'s college teaching program could easily have served as the model for the doctor of arts degree program that was heavily subsized by the Carnegie Foundation in the late 1960s and adopted by many universities around the nation. The only difference was that enthusiasm for the doctor of arts faded while the commitment to interdisciplinary doctoral work was sustained in Stillwater. The combined college teaching program continues to be one of the largest producers of doctoral graduates, who are widely sought by colleges and regional universities that have teaching—rather than original research—as their major mission.

The importance of this work in graduate education both to the College of Education and to the Graduate College needs to be emphasized. By the time Dean Holley was about to retire, education—with a relatively small faculty—was producing well over half of the student credit hours at the graduate level, doing far more in that area, for example, than the faculty of the much larger College of Arts and Sciences. This meant that there was a burdensome advising load, especially at the doctoral level. It also explains in large part why faculty research efforts were restricted almost totally to dissertation supervision.[15]

New educational programs obviously put added pressure on available space for instruction, laboratories, and clearinghouses. To a degree, Dean Holley's cry for facilities was heard and answered. In 1959, he was delighted to announce that the College of Education had made a major stride forward in regard to its physical facilities, for he and his staff would be vacating quarters that had long been used in Morrill Hall and would move across the street into Gundersen Hall. Education was assigned about half of the first floor, sharing the rest of the space with personnel from the Department of Physics. The college had all of the second floor, where there were two up-to-date elementary education laboratories, a combination seminar-materials laboratory, an efficient art education laboratory, and an ultramodern reading clinic. None of the third floor was available because architecture was still to be quartered there.[16]

The architecture students proved to be a constant problem for Dean Holley. Typically those students worked into the wee hours of the morning, staying long after all others had vacated the building. In order to get some relief from the tedium of the drafting table, they would take advantage of the lack of supervision, sneak down to the first floor, and steal the sign that identified the Office of the Dean of the College of Education. After several such sorties, Dr. Holley finally laid the problem to rest by having the sign bolted completely through the wall and fastened from the inside.[17]

Although Carl Gundersen had only indirect contact with people enrolled in education while he taught at Oklahoma A. and M. College,

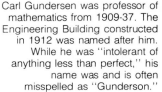

Carl Gundersen was professor of mathematics from 1909-37. The Engineering Building constructed in 1912 was named after him. While he was "intolerant of anything less than perfect," his name was and is often misspelled as "Gunderson."

nonetheless his name today is closely associated with the college. He was born in Kragero, Norway, on January 10, 1864. Although he started his education in his native land, he completed his undergraduate work at Stanford University in 1897. He followed that A.B. with an A.M. in 1899 and then a Ph.D. in 1902 in mathematics from Columbia University. He served as professor of mathematics at LaGrange College in Missouri from 1902-04 and later moved to the Michigan Agricultural College in East Lansing. He joined the Oklahoma A. and M. College staff in 1909. Dr. Gundersen stayed with the institution until he retired in 1937, at which point he held the record for the longest number of years of service to the Oklahoma Agricultural and Mechanical College. He was succeeded by A. H. Diamond as head of the Department of Mathematics. Following retirement, he moved to Saratoga, New York, and lived in the Catskill Mountains. He died at the age of seventy-four in the New York Medical Center on April 11, 1938.[18]

As a respected professor of mathematics, Dr. Gundersen was responsible for teaching courses required of all the students enrolled in the School of Engineering. But "Doc Gundy" was more than mathematics. He also taught astronomy and had his telescope in Old Central, which also housed the offices of the O'Collegian. An O'Collegian editor, Walker Stone, class of 1926, said: "One night, he covered up his telescope, closed his office, and came into my office. Dr. Gundersen, in his fastidious manner, buttoned up his coat, sat down in a straight chair beside me, and said: 'Meester Stone, I cannot understand vy you vaste your time on vords, ven all der poetry is in der starts.'"[19]

Students "enjoyed his inspired teaching of calculus, differential equations, and other adventures into the pure beauty of mathematics . . . and his kindly smile, his nice intolerance of anything less than perfect, of anything not exact."[20] Consequently, it was quite fitting that the Oklahoma State Board of Agriculture renamed the Old Engineering Building in honor of "Doc Gundy" shortly after his death.

Once the Engineering Building was converted to Gundersen Hall, there was confusion over the spelling of his name, and "Gunderson" prevailed for several years. This was not the first time there had been such problems. From 1909-21, the college catalog listed "Gunderson." A plaque, to be made of bronze and of substantial proportions, was designed and was to be affixed to the building, explaining who Professor Gundersen was. Although the blueprint made by college architect Philip Wilbur still exists, for some reason the plaque was neither cast nor installed.

Shortly after assuming the deanship, Dean Holley recognized, as had his predecessors, that the summer was useful not only for serving the needs of pre-service clients but also for meeting special needs of practicing administrators. He brought to a high level of sophistication the old practice of identifying problems, marshalling or attracting resources, and marketing to a specific population. In the 1980s, that approach is called "market segmenting," but in 1953, Dean Holley probably just called it good business. He was cognizant of the fact that school administrators served year-round and would not find a four- or eight-week session attractive, or even possible. But he felt they could arrange to delegate their responsibilities for a single week to attend a workshop offered by the college if the topic were right and the workshop leaders were of stellar quality. He moved to provide a series of five workshops, each with its own focus and with its own external expert in charge.

The first two sessions, led by Simon McNeeley, a school health and physical education specialist with the United States Office of Education, were to deal first with school health programs and then with the administrator's role regarding physical education and athletic programs. J. P. Causey, a principal from Oak Ridge, Louisiana, was scheduled to lead the third workshop, which considered the administrator and instructional programs. Finally, the last two sessions were offered under the direction of Howard Dawson, director of the National Education Association's Department of Rural Services. Ironically, he was based in Washington, D.C. His topics were the development of a comprehensive program for school-community relations. The series proved to be of great interest to practicing administrators. The format was repeated the following summer but limited to Dr. Dawson's dealing with the relationship of public education to local, state, and federal governments.[21]

In earlier years, the director of the summer session had emphasized that the college sported a swimming pool, that the campus was tree-shaded, and that area lakes were available for boating and picnicking. Dean Holley could now forget ways to beat the Oklahoma heat by swim-

1955 REDSKIN

"I just never model unless I can wear my fur!" Although this feline seems to be the center of attention of these students in elementary art, he (or she?) might be surprised at some of the creations he inspired!

ming or escaping to the out-of-doors, for he highlighted the fact that Oklahoma A. and M.'s summer program was offered in air-conditioned comfort made possible through the new Library, the new Classroom Building, and the new Student Union.[22]

While Stillwater students were being cooled by air conditioning, a great social issue was getting hot—racial integration. While desegregation in both the North and South was a violent and nasty event in many places, Oklahoma State University has the right to hold its head high. In the spring of 1949, when education in the state was still legally segregated, Oklahoma Agricultural and Mechanical College had its first brush with integration. Henry W. Floyd and Jane Ellison, both undergraduates from Langston University, the black institution of higher learning in Oklahoma, approached Dean Herbert Patterson to enroll in international relations (political science) and textiles (home economics), respectively. Dr. Patterson accepted the applications and forwarded them to the president's office for action. President Bennett, in turn, referred the matter to the board of regents and asked the attorney general for an opinion.[23] In the final analysis, the attorney general said the applicants should attend Langston because that institution had programs in both political science and home economics.

Although the initial attempt failed, a positive attitude on campus was evident. On February 25, 1949, Lloyd Murphy, editor of the *O'Collegian*, wrote: "I think that most A. and M. students have taken rather a broad-minded outlook on the subject. Of course, there are a few extreme radicals among the students, but the general over-all effect to me has been that Aggie students feel that if the Negro students sincerely want to enroll here, and cannot get the courses they want at Langston, then let them come. Most of the students have been rather disgusted over the disturbance at Oklahoma University the past two years."[24]

Conger shared the views of the *O'Collegian*. "Right-thinking people everywhere would like to see prejudices of all kinds disappear but wholesale condemnation of one section of the country is not the way to do it." He feared that resentment would put blacks at a greater disadvantage than segregation if integration were forced on the country.[25]

In the spring of 1952, the question of integration was brought much closer to the School of Education. In the late 1940s, George Washington McLaurin, a retired professor from Langston University, had applied for admission to the doctoral program in education at the University of Oklahoma. In September 1948, the federal district court ordered that he be admitted. The University of Oklahoma complied with the order but followed a plan devised by the Oklahoma State Regents for Higher Education whereby blacks were "roped off" or "railed off" from their white counterparts. For reasons that were not stated publicly, McLaurin transferred to Stillwater and enrolled in January 1952. This event was not of sufficient magnitude to warrant even a note in the student paper. While McLaurin earned hours in doctoral dissertation, he did not complete his degree.[26]

On May 17, 1954, segregation was abolished nationally by the Supreme Court through the case of *Brown vs. The Topeka Board of Education*. That summer, Stillwater's chapter of Phi Delta Kappa was sponsoring panels to discuss the implications, with the panels having both blacks and whites participate. The panels were fully in favor of integration. If the college were to integrate, the decision was made to do so totally. All facilities—classrooms, dormitories, and cafeterias—were available to blacks from the first. The only restriction was that blacks and whites would not be assigned to the same dormitory room unless they requested it.[27]

Two years later, the summer session was still addressing the question of integration but had also added a focus on the space race which was well underway even though the shock of the Soviet Union's success with *Sputnik* was still some months away. Four special workshops were offered by Dr. Dawson, who was ever ready to leave Washington in order to teach in Stillwater. He conducted one workshop on problems of integration, which was intended for school administrators. For the teachers, a program was developed which focused on science for elementary education. That was fairly easy to organize since that was the year that Oklahoma A. and M. launched its National Science Foundation program during the regular academic year. The offerings that pertained to more routine matters were school district organization, taught by Dr. Dawson, and an educational leadership seminar directed by Russell T. Gregg, professor of education at the University of Wisconsin and past chairman of the National Conference of Professors of Educational Administration.[28] The tradition of timely topics and topnotch leaders was alive and well in Aggieland's School of Education.

While it is known widely that the United States initiated the major drive in science education in the years following the launching of *Sputnik*, what is less well known is that the National Defense Education Act (NDEA) also had provisions which allowed the United States Office of Education to contract with institutions to develop effective programs for preparing educational professionals in counseling and guidance techniques. Many able high school students were capable of performing well in the new science curricula, but they also often had the natural inclination of normal adolescents to shy away from tough courses in the hard sciences and advanced mathematics. Without professionals to counsel the students, would those classes be populated?

Beginning in 1959 and supported by an NDEA grant, Harry K. Brobst, director of the Bureau of Tests and Measurements, was appointed to direct a summer institute, which was to provide public school teachers

Dr. and Mrs. Ware Marsden visit with students concerning their future careers as teachers. Dr. Marsden served the College of Education in various capacities including director of teacher education. In 1957 he became chairman of the campus-wide Council on Teacher Education, thus moving that organization closer to the College of Education. Mrs. Marsden also served on the education faculty.

with theories and techniques of counseling, diagnostic methods, and supervised clinical experiences. Following tried and true practices, he augmented his on-campus staff with other experts brought in from the outside—including Arthur Combs from the University of Florida, Ralph Berdie and Henry Borow from the University of Minnesota, and Amanda Herring from the University of Tulsa. As with the science institutes sponsored by NDEA funds, the counseling and guidance participants received a stipend of $75 per week plus $15 for each dependent. This program continued for several years.[29]

In the summer of 1961, the College of Education expanded its offerings to accommodate the increased emphasis nationally on the "new mathematics." Thirty-five Oklahoma elementary teachers and principals were invited to participate in a two-week seminar which would attempt to get them to teach mathematics as a way of thinking rather than as simply computation. Special attention was given to showing how newly developed mathematics programs—especially the one created by the Yale University School Mathematics Study Group—could be integrated into existing school programs. Ware Marsden and Edward Vodicka, both of the College of Education, coordinated the institute. They were reinforced by Vivian Haynes, an elementary mathematics specialist who worked with the Oklahoma City school system, and Maurice Hartung, a professor of education from the University of Chicago.[30]

During these same years, the Bureau of Tests and Measurements continued to clip along at a healthy rate, but Old Central, the building in which it was housed, was decaying. In the summer of 1957, a 20 by 25 foot section of the auditorium ceiling on the second floor fell, breaking a table and damaging some eighty chairs. Luckily, the room was not used in the summer. It should be said that such ruin was not novel to Old Central. Condemned for class use in 1921 and for all use in 1927, it would again fall to condemnation in the early 1970s.[31] When Old Central was condemned, the bureau moved across campus first to occupy space in Hanner Hall and later to its present site in North Murray Hall where it resides with the Department of Applied Behavioral Studies in Education and the Department of Psychology. Each has academic interests that complement at least a part of the bureau's service functions.

In the summer of 1957, the bureau was called into service by J. N. Baker and King Cacy, the dean and assistant dean of students, respectively. They operated a series of two-day educational counseling clinics to help high school graduates formulate their educational plans. The bureau administered, scored, and interpreted tests measuring college ability, aptitudes, reading level, language usage, and mathematics skills. Dr. Brobst provided group interpretation of results but could not avoid individual counseling when it came to possible majors, vocations, and appropriate courses. The program was so successful that it was made mandatory two years later.[32]

While the Bureau of Tests and Measurements was concerned that college students be properly counseled and placed in academic work, there were those who were convinced that students would do better in college if they were properly stimulated while in their early years of formal schooling. One such person was Edmon Low, who was brought to Stillwater in 1940 by Henry Bennett to serve as the college librarian. Mr. Low had an abiding philosophy that librarians should be trained for the public schools so that they would cooperate with the teachers and pupils in enriching classroom activities through library materials. He worked with Ruth Hammond, who held the rank of assistant professor of library science, and was able to begin a rudimentary library education program.

In 1957, the year before Ms. Hammond retired, Mr. Low was able to entice Della Farmer Thomas to join the staff, first as assistant professor and later as associate professor of library science. Mrs. Thomas was head of the education area of the library and was responsible for the day-to-day operations of the library education program, even though Mr. Low was designated as head in addition to his other duties.

Initially, library education courses were offered on an occasional

Providing books, records, filmstrips, and other audio-visual materials, the Curriculum Materials Laboratory is a Mecca for educators. Under the watchful eye of longtime mascot, "The Cat in the Hat," the facility enabled a fledgling library education program to blossom.

basis. Gradually demand increased to the point where a battery of courses—including orientation, reading guidance for young people, book selection, and cataloging—was available each year. In developing the program, Mrs. Thomas worked closely with faculty and administrators in the College of Education, especially Ware Marsden. She was very proud of a course on the use of school libraries for teachers, developed through conferences with the education department. Quickly, that course mushroomed to as many as five separate sections a term. Increased activity in library education led to a more developed structure. Mr. Low dedicated some space on the Library's fourth floor for a Curriculum Materials Laboratory. Still later, additional success dictated a relocation of the laboratory on the fifth floor, which Mrs. Thomas described as a "huge, nearly deserted corner." The laboratory was off to a good start in part because a grant proposal written by Mrs. Thomas was funded by the federal government for $8,543 in 1967-68.[33]

In addition to books, the Curriculum Materials Laboratory had filmstrips, records, programmed materials, 8-mm films, and audio-visual materials. Before long, the Curriculum Materials Laboratory was regarded as a Mecca for area educators. Mrs. Thomas said, "Because former students tell others what's available, an increasing number of area educators are discussing our lab and its services."[34] Here again is an example of educators in Stillwater responding to and serving a need, for graduate schools of library science gave little or no attention to the preparation of librarians for public schools.

If area librarians regarded Stillwater and the Curriculum Materials Laboratory as a Mecca, Mrs. Thomas saw it as an oasis in a far larger world. Working through J. C. Fitzgerald and the Division of Continuing Education, she organized a series of summer study tours to Europe and Asia. Each lasted from four to six weeks, focused on four to six countries, carried graduate credit, and was demanding. For example, the 1970 tour visited Spain, Greece, Yugoslavia, Austria, and Scandinavia. Mrs. Thomas developed a fifty-page publication which dealt exhaustively with each nation's place in children's literature. These tours were so successful and so professional that they received coverage in national library science journals. Over the years, other professionals, including Nancy Amis, Anne Hoyt, Elizabeth Max, and Carolyn Bauer, were involved as the program expanded.[35]

Another modification which occurred in the early 1960s concerned student teaching. Typically, that portion of the teacher preparation program came in the senior year. In 1960, the college received a $6,000 grant from the American Association for the Advancement of Science to place juniors in practice teaching situations in order to see if such students would discover areas which needed strengthening. Steps were then taken to correct such weaknesses during the senior year. Twenty-two elementary education majors enrolled in the program. Of the six interviewed upon completion, all stated they had newly-discovered needs, ranging over a surprisingly large number of areas, including mathematics, science, psychology, phonetics, English, music, and art.[36]

Three years later, the student teaching program was again altered. It was decided that the college student missed out on many important steps in classroom organization if he or she joined the classroom halfway through the semester. To remedy this, Paschal Twyman, acting director of student teaching, announced there would be a "September Experience" which would enable the person who would be student teaching later in the fall to observe a practitioner one week before classes began and for the first week of classes to see how the school year started.[37]

Clearly, the School of Education was continuing to evolve in a positive fashion under Dean Holley's leadership. One sign of the respect in which Dr. Holley was held was his appointment by Governor Henry Bellmon to an eight-member special Commission on Education, a commission to which the Governor could make only two appointments. Others on the commission included Oliver Hodge, the state superintendent of education, and E. T. Dunlap, the chancellor of the Oklahoma State Regents for Higher Education. The commission was assigned two purposes by the legislature: to study and make recommendations regarding strengthening and improving technical skills training, and to study and make recommendations on improvements in the curriculum of the public high school. It decided to survey high school dropouts and to study job needs through the decade of the 1980s, as well.[38]

As Dean Holley advanced through his career, his expertise brought some other special appointments. His dedicated service to the profession of education was recognition. In 1963, the U.S. Department of State and the American Association of Colleges for Teacher Education jointly sponsored a project to study and exchange ideas about teacher education in colleges and in elementary and secondary schools in the United Arab Republic, which at that point consisted only of Egypt.[39] Dean Holley was one of seven nationally-known educators invited to participate in the program. After spending a month in the United Arab Republic, he proceeded to travel to both East and West Pakistan (later Pakistan and Bangladesh) to visit a home economics project that was sponsored by Oklahoma State University and the Ford Foundation. He then continued on home via Hong Kong and Honolulu.

Once back in the United States, he attended the sixty-eighth annual meeting of the North Central Association (NCA) in Chicago. This was not unusual as Dr. Holley had served that accrediting organization for thirty-four years. He went, no doubt, expecting routine meetings. He was surprised to learn that the 4,106 institutional members had elected him as an honorary member of the association. This special honor was accorded only two people each year. To complete the surprise, President Willham flew to Chicago for the sole purpose of helping recognize

1955 REDSKIN

By the mid-1950s, the School of Education was making significant improvements in curriculum development and public service projects. Faculty involved in these new courses and programs included (*front row, left to right*) I. T. Smith, M. S. Everett, Virginia Marsden, Harry Brobst, Myrtle Schwarz, and Helmer Sorenson; (*back row, left to right*) Ernest Dewey, W. B. Ramsey, William Hardy, Roy Gladstone, Guy Lackey, Millard Scherich, and E. C. Foster.

and honor the dean. President Willham had good cause to go out of his way to honor Dr. Holley at the NCA convention. A decade earlier, in Willham's early years in the presidency, Oklahoma A. and M. College had its NCA accreditation suspended because of athletic discrepancies. At that time, Dean Holley played a key role in leading the college back to accreditation.[40] This was not Dr. Holley's first national recognition. In 1954, while he was serving as departmental head of business education, the National Association and Councils of Business Colleges of the United States and Canada had elected him as its Man-of-the-Year.

In 1964, Dr. Holley retired from the deanship after having served Oklahoma A. and M. College and Oklahoma State University for nearly a quarter of a century. During his thirteen years as dean of the College of Education, he had fought tirelessly for higher standards and for a more elevated professional status for educators at all levels. Over those years, he had seen enrollments in his college triple, along with increasing faculty positions and financial resoures. Of greater significance to him, he believed the quality of the students had improved and that the relationships between the College of Education and the other collegiate units in the university had been strengthened. Because he considered that the institution was graduating superior teachers, it was thus not surprising that those teachers, in turn, were sending higher quality high school graduates to the university. Even though he left Stillwater with a sense of pride and accomplishment, he did not leave education since he went directly to the national headquarters of the National Council for the Accreditation of Teacher Education (NCATE) in Washington, D.C. As associate director of NCATE, his job was to help set up visitation teams that would make on-site inspections of teacher education programs and to examine the reports they submitted to the organization's headquarters for completeness and relevance. He stayed with NCATE until 1970 and then returned to Stillwater. Dr. Holley died in 1976 following a lengthy illness.[41]

In the final analysis, Dr. Holley was the first dean of education who lived in what might be called a "normal" period. He did not need to fight for a place in the sun. Also, he had not had to contend with the economics of severe depression or the dislocation of war. That is not to say, however, he had "an easy row to hoe," for that was never the case. He had inherited a school on a solid foundation. He moved ahead to build on that foundation in such a way that it would keep pace, not with an old-style land-grant college, but with an emerging comprehensive land-grant university.

Endnotes

1. Oklahoma A. and M. College *Daily O'Collegian*, 15 May 1951, p. 10.

2. *Daily O'Collegian*, 26 July 1955, p. 1.

3. Andrew Holley, "Critical Issues in Education," *Oklahoma A. and M. College Magazine*, vol. 24, no. 2 (October 1952), p. 5.

4. Holley, "Critical Issues in Education," p. 5.

5. *Daily O'Collegian*, 19 December 1935, p. 1.

6. *Daily O'Collegian*, 13 November 1951, p. 3, 8 July 1952, p. 1.

7. *Daily O'Collegian*, 6 January 1943, p. 1; "Faculty News," *Oklahoma A. and M. College Magazine*, vol. 3, no. 1 (October 1931), p. 4.

8. *Daily O'Collegian*, 15 January 1955, p. 1.

9. *Daily O'Collegian*, 13 April 1955, p. 8.

10. Andrew Holley, "Teacher Shortage Looms High on Education Horizon," *Oklahoma A. and M. College Magazine*, vol. 27, no. 6 (February 1956), p. 17.

11. Holley, "Teacher Shortage Looms High on Education Horizon," p. 17.

12. Holley, "Teacher Shortage Looms High on Education Horizon," p. 16.

13. Andrew Holley, "Obtaining and Retaining Competent Teachers," *Oklahoma State University Magazine*, vol. 2, no. 10 (April 1959), pp. 18-19.

14. Author interview with Helmer Sorenson, 25 July 1986, Centennial Histories Oral Interview Collection, Special Collections, Edmon Low Library, Oklahoma State University, Stillwater, Oklahoma. When Sorenson was being interviewed to gather material for this book, he frequently referred to Holley as "J. Andrew." When asked if that was the way he was addressed, he replied, "Well, I do not think many people called him that to his face. He was too dignified; they called him Dean Holley."

15. Sorenson interview.

16. *Daily O'Collegian*, 4 April 1959, pp. 1, 6.

17. Author interview with John Tate, 22 March 1986, Centennial Histories Oral Interview Collection.

18. *Daily O'Collegian*, 13 April 1938, p. 1.

19. Walker Stone, "Memorable Times," *Oklahoma State University Magazine*, vol. 2, no. 4 (October 1958), p. 30.

20. Robert E. Wardsock, "A Small Grey Man," *Oklahoma A. and M. College Magazine*, vol. 9, no. 8 (May 1938), p. 12.

21. *Daily O'Collegian*, 2 June 1953, p. 1, 7 June 1954, p. 3.

22. "The Stairway to Knowledge," *Oklahoma A. and M. College Magazine*, vol. 25, no. 9 (May 1954), p. 11.

23. *Daily O'Collegian*, 23 February 1949, p. 1, 24 February 1949, p. 1.

24. *Daily O'Collegian*, 25 February 1949, p. 1.

25. N. Conger, "The Renegade South," p. 2, N. Conger Collection, Special Collections, Edmon Low Library.

26. Philip Reed Rulon, *Oklahoma State University—Since 1890* (Stillwater: Oklahoma State University Press, 1975), p. 291. Regarding the *Daily O'Collegian's* non-response to McLaurin's admittance, it should be noted that President and Mrs. Henry G. Bennett had been killed in a plane crash only days before the end of 1951. When the spring semester began in 1952, the campus was deep in mourning and preoccupied with funeral plans. Also, because McLaurin was not the first black to gain admittance to Oklahoma A. and M. College, the newspaper may not have seen his enrollment at the college as newsworthy.

27. *Daily O'Collegian*, 13 July 1954, p. 1, 10 June 1955, p. 6.

28. Actually, the first National Science Foundation summer institute offered on the Oklahoma A. and M. campus was under the leadership of James H. Zant, who was professor of mathematics in the School of Arts and Sciences. It was held in 1955. It was also the first NSF institute offered west of the Mississippi. *Daily O'Collegian*, 11 January 1961, p. 3, 24 February 1956, p. 1, 5 June 1956, p. 1.

29. *Daily O'Collegian*, 5 June 1959, p. 6, 6 June 1961, p. 6.

30. *Daily O'Collegian*, 16 June 1961, p. 8.

31. *Daily O'Collegian*, 26 July 1957, p. 1.

32. "Education Counseling Clinic," *Oklahoma State University Magazine*, vol. 1, no. 3 (September 1957), p. 8; Gordon Hart, "Summer Clinics Benefit Freshmen," *Oklahoma State University Magazine*, vol. 3, no. 2 (August 1959), p. 4. The Bureau of Tests and Measurements is currently known as the University Testing and Evaluation Service.

33. Author interview with Della Thomas, 15 June 1989, Stillwater, Oklahoma; Oklahoma City *Daily Oklahoman Orbit*, 23 February 1969, pp. 4-5.

34. *Daily Oklahoman Orbit*, 23 February 1969, p. 5.

35. Please refer to "Children's Literature as a Bookman's Holiday," *Library Scene*, vol. 3, no. 1 (March 1974), pp. 14-18.

36. *Daily O'Collegian*, 7 June 1960, p. 4.

37. *Daily O'Collegian*, 19 December 1963, p. 5.

38. *Daily O'Collegian*, 9 October 1963, p. 1.

39. Lest this be confusing, it should be noted that the United Arab Republic was a short-lived political alliance of Egypt and Syria, lasting from 1958 until 1961, when Syria broke off the association. However, officially Cairo continued to refer to itself as the "United Arab Republic" until 1971 when it became the Arab Republic of Egypt.

40. "Dean Holley Retires: Has New Position," *Oklahoma State Alumnus Magazine*, vol. 5, no. 7 (July 1964), p. 18.

41. *Daily O'Collegian*, 12 June 1964, p. 1; *Stillwater NewsPress*, 5 September 1976, p. 2.

6 Seeking and Achieving Quality

With the arrival of each dean of the School/College of Education at Oklahoma State University, there had been a slow but fairly steady growth in the faculty, although the rate varied depending on events taking place in the state and nation. With the expansion of the faculty, it was possible to expand course offerings and non-instructional services to a broader clientele. Unlike the presidents of the institution, the deans of education, with the exception of Wilson Little, had long tenures. All of these features continued as Helmer E. Sorenson, the sixth dean, succeeded J. Andrew Holley. In addition, the new leader was able to give greater emphasis to something that both Deans Napoleon Conger and Holley reached for but could not grasp firmly—quality.

By the time Dr. Sorenson was installed as dean in 1964, he was no stranger either to the college or to educators in the state. He was the first person to be installed as dean of the College (rather than the School) of Education. Dean Sorenson completed his bachelor's degree at Eau Claire State Teachers College and then proceeded to earn both his Ph.M. and his Ph.D. at the University of Wisconsin-Madison. After serving as a teacher and administrator in Wisconsin and as an assistant professor of education at the University of Northern Iowa, he was ready to relocate. Although he was offered a deanship at an Alabama institution, he declined partly because of the way that state funded education.

In 1949, Professor Sorenson came to Stillwater as an associate professor of education. As natives of Wisconsin, the Sorensons were in for a shock as air conditioning was still not yet widely available on campus.

He was attracted to Oklahoma A. and M. College because the School of Education had a doctoral program in place in his academic field of educational administration, although he was quick to admit that that program had become essentially a stepchild and "had almost gone to pot completely."[1]

Joining a faculty of about thirty people, Dr. Sorenson set out to rebuild the program. For a while he experienced a series of promotions or title changes every other year. The associate professor of 1949 became the professor of education in 1951 only to become professor of education and vice dean of the School of Education in 1953. In 1955, he earned his longest string of titles: professor of education, head of the Department of Educational Administration, and vice dean of the School of Education, which he retained until he became the sixth dean in 1964. He stressed, though, that the addition of "head" to his titles had little meaning, for the school continued to operate largely as a single unit with the dean being the only bona fide administrator. As a professor, he had two activities which he especially enjoyed: working with the doctoral students in educational administration and working with the practitioners in the field. In regard to the latter, he typically teamed up with men such as Gerald Stubbs, Morris Wallace, Richard Jungers, and Kenneth St. Clair as well as advanced graduate students to attack problems faced by school superintendents and school boards throughout Oklahoma.

A year after he assumed the deanship, he developed a position paper about the state of the college as the university was engaged in a search

1966 REDSKIN

Dean of the College of Education from 1964 to 1972, Helmer E. Sorenson increased the professional focus of the college by relocating several ancillary units in other colleges.

to find a successor for President Oliver S. Willham. From that paper, it is possible to identify some of the goals he set. Foremost, he hoped that a rational alignment of departments could be achieved. He noted that the college consisted of a variety of departments, not all of which were usually found in a college of education—educational administration, aviation education, education, library education, philosophy, psychology, industrial arts education, technical education, trade and industrial education, and religion. Meteorology and photography, though, were no longer with the college, so some progress toward a more rational alignment had taken place. Four of the departments, in Dr. Sorenson's judgment, were not centrally tied to the mission of preparing teachers and educational administrators for the public schools—philosophy, psychology, aviation education, and religion.[2]

He also said that "one might assume that all departments made up of faculty who primarily deal with professional aspects of preparation of teachers throughout the University would be departments in the College of Education," but that assumption also was not true. Although there was no elaboration on that point, it silently called for at least the programs in home economics education, agricultural education, and business education to be brought under the aegis of the College of Education. Still, even without those programs, the college had recently experienced a rapid increase in the size of the faculty. From 1917 to 1945, the staff grew by 400 percent, which sounds large but in real numbers was a leap from three to thirteen people. In 1954, the total was thirty-three, and Dean Holley could still operate the school—albeit awkwardly—much like a large department. But in 1964, seventy-eight people were involved, which was a challenge, a blessing, and a bane.[3]

It was a blessing because a larger professional staff automatically added depth, breadth, and richness to the academic programs and to the professional interactions within the college as distinct specializations were championed. It was a challenge because all of higher education, including Oklahoma State University, was experiencing an era of rapid expansion, and there was the stiff competition for employing qualified staff. Unlike more leisurely eras, by the 1960s applicants for faculty positions expected not only adequate salaries but also suitable classrooms, offices, and laboratories plus time and support for research. Throughout his tenure as dean, Dr. Sorenson was constantly plagued by the fact that resources available to him were never adequate to enable him to develop the college to its potential.

It was a bane for two reasons. A faculty of seventy-eight could no longer be treated as a happy family or large department. Yet administratively, the college consisted of only three academic units: the Department of Psychology, the School of Occupational and Adult Education, and the hodgepodge Department of Education which included everything else. It was extremely difficult to manage the last unit, which in no small regard resembled the Holy Roman Empire with each program interest group—such as reading or counseling—being like a principality with the "coordinator" as the prince. Few people aspired to the position of head of that department for obvious reasons. Second, blending natural growth with regular staff turnover plus scarce resources frequently meant that the college was forced by circumstances to forego hiring the tested and seasoned veteran professor in favor of the more affordable but generally less proven person straight out of a graduate program. In spite of trying to use great care in screening applicants, it was inevitable that mistakes were made from time to time. People who at first blush appeared to have substantial potential sometimes failed to blossom.

Clearly, Dean Sorenson wanted to have an orderly college comprised of academic and service units. He also wanted a college that had recognized high quality staff. One academic program which did not neatly fit into education was philosophy. While this program had been associated with the college for decades largely because of the early work in the philosophy of education, the curriculum gradually broadened to include topics that were more appropriate to philosophy per se rather than to a specific professional affiliation. This was the natural consequence of hiring faculty who would be willing to teach the philosophy of education provided they were also able to slip in courses which reflected their own professional specialization in the discipline of philosophy. By the time Dr. Sorenson arrived in Stillwater, philosophy had been informally separated from the more generic education group, as Millard Scherich was designated both as professor of education and as chairman of the Department of Philosophy in 1948. In spite of that action, the autonomy of the new department was probably marginal. The chairperson recommended which courses and sections should be staffed with which faculty, but for all practical purposes all other faculty matters were handled directly by the Office of the Dean, as was generally true of the other academic areas within the college. The school was still small enough for that style to be acceptable.

All agreed, that having philosophy in education was not a practical problem, as personal and professional relationships were always positive. Yet, at the same time, all were equally aware that philosophy was operating in a manner that gave it stronger ties to arts and sciences than to education. By Dean Sorenson's early years in the deanship, negotiations were opened with the dean of arts and sciences. By mutual agreement of the deans and the philosophy faculty, it was decided that philosophy would be relocated administratively in arts and sciences. The transition was made smoothly. Since that time, the Department of Philosophy in the College of Arts and Sciences has regularly offered

1965 REDSKIN

During the deanship of Helmer Sorenson, the education faculty grew from a small cadre of dedicated educators working nearly in a family environment into a far larger group of professionals offering complex curricula. Seated left to right are Tiner Lapsley, Pete Chapman, W. Price Ewens, L. H. Bengston, M. W. Roney, Harry Brobst, Helmer Sorenson, Ralph Brann, Della Thomas, Tom Mayberry, Robert Scofield, Walter Scott, and Kenneth St. Clair

courses in the philosophy of education, thus maintaining a service linkage with its former collegiate home.

Another academic unit which did not clearly "fit" within the school's mission was psychology. Like philosophy, it developed out of an early interest in educational psychology, with that emphasis dominating course offerings and faculty interests until after World War II when men such as Harry Brobst and Roy Gladstone joined the staff.

Psychology was becoming a very popular field of study, not only for people in education but for many students on the Stillwater campus. Such growth eventually required that psychology be treated as something other than a part of undifferentiated education.

In 1956, William J. Griffiths was employed by Dean Holley as professor and head of psychology. The College of Education was able to add to its graduate offerings when Dr. Griffiths announced in 1958 that his department had won approval to engage in work leading to the Ph.D. He was especially pleased with this advance because now graduate students trained at Oklahoma State University would qualify for jobs in the state that had previously been filled by out-of-state Ph.D. degree holders. Not only would the degree program make the faculty more competitive in the quest for grants and fellowships from private and public sources, but also such research would be facilitated because of the increased number of advanced, research-oriented graduate students.[4]

Following Dr. Griffith's resignation in the mid-1960s, Arthur E. Harriman became departmental head. With that appointment, the department began to track on a somewhat different line. Although Dr. Harriman was interested in administration and teaching, his real passion was for research, which, at that time, was earning a more respected place within the college.

Within a year, Dr. Sorenson worked to have Professor Harriman reassigned to a major role in research. That was accomplished when Marvin Edmison of the Research Foundation matched college salary dollars which established Dr. Harriman as research professor of psychology. With the headship again vacant, a new search resulted in the appointment of William E. Jaynes. Under Dr. Jaynes' leadership, the department expanded into the areas usually associated with a modern department of psychology, such as clinical and experimental. Dean Sorenson relied on Dr. Jaynes as the administrator responsible for departmental affairs.

Eventually, the department boomed and became a resource with which to be reckoned. The college budget was largely enrollment-driven, which meant that student-credit-hours were the "coin of the realm." Psychology, with its very popular and large introductory sections, frequently produced nearly a third of the college's student-credit-hours. This level of success complicated, at least to a degree, Dean Sorenson's dream of making the college a unit having only logically related departments and programs. On the one hand, psychology was a discipline almost always associated administratively with colleges of arts and sciences in American universities, for educational psychology was but one small sub-field. On the other hand, losing the undergraduate student-credit-hours could adversely affect the college's budget while losing the research- and grant-oriented graduate efforts could negatively affect the college's reputation for scholarly work.

As the Department of Psychology grew and diversified, the faculty, nearly all of whom were products of arts and sciences programs, increasingly identified with the College of Arts and Sciences. They began talking among themselves about the perceived advantages of being linked administratively with the college with which they identified "psychologically"—if the use of that term may be allowed. When Dean Sorenson retired, it appeared that the idea of relocation might be laid to rest, for Donald Robinson, the new dean, held degrees in both psychology and education. When James Philips became head of psychology in 1977, conversations were opened among the departmental faculty and the deans of education and arts and sciences. By 1982, it had been agreed that an amiable reorganization would occur with psychology moving administratively to a new home. It speaks well for all involved with the shift that it was executed without negatively effecting the continued operation of any of the units.

Under Deans Holley and Sorenson, steps were underway which led to the School/College of Education's releasing departments not tied closely to its mission. Yet, the other side of the coin, so sharply articulated by Dean Sorenson, was that academic units *having* a strong professional interest in teacher education were still not under the aegis of the college.

The preparation of educators had developed in a pragmatic and uncoordinated fashion during the early decades of Oklahoma A. and M. College. Agriculture, business, home economics, arts and sciences as well as education acted in splendid isolation from the others. Each dean protected his or her education department. Yet, as time passed, teacher educators on-campus and professional accreditation organizations such as the National Council for Accreditation of Teacher Education (NCATE) off-campus were increasingly uncomfortable with that state of disarray. The problem was clear, but the solution had to be forged within the political arena of the day. The other deans were against surrendering their academic units—that is, home economics education, agriculture education, and business education—to the School of Education. Likewise, they did not want to accept any organizational structure which suggested that their faculty reported to the dean of education.

After a great deal of arguing and cajoling, the final compromise was to create a campus-wide Council on Teacher Education that included all faculty involved in the professional preparation of teachers and headed by the director of teacher education. While logically that officer should have been the dean of education, politically that was unacceptable. The assignment fell to Gerald Stubbs, who was an excellent choice. Working out of the president's office, he had served for years as Oklahoma A. and M.'s director of public school services. Even though he then had no official tie to education, he had exceptionally close working relations with the school.

The creation of the council tells a great deal about college politics. In 1950, the council consisted of fifteen faculty appointed by the president to staggered three-year terms. Agriculture, business, and the Oklahoma Institute of Technology (engineering) had one representative each, home economics had two, education had four, and arts and sciences had six. Director Stubbs chaired and reported to the vice president for academic affairs who was also the dean of the Graduate College. Serving as ex officio members were the vice president, the dean of the School of Education, and the director of teacher certification. Not only was Dean Holley not an officer, he was also not a regular voting member. It was several years before he was granted the status of vice chairman and voting member. Still, some progress had been made toward integrating the various teacher education programs at Oklahoma Agricultural and Mechanical College into a coordinated unit, even though that had to be at the supra-college level.

The council had five major responsibilities. It was to evaluate cur-

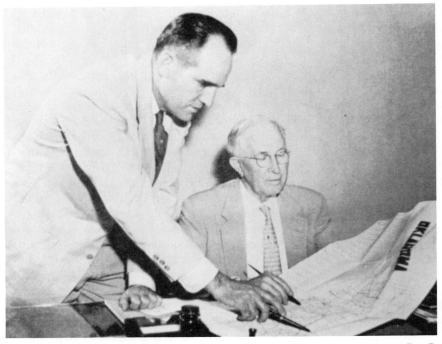

Truly giants in the field of continuing education, J. Conner Fitzgerald (*standing*) and Roy R. Tompkins believed that extension programs should be made available to all people of Oklahoma regardless of their distance from the Stillwater campus.

rent programs and develop new ones as they were needed, to plan for counseling and guidance through official advisors in all teaching fields, to plan for and coordinate accreditation visits by the State Department of Education and NCATE, to establish supervisory committees to monitor each academic program, and to coordinate practice teaching. When Director Stubbs left the post of chairman of the Council on Teacher Education, it was moved slightly closer to education. The new director was Ware Marsden, who held academic rank in the School of Education but reported to the vice president for academic affairs when it came to the work of the council.

While educators on campus were busy trying to develop a more coordinated internal governance structure, most units were simultaneously looking outward to their respective publics. Postwar prosperity had brought another problem with which educators eventually had to deal—the automobile. America's teenagers increasingly had access to wheels, and apparently they were not totally equipped to use them prudently. As early as 1946, Dean Conger—always ready to respond to perceived need—announced that a one-week short course would be offered to introduce teachers to a program in driver's education. This offering was repeated in the summer, offered either for undergraduate or graduate credit, and had the prerequisite of a driver's license and two years of driving experience.[5]

In spite of early efforts to promote safety on the highways and byways, the situation deteriorated and became a national concern, reaching the point where the United States Senate established the Special Committee on Traffic Safety Research and Education with Oklahoma State University's President Willham serving as a member. Both the National Safety Council and the National Association of State Universities and Land-Grant Colleges called for the creation of safety centers. Oklahoma State University responded by transforming the driver's education program into the university-wide Southwest Center for Safety Education and Research—the first in the region. Administratively, the center was placed under J. C. Fitzgerald in the Division of Continuing Education and was designed to deal with safety in general, not just auto safety. Dr. Fitzgerald committed the center to coordinating the efforts of all relevant departments on campus in order to teach safety techniques, to conduct research about safety and disseminate the findings, and to provide public service regarding all aspects of safety. The center worked with schools, with agencies at the city, county, state, and federal levels, and with business and industry.[6]

In spite of the plans to attack safety problems on a broad scale, the genesis for and the focus of the program was always on driver education, because that was the major problem during the late 1960s and early 1970s. Eventually, the center added a driving range, built a driver simulation laboratory, and purchased a dual-control car for on-the-street driving. By the 1980s the program had built such a strong reputation that Stillwater High School contracted to have each of its driver education students provided six hours of driving on the range. The Payne County Misdemeanant Program gave offenders the option of getting counseling and taking a driver improvement course at the center. In addition, the Oklahoma Department of Public Safety would cancel points for people with traffic violations if they took a course at the center.[7] The latter role is one of the few remaining remnants of the driver education program.

The need for expansion was also felt in areas more closely related to traditional educational programs. While the need for teachers expanded, the same can be said of the educational programs. In 1958, a non-credit, ungraded program in remedial reading was established to help students and adults become more efficient and effective readers. This ten-week course, under the direction of Walter Hill, was available for a $5 fee and claimed a participant could improve his or her reading skills by 50 to 250 percent. It was offered through the Division of Con-

In the post World War II years, the School of Education began offering a program in driver's education to teachers. Over the years, increased efforts to promote safety on the highways led to the university's transforming the driver's education program into the university-wide Southwest Center for Safety Education and Research. In addition to having access to a driving range, classes used driving simulators.

tinuing Education in cooperation with the College of Education.[8]

Another new program, and one which would eventually bring national recognition to the College of Education, was in vocational rehabilitation. OSU had been actively involved in vocational rehabilitation for decades in a way that is fondly remembered by thousands of its alumni. In 1933, Ralph Jackson was in an automobile accident which left him both blind and paralyzed. After two years of intensive physical therapy and several operations, he gradually regained his ability to walk, but his sight was gone forever. That he might be gainfully employed, the Oklahoma Service for the Blind taught him to run a shop, and the Oklahoma A. and M. College donated space in the white frame building called the Y-Hut, which was located east of where the Classroom Building now stands. Jackson operated that little cafe for thirty-one years, with the aid of his wife Velma—who was also partially blind as a result of a drug reaction when she was a small child—and his seeing-eye dogs—first Crissy, then Babe, and finally Sunny. In 1969, the Jacksons closed the Y-Hut.[9]

Twenty years before vocational rehabilitation was created as a separate academic program, the School of Education was involved with special efforts to aid the handicapped. For a number of years, the school employed Margaret Hunt, audiometer counselor and lip reading teacher for the Oklahoma City public schools, to offer a lip reading course during the summer. The course was designed to equip hearing teachers to work with pupils who had only partial hearing.[10]

The academic program in vocational rehabilitation was established in 1959 as a two-year master of science degree program emphasizing rehabilitation counseling. It was offered in cooperation with the U.S. Office of Vocational Rehabilitation. The goal of the program was to prepare counselors who could help handicapped persons find the level of personal, vocational, and social adjustment needed for a productive life. Clayton A. Morgan, coordinator of the program, stated that it blended four areas: specialized information regarding rehabilitation, practical application of theory, basic facts and principles, and field training experiences. The last area was the vocational rehabilitation equivalent of student teaching, for the student spent a semester working at the Oklahoma State Tech Rehabilitation Center in Okmulgee and also spent one day a week in Oklahoma City visiting agencies which served the handicapped.[11]

The vocational rehabilitation program at OSU experienced two significant expansions of focus over time. In 1962, the procedures for train-

Although programs and facilities for the physically challenged have especially come to the forefront in the last twenty years at OSU, the campus was home to the Y-Hut, a popular business operated by a blind couple. Proprietors Ralph and Velma Jackson prepared thousands of hamburgers and cups of coffee for Aggies through the years. The hut was located east of where the Classroom Building now stands and was adjacent to the old power plant.

ing vocational rehabilitation counselors were well developed with the counselors and clients operating effectively. But getting a client ready for a productive career and getting the person placed were two separate matters. In that year, Oklahoma State was one of four institutions nationally that was selected to develop a program to enhance the counselor's skills in placement, working with practicing counselors on an in-service basis. The other institutions were New York University, Kent State University, and San Francisco State University. Although the placement training program was integrated with the counselor training program directed by Dr. Morgan, it was administered by Seth W. Henderson.[12]

While Henderson's responsibilities were regional in scope, Dr. Morgan advanced vocational rehabilitation to the national scene. While attending a national conference of vocational rehabilitation professionals, he found they were informally swapping information about what worked and what should be avoided. He volunteered to coordinate the exchange of such materials, and the Vocational Rehabilitation Clearinghouse was born. It was operated on a shoestring by Dr. Morgan, with users providing some voluntary support plus some aid from small federal grants, until he and Harry Brobst wrote a funding proposal in 1971 to the Rehabilitation Service Administration. When the proposal was funded in 1972, Paul Gaines became the first full-time administrator of the clearinghouse. It grew to the point where it operated internationally,

OSU PUBLIC INFORMATION

The coordinator of an academic program to prepare counselors to assist in vocational rehabilitation, Clayton A. Morgan expanded his work to the national level. Through his efforts, the Vocational Rehabilitation Clearinghouse was established at OSU.

responding each year to thousands of requests for hands-on training materials. Beginning around 1980, the clearinghouse assumed the additional responsibility of distributing materials related to special education as well. In 1988, with a staff consisting of a director, one full-time staff member, and seven part-time workers, the clearinghouse has over 10,000 titles of vocational rehabilitation and special education materials available and continues as the only center of its kind in the nation funded by the Rehabilitation Service Administration.[13]

Special education was not addressed solely by the Vocational Rehabilitation Clearinghouse, however, for advocates of care for children with special needs became increasingly active during the 1960s. To respond to this need, Rondal Gamble was added to the college faculty in 1966. By the following year, the Oklahoma State Regents for Higher Education approved a degree program for teachers of exceptional children. Such a program was especially needed because of the social trend which led to the passage of Public Law 94-142. This statute called for keeping handicapped children in the public schools instead of institutionalizing them or segregating them completely in separate classrooms. If they were to be in the common schools, however, there had to be educational professionals to work directly with the children and to provide assistance and counsel to the teachers who had no previous work in special education. Dr. Gamble estimated that at least 10 percent of the school population could be classified as exceptional, with 1 percent considered mentally retarded and the rest either physically handicapped or emotionally disturbed. Initially, Professor Gamble intended to focus on the trainable and the educable mentally handicapped. In the first year of the program, he could already boast of forty majors. He planned to expand into work with the physically and acoustically handicapped.[14]

The late 1960s and early 1970s saw another operation grow within the College of Education that combined the clearinghouse concept of the vocational rehabilitation program with the idea of serving people with deficiencies. For years, the college had a reading center that offered reading improvement courses designed to increase reading speed and comprehension for college students, public school students, and parents of younger children with reading problems. In 1970, the reading center added a resource center and became one of seventy-two such centers across the nation that were to provide information and research findings about reading to teachers in the field. Darrel Ray, director of the reading resource center, stated that the national chain of reading centers had been established by the United States Office of Education and would operate under the leadership of ERIC/CRIER (Educational Resources Information Center/Clearinghouse on Retrieval of Information and Evaluation on Reading), which was the model clearinghouse responsible for organizing and distributing research and related information.

Unlike the reading center, the resource center dealt not with learners but with the professionals who were teaching reading.[15]

In 1959, the College of Education grew as a result of an administrative reorganization. Originally, industrial arts education and engineering workshops had been housed within first the School and later the College of Engineering. For the first half of the twentieth century, all of the engineering students were expected to have work in the shop, with emphasis placed especially on pattern making. As engineering developed as a profession, the shop work was gradually squeezed out of the curriculum. Eventually the remainder of the program—industrial arts education—was reassigned to the College of Education under Dean Holley's leadership. At the time, two of the departments in the School of Industrial Education already existed—industrial arts headed by Cary Hill and trade and industrial arts education, which was to be headed by Joe Reed after Glenn Smith retired. To round out the program, the new area of technical education was added.

It would appear that engineering was unwilling to settle for only an administration change, though, for the academic unit was essentially evicted from its quarters in the Industrial Arts Building and physically relocated in space provided by the State Department of Vocational-Technical Education on Sixth Street. Eventually, the program migrated back to the campus, initially to space in South Gundersen and finally back to its original domicile—the Industrial Arts Building.

When the shift to education was made, the director of the school was Maurice W. Roney, who was also serving as the acting director of the OSU Technical Institute. Offering four-year and graduate programs, technical education prepared individuals to teach in the junior high schools, the senior high schools, or technical schools, and to work with industry.[16] After Professor Roney resigned in 1969, he was succeeded by Lloyd D. Briggs, who had been associated with the school in a variety of ways since 1962. He had joined the faculty as an assistant professor of technical education in 1968.

With more programs and a larger faculty, Dr. Sorenson reopened the call for larger space. In 1959, Dean Holley had greatly improved the college's physical situation by taking over about half of Gundersen Hall. Six years later, with Dr. Sorenson at the helm, it was announced not only that the College of Education would have all of that building but that it was to be renovated—the first major overhaul it had had since being erected in 1910-12. U.S. Senators A. S. "Mike" Monroney and Fred Harris and U.S. Representative Tom Steed stated that the United States Office of Education had awarded $357,885 to Oklahoma State University with $60,000 earmarked for Gundersen. Eugene Swearingen, the vice president for development, believed the total cost for the work on Gundersen would run about $300,000. In 1912, it had cost $100,000 as new construction. To accommodate the remodeling, most of the College of Education faculty were relocated temporarily in the Physical Sciences Building, squeezing into any space available. Richard Jungers recalled that his office away from Gundersen was a long storage closet. With the first floor of Gundersen totally gutted, he said the campus joke was that they were either making an indoor parking garage or a bowling alley out of the building.[17]

Although the building was remodeled, a substantial block of federal monies earmarked for Gundersen was diverted into the College of Business Administration Building, which was being built north of Gundersen on the site of the old Student Services Building. This left Dean Sorenson—always strapped for adequate resources—unable to do all that he had wanted. While those funds were not recaptured, the situation did cause the Oklahoma State Regents for Higher Education to adopt a policy which would prevent a similar diversion in the future.[18]

In spite of the chaos that is always associated with temporary quarters and remodeling, it was still worth it. For the first time since the school was established in 1913, it had a building it could call its own. Once all of the dust settled, the College of Education had a building with new ceilings, floors, partitions, lights, and windows. Display cases had been added for the Art Education Center, the Media Center had been modernized, a Science Education Center had been installed, forty offices and five classrooms were in place, and there was a new heating and cooling system.[19] While the new space did not allow all of the college staff to work under one roof, it did bring most of them together for a few years. Ironically, as the college grew, the trend to consolidate reversed itself and became a move to spread all over the campus. By the 1980s, the college had Gundersen but also used the Industrial Arts Building, the Edmon Low Library, the Classroom Building, North Murray, North Cordell, the Poultry Building, the airport, the USDA Building, and Murray Hall, plus occasional forages into the Public Information Building and the College of Business Administration Building.

Partly because of the interesting special projects that continued to be developed and partly because of the high demand for extension classes in the field, the late 1950s through the 1960s were golden years for the college's extension program. In 1957, Oklahoma A. and M. College was so heavily involved with off-campus programs that President Willham approved the creation of a separate office of extension for education which was officially called Educational Extension and Public School Service. The program was to be directed by Stubbs. This man of many talents gave up his titles of director of public school services and director of teacher certification in favor of professor of education, director of teacher education, and director of Educational Extension and Public School Service. This action was effective on February 1. It was only five

A highly experienced educator, Gerald T. Stubbs served Oklahoma A. and M./Oklahoma State University in many capacities. As the director of the Department of Public School Services, he worked with schools throughout the state to improve their programs and facilities. Although he was not officially a member of the education faculty until later in his career, he served as the first director of the Council on Teacher Education. In 1957, he became the first director of extension in the College of Education.

months later that Oklahoma A. and M. College evolved into the comprehensive, higher education institution, Oklahoma State University.[20]

Professor Stubbs obviously was no newcomer to the world of professional education as he was one of the individuals who "trailed" President Bennett to Stillwater. Dr. Bennett was profoundly a "schoolman" who used his office and his chief lieutenants to serve the schools. Consequently, especially in the area of education, personnel tended to float back and forth between college and school responsibilities without always differentiating between the two. Director Stubbs illustrates that situation well, for even while he was earning a salary out of the president's office, one would have assumed from his titles that he was a member of the School of Education. President Willham's action helped clarify the situation. To be sure, the Office of Educational Extension continued to offer services which were performed in the past such as helping school districts evaluate curricula and facilities and providing in-service for administrators and faculty as the flood of baby boomers swept through the educational system. Yet, the office was also willing to face totally new challenges.

The college was always asked to deliver far more off-campus classes than it was able to staff. Two factors worked together to create a bonanza for extension. First, educational standards throughout the state were increasing, which meant that certified school teachers holding the bachelor's degree were being encouraged to earn their master's. Second, at that time Oklahoma State University and the University of Oklahoma were "the only games in town" when it came to public graduate education. The state was truly the college's campus, and faculty were flown to distant places, using the fleet of university planes that President Henry Bennett had created in Stillwater. In any given semester, faculty from Stillwater could be found from Idabel to Goodwell and from Miami to Altus, and at least one course was offered for the inmates incarcerated in the penitentiary at El Reno. During much of this time, Dr. Jungers served as the director of the College of Education's extension and field services program. Appointed in 1964, Dr. Jungers was the first person on the college's payroll who exclusively handled extension.[21]

Yet, gradually those heady years ended, not because Oklahoma State University's educational extension program was failing to provide high-quality services but because of political considerations. In America, growth is typically regarded as one criterion by which the health and utility of an organization is judged, and education is no exception to that understanding. Junior colleges strive to obtain the upper-division years; institutions with a focused mission try to become comprehensive; baccalaureate colleges lust after a graduate program. It was the last factor that adversely affected the Office of Educational Extension in Still-

In 1964, Richard Jungers became the first person on the College of Education's payroll who handled extension exclusively. To Dr. Jungers, if a project had at least a 51 percent chance of succeeding, it should be attempted. Thus, he often had as many courses for credit in progress as all other campus extension offices combined.

water. The Oklahoma State Regents for Higher Eucation were extremely effective under the leadership of E. T. Dunlap in preventing the spread of doctoral programs beyond Oklahoma State University and the University of Oklahoma. But political pressure was such that they could not refuse to authorize master's programs at the regional colleges, which were then transformed into regional universities.

From an educational point of view, it is difficult to fault the action taken by the state regents. If graduate education were restricted to two institutions in the central part of the state, Oklahoma's great geographical spread would cause a real hardship on those seeking to advance themselves educationally. When a college expands into graduate work, almost without exception the first fields developed are education and business. Typically, there is a ready pool of both students and instructors in those areas—even at the graduate level. In addition, they are relatively inexpensive programs to offer.

Once the regional institutions were authorized to offer graduate programs, they proceeded to "freeze" Oklahoma State University out of much of the extension class market. That was easily accomplished because of the procedures of the state regents. In order to offer a course off-campus, it had to be submitted to the regents for approval at an open meeting. In such meetings, officials from the regional public institutions as well as private schools could and did object, saying such an extension course duplicated what they offered in the geographic region. Virtually without exception, the objection was sustained, and the class would not be offered—at least not by OSU's College of Education. As a consequence, even when the regionals could not teach classes off their campuses, they could keep university courses out of their geographic area. Graduate work at the master's level was quickly regionalized.

If the College of Education were being affected by the pains of significant growth by the mid-1960s, the same can be said for the entire campus. Things were crowded, and facilities were being bombarded by too many people all at once. A partial solution was to change the class schedule so that the academic day would begin at 7:30 A.M. instead of 8:00 A.M. This added two extra hours for classes, thus easing the pressure on classroom space. It also relieved the campus traffic problem since students and faculty would arrive and leave on the half-hour while support staff would travel on the hour. Finally, it was hoped that not everyone would stampede the Student Union Cafeteria at noon. Although this was a simple change, it is a good example of a minor organizational shift which enabled the institution to serve its people more smoothly and to utilize its facilities more effectively without adding to either the plant or staff.[22]

During the early years of Dr. Sorenson's deanship, education both nationally and in Oklahoma was again facing a crisis in the form of an

Occupational and adult education grew out of programs once housed in the School of Industrial Education. It is intended for individuals pursuing careers in vocational education, adult and continuing education, and employee development and training. Longtime trade and industrial professor Clyde B. Knight prepares a videotape for instructional purposes.

acute teacher shortage on all levels, which Professor Marsden characterized as one of society's outstanding problems. The situation in elementary education was especially serious. Nationally, an additional 150,000 teachers would be needed each year between 1964 and 1970, while only 60,000 would be graduated. In secondary education, an additional 90,000 teachers could be placed each year, but only about 60,000 would be available. Clearly, it was a seller's market, but Dr. Marsden said the field was not able to attract people because of the relatively low salaries. Although teacher's salaries had increased considerably faster than those of the average wage earner, the typical elementary and secondary teacher was able to command only an average yearly salary of $4,835 and $5,334 respectively.[23]

The teacher supply situation in Oklahoma in the mid-1960s was perilous. In 1965, almost half of OSU's graduates in education left the state—230 of 506 were placed outside of Oklahoma. Although Oklahoma's practicing teachers ranked highest in the United States in regard to college training, with 99.7 percent holding the bachelor's degree and 37 percent having the master's, their salaries were $1,000 below the national average. The Oklahoma Education Association (OEA) responded to this situation in March of 1965 by sanctioning all of the state's school districts, and the National Education Association (NEA) quickly followed suit. Within four months, the Oklahoma Legislature took steps to correct the situation at least partially by authorizing an average raise of $550. In September, Oklahomans voted, by a 2 to 1 margin, to authorize local districts to raise taxes to support the schools. With that, the OEA and NEA sanctions were lifted.[24]

By 1970, the matter of supply and demand in education had reversed itself significantly, and research showed there was "a great surplus of teachers." Dean Sorenson responded to those data by saying the researchers gave too much attention to quantity and not enough to quality, for there was always a shortage of good teachers.[25]

Teacher supply was not the only problem emerging in the late 1960s and 1970s. These were years when great social issues, including the civil rights movement and the anti-Vietnam War effort, were brewing across the nation. While the situation in Stillwater was very tense several times, the campus bubbled but did not explode. Not all students were involved in social movements, but many were adrift, without clear goals for their academic, vocational, and personal lives. In these years it was the vogue for college students to disdain "The Establishment" and to suspect anyone older than thirty. As a consequence, there was a great need for professional counseling, but the students tended to avoid the regular staff. Charles E. Larsen, director of counseling services, developed a novel program of putting professional counselors in the residence halls and reinforcing them with psychology graduate students who helped with psychological testing and individual counseling. Eight offices were established in the halls. Not only did this make it very easy for a student to get advice and counseling almost on the spur of the moment, but he or she could get such information from a person near his or her own age if that were preferred. The arrangement had the added academic advantage of providing the graduate students direct experience in working with clients.[26]

Another movement growing in the 1960s involved increasing opportunities for women. This had many implications for the college because of its large proportion of women, especially at the undergraduate level. During the early years of Oklahoma A. and M. College, women had been assigned a clear role with early college catalogs usually including a section entitled "Girls, of Interest to." In 1909, the catalog stated that women comprised about one-third of the student body and could take any courses offered by the college. However, it went on to note that "the course in Domestic Science is of the greatest practical value to young women because it is carefully arranged to give science with practice in the best possible proportion and order. This course affords a complete education in hygiene, designing, art work, cutting and fitting, plain and fancy sewing, and includes the subjects needed in a liberal education—English, history, mathematics, physical culture and a number of forms of music.

"In order to meet the demand for a more general course, [the] 'Science and Literature' course has been established. This course will be found to be especially adapted to needs of young women desiring higher education in literature, languages, history . . . , and offering training in music, elocution, and domestic science."[27] By 1913-14, women were encouraged to take note that "a complete 'Teachers' Normal Course' of collegiate grade is offered to those who desire professional training for teaching in high schools and colleges."[28]

As the decades rolled along, the attitude of men toward women did not change a great deal. As late as 1965, a ranking Oklahoma State University administrator stated quite frankly that teacher education curricula were especially attractive to women, particularly the program for preparation of teachers for the elementary grades because it gave a good general education for a prospective housewife and mother. It also provided a kind of insurance policy in the form of preparation for a profession which could be used if the person chose to work. To this administrator, many women enrolled in college with more than one purpose in mind, including finding a suitable life mate. Because Oklahoma State included several colleges in which the enrollment was virtually all male, it was particularly important that a variety of strong programs

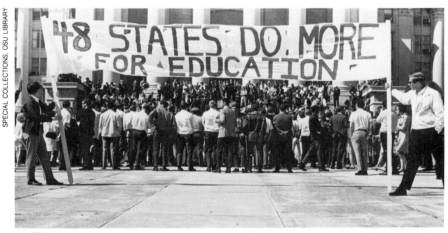

During the 1960s, there were many instances of student protests across the U.S. Although OSU students were sympathetic to many social concerns of the time, for the most part, the campus only rumbled—never erupted. In 1967, OSU students joined others from across the state in a peaceful protest at the state's capitol. The group opposed a multimillion-dollar budget reduction for higher education.

of interest to women be provided. This suggested, of course, that males were of single purpose regarding college attendance and that women's programs were needed for balance.

The situation was starting to change, though, as evidenced through the battle of the Bermuda shorts. Edmond Low, the university librarian, had banned shorts in the library during the 1950s, doing so with the approval of the Library Committee, the deans of men, women, and students, and the president. Mr. Low recognized that "a certain dignity of dress should be observed in the library due to the nature of the place. There was also the practical matter of limiting the scanty attire worn by men and women in the summer, such as wet bathing suits." That was fine until the Reserve Officers Training Corps units on campus issued shorts as a part of the cadets' standard summer uniform. When the library staff did not object to that uniform, men, other than cadets, began to wear Bermudas in the library. When women tried to follow suit, all shorts were again banned. After Roscoe Rouse succeeded Mr. Low, all students were allowed to wear Bermudas in the library.[29]

While many social groups were voicing their concerns about equal opportunity and the threat of sexual or racial discrimination, teachers in Tulsa's classrooms objected to what they perceived to be exploitation by OSU's College of Education. In late 1970, the Tulsa Classroom Teachers Association's (TCTA) negotiating agent took the position that teachers should not cooperate with student teachers without some form of tuition compensation. One suspects that relations between the college and the TCTA were less than warm and open since college officials learned of the situation only by reading the *Tulsa Tribune*. In the spring of 1971, the college offered John Haynes, president of the TCTA, a proposal that would provide cooperating teachers with three hours of tuition. At that time, however, there was significant inflation, and President Richard M. Nixon was about to freeze wages and prices. The fiscal situation was unstable enough so that the college withdrew the offer, saying the program could not be funded that year. Not knowing whether the TCTA would be understanding, thirty-one students scheduled for Tulsa were reassigned so that neither side would lose face.[30] Eventually, the situation was resolved, and cooperating teachers routinely received tuition waivers good for classwork taken at Oklahoma State University.

In 1972, after serving Oklahoma A. and M. College and Oklahoma State University as a faculty member and administrator for twenty-one years, Dr. Sorenson decided to resign. He called for universities generally to take the training of teachers more seriously and for society to value education, rather than simply give it lip service. He especially called on Oklahoma State University to develop a more integrated approach to the way teacher education was administered. At sixty-one years of age, he did not have to retire, but he did so for the good of the program.[31]

Dean Sorenson was schooled in educational administration and believed in administrative order. It was for that reason that he campaigned throughout his career to free the college of non-education programs and to unify all teacher preparation programs under one administrator. True, the university had been able to replace the multi-headed educational hydra with only a two-headed structure, personified in the dean of the College of Education on the one side and the director of teacher education on the other. Dr. Marsden, the director of teacher education was scheduled to retire in June of 1972. Dean Sorenson believed strongly that if one person were both the dean of the College of Education and the director of teacher education the governance system within professional education would be greatly improved. Even if the dual structures could not be collapsed because of political reasons, maybe the environment was such that greater unity could be achieved by placing both organizations under the same individual. But to do that would require that the deanship of education and the directorship of teacher education both fall vacant at the same time. Through his retirement, he forced the university educational community either to articulate cogent reasons for maintaining the awkward existing system or for opting for a better one. If both positions were vacant at the same time, they could be combined.

In a memo to the faculty, Dean Sorenson stated:

"Formal organization becomes much more important as an institution increases in size and complexity. Appropriate organization facilitates communication. Unfortunately appropriate organization does not insure that an agency will be effective, but awkward organization can do much to prevent effective utilization of scarce resources. Change is a constant in our society. Change, therefore, is a constant in our University. A department, a college, or a University Faculty which expects to be relevant can most effectively accomplish the mission dictated by societal changes by appropriate reorganization. Therefore one should not be alarmed that reorganization of a college, or for that matter the entire University, is needed. Reorganization involving professional personnel whose primary assignments are in teacher education at OSU is needed.

"In order to fix responsibility and to secure better utilization of faculty in teacher education, the Director of Teacher Education and the Dean of the College of Education should be one and the same person. However, fixing responsibility for Teacher Education in one individual will not by itself accomplish much. Other reorganization and clarification of the nature and role of the Council on Teacher Education is also needed for the new Director and Dean must also have clear authority if he is to be held responsible. You may know that Dr. Marsden will retire at the end of this academic year. Thus, the natural time to accom-

1970 REDSKIN

The beams quivered. The floors quaked. The turrets cracked— paused—but slowly fell to earth in a cloud of debris. The castle-like Williams Hall which had graced the old quad was razed to make room for the Seretean Center for the Performing Arts.

plish a portion of the needed reorganization is at hand."[32]

In the final analysis, it can be said that Dean Sorenson served his college well. Under his tutelage and following the path begun by Dean Holley, education grew from being a small cadre of dedicated educators working within nearly a family environment into a far larger group of professionals who were responsible for offering broader, more complex curricula.

During his tenure, he was not successful in establishing an administrative reorganization of the Department of Education or in bringing all of education into the college. But he surely had increased the professional focus of the college by helping to relocate several ancillary units in other colleges. He had made greater articulation among educational programs a *fait accompli* through his well-timed retirement.

Like other deans before him, Dr. Sorenson's retirement from Oklahoma State did not mean retreating to the rocking chair and lap robe. Instead, he enthusiastically accepted the offer from the University of Nebraska at Lincoln to supervise its program in higher education. This added still another dimension to his career. Dean Sorenson ably fulfilled that role until 1976, when he and Mrs. Sorenson replaced the harsh northern winters for the more mild clime of Stillwater, where they continue to take a deep interest in the evolution of the college.

In a very real sense, Deans Conger, Holley, and Sorenson form an educational trilogy and jointly were responsible for leading education in Stillwater to new heights. From 1936 until 1972 may be character-ized as the age of schoolmen, for all three were openly and avowedly advocates of service to the schools, especially through high-quality instructional programs and through purposeful extension/advis-ing/counseling. Dr. Conger had the dual advantage of public school ties and strong links to the president's office. Likewise, Dean Holley had a firm network into the schools through state department work. Dr. Sorenson, while lacking Oklahoma public school service, had both credi-bility as a school administrator and an excellent mentor in Dr. Holley. All three capitalized on college/university-wide offices such as the Department of Public School Services, University Extension, and the Placement Bureau to keep in touch with the field. Few of Oklahoma's counties were untouched by the education octopus living in Stillwater.

Yet, the three schoolmen launched their careers when the mission of the school/college was almost totally instruction and extension. As Oklahoma A. and M. College and early Oklahoma State University expanded and consolidated into an organization of statewide influence, the school followed suit. In 1972, the university was operating quite eas-ily on national and international stages, which paved the way for edu-cation to complete its tripod mission by strengthening the leg of research, which had started to grow with the emergence of graduate programs.

Endnotes

1. Author interview with Helmer Sorenson, 25 June 1986, Centennial Histories Oral Interview Collection, Special Collections, Edmon Low Library, Oklahoma State University, Stillwater, Oklahoma.

2. Helmer Sorenson "College of Education," unpublished manuscript, Materials for the Cen-tennial Histories volume on the College of Education, Special Collections, Edmon Low Library.

3. Sorenson, "College of Education."

4. Oklahoma State University Daily O'Collegian, 28 March 1958, p. 8.

5. Daily O'Collegian, 1 January 1947, p. 1.

6. Daily O'Collegian, 4 April 1961, p. 4.

7. Stillwater NewsPress, 11 October 1981, p. 6D.

8. Daily O'Collegian, 1 October 1958, p. 7.

9. "Y-Hut Closes Doors," Oklahoma State Alumnus Magazine, vol. 10, no. 3 (March 1969), p. 28.

10. Daily O'Collegian, 21 June 1938, p. 1.

11. "Restoring our Human Resources," Oklahoma State University Magazine, vol. 3, no. 5 (November 1959), p. 4.

12. *Daily O'Collegian*, 23 October 1962, p. 8.

13. Author interview with Paul Gaines, 4 December 1987, Centennial Histories Oral Interview Collection.

14. *Daily O'Collegian*, 25 February 1967, p. 2.

15. *Daily O'Collegian*, 23 June 1970, p. 5.

16. *Daily O'Collegian*, 15 July 1959, p. 6.

17. *Daily O'Collegian*, 25 June 1965, p. 1, 13 January 1949, p. 8; Author interview with Richard Jungers, 3 July 1986, Centennial Histories Oral Interview Collection.

18. Sorenson interview; Author's personal communication with E. T. Dunlap, 30 May 1986, Stillwater, Oklahoma.

19. *Daily O'Collegian*, 2 February 1967, p. 2.

20. *Daily O'Collegian*, 3 May 1957, p. 1.

21. "Continued Learning, Public Education, In-Service Stressed," *Oklahoma State University Outreach*, vol. 15, no. 4 (April 1974), p. 32.

22. "Campus Briefs," *Oklahoma State Alumnus Magazine*, vol. 6, no. 2 (January 1965), p. 30.

23. *Daily O'Collegian*, 13 March 1964, p. 3.

24. *Daily O'Collegian*, 10 February 1966, p. 8.

25. *Daily O'Collegian*, 20 October 1970, p. 9.

26. *Daily O'Collegian*, 5 December 1967, p. 9.

27. *Annual Catalog, Oklahoma A. and M. College, 1909-1910*, pp. 20-21.

28. *Annual Catalog, Oklahoma A. and M. College, 1913-1914*, p. 25.

29. *Daily O'Collegian*, 12 June 1964, p. 2.

30. *Daily O'Collegian*, 10 March 1971, p. 1.

31. "Campus Compendia—Education Dean Steps Down," *Oklahoma State Alumnus Magazine*, vol. 13, no. 1 (January 1972), p. 12; *Daily O'Collegian*, 21 July 1972, p. 1.

32. Helmer Sorenson to Faculty of College of Education, 23 November 1971, p. 2, Materials for the Centennial Histories volume on the College of Education.

7 Toward the Centennial Year

When Helmer E. Sorenson announced his retirement in 1972, President Robert B. Kamm initiated a national search to locate a new dean. The successful candidate was Donald W. Robinson, a native of Rockford, Illinois. Dr. Robinson earned his B.A. in psychology from Carthage College in 1950 and went on to receive an M.S. in psychology in 1951 and the Ph.D. in educational psychology from Bradley University in Peoria, Illinois. Before joining OSU's College of Education as its seventh dean, he had served as director of guidance, tests, and measurements for the Bradford, Connecticut, public schools and had been a faculty member at Southern Illinois University in Carbondale. He later accepted the responsibilities of dean of students, initially at Carthage College and then at the Indiana Institute of Technology in Fort Wayne. He then left the Great Lakes region, heading east to Washington, D.C., where he served in both the United States Office of Education and the National Institutes of Health in Bethesda, Maryland.[1] His federal service ended when he agreed to serve as the dean of the College of Education at Youngstown State University.

Dr. Robinson's move to Stillwater actually was the result of a fortunate happenstance. By 1972, he had decided he would leave Youngstown State and was seriously considering the presidency of a small, independent college. At the same time, he and George Gries, then dean of Oklahoma State University's College of Arts and Sciences, happened to serve on the same North Central Association review committee. Over dinner, Dean Gries encouraged Dr. Robinson to apply for the position

Donald W. Robinson, dean of the College of Education from 1972-88, reorganized the college in such a way that faculty energy built up under his predecessors could be released and channeled not only into instruction and extension/service but also into research and participation in national circles of scholars.

in Stillwater. A few days later, President Kamm called Dr. Robinson with the same suggestion. After on-campus interviews with faculty and administrators, he was offered the position and accepted.[2] It was the first time since the appointment of Herbert Patterson that an education dean was appointed who did not have prior and sometimes lengthy association with the institution in Stillwater.

Dr. Robinson was installed in office in August of 1972, and, with that event, Dr. Sorenson's last recommendation to the university administration was realized. The new dean of the College of Education was also named as director of teacher education. President Kamm said: "I think Dean Robinson is especially well qualified to provide leadership in teacher education on this campus. He has served as an education dean, has experience as an administrator, has been associated with public schools, served in Washington, is a consultant-examiner for the North Central Association, and knows education both regionally and nationally . . . and he is a person with a strong background in both psychology and education—and this is important, in that our department of psychology is located administratively in the College of Education."[3]

When the new dean arrived in Stillwater, William Jaynes was head of the Department of Psychology, the School of Industrial and Adult Education was without a head, and Price Ewens served as acting head of the Department of Education. It did not take Dean Robinson long to realize what his predecessor had known for years—the Department of Education was unmanageable; nobody wanted the responsibility of being its administrator. In less than six months, Dr. Robinson was able to divide the Department of Education into more rational administrative units. Wisely, he did not suggest that his proposed college organization would be irrevocable. Instead, he informed the faculty that the department would be divided into three units, but on an experimental basis with acting heads. If the system worked, it would be kept; if not, it could be altered and improved. As a result, the Departments of Applied Behavioral Studies in Education (ABSED), Curriculum and Instruction in Education (CIED), and Educational Administration and Higher Education (EAHED) emerged under the leadership of Robert E. Mangum, Idella Lohmann, and James B. Appleberry, respectively. It was not surprising that the new administrative structure was a vast improvement over the former one even though each of the new departments still encompassed more than a single academic focus.

The new regime was put in place in January of 1973. When the next fiscal year began in July, Drs. Mangum and Appleberry were made permanent heads, and Dr. Lohmann—who was not interested in a long-term administrative position—was succeeded by Donald Myers. While no one had wanted to head the Department of Education, thus leaving it quite unstable, "stability" is the word to characterize the new departments. Bill F. Elsom succeeded Dr. Mangum when the latter moved to Mississippi; Douglas B. Aichele succeeded Dr. Myers when the latter accepted the deanship of the College of Education at the University of Nebraska-Omaha; and Thomas A. Karman followed Dr. Appleberry when he left Stillwater to become the assistant to the president of the University of Kansas. Dr. Appleberry, a doctoral graduate in educational administration from OSU, went on to become a university president, first at Pittsburg State University (where Dean John H. Bowers had gone in 1919) and later at Northern Michigan University. In 1987, applied behavioral studies was the first of the three new departments to move to a third head. After Dr. Elsom's sudden death in July 1986, Dale R. Fuqua, an educational psychologist from North Dakota, was appointed as the new head of that department. N. Jo Campbell had served ably as interim head during the 1986-87 academic year.

While the reorganization of the Department of Education was underway, the same was true of the School of Industrial Education. In 1972, each of the departments of the school—technical education under Don Phillips, trade and industrial education under Pete Chapman, industrial arts under Harold Polk, and aviation education under Orrin Tatchio—reported directly to the dean. In early 1973, Lloyd Briggs was named acting director of the now renamed School of Occupational and Adult Education (OAED) and succeeded as director in 1974. Subsequently, the school was reorganized. Because each of the previously existing depart-

OSU PUBLIC INFORMATION

N. Jo Campbell (*seated*), professor of ABSED, has infected generations of students with her love for statistical analysis and research design. Outside of the classroom, she has administered the University Testing and Evaluation Service, assisted Kenneth McKinley in the Office of Research and Projects, and served as interim head of ABSED. Assisting Dr. Campbell is Marilyn Ford.

ments was very small and because of the considerable overlap in curriculum and use of the faculty, departments were eliminated. At the same time, the non-vocational adult education and human resource development emphasis in the department was given higher priority and program emphasis.

If the reformation of the old Department of Education resulted in greater order and stability, the same applied equally to the School of Occupational and Adult Education. That administrative unit remained under the leadership of Dr. Briggs until he was lured away from Stillwater by the offer of a position with the World Bank in Washington, D.C. In 1981, Melvin D. Miller succeeded Dr. Briggs as professor and director of the school.

The restructuring of both teacher education and the College of Education was noted positively not only inside the university but by significant outside agencies as well. In 1981, the National Council for the Accreditation of Teacher Education (NCATE) made its regular periodic visit to Oklahoma State University and granted the maximum seven-year accreditation to all of the academic programs of professional education which had been submitted for review. At the exit interview, Vice President for Academic Affairs and Research J. H. Boggs said it was "the most positive teacher education report received by this institution in the past twenty years." The team noted that significant progress had been made especially over the last five years and drew attention to the "decided improvement in the governance of the teacher education system under the direction of Dean Robinson."[4] The team especially commended the college for its multicultural education program and for revisions in the

By the mid-1970s, the College of Education had emerged with strong, stable administrative units. The old Department of Education gave way to Departments of Applied Behavioral Studies, Curriculum and Instruction, and Educational Administration and Higher Education. Faculty members included (*seated*) Donald Robinson, Donald Phillips, Bill Elsom, Richard Jungers and (*standing*) Frank McFarland, Donald Myers, Robert Mangum, Lloyd Briggs, Lloyd Wiggins, Kenneth McKinley, James Appleberry, Robert Brown, and Ralph Brann.

curriculum to sensitize all teacher education students to the needs of the handicapped.

As a land-grant institution, research has always been a central focus for at least some units at Oklahoma A. and M./Oklahoma State University. Contrary to popular belief, the first building erected on the campus was not Old Central but rather three frame structures associated with the Agricultural Experiment Station, which suggested the priority of research over both administration and instruction. In the School/College of Education, however, research was given de facto low priority for decades. Although some research was done as early as Dr. Patterson's deanship, usually such work was related to practical matters of concern to professional educators. Examples of such research are the school surveys which were conducted so frequently under Deans J. Andrew Holley and Sorenson, although today such work would be regarded as extension.

The research and scholarly work that was done within the school/college was usually "bootlegged" since the Oklahoma A. and M. College lacked a formal mechanism to support and encourage research in education until the late 1940s. At that time, President Bennett asked the board of regents to approve a charter for what was to be called the Research Foundation. He believed such an organization would "recognize and encourage research ability in fields as yet not recognized in this institution [that is, fields other than agriculture and engineering] . . . . It will fill a gap in our present organized research, and in time this will furnish a sound basis for the integration of all of the Institution's research activities."[5] Once established, the Research Foundation was the administrative office charged with helping all of the schools except agriculture and engineering to secure funds for research from public and private sources and with monitoring the expenditure of those resources.

Although faculty in education were regularly involved in research work administered through the foundation, it was not until 1964 that the education college garnered its first major, nationally-funded project. This project, funded for $600,000 through the Federal Manpower Development and Training Act and the Ford Foundation, was designed to discover what learning experiences would make school dropouts more likely to become and remain economically productive and personally satisfied. The directors of the project were J. Paschal Twyman and Victor O. Hornbostel, who were both associate professors of education. Dr. Twyman went on to become president of the University of Tulsa, and Dr. Hornbostel later became the dean of education at that same institution. This study was a cooperative effort of the OSU Research Foundation, the Oklahoma City public schools, the State Board of Vocational Education, and the Oklahoma Employment Security Commission. It involved about 350 Oklahoma City youth between the ages of nineteen and twenty-one who had dropped out of school after the tenth grade, who had been out of school at least two years, and who were either unemployed or underemployed. These subjects were assigned to four groups for a yearlong instructional phase of the program—100 received both vocational and academic instruction; 100 received only vocational training; 50 were given only academic instruction; and 100 received no training at all but served as the control group.

Dropouts were accepted into the project only after they passed an aptitude test and gave good indication that they could succeed in one of the vocational areas. Once admitted, they were involved in intramural athletic events, heard outside speeches, and went on field trips and to cultural events in order to build a cohesive group and spur peer support. Drs. Twyman and Hornbostel were able to utilize an additional incentive for 200 of the participants, for the youth allowance provision of the Federal Manpower Development and Training Act authorized a stipend of $14 a week for those who received either vocational only or vocational plus academic instruction. But the law did not provide similar support for the "academic only" group. The researchers successfully appealed to the Ford Foundation for $185,000 so that they could keep all three sections equal in terms of external motivation.[6]

Frank E. McFarland retired from OSU as professor of applied behavioral studies in education and director of student services for the College of Education. He had previously served as director of student services for the College of Arts and Sciences and as dean of student affairs. In 1968, the OSU Student Government Association created the "Dean Frank McFarland Award" to recognize an outstanding administrator. Also, pictured above are Carolyn Gang, Linda Buffa, Pat Stuever, Jo Ellen Fenimore, Anne Hardy, and James Puckette.

The second phase of the project was a two-year follow-up to determine how successful each group was. In the spring of 1967, it was reported that those dropouts who received vocational training, whether with or without academic instruction, fared best in terms of average weekly wages earned. The "academic and vocational" group earned $66.73 a week, the "vocational only" earned a dollar less, and the "academic only" earned $10 less.[7] While a difference of $10 seems small in absolute terms, it did figure to be nearly 15 percent less.

By the mid-1960s, research was becoming a much more significant undertaking by faculty in the College of Education. In 1965, the Research Foundation, under the direction of Marvin T. Edmison, reported that 166 funded projects were underway in the university. The Bureau of Applied Social Research at Columbia University, basing its conclusions on a national survey of deans and research coordinators, ranked Oklahoma State University eleventh out of 107 doctoral schools of education "for competent and worthwhile research in the area of education." John C. Egermeier, associate professor of education, believed that research was a dynamic feature of the college, at least in part, because faculty were interested in cooperating both with outside agencies, such as the Office of Economic Opportunity, and with other non-education departments, such as family relations and child development, to solve practical problems.[8]

Obviously, research and development had become far more significant priorities in the college than had been the case under earlier deans.
The same, however, may be said of the other colleges which had research
administered through the university's Research Foundation. The upshot
was that this central office was badly overburdened. In 1973, the colleges moved to establish their own research offices. In that year, Kenneth McKinley was brought from Youngstown State University, where
he had worked with Dean Robinson as director of education research
and projects. He was shoehorned into space in the northwest corner of
the first floor of Gundersen, which he shared with Richard Jungers, director of the college's extension office. After several years of a very close
association in both the literal and the figurative sense, the two offices
were assigned separate space. The Office of Education Research and
Projects was relocated on the fourth floor of the Classroom Building.

One of the college's earliest major training projects was triggered by
the Educational Professional Development Act (EPDA), which authorized the Division of Vocational Education in the United States Office
of Education to provide support for the preparation of leaders in the field
of vocational education. Running from 1971 through 1978, Lloyd Wiggins and Lloyd Briggs of the School of Occupational and Adult Education organized a class of ten to twelve fellows each year. The goal was

The School of Occupational and Adult Education led the way for the College of Education in
international projects designed to advance technological development. Lloyd Wiggins (*left photo*)
was a participant in many projects and was responsible for coordinating the Jordan proposal
and the early phases of the project. In the right photo, Donald W. Robinson (*right*) and Lloyd
Briggs (*middle*) director of the School of Occupational and Adult Education, confer with an educator from abroad.

to move each cohort through an interdisciplinary program at the doctoral level. Cooperating with occupational and adult education were the Departments of Agricultural Education, Home Economics Education, and Business Education and Administrative Services. Fellows were recruited from across the nation, coming from collegiate vocational/educational units, from state departments of vocational-technical education, and, in some cases, from public school faculties. In light of the rigorous screening, it was not surprising that graduates moved on to positions of great influence. Most opted for policy-making positions in state departments of vocational-technical education, but one became a director of a school of home economics, and two became directors of state departments of vocational-technical education. The success achieved through this program greatly enhanced the stature of the college's School of Occupational and Adult Education and made it a factor to be reckoned with on the national scene.

Over the years the Office of Education Research and Projects has administered thousands of funded and unfunded scientifically designed research studies and creatively designed applied projects which have been developed and executed by the faculty. These projects have led to an equal number of papers presented and articles published. Clearly, there is inadequate room here to report on each, let alone comment on the designs and findings of such studies. Also, in the world of professional education, it is a fact of life that funding sources are usually far more interested in supporting research and development programs, training projects, and outreach/public service efforts, instead of pure research. Some of these projects are noted below.

Throughout the history of the School/College of Education, many faculty have devoted considerable time to work in countries around the world. In 1965, the Ford Foundation selected the college to administer an $800,000 award to work with the Federal Technical School in Rio de Janeiro, Brazil, to develop a model vocational-technical education center. This project, which was spread over a five-year period, involved planning, renovating, and remodeling existing Brazilian facilities as well as establishing laboratories, purchasing equipment, developing criteria for recruiting and hiring faculty, and evaluating the program. Dr. Briggs, a professor of technical education and later head of the School of Occupational and Adult Education, spent several years in Brazil helping establish the program.

In addition to sending OSU faculty to Brazil, the project also sponsored Brazilian nationals who came to Stillwater. At OSU, they studied in the English Language Institute if their command of English were weak. Then they enrolled in a combination of courses given by the OSU Technical Institute and the College of Engineering, as well as moved through the technical teacher education program offered by the College of Education. Typically, graduates of the program returned to Brazil as directors or departmental heads of the new institutions. In the final analysis, the total cost of the project was about $2 million.

Once in Stillwater, regardless of how diligently the Brazilians studied English, they still had understandable difficulty dealing with the idiomatic use of the language. One day, Jon Bookout, a professor of foreign languages and a staff member with the English Language Institute, was confronted by a delegation of Brazilians who demanded that he explain what "chew" meant. When he responded that people chew food and chew gum, they rose to a person, saying they knew *that* "chew" and wanted to learn the *other* kind of "chew." Baffled, Dr. Bookout asked them to use it in a sentence. After a second, the spokesman said, "What chew doing tonight?"

When the Brazilian project ended, the memory of close cooperation did not vanish. For example, when the Federal University of Rio Grande Do Sul in Porto Alegre, Brazil, was seeking a consultant with expertise in higher education systems, they engaged the services of William B. Adrian. Dr. Adrian, an associate professor of educational administration and higher education, not only knew planning and management techniques but also Portuguese.[9]

The Brazilian project was so successful that the college quickly gained an international reputation, especially for its ability to develop vocational-technical programs through the School of Occupational and Adult Education. Over the years, the college has worked on similar projects in many parts of the globe. In 1968, the college initiated its first major international project, in concert with the royal Thai government, the World Bank, and the United States Agency for International Development (USAID). Spadework was done by Maurice W. Roney, who was on the faculty of the School of Industrial Education and who earlier had been heavily involved in the Ethiopian project. Dr. Kamm lent presidential stature to early negotiations when he paid a visit to Bangkok in 1969.

As the Ethiopian project had focused on agricultural development, the Thai project stressed vocational education and emphasized especially programs offered through trade and industrial education. Headquartered in the Thewes Vocational Teacher Training School located in Bangkok, first Clyde B. Knight and later Richard W. Tinnell served as chief of party and supervised curriculum development, facility planning, workshops for faculty and administrators, and especially the procurement of appropriate equipment. The last responsibility proved to be quite an ordeal because of bushels of international red tape, but it was essential that the right equipment be obtained and placed at the right place if the curricular and planning efforts were to bear fruit. The project interestingly was called "LIVE" for "Loans for the Improvement of Vocational Education" and referred to the World Bank loans supporting the effort.

Oklahoma State University personnel such as Cecil W. Dugger, Jimmy V. Wilson, Neal I. Vest, John R. Bayless, Richard L. Castellucix, and Jimmy R. Sloan developed model programs not only for the headquarters school but for fourteen vocational schools scattered throughout the kingdom.

In no small way, the project was a showpiece. It attracted the personal interests of the royal Thai family and was a magnet attracting many Oklahoma leaders, including President Kamm, Dean Sorenson, James H. Boggs (vice president for academic affairs), William Abbott (director of international programs at Oklahoma State University), and Francis C. Tuttle (director of the Department of Vocational and Technical Education for Oklahoma). Dr. Dugger said: "[The project] was very rewarding for us as advisors, and in my opinion the Thai people were very pleased to have Oklahoma State University there." The Thai continue to refer to the Bangkok (OSU) campus and the Stillwater (OSU) campus."[10] One index of the regard in which Oklahoma State University was held was the fact that Dr. Dugger organized an informal Oklahoma State alumni branch in Bangkok, with President Kamm as the featured speaker at the first meeting in 1969. Those alumni ties have flourished, and Thai students continue to migrate to Stillwater as the place to receive both a solid education and a warm welcome.

By far the largest and most ambitious international project undertaken by the College of Education was in Jordan. Under the leadership of Lloyd Wiggins and later Dr. McKinley, the project was sponsored by the World Bank in excess of $3.6 million. It took about a dozen OSU

Through the Jordan projects, OSU personnel traveled to the Middle East while wave after wave of Jordanian educators arrived in Stillwater for specially designed development programs. Pictured is a group of public school and community college administrators. Thomas Karman and J. Kenneth St. Clair, both faculty members in EAHED, are on the back row.

and non-OSU experts from across the United States to Jordan for periods ranging from a few months to a year. Other education faculty who went to Jordan included Wilbur "Deke" Johnson, William B. Adrian, Clyde B. Knight, and Larry D. Jones. It brought scores of Jordanian trainees to the United States for education not only in Stillwater but in many places throughout the nation. Two especially challenging elements of this project were the development of an applied research and evaluation unit and a computer unit for the ministry of education in Jordan.

In these various international projects, the College of Education worked with an impressive string of organizations. Besides the Ford Foundation and the World Bank, these included the Brazilian Ministry of Education, the United States Agency for International Development, the royal Thai government, and the Asian Development Bank. One index of success was the fact that, in 1981, Dr. Briggs was enticed by the World Bank to leave Oklahoma State University to work for them.

One unique international project of the college was an exchange program with Carabobo University in Valencia, Venezuela, which also involved the University of Kansas. Dean Robinson and Dean Dale Scanell of the University of Kansas led a team which developed a master's degree program to upgrade the faculty of Carabobo University, an institution of 30,000 students. Then the American universities supplied professors who went to Venezuela for a semester or two to teach in the program and otherwise advise the dean of the Institute for Post-graduate Studies and the rector (or president). Traffic flowed both ways with the Venezuelan project, for many faculty and administrators from Carabobo traveled to Stillwater to earn master's and sometime doctoral degrees. Such students were almost always provided with generous support by the government through *Fundacion Gran Mariscal de Ayacucho* (GMA) scholarships.

Without a doubt, the high point of the Venezuelan project was when Oklahoma State University sent its "big guns" to Valencia to work with advanced postgraduate students in a special intensive capstone seminar. This two-week seminar was sponsored by the Venezuelan Ministry of Education and focused on higher education planning and evaluation. The American team was led by President Kamm and Dean Robinson, both of whom brought a certain luster to the sessions because they could operate from the perspective of scholars of academic administration as well as from a base of long years as practicing university administrators. It was around this point in time that Dr. Kamm retired from the OSU presidency. With an undergraduate degree in teacher education and a master's and doctorate in educational psychology and higher education, Dr. Kamm had a special kinship to education. Thus, he decided to return to the classroom in OSU's College of Education where he taught courses in higher education until he "retired" a second time in Decem-

Following his retirement from the university presidency, Robert B. Kamm joined the College of Education as university professor in the higher education program. John Gardiner, Dale Barnett, Dr. Kamm, and Margaret Payne visit following announcement of the first recipients of the Robert B. Kamm Fellowship in Higher Education Administration. Mr. Barnett and Mrs. Payne were the initial winners. Dr. Gardiner coordinated efforts to endow both the fellowship as well as the Kamm Lectureship.

ber 1987. Dr. Kamm was succeeded in the presidency by Lawrence L. Boger, who had served as provost at Michigan State University.

Regrettably, when Venezuelan oil revenues decreased, the program was terminated. To this day some faculty from Carabobo still matriculate for doctoral studies at Oklahoma State University.

Finally, the College of Education also had projects in Indonesia and Jamaica. When Dean Robinson came to Stillwater, he already had strong ties with the American Association of Colleges for Teacher Education (AACTE). That organization was deeply involved with international administrative internship programs that brought scholars from developing countries to the United States. The program was financed by USAID. In 1974, Dr. Robinson traveled to Indonesia to interview prospective interns. The following year, administrators from the Institute for Education and Teacher Training at Padang, Sumatra, arrived in Stillwater for a two and a half month specially tailored internship. This was so successful that it was repeated in 1976, that time with support from the United Nations Educational, Scientific, and Cultural Organization (UNESCO). Unlike most of the other international programs which were oriented toward vocational-technical education, the one in Indonesia featured administation.

The Jamaican project was the result of cooperation among the College of Education, the government of Jamaica, RCA Corp., and USAID.

The initial negotiations involved Dean Robinson, Dr. Dugger, and Archibald Alexander of the State Department of Vocational Education. For the 1984-85 academic year, Dr. Dugger worked with the permanent secretary of the Ministry of Youth and Community Development to develop curriculum, plan facilities, and write specifications for equipment purchases. The stress was on further developing non-formal skills training for the country.

As is obvious from the above, over the past several decades the College of Education has developed an impressive record of international development activities and has achieved a position where interested parties actively seek out the college and ask that it present a proposal in the competition for projects. Today, it is not unusual for other institutions and organizations to withdraw from such competition if they know the college plans to participate, for it is known in the international community that the college will not only propose solid experiences but will also staff the project with senior faculty and staff who frequently go well beyond the letter of the agreement to ensure success. Since virtually the day education was recognized as a separate school, service was an important thrust. The focus on the service area has broadened to the world.[11]

Another major program that is nearly synonymous with Oklahoma State University's College of Education concerns the National Aeronautics and Space Administration (NASA). Although NASA was established in 1957 with the advent of *Sputnik* and the accelerated race into space, as late as 1964 it was reported that a majority of American citizens associated the acronym either with a Caribbean island (Nassau) or with an Egyptian president (Nasser). To correct that deplorable situation, NASA launched not only spacecraft but also a major public relations campaign to bring itself to the attention of the American people by acquainting them with the research findings that were of direct benefit to them.

The relationship between OSU and NASA began in 1968 when OSU was selected to conduct NASA's mobile space-age education demonstration program in eight states on behalf of the NASA Johnson Space Center in Houston, Texas. This task was given to the College of Education. The goal of this $94,500 project was to provide in-service and pre-service assistance to teachers by developing space-related instructional materials and activities and by working with teachers so that they could deal effectively with space education in the classroom. This relationship was strengthened the following year when the College of Education won a $600,000 contract to manage the nationwide Space Science Education Project (SSEP). Under the direction of Kenneth Wiggins, who was then co-director of OSU's Science Teaching Center and associate director of the Research Foundation, this project helped explain to school children, their teachers, and other publics the how's and why's of the

Work and play combine as students in an aviation workshop create and decorate a miniature hot air ballon. "Teachers Have Class" caught on and was the theme for one of the college's honors and awards banquets.

space program. With two doctoral students who had experience working with NASA—Ronald Oines and Robert Helton—Dr. Wiggins developed nine regional space education centers in the United States and employed a staff of twenty-seven, all of whom had backgrounds in science teaching. Although the staff worked all over the nation, each held academic rank in Oklahoma State University's College of Education.[12] Functionally, however, during this first period, the NASA project was administered by the OSU Research Foundation, and it was not until the college established its own research administration unit in 1973 that the project officially became an activity of the College of Education.

Oklahoma State has the privilege of having an astronaut among its alumni. William R. Pogue served as an officer in the Korean conflict and was a part of the USAF Thunderbirds before enrolling in OSU and earning a master's degree in mathematics in 1960. He then served as a mathematics instructor at the Air Force Academy in Colorado Springs and went on to graduate from the Empire Test Pilot's School in Franborough, England. After serving as a test pilot for the British Ministry of Aviation for two years, he became an instructor at the Air Force Aerospace Research Pilot School at Edwards Air Force Base and later joined the Johnson Space Center. He was a member of the support crew for the

Apollo VII, XI, and *XIV* missions and is now retired and living in Oklahoma again.[13]

The NASA project was appropriately subject to periodic competitive bidding, and in 1975 the contract left OSU's College of Education and was assigned to the California State University at Chico. In Stillwater, tongues wagged with rumors of political power plays and Congressional pressure to explain what had happened. But regardless of the reason, the separation was at best brief. With the financial, moral, and personal support of Dean Robinson and countless others, Dr. Wiggins worked tirelessly to regain the contract, and in 1979 it was restored to OSU and has stayed ever since.[14] As long as the college continues to direct the project in the future as masterfully as it has in the past, it would be difficult for any other institution to make a serious bid to take it away.

From centers located throughout the United States, the NASA teams sally forth in specially equipped vans loaded with the paraphernalia needed to put on expert demonstrations in schools at all levels. But the personnel associated with NASA are far more than simply "show and tell," for they develop and test curricular materials which are then shared with teachers in the field. One goal is to ensure that the public in general is kept fully apprised of what the space agency is about, but an equally important goal is to guarantee that today's teachers have the best possible curricular materials to enable them to prepare scientists for the nation in the twenty-first century.

In 1985, when President Ronald Reagan made the decision that the first civilian in space was to be a teacher, NASA asked Oklahoma State University to assume the additional responsibility of supervising and managing the Teacher in Space program. The Council of Chief State School Officers selected ten finalists. For two years the finalists were on leave from their local school districts, being supported by OSU with funds provided by the space agency. They were assigned to the various NASA centers across the country, and OSU personnel were responsible for training them, for developing instructional materials, for designing and manufacturing the experiments that were to be conducted in space, for working with the Public Broadcasting System inasmuch as some lessons were to be broadcast live, and for doing the logistical work associated with public appearances and speaking engagements. Oklahoma State University faculty and staff worked especially closely with the two finalists, Christa McAuliffe and Barbara Morgan, at the Johnson Space Center. Mrs. McAuliffe agreed to be the featured speaker at the College of Education's 1986 Honors and Awards Banquet, which was to be her first major public appearance after her flight.

The *Challenger* was scheduled to be launched from Florida on January 24, 1986. A large contingency from Stillwater, including Dean Robinson and Dr. Wiggins, was on hand for the event, but weather caused

Through the leadership of Kenneth Wiggins, OSU's College of Education has been inseparable from NASA's educational activities. The entire nation was deeply involved emotionally as the Teacher in Space program advanced, and all were shocked when the flight of the *Challenger* ended in disaster and the death of Christa McAuliffe (*right*). In spite of the setback, the program continues with Barbara Morgan (*left*).

delay after delay. Finally, the launch began at 10:38 A.M. on January 28, and, as is well known, it burst into an awful fireball seconds after lift-off, killing all on board. In spite of that disaster, the Teacher in Space project continues, with Barbara Morgan having agreed to take part in the mission. Ms. Morgan was on campus for a series of programs in the spring of 1987.[15]

The growth and success of the NASA program eventually had structural implications for the college with the creation of the Department of Aviation and Space Education in the fall of 1987, although both flight service and aviation education had their origins at Oklahoma A. and M. College before the onset of World War II. To anyone familiar with the history of Oklahoma A. and M. College, it would be a decided understatement to say that Henry Bennett was forward-looking and progressive. After all, he envisioned a huge physical plant that must have appeared to be insanity to others "slogging" through the Depression. But if man's imagination could soar, his body could also fly. Literally, he *believed* in flight. He was responsible for creating the college flight service, adding it to the already existing college motor pool, and gradually building up a fleet of small planes. Russell Babb, who flew for Presidents Bennett, Willham, Kamm, and Boger, said, "Dr. Bennett would not drive fifteen miles if he could fly."[16]

In point of fact, though, President Bennett was flying before the college owned any planes. Initially, Al Guthrie operated a private charter service and employed Mr. Babb, who had learned to fly during World War II. One day, Dr. Bennett asked Mr. Babb why the college did not own its own aircraft. His off-hand reply was that that would have advan-

Henry Bennett's zeal for flying resulted in flight service, flight education, and the Flying Aggies. This organization of flyers regularly flew away with first place trophies in national competitions and was easily recognized nationally among people in aviation. From left to right are Glen Nemecek, coordinator of aviation education; Mary Wallace "Wally" Funk; Paul Burrell, coach of the Flying Aggies; Kenneth Wiggins, head of the Department of Aviation and Space Education; Arlene Walkup, widow of Hoyt Walkup, who originally founded the Flying Aggies; Tiner Lapsey, former sponsor of the Flying Aggies and former coordinator of the aviation department; and Gary Heartsill.

tages given the amount that the president flew. A month later, President Bennett called Babb to tell him that the college had signed a contract with the city to operate the airport and had a fleet of six training aircraft plus two charter planes. That agreement was effective as of September 1, 1947.

Working with Mr. Babb was Hoyt Walkup, who also had been trained to fly during World War II and who came to the college when the airport was taken over. Within a year, Mr. Walkup had established the Flying Aggies, which was an organization of college students who had at least private pilot licenses. The Flying Aggies very rapidly climbed to national prominence by regularly winning competitions sponsored by the National Intercollegiate Flying Association.

In 1951, Dr. Bennett decided to reorganize the airport operations by reassigning Glenn Rucker from airport manager to campus responsibilities and by putting Mr. Babb in charge of flight service and Mr. Walkup in charge of management and flight training. The two men worked well together and would regularly pinch-hit for each other if circumstances demanded. While the flight service still reported to the president through the business office, flight training was placed under the School of Engineering because it was part of an academic program through which students could earn up to twenty-two credit hours of electives. Within a couple of years, though, flight training was shifted to Dean Holley's School of Education because it was clearly an educational program and not aligned with the mission of engineering. Once in education, the flight program was administered as a part of what became the School of Occupational and Adult Education and grew to a full-time staff of nine, augmented by half a dozen qualified students serving as instructors.

By the late 1970s, the city of Stillwater elected a mayor who aggressively challenged the university's off-campus prerogatives, including the ownership of Lake Carl Blackwell, a chief source of water for the city, and the right to operate the airport. Eventually, it was agreed that the airport would revert to the city with Mr. Walkup staying on as manager. That had the effect of separating the facility from the training program. Orrin Tatchio was made head of aviation education. He was later joined by men such as Ricky Gladden, James Vandegrift, and Bruce Hoover.

When Mr. Hoover resigned as head of aviation education, there was agreement at both the university and college levels that the programs related to space education and aviation education should be merged. This was accomplished by appointing Dr. Wiggins as head of the fifth college department and by drawing faculty from occupational and adult education and curriculum and instruction. As a result of this step, it is anticipated that two strong, national programs will only grow stronger.[17]

Another example of research, development, and training projects is the Teacher Corps program which had a life of six years (1975-1981). Funded by the United States Department of Education, it was divided into two phases. The project was initiated cooperatively between the public schools in Sapulpa and the College of Education, with the college's efforts coordinated by Kenneth Wiggins. Throughout the project, some twenty-five college faculty were charged with the responsibility of developing in-service programs that were designed to enhance the teachers' abilities to work successfully and comfortably with minority pupils and/or disadvantaged youth. After operating very successfully at Sapulpa, the college was invited to do a repeat performance in Shawnee, under the direction of Vernon Troxel. While the major goal of the Teacher Corps was directed toward developing teachers, a secondary objective was to stimulate recruitment of minorities, to encourage them to enroll in collegiate teacher education programs, and ultimately to place them as leaders and role models in the public schools.

While the Teacher Corps dealt primarily with public school personnel, the Dean's Grant Project was focused on faculty in higher education. Funded by the U.S. Office of Special Education and spearheaded by Dean Robinson, Professors Darrel Ray, Kay Bull, and Imogene Land, this project was unique inasmuch as it was designed to impact on all faculty involved with teacher education and not simply College of Education faculty. In some respects, the Teacher Corps and the Dean's Grant projects were companion efforts since both included segments pertaining to minorities and multicultural education.

The Dean's Grant program was funded at Oklahoma State University for seven years and was intended to assist college faculty in redesigning classes and in developing skills needed to deal successfully with minorities and the handicapped. Such efforts were necessary because of Public Law 94-142, which mandated that handicapped students be "mainstreamed" to the greatest extent possible. The consequence was that teachers in "regular" classrooms—at all levels of education—would soon be facing students with special needs who had previously been segregated in special education classrooms, if they had been admitted to the public schools at all.

Another minority group served by faculty of the College of Education were the Indians. In 1976, under the leadership of Kenneth McKinley and supported by other university faculty such as Donald Brown of the Department of Sociology, the college undertook a major analysis of the the status of Indian education in Oklahoma, ranging from pre-school through graduate school. It focused especially on three programs: the Johnson-O'Mally Program, which was administered by the Bureau of Indian Affairs and dealt with the public schools; the Title IV programs operated by the Indian Education Office; and the Bureau of Schools Office, which was also administered by the Bureau of Indian Affairs.

More recently, under the leadership of Russell Dobson and Larry Foreman, the college has become involved in a Title IV project entitled "American Indian Education Personnel Development," which was designed to prepare Indians at the graduate level to serve in leadership roles in the public schools in the fields of school administration, curriculum supervision, school guidance and counseling, and clinical psychology. A special feature of this project was the availability of nine fellowships to enable participants to study full-time. The fellowships were funded through the combined efforts of the U.S. Department of Education, the Oklahoma State University Graduate College, and the Colleges of Education and Arts and Sciences.

During the first year of funding, the College of Education was in the company of Harvard, the University of California at Los Angeles, Pennsylvania State University, and the University of Minnesota, all of which had similar programs. But, as with the Dean's Grant, only OSU's exemplary program was approved for further funding after the initial year.

Phil Caskey, Stillwater Middle School teacher (*far left*), demonstrates chemical reactions to sixth grade students. Observing the demonstration are elementary science major Raegan Rethard, secondary science major Diana Emmert, and DIRECT Project staff Suzanne Cowley and Terence Mills.

Another effort directed at the Indian population was originally proposed and directed by Helen Cheek and continued after her untimely death by Douglas Aichele and Darrel Ray of OSU and Carl Downing of Central State University. Funded by the National Science Foundation, the project was designed to increase the participation of Indian students in high school and college mathematics. The project included reducing mathematics anxiety and increasing expectations in mathematics of students, teachers, counselors, and parents through special videotaped programs and conferences. One product of the grant was a supplementary, culturally-based curriculum for grades K-10, as well as curricula for K-3 and 7-8.

Still another project which aimed at improving school science and mathematics programs was "DIRECT"—Development, Implementation, and Research for Educating Competent Teachers. This interdisciplinary effort, involving Terence Mills of curriculum and instruction, James Choike of mathematics, and Dwaine Eubanks of chemistry, was the result of a concern that many teachers in middle schools were trained as either elementary or secondary school teachers but were assigned to science and mathematics classes in the middle schools. Because of this, the OSU professors developed an innovative middle school mathematics and science pre-service teacher education program. This program consisted of specially designed laboratory sections of existing science courses, capstone content and companion teaching methodology courses coupled with appropriately placed field experiences, a mentor system, and informal but structured learning activities incorporating applied mathematics and science concepts from the real world into the middle school curriculum. The National Science Foundation awarded only two grants to large universities under this initiative to design experimental middle school math and science teacher education curricula.

A final example of the college's involvement in program and curriculum development was one proposed by Michael Warner of applied behavioral studies and David Yellin of curriculum and instruction. Funded by the U.S. Department of Education for nearly $100,000, it was entitled "Preparing Teachers to Serve Mildly Handicapped Students in Rural School Districts: A Unified Regular-Special Education Pre-Service Curriculum." This program identified and recruited qualified undergraduate students into a course of study which included work in both elementary and special education, which led to dual certification, and

Graduates of the College of Education are regularly nominated for and selected as Teachers of the Year. Sherleen Sisney became the first graduate of the college to be recognized as National Teacher of the Year. While she was pleased with her award, she was deeply torn because she did not like to be away from her classes in Louisville while she traveled the country speaking on behalf of America's educators. Mrs. Sisney speaks to a CIED class taught by Daniel Selakovich (*right*).

which featured a special seminar focusing on the development of reflective thinking skills of pre-service teachers. In conjunction with the seminar, there was a specially arranged field observation participation experience for all of the students. This unique preparation program was especially timely in light of the need to deliver special education to the state's rural schools and was very much in harmony with Oklahoma State University's land-grant mission.

The aforementioned projects are by no means a complete listing of the research and development activities undertaken by faculty in the College of Education. In fact, the list represents only a tiny fraction of faculty efforts, and many worthwhile projects have been omitted. An index of the spectacular growth in this area may be seen in the fact that in 1975, when the Office of Education Research and Projects was established within the college, its staff consisted only of one director, one professional staff person (reassigned from the OSU Research Foundation when it was dissolved), and one clerical worker. This staff was responsible for grants and contracts totalling about $750,000 per year and involved the submission of a dozen proposals per year and the oversight of six to eight projects. As the college approaches the centennial year, the staff has grown to seven people, the annual total of grants and contracts has increased to $4.5 million, about fifty proposals are processed each year, and anywhere from twenty-five to thirty grants or contracts are underway at any given time. Furthermore, the office has also assumed the responsibility of monitoring the college budget.

During this period of far greater activity involving grants and profits, the college did not neglect its mission of extension, but the traditional program in that area had been badly dented by the regionalization of the state by the State Regents for Higher Education and was subsequently drastically reduced in scope. The state was no longer automatically recognized as the college's campus. Faced with a significant new challenge, the college shifted gears and bounced back with a variety of new thrusts, for the college was always exceptionally adroit at identifying and meeting new needs. For example, the CE/MORE (Continuing Education/Multiple Option Renewal Experience) program was initiated, which took almost all of a master's program to cities where there was adequate demand. This program worked exceptionally well when a district had a group of classroom teachers who wanted to earn a degree in curriculum and instruction. Even though these teacher-students rarely had to travel to Stillwater for classes, they developed considerable camaraderie by moving through the program as a cohort.

Although the college was frozen out of entree to a large part of the state by the regional institutions, no one could refuse to authorize the travel of practicing teachers, administrators, and counselors to Stillwater. Needs, once addressed by extension, were taken up via the weekend

Oklahoma Teacher of the Year Michael Adkins is no Mr. Chips when he combines history with histrionics by dressing in period garb and speaking in period dialect to teach his students about ordinary people of the nineteenth century. Pictured above are Greg Grafman, president of the Education Student Council; Danny Tanner, past president and first recipient of the Education Alumni Association Scholarship; Thu-Hue Tran, Education Queen; Adkins; and Wendy Husby, scholarship chairman.

workshops. Almost immediately the faculty developed a catalog of dozens of tightly focused offerings that met on Friday evenings and Saturdays and met staff development requirements of teachers. Since these programs were highly popular, they served as a vehicle for introducing hundreds of Oklahoma's educators to the College of Education faculty and the Oklahoma State University campus. But this was not the first time that weekends were used for professional development.

In the early 1960s, Della Farmer Thomas, associate professor of library science, organized one-day workshops/conferences for children's literature. While formats varied, they were always built around a luncheon speaker of national stature and usually included a fair where area educators could display projects that resulted from the cooperation of pupils, teachers, and the school library. Earlier, Dean Patterson had "stolen a page" from the teachers' colleges by adding featured speakers to the summer session. In the late 1970s and 1980s, the faculty simply built on the model employed successfully by Mrs. Thomas.

Over the years, the college has been gradually inched away from earth, first with flight training or aviation education and later with the great leap into outer space with NASA. It was only natural that these early ventures would lead to experimentation with and mastery of a dramatic new technology that would expand the sphere of instruction from the campus to the world—telecommunications. Under President Boger, use of telecommunications was designated as a high priority for the university, and by 1984 the college was moving into that new frontier. Even though producing uplink programs (that is, broadcast from Stillwater throughout the world by satellite) is extremely expensive and requires an incredible amount of faculty time, the college has produced on the average of ten such programs each year. During that time the college has served over 27,000 educators in more than 1,350 sites.

In most cases, the OSU-generated program is used as an interactive teleconference, with people in the field being able to communicate directly with participants in Stillwater via telephone hookups. Generally, the broadcast becomes the central feature of a "wrap around" conference at local receiving sites. In such instances, coordinators at receiving sites will develop their own local program (for example, additional speakers, panels, and discussion groups) that usually introduce the OSU segment and then delve into implications or implementation at the end of the transmission.

From a technical point of view, one of the more complicated programs was aired in October 1985. It focused on state-mandated student assessment programs and was to feature Terrell Bell, former U.S. Secre-

OSU PUBLIC INFORMATION

National and international teleconferences demand months of preparation to wed academic content with technological possibilities. In a wonder of split second timing, Terrence Bell was downlinked from Salt Lake City to the studio in Stillwater, and then the conference—coordinated by Katye Perry of ABSED—was uplinked to the world.

tary of Education. When Dr. Bell found he could not travel to Stillwater to join his colleagues for the live broadcast, steps were taken to have him speak from his office in Salt Lake City, but it appeared as though he were physically a part of the Stillwater group. This program, consisting of the one-day national teleconference followed the next day by an on-campus conference to explore issues surrounding competency testing, was coordinated by Katye Perry, David Lane, and N. Jo Campbell, associate professors and professor respectively, in ABSED. On-campus participants included Larry Zenke, superintendent of the Tulsa Schools; Karen Leveridge, president of the Oklahoma Coalition for Public Education; and Nancy O'Donnell, OSU graduate and Oklahoma Teacher of the Year for 1982.

While each program has been a great success in its own right, three particular offerings need to be highlighted. First, the program entitled "Educational Microcomputer Software: Identification, Evaluation and Integration," coordinated by Joyce Friske, associate professor in CIED, and Dr. Aichele, professor and head of CIED, won the Creative Programming Award by the National Continuing Education Association. Second, the Oklahoma State Regents for Higher Education approved the college's request to offer a complete graduate course for credit via the satellite. This was the first time Oklahoma State University offered college credit for participating in teleconferences. This telecourse was delivered in eight segments during the fall of 1988. Entitled "Contemporary Issues in the Profession of Teaching," it was coordinated by David S. Lane, associate professor of ABSED, and Adrienne E. Hyle, assistant professor of EAHED. Third, another first was captured when the Oklahoma State Regents for Higher Education agreed to fund a program called "Classroom Integration of Telecommunications: Focus Bulletin Boards, Electronic Model and Data Bases." This conference was coordinated by Dr. Friske.

The college's active and successful involvement in telecommunications led logically to participation in a far larger and more ambitious effort. When President Ronald Reagan began speaking of his Strategic Defense Initiative (popularly dubbed "Star Wars"), Senator Edward Kennedy of Massachusetts countered that the nation should at least parallel Star Wars with Star Schools. Senator Kennedy shepherded legislation through the Congress. Springing into action, Oklahoma State University's College of Education helped establish the Midlands Consortium Star Schools Project, in cooperation with the Oklahoma State Department of Education, the University of Alabama at Birmingham, the University of Kansas, Kansas State University, the Missouri School Board Association, the Missouri State Department of Education, and the University of Mississippi. Of sixty-eight applications submitted, the Midlands Consortium was one of four funded. Oklahoma State University's

For decades, the College of Education has been applauded for taking the lead in forging inter-departmental and intercollegial partnerships to address compelling problems in education. Jeanne Agnew, professor of mathematics (*left*), Douglas Aichele, professor and head of CIED (*middle*), and John Jobe, professor of mathematics (*right*), settle last minute details before going on the air with a national mathematics education teleconference.

College of Education is the administrative headquarters for this $10 million project, and Kenneth McKinley serves as director of the five-state project. Project funds will support equipping at least 300 schools to participate fully; produce satellite programming through over twenty individual courses ranging from basic English through science, mathematics, and foreign languages; provide technical assistance and staff development to teachers and administrators; help identify and disseminate information relevant to satellite programming; and enable the conducting of research and evaluation activities related to the project. Clearly, while keeping its feet firmly on the ground, the college had already reached for and seized the stars.

During Dr. Robinson's deanship, the college not only moved ahead aggressively with funded projects and new extension opportunities but also seized the leadership in getting statewide policy makers to take the necessary steps to enhance education in Oklahoma. In the late 1970s, State Superintendent of Public Instruction Leslie Fisher created a large committee, which included the deans of education from Oklahoma State University, the University of Oklahoma, Central State University, Southwestern Oklahoma State University, and East Central University, "to look at education." Although Dr. Fisher was interested in very small and quite specific details related to certification, the five deans were successful in getting the committee to change its focus to long-range planning. Eventually, five sub-committees were created, position papers were developed, discussions took place, and revisions were made. After three years of considering, reconsidering, and negotiating, the results were forwarded to the legislature and promulgated in House Bill 1706. This measure, passed in 1980, became both the foundation for making significant advances in Oklahoma and also the model for professional development for the other states in the Union. House Bill 1706 is an excellent example of purposeful and positive collaboration among university administrators, public school leaders, state department personnel, and legislative leaders.

This legislative landmark should be outlined at least briefly because of its significance in the development of professional education in Oklahoma and because of the major role Oklahoma State University's College of Education personnel—especially Drs. Robinson, McKinley, and Kenneth King—played in its creation. In order to attract talented people into the profession, the state mandated that beginning teachers' salaries be increased by $1,000, or by nearly 10 percent. That would have pleased Deans Patterson, Conger, Holley, and Sorenson, all of whom had bewailed the low priority society placed on teacher compensation. Furthermore, there were financial incentives to encourage practicing teachers to earn the master's degree. Standards of admission to and retention in teacher education programs were raised, such as having a grade point average of 2.5 and being in the upper half of one's class. It was no coincidence that the new state-mandated standards were those already in effect in Stillwater.

The bill also called for a more rigorous screening process for students seeking admission to teacher education, and this included not only a battery of tests but also a personal interview. In the interview, it was not unusual for faculty to counsel students to choose other fields if they were not well-suited for education. Next, the law required early school-based practice to ensure that the prospective teacher had a clear and recent concept of what schooling actually entailed. Again, this had already been a feature of Oklahoma State University's program for an extended period of time.

Yet another aspect of the law, which was unique and highly creative, was the role of the Entry Year Assistance Committee (EYAC). With the passage of House Bill 1706, a graduate in education was issued a license to teach but not a certificate. During the entry year, the new teacher would work closely with a master teacher in his or her building and would also be supervised and assisted by a building administrator and by a university faculty member. Throughout the year, the team operated in a formative fashion, helping the beginning teacher strengthen weaknesses through coaching, encouraging, and cheerleading. At the end of the year, the committee moved to summative evaluation by recommending to the state department that the newcomer be certified, be continued in a second year of supervision, or be discontinued. One unique feature was that university faculty were directly involved with the student after he or she left the campus.

Another unique and precedent-setting aspect was that the legislature provided line-item funding to teacher education programs to support faculty participation in EYAC's, and that, in and of itself, was highly significant. So often in the past, the legislature had issued mandates to the profession which increased responsibilities but offered no additional resources. Dean Robinson staunchly maintained, and rightfully so, that faculty were already working under overloads and needed relief if the program were to succeed. To the surprise of some, the legislature agreed and earmarked EYAC dollars to the state regents, who, in turn, saw that the resources were channeled directly to the director of teacher education on each campus for allocation within the teacher education program. This was the first—and so far the only—time the legislature earmarked permanent funding for teacher education. Although several other states have now developed similar entry-year assistance programs for new teachers, no other state has as yet provided special earmarked funding to support college of education participation in this important teacher education improvement initiative.

The law also stipulated that prospective teachers would be required to pass an examination, called a curriculum examination, in each field before they would be certified to teach in that discipline. This step alone would have pleased Dean Holley who, nearly half a century before House Bill 1706 was enacted, said that "the time will come when teachers will be required to be certified on the basis of examinations in their subject field and on general background. Teachers must have a good all-around knowledge of almost everything, if they are to succeed."[18]

Finally, the law not only stipulated that continuing professional development would be required for educators in the public schools but also that teacher educators at the college level would be required to participate in professional activities in those schools. Clearly, House Bill 1706 made major advances in strengthening teacher education and continues to be a model adopted by other states.

Having made great headway in the state, it was not surprising that a few years later Oklahoma State University's College of Education was highly visible nationally as a member of the Holmes Group, a consortium of the top 100 research colleges of education in the nation. While the goals of the group are still evolving, it is reasonably safe to say it will champion an extended program of teacher education, encourage improved quality of the undergraduate experience generally, nurture

Every discipline would like to "hook" children when they are young. OAED combined hands-on learning, team building, creativity, and competition in the Technology Festival. A team of young inventors hopes its creation will beat the competition across the gym floor.

If football teams could compete in bowl games, William Segall, a professor of CIED, believed the same should be true for high school scholars. Beginning in 1985, Dr. Segall organized the Academic Bowl, which five years later was televised over Cox Cable with sponsorship from Texaco. The teams which survived the competition in Stillwater went to the National Academic Championship in New Orleans. Rarely have these teams placed less than third nationally.

Centennial Histories Series

closer relationships between the schools and teacher education groups, and restructure the teaching profession through the introduction of a career ladder. Dean Robinson was elected to the national board of directors of the Holmes Group and represented member colleges in Kansas, New Mexico, Oklahoma, Arkansas, Texas, Louisiana, Mississippi, and Missouri.[19]

Changes were taking places in teacher education on both the state and national levels, and changes were also occurring in the demographics of the state system of higher education. One of the anomalies of Oklahoma higher education was the fact that initially the system had provided for public higher education in neither of the major metropolitan areas—Oklahoma City and Tulsa. The former had Oklahoma City University while the latter had the University of Tulsa and Oral Roberts University, but those were private schools and consequently relatively expensive. By the 1960s, pressure was building to remedy that situation even though the Oklahoma State Regents for Higher Education was hard pressed to find the resources to maintain the existing system adequately let alone fund expansion. Eventually, the demand for public higher education and the reality of scarce resources were reconciled by establishing the first tier of higher education—junior colleges—in both of the cities. The Greater Oklahoma City area was served by two schools—South Oklahoma City Junior College (later renamed Oklahoma City Community College) and Oscar Rose Junior College (later renamed Rose State College). Tulsa was served by Tulsa Junior College, which kept that name and eventually expanded to three campus in Tulsa. These three metropolitan institutions were established in the late 1960s and opened their doors to students in the early 1970s.

The compromise was accepted by constituents in Oklahoma City, for it was not unreasonable to expect upper-division and graduate students to commute the short distance either to the University of Oklahoma in Norman or to Central State University in Edmond. But for Tulsans, the nearest upper-division, state-supported work would be found in either Tahlequah or Stillwater, both of which were at least an hour's drive even after the Cimarron Turnpike was completed. Pressure continued to build, and the Tulsa delegation in the state legislature became more strident as Oklahoma rode the financial crest of the bonanza created by the Organization of Petroleum Exporting Countries' (OPEC) manipulation of the price of crude oil. With the state coffers recording surpluses running into the hundreds of millions of dollars, surely the state could afford to do right for Tulsa by meeting her legitimate need for a free-standing university. Whatever was Tulsa's fate would have serious possible implications for Oklahoma State University and its College of Education.

The battle lines were drawn, with Tulsa's legislative delegation saying "Tulsa State University" and with the powerful Speaker of the House Dan Draper of Stillwater, saying "No." Clearly, it was time for another compromise, and both sides gave. Many possible accommodations were considered, and eventually it was agreed that a university center would be established in Tulsa with instruction at the upper-division and master's level being provided by a consortium of four institutions—Oklahoma State University, the University of Oklahoma, Northeastern Oklahoma State University, and Langston University. This gave Tulsa similar entree to higher education that had been afforded to much smaller communities such as Idabel and Ardmore. Once that was resolved, the only matter remaining was to carve up the academic pie and to assign pieces to the four schools. That was done through the coordinating board, the Oklahoma State Regents for Higher Education.

When the state regents asked the members of the consortium to identify priorities, the university administrators at Oklahoma State placed the M.B.A. program as first, which neatly paralleled the preferences of the business leaders in Tulsa. By the time Dean Robinson was notified, it appeared as though final action had already been taken in areas relevant to the College of Education. Oklahoma State University was assigned the M.B.A. program; Langston University was authorized to offer work in education and business at the undergraduate level; and Northeastern Oklahoma State University was cleared to offer education courses at both the undergraduate and master's levels. It appeared that Oklahoma State University's College of Education might be frozen out of Tulsa. While Dr. Robinson had been willing to agree that education did not have to be the top priority, he was unwilling to accept the status of no priority and immediately joined in a flurry of eleventh-hour negotiations that altered the final decision. Eventually, the College of Education was authorized to offer graduate programs at the University Center.

That decision was of great importance to the college, for a substantial portion of its students was drawn from the Tulsa area, but it was equally important to the university. For education faculty, to drive to the University Center at Tulsa (UCT) to offer classes in the late afternoon or evening differed not at all from what they regularly did in relation to the once healthy and very active program offered through Education Extension. Consequently, from the beginning the college offered a broad array of courses from which students could select. Other units in the university, however, found that Tulsa required them to make difficult adjustments—they were not used to teaching outside of Stillwater; they were fond of teaching Monday-Wednesday-Friday for one hour in the morning and, of course, that was not where or when the UCT students were generally available.

In the early years of UCT, the Oklahoma State University presence

190

While Oklahoma Agricultural and Mechanical College originally had a land-grant mission focused on agricultural and rural life, the emphasis broadened into urban concerns with the technical branches in Oklahoma City and Okmulgee. In the early 1980s, the University Center at Tulsa was opened and became a major vehicle through which the College of Education offered graduate programs in Oklahoma's "second capital." Thomas Smith, director of extension for the College of Education, played a critical role in the development of the UCT.

would have been virtually invisible if it had not been for the College of Education. Even as late as the spring of 1988, when the M.B.A. program was in full operation, education still accounted for 57 percent of the UCT students with business—a distant second—accounting for 31 percent. With these two colleges having 88 percent of the Oklahoma State University enrollment at UCT, it was clear that the other colleges, including the vastly larger College of Arts and Sciences, had not adapted to opportunities in Tulsa.

Because education was such a potent force at UCT, and because the college's program in extension had by that time been greatly curtailed due to the regionalization of the state, it was decided to take full advantage of Director of Extension Thomas Smith's talents by appointing him as OSU's representative to UCT. Dr. Smith, who had served as superintendent of the Oklahoma City public schools, succeeded Richard Jungers as director of education extension in 1979. Because UCT was largely an outreach operation, the two positions fit together well. Dr. Smith played an especially critical role, for UCT burst on the scene late in the summer of 1982, leaving almost no time to plan. Because of that, the major players—the four institutions and the state regents—were engaged in endless negotiations as policies and procedures were developed, as responsibilities and prerogatives were established, and as academic turf was carved out. Dr. Smith was ideally suited for those tasks and served the university and college with great skill until he retired at the end of 1987.

In retrospect, much as Tulsa wanted a school of its own, it was fortunate for all of Oklahoma higher education that such a move was diverted, for no sooner had UCT begun than the state had its fiscal socks knocked off. The heyday of heavy state spending increases collapsed when OPEC no longer was able to control its members and set oil at a high price. Had Oklahoma been supporting an additional university, a difficult situation would probably have been critical when higher education budgets were rolled back.

From time to time throughout the history of the School/College of Education at Oklahoma State University, deans and faculty colleagues had worked to establish a viable student organization, and eventually those efforts took root and flourished. When such students were graduated, they were transported into the ranks of the alumni and became the concern especially of the Alumni Association. But as alumni of the university grew into the thousands and then tens of thousands, it was difficult for the association single-handedly to maintain appropriate liaison with the alumni. The problem of sheer size was addressed through downsizing and decentralizing, with many responsibilities being delegated to college constituency groups. It was concluded that alumni were graduates of both the university and the college, and alumni organizations tied to each could provide complementary services.

In the spring of 1987, Thomas Karman agreed to do the spade work to get a College of Education Alumni Association off the ground. After contacting selected alumni to see if there was interest in the idea, a steering committee was brought together to develop a set of bylaws. The first college association meeting was held in conjunction with graduation in 1987, and the steering committee was duly elected as the association board. Original board members and officers were: Bill D. Hindman, president; Nancy O'Donnell, vice president; Jerrilee Mosier, secretary; Becky Rodgers, treasurer; Russell Conway; Kathy M. Dearinger; William Hodges; Edna Jungers; Mary Meritt; Bernice Shedrick; Thomas J. Smith; Lori A. Downey; Pat Graff; and George A. Rowley.

As Oklahoma State University approached the Centennial year, the Education Alumni Association established itself as a viable organization. Interest in its activities and willingness to invest time, talent, and energy in board service expanded hand in hand. Under the leadership of Sherry Morgan, Jerrilee Mosier, and Becky Rodgers, president, vice president, and secretary of the association, respectively, the board for the Centennial year has achieved representation from a broad cross section of Oklahoma educators and has involved alumni from states in the surrounding region. Board members are Mike Adkins, Mignon Bolay, N. Jo Campbell, Ceila Card, Norma Cole, Russell Conway, Janet Cundiff, Kathy Dearinger, Lori Downey, Pat Graff, Leasa Hansen, Susan Hart, Georgianne Heath, William Hodges, Jim Jones, Edna Jungers, Lynn Kinnamon, Mary Meritt, Nancy O'Donnell, Rebecca Ann Parrack, Karel Payne, Linda Powers, Randall Raburn, George Rowley, Bernice Shedrick, Carol Simmons, Linda Skinner, Thomas J. Smith, Mary Stroemel, Sandina Stallard, Frank Taylor, and Jana Vermilion.

Once the association was underway, Dr. O'Donnell ably assumed the position of executive director of the association. A member of the original board, she had taught in the Perry School System and was selected as the Oklahoma Teacher of the Year for 1982. The Education Alumni Association has developed a healthy head of steam, with alumni visiting campus both at homecoming and graduation. As was hoped at the outset, a productive symbiotic relationship has been fostered with the professionals in the field and the professionals on campus working with each other for the mutual advantage of and advancement of professional education in Oklahoma. Among other goals, the association plans to organize outstanding graduates of the college and encourage talented high school students to pursue a career in education and to support students who demonstrate high scholastic and leadership potential. At the Annual Honors and Awards Banquet, the first Education Alumni Association Scholarship was awarded to Danny R. Tanner, an elementary education student.

The year 1988 proved to be one of significance to OSU and the College of Education. President Boger announced his retirement as university president as of July 1. In the late spring, the board of regents named John R. Campbell, formerly a dean at the University of Illinois, as Oklahoma State University's fifteenth president.

On June 3, Dean Robinson notified the faculty that he had decided to retire, effective August 15, in order to give the college an opportunity for selecting new leadership. He felt the timing was appropriate, since the college was in good shape and operating smoothly. However, retiring from the deanship did not mean he would while away empty hours playing with his pet possoms and listening to his collection of jazz records. Dr. Robinson became dean of the College of Education at the University of Missouri-St. Louis. In order to make sure that the College of Education was in the best possible position to meet a new president, the first major planning retreat for the college in nearly a decade was held at the Marland Mansion in Ponca City in late June.

At that gathering, Dean Robinson made the following remarks in which he expressed his hopes for the future of the College of Education as well as reflected on past accomplishments in the college:

"It is an important time for the OSU College of Education to review where it is now and where it should be heading. The college stands at a crossroads in terms of new leadership, not only at the college level, but at the Oklahoma state education system level. We are privileged to have a new chancellor for the State Regents of Higher Education, a new

Kenneth L. King joined the faculty of the College of Education in 1972. Appointed dean in 1989, Dr. King will lead the college as OSU takes its first steps into the second century.

state superintendent of public instruction, a new secretary of education reporting directly to the governor, and a new president of the Oklahoma State University. The OSU College of Education enjoys a position of acclaimed leadership in the state and region. This is based on your willingness (as faculty) to change as the needs of society and our practitioner/colleagues in the schools change with those needs. The college is currently considered a national leader in the delivery of in-service education through satellite telecommunications, in teacher education reform, and in national and international technical assistance and training work with the National Aeronautics and Space Administation, the World Bank, and the U.S. Department of Education.

"As your outgoing dean, I think it is important for you to be cognizant of several national, regional, and local issues as you, the faculty, examine your stake in the future of the college. At the national level, I would submit to you five evolutionary themes that are currently under discussion with regard to the role of university teacher preparation. It is my advice to you to be aware of the public's resurgence of interest in teaching as a career option; be cognizant of the recommendations of several of the nationally prominent teacher education reform reports (for example, the Holmes Group, the Carnegie Reports, and the National Board for Certification); continue to dialogue with arts and sciences faculty and experts in the disciplines . . . ; to maintain a stakeholder position in defining requirements for teacher education, curriculum, and certification; be aware of the professional teacher organization's continued push for autonomous, professional standard boards and guidelines for entry and exit into the teaching profession; and be not dismayed that colleges of education are not tranquil places currently because of the cacophony of voices from various public and professional groups as to what the role of higher education in the preparation of classroom teachers and in-service professionals should be.

"At the regional level, the Southern Regional Educational Board (SREB) is an influential group which continues to support studied change in education and, along with the Southern Regional Holmes Group Board, will be an important entity with which to maintain contact. A continuation of the coalition building and work through the Oklahoma Association for Colleges of Teacher Education (OACTE) to influence teacher education policy formulation in the legislature is important.

"In the long run there are many directions that a mature college of education may take. In the final analysis, regardless of what route you take, it is imporant, in my perspective, to remain in touch with the profession of education rather than trying to assume or be assimilated by the arts and sciences model.

"Several recent research reports and case studies have documented the demise of colleges of education at major universities in the United States because the faculty did not identify with the profession but did embrace the arts and sciences model. Thus, it is my position that we in colleges of education in the future must take the profession of education, not academia, as our main point of reference. Our commitment must be to the preparation of excellent practitioners. Our scholarship should be directed to the improvement of the schools and learning, and our service should center around the direct improvement of student learning and/or the enhanced performance of practicing education professionals."[20]

On June 16, 1989, the OSU Board of Regents appointed Kenneth L. King as the eighth dean of the College of Education. Although Dr. King was reared in Reydon, Oklahoma, in the Black Kettle National Grassland in far west Roger Mills County, he actually is a native of Texas since his parents preferred the better hospital facilities located in Wheeler, Texas, and slipped into the Texas Panhandle for his birth. In 1964, Dr. King received his bachelor's degree in elementary education from Southwestern State College at Weatherford. He earned his master's in secondary education and his doctorate in higher education curriculum/media from the University of Oklahoma in 1968 and 1969 respectively. After teaching in the Pampa, Texas, public schools and at the University of Oklahoma and Kansas State University, he joined the Oklahoma State University faculty in 1972 as associate professor of curriculum and

The College of Education's administrative team as it enters the second century consists of (*left to right*) Kenneth McKinley, education research and projects; Kenneth Wiggins, aviation and space education; Melvin Miller, OAED; Thomas Karman, EAHED; Dale Fuqua, ABSED; Douglas Aichele, CIED; and Kenneth King, dean.

instruction and has subsequently served as director of educational student services, associate director of teacher education, and associate dean. Since Dean Robinson's retirement, Dr. King served as interim dean. In a memo to faculty, staff, and students, President Campbell stated: "It is my belief that under the direction and guidance of Dr. King, the OSU College of Education will continue to grow and excel. I look forward to working with Dr. King, as well as with you, toward our common goal of moving the level of excellence in education throughout the state upward a few notches."[21]

The history of the School/College of Education in Stillwater paralleled to a great extent the development of Oklahoma A. and M. College/Oklahoma State University itself. Sure, it had small, meager beginnings, starting as a Johnny-Come-Lately, one-man show with John Hugh Bowers. But even in those days, a large proportion of the alumni entered teaching as a career, and many others used teaching as the means of acquiring enough money to resume their own collegiate education. For literally decades, Oklahoma A. and M. College should have looked at its School of Education and preparatory school and said—to quote an ad popular in the late 1980s—''I couldn't have done it without you!''

From the beginning, the story of education has been one of growth and increasing strength. That growth was often painfully slow and was set back several times by factors beyond the school's control, such as wars and depressions. But as early as 1938, when the school and its faculty were still tiny, professors felt confident that it was on its way to being the School of Education in Oklahoma. Nearly thirty years later, Dean Holley could state that academic standards, staff qualifications, and student abilities had definitely increased during his twenty-four years of association with the school.

In all fairness, it can be said that all of the deans before Dr. Sorenson had to nurse and nurture the small but growing institution. Under his direction and with encouragement and support from top administrators, education became a robust adolescent, reached its growth spurt, and developed with great rapidity. During those years of sometimes chaotic advances, Dean Sorenson was chronically plagued with too many students, too few faculty, and too few resources. But he always kept his eye on the goal established earlier by Deans Conger and Holley— quality—and he made progress in spite of continuing problems.

Finally, adolescence passed, and the college blossomed into a mature, modern, and complex structure that for the first time in its history was able to launch a balanced program of not only instruction but also research and service. That, in turn, gave it the ability to be a force to be reckoned with among leadership and decision-making circles in the state and nation. Its leadership role was recognized not only nationally but internationally.

When many people who had served Oklahoma State University for extended periods of time were asked if a dean made a difference, the vast majority replied that they did not think so. Yet, as one looks back over the past decades, it is difficult to accept that judgment. Perhaps, no dean made sudden and dramatic changes in the college, but it is clear that each individual dean's focus had a subtle yet profound influence on the orientation of the organization as a whole. To be sure, every dean with the possible exception of Dr. Bowers was involved to a certain degree with national organizations. The emphasis through Dean Sorenson's tenure was on the preparation of professional educators and on service to the public schools of Oklahoma, with the dean frequently leading his people personally into the field to help conduct school surveys. Because that was a valuable and high-priority activity for the dean, faculty—realizing it consciously or not—generally followed suit by focusing on the instruction, service, and extension roles and not by stressing research.

With the advent of Dean Robinson, the value structure started to shift, not quickly, but pervasively. Dr. Robinson surely did not ignore the significance of the public schools or take them for granted, but it was equally clear that the college's role in offering services to its clientele changed somewhat. As new fiscal and human resources were obtained, it was possible for faculty to find the time and money to become more heavily involved with research, scholarship, and national professional associations, areas which had typically been on the back burner in earlier years. These types of professional activities were of great personal interest to the dean, and gradually the members of the faculty flowed into the wake created by the dean through his own example. Consequently, it can be concluded that, on the eve of the Centennial, the college has a better balance of instruction, research, and extension then it ever had before. It is obvious that OSU's College of Education has seized the leadership role in regard to shaping policy to a great degree within Oklahoma and to an increasing degree nationally. Deans, it would seem, do make a difference.

Thus, near the end of the first century, as the eighth deanship begins, it is an understatement to say that Oklahoma State University can truly be proud of its College of Education. It has succeeded in becoming THE college of education in Oklahoma and one of the most respected colleges of education in the nation.

Endnotes

1. *Stillwater NewsPress*, 25 July 1972, p. 1.

2. Author interview with Donald W. Robinson, 14 January 1988, Centennial Histories Oral Interview Collection, Special Collections, Edmon Low Library, Oklahoma State University, Stillwater, Oklahoma.

3. "New Dean of Education," *Oklahoma State Alumnus Magazine*, vol. 13, no. 8 (November 1972), p. 20.

4. "Education," *Oklahoma State University Outreach*, vol. 53, no. 2 (Winter 1981), p. 10.

5. Minutes, Board of Regents for the Oklahoma Agricultural and Mechanical College, 2 December 1944, p. 18, Special Collections, Edmon Low Library.

6. "What Can be Done About Dropouts," *Oklahoma State Alumnus Magazine*, vol. 5, no. 3 (March 1964), pp. 10-11.

7. Oklahoma State University *Daily O'Collegian*, 20 April 1967, p. 3.

8. *Daily O'Collegian*, 22 July 1966, p. 3.

9. "Brazil Development Project, 1966-1976," Fall 1987, Special Collections, Edmon Low Library; *Daily O'Collegian*, 28 September 1965, p. 1.

10. Author interview with Cecil Dugger, 14 June 1989, Stillwater, Oklahoma.

11. Jerry Leon Gill, *The Great Adventure: Oklahoma State University and International Education* (Stillwater: Oklahoma State University, 1978). Readers should consult this valuable work for a more detailed account of the college's international programs up through the mid-1970s. It is telling that Dr. Gill dedicated a complete chapter to the work of the College of Education.

12. "NASA Space Science Education," *Oklahoma State Alumnus Magazine*, vol. 10, no. 8 (November 1969), p. 7; "Telling 'How's' and 'Why's' of NASA," *Oklahoma State Alumnus Magazine*, vol. 11, no. 1 (January 1970), p. 16.

13. Phyllis Luebke, "Schedule a Skylab Mission," *Oklahoma State University Outreach*, vol. 14, no. 8 (November 1973), pp. 12-13.

14. "Education," p. 10.

15. Author interview with Kenneth Wiggins, 8 December 1987, Centennial Histories Oral Interview Collection.

16. Author interview with Russell Babb, 6 March 1989, Stillwater, Oklahoma.

17. It should be noted that over the years the college had some departments, such as meteorology, religious education, philosophy, and psychology, either die or move to other administrative units. Other departments, usually those that were quite small, such as library science education, industrial arts education, technical education, trade and industrial education, and photography, were reorganized into larger departments.

18. *Daily O'Collegian*, 19 December 1935, p. 1.

19. Robinson interview.

20. Remarks made by Donald W. Robinson at the College of Education retreat in June 1988.

21. John R. Campbell to Faculty, Staff and Students, College of Education, 16 June 1989, Personal files of the Author.

Appendices

Deans of the College of Education

1909-1919	John Hugh Bowers
1919-1936	Herbert Patterson
1936-1948	Napoleon Conger
1948-1951	Wilson R. Little
1951-1964	James Andrew Holley
1964-1972	Helmer Ellsworth Sorenson
1972-1988	Donald Walter Robinson
1989-	Kenneth Lee King

Appendix 2

Faculty of the College of Education*

James Franklin Acord, B.S. (Ball State University), M.S. (Southern Illinois University), Ph.D. (Southern Illinois University); Assistant Professor of Trade and Industrial Education, 1977-78

William B. Adrian Jr., B.S. (Abilene Christian College), M.S. (University of Denver), Ph.D. (University of Denver); Associate Professor of Educational Administration and Higher Education, 1978-83

Douglas B. Aichele, A.B. (University of Missouri), A.M. (University of Missouri), Ed.D. (University of Missouri); Assistant Professor of Education, 1969; Associate Professor of Education, 1972; Professor of Curriculum and Instruction and Director of Student Teaching, 1976; Professor and Head of Curriculum and Instruction, 1979-

Robert Thomas Alciatore, A.B. (Spring Hill College), S.T.L. (St. Louis University), Ph.D. (University of Minnesota); Associate Professor of Education, 1967; Professor of Education, 1971-73

Thomas H. Allen, A.B. (University of Tennessee), M.A. (University of Chicago), Ph.D. (University of Chicago); Associate Professor of Education, 1948-49

Nancy Amis, Instructor of Library Science, 1961; Assistant Professor, 1964; Acting Coordinator and Associate Professor of Library Science, 1968; Associate Professor Emeritus of Curriculum and Instruction, 1972

Carl R. Anderson, B.M.E. (University of Kansas), M.A. (University of Kansas), Ed.D. (Oklahoma State University); Assistant Professor of Education & Assistant to the Graduate Dean, 1970; Associate Professor of Educational Administration and Higher Education, 1975; Associate Professor of Educational Administration and Higher Education and Program Specialist, Education Extension, 1977-82

Craig K. Anderson, B.S.Ed. (Oregon College of Education), M.Ed. (Colorado State University), Ph.D. (Colorado State University); Assistant Professor of Occupational and Adult Education, 1982

Alexis M. Anikeeff, A.B. (University of Michigan), A.M. (University of Michigan), Ph.D. (Purdue University); Associate Professor of Psychology, 1953-56

James Bruce Appleberry, B.S. (Central Missouri State College), M.S. (Central Missouri State College), Ed.S. (Central Missouri State College), Ed.D. (Oklahoma State University); Assistant Professor of Education, 1968; Associate Professor of Education, 1971; Associate Professor & Head of Educational Administration and Higher Education, 1974; Professor & Head of Educational Administration and Higher Education, 1975-75

Lynn K. Arney, B.S. (University of Tulsa), M.Ed. (Northeastern Oklahoma State University), Ed.D. (Oklahoma State University); Assistant Professor of Educational Administration and Higher Education, 1985; Associate Professor of Educational Administration and Higher Education, 1988-

Tom W. Ash, B.S., Instructor in Occupational and Adult Education, 1978-80

Ann Elizabeth Austin, B.A. (Bates College), M.S. (Syracuse University), M.A. (University of Michigan), Ph.D. (University of Michigan); Assistant Professor of Educational Administration and Higher Education, 1984-86

Frederick L. Bagley, Commercial Pilot and Instructor Ratings, Flight Instructor in Aviation Education and Flight Training, 1955-57

John Lawrence Baird, B.S. (Washburn University), M.S. (Kansas State University), Ed.D. (Oklahoma State University); Director of Educational Development and Adjunct Associate Professor of Educational Administration and Higher Education, 1977; Associate Professor of Occupational and Adult Education, 1980-

Harry Leigh Baker, A.B. (Baker University), B.S. (Kansas State University), A.M. (University of Chicago), Ph.D. (Yale University); Associate Professor of Psychology, 1938-39

Isabel K. Baker, B.S. (Northeastern Oklahoma State University), M.S. (Oklahoma State University), Ed.D. (Oklahoma State University); Visiting Assistant Professor of Curriculum and Instruction, 1980-81

William R. Baker, B.S. (University of Oklahoma); Instructor in the Training High School, 1925-28

John C. Barrett, Flight Instructor, Flight Training Department, 1964; Contract Instruction, 1974-83

Gerald Richard Bass, B.S.Ed. (University of North Dakota), M.Ed. (University of North Dakota), Ed.D. (University of North Dakota); Assistant Professor of Educational Administration and Higher Education, 1985; Associate Professor of Educational Administration and Higher Education, 1988-

Carolyn June Bauer, B.S. (Oklahoma State University), M.S. (Oklahoma State University), Ed.D. (Oklahoma State University); Instructor in Library Science, 1966; Assistant Professor of Curriculum and Instruction, 1972; Associate Professor of Curriculum and Instruction, 1977; Professor of Curriculum and Instruction, 1985-

Robert S. Beecroft, B.A. (State University of Iowa), Ph.D. (State University of Iowa); Associate Professor of Psychology, 1964-66

Ronald Stephen Beer, B.S. (Illinois State University), M.A. (Michigan State University), Ph.D. (Kent State University); Professor of Educational Administration and Higher Education and Vice President for Student Services, 1980-

Bernard R. Belden, B.Ed. (State University of New York), M.A. (New York University), Ph.D. (Syracuse University); Associate Professor of Education and Director of Reading Improvement Center, 1959; Professor of Education and Director of Reading Improvement Center, 1964; Professor of Curriculum and Instruction, 1964; Professor Emeritus, Curriculum and Instruction, 1987

Leroy H. Bengston, B.S. (Central State College), M.S. (Oklahoma State University); Associate Professor of Industrial Arts Education, 1953; Associate Professor and Acting Head of Industrial Arts Education, 1963; Associate Professor Emeritus and Acting Head Emeritus of Industrial Arts Education, 1969

Ann Benson, B.S. (Oklahoma State University), M.S. (Oklahoma State University), Ed.D. (Oklahoma State University); Research Associate, 1972; Instructor in Occupational and Adult Education, 1977-79

Jack P. Berry, B.S. (University of Oklahoma), M.S. (Oklahoma State University); Temporary Assistant Professor of Trade & Industrial Education, 1971; Assistant Professor of Trade & Industrial Education, 1974-76

Gary R. Bice, B.S. (Cornell University), M.S. (Cornell University), Ph.D. (Ohio State University); Associate Professor of Occupational and Adult Education, 1985-

Edwin L. Biggerstaff Jr., B.S. (North Texas State University), M.S. (North Texas State University), Ed.D. (North Texas State University); Professor and Head of Education, 1969-72

Jacob Watson Blankenship, B.S. (Southeastern State College), M.Ed. (East Texas State College), Ph.D. (University of Texas); Assistant Professor of Education, 1964; Associate Professor of Education, 1966-70

Donald M. Boehnker, B.S. (University of Cincinnati), M.S. (University of Cincinnati), Ed.D. (Indiana University); Assistant Professor of Curriculum and Instruction, 1976-79

Barbara McGill Bond, B.A. (University of Tulsa), M.A. (University of Tulsa), Ph.D. (University of Chicago); Assistant Professor of Educational Psychology, 1960-64

John Richard Bosworth, B.A. (University of Illinois), M.A. (University of Illinois); Assistant Professor of Philosophy, 1962-84

John Hugh Bowers, A.B. (West Virginia University), L.L.B. (West Virginia University), A.M. (Illinois Wesleyan University), Ph.D. (Illinois Wesleyan University); Professor of Pedagogy and History, 1909; Professor of Pedagogy and Social Science, Dean of Normal Division, and Acting Dean of Domestic Science and Arts Division, 1914-19

Rolland Argene Bowers, A.B. (Kearney State College), M.A. (Colorado State College), Ed.D. (University of Nebraska); Professor of Educational Administration and Higher Education and Associate Dean of the College of Education, 1975-84

Paul V. Braden, B.A. (Michigan State University), M.A. (Michigan State University), Ph.D. (Michigan State University); Associate Professor of Technical Education, 1966; Acting Director, Occupational and Adult Education, 1969-72

Ralph A. Brann, B.S. (Bethel College), M.S. (Oklahoma State University), Ed.D. (Oklahoma State University); Assistant Professor of Education, 1967; Associate Professor of Education and Assistant to the Dean of the College of Education, 1970; Professor of Educational Administration and Higher Education, 1978; Professor Emeritus of Educational Administration and Higher Education, 1979

Lloyd Delano Briggs, B.S. (Oklahoma State University), M.S. (Oklahoma State University), Ed.D. (Oklahoma State University); Assistant Professor of Technical Education, 1968; Associate Professor of Technical Education, 1972; Professor of Technical Education and Head of Occupational and Adult Education, 1973; Professor and Director of Occupational and Adult Education, 1976-81

Charles W. Briles, B.L. (University of North Carolina); Associate Professor of Education and Social Science, 1915; State Director of Vocational Education, 1921

Harry Kern Brobst, A.B. (Brown University), M.A. (University of Pennsylvania), Ph.D. (University of Pennsylvania); Assistant Professor of Psychology, 1946; Assistant Professor of Psychology and Director of the Testing Bureau, 1948; Associate Professor of Psychology and Director of the Bureau of Tests and Measurements, 1951; Professor of Psychology & Director of the Bureau of Tests and Measurements, 1955; Professor Emeritus of Psychology, 1974

Wheeler E. Brock, B.S. (Northeastern State College of Oklahoma), M.S. (Northwestern State College, Louisiana); OSU Pakistan Education Program, Dacca, Pakistan, 1965; Assistant Professor of Trade and Industrial Education, 1969-72

Larry T. Brown, B.A. (University of Kentucky), Ph.D. (Princeton University); Assistant Professor of Psychology, 1961; Associate Professor of Psychology, 1965; Professor of Psychology, 1973-

Robert Storey Brown, B.S. (University of Texas), M.Ed. (University of Texas), Ph.D. (University of Texas); Associate Professor of Education, 1968; Associate Professor of Education and Assistant Director of Teacher Education, 1973-75

Kenneth Alton Browne, A.B. (Hastings College), A.M. (Stanford University), Ph.D. (University of Pennsylvania); Professor of Education, 1965-66

Kay Sather Bull, B.S.B.A. (Roosevelt University), M.B.A. (Roosevelt University), Ph.D. (University of Wisconsin); Visiting Assistant Professor of Applied Behavioral Studies in Education, 1978; Assistant Professor of Applied Behavioral Studies in Education, 1979; Associate Professor of Applied Behavioral Studies in Education, 1983; Professor of Applied Behavioral Studies in Education, 1988-

Gerald Burns, B.A. (University of Northern Colorado), M.A. (University of Northern Colorado), Ed.D. (University of Denver); Visiting Assistant Professor, 1983-

M. Doyle Butler, B.S. (Oklahoma State University), M.S. (Oklahoma State University); Instructor, Building Construction, 1967; Assistant Professor of Trade and Industrial Education, 1968; Thailand Industrial Education Contract, Bangkok, 1970-72

Jack Alvin Byrom, B.S. (Southeastern State College), M.A. (Teachers College, Columbia), Ed.D. (Teachers College, Columbia); Assistant Professor of Education, 1947; Associate Professor of Education, 1949-60

H. Stephen Caldwell, A.B. (Hanover College), M.S. (DePauw University), Ph.D. (Purdue University); Assistant Professor of Psychology, 1971; Associate Professor of Psychology, 1974; Professor of Psychology, 1980-

James Henry Caldwell, Graduate (North Arkansas College); Instructor in Mathematics, Secondary School, 1912; Assistant Professor of Mathematics, Secondary School, 1915; Assistant Professor of History, 1920; Assistant Professor of History and Instructor in Education, 1921

William E. Camp; B.S. (Texas Technical University), M.S. (Texas Technical University), M.B.A. (Virginia Technical University), Ed.D. (Virginia Technical University); Assistant Professor of Educational Administration and Higher Education, 1984-86

James Robert Campbell, B.A. (Antrim College), M.A. (Antrim College), M.A. (University of Oklahoma); Director of Correspondence Study, 1921; Dean of Correspondence Study, 1922; Professor of Education, 1923-30

Noma Jo Campbell, B.S. (Oklahoma State University), M.S. (Kansas State University), Ed.D. (Virginia Polytechnic Institute); Assistant Professor of Applied Behavioral Studies in Education, 1975; Associate Professor of Applied Behavioral Studies in Education, 1977; Professor of Applied Behavioral Studies in Education, 1981-

Olen Kenneth Campbell, A.B. (Southeast State College), M.A. (Teachers College, Columbia University), Diploma, Superintendent of Schools (Teachers College, Columbia University); Assistant Professor of Education and Educational Adviser, Cordell Hall, 1939; Military Leave, 1942; Associate Professor of Education, 1946; Associate Professor of Education and Dean of Students, 1948; Dean of Students, 1949-50

Raymond Guy Campbell, A.B. (University of Nebraska), M.A. (Teachers College, Columbia University); Assistant Professor of Education, 1930

Alfred Carlozzi, B.A. (Iona College), M.A. (Trinity University), Ed.D. (University of Houston); Assistant Professor of Applied Behavioral Studies in Education, 1979; Associate Professor of Applied Behavioral Studies in Education, 1983-

Chester Col Carrothers, A.B. (Upper Iowa University), A.M. (Drake University), Ph.D. (Ohio State University); Assistant Professor of Secondary Education, 1942; On leave with U.S. Government on Wartime Industry, 1944

Owen L. Caskey, B.S. (Texas Technical College), M.Ed. (Texas Technical College), Ed.D. (University of Colorado); Associate Professor of Psychology, 1963-64

Kathryn S. Castle, B.A. (University of Oklahoma), M.A. (Emory University), Ed.D. (University of Virginia); Assistant Professor of Curriculum and Instruction, 1975; Associate Professor of Curriculum and Instruction, 1979; Professor of Curriculum and Instruction, 1985-

Ed Chandler, B.S. (University of Wisconsin), M.S. (Oklahoma A. and M. College); Teacher Trainer, Trade and Industrial Education, 1943-51

Marie D. Chaney, A.B. (Central State College), M.L.S. (George Peabody College); Instructor of Library Science, 1966; Assistant Professor of Library Science, 1970-71

Theodore Pete Chapman, B.S. (Southwestern State College), M.S. (Oklahoma State University); Associate Professor and Head of Trade and Industrial Education, 1959; Professor Emeritus of Trade and Industrial Education, 1978

Marlin Ray Chauncey, A.B. (Kansas State Teachers College), A.M. (Teachers College, Columbia University), Ph.D. (Columbia University); Assistant Professor of Education, 1923; Associate Professor of Education, 1925; Professor of Education, 1937; Head of Secondary Education, 1938; Professor Emeritus of Education, 1957

Helen Neely Cheek, B.A. (Arizona State University), M.A. (Arizona State University), Ph.D. (Arizona State University); Assistant Professor of Curriculum and Instruction, 1980; Associate Professor of Curriculum and Instruction, 1980-85

Bee Chrystal, B.S., (Oklahoma Agricultural and Mechanical College), M.S. (Teachers College, Columbia University), Additional Study (University of Colorado, University of Chicago, University of California, Los Angeles, and Peabody College); Instructor in the Training High School, 1923; Assistant Professor of Mathematics, 1932; Associate Professor of Mathematics, 1947; Associate Professor Emeritus of Mathematics, 1950

James Clement, Commercial Pilot Certificate (FAA); Flight Instructor, 1973-75

Dora Irene Clements, B.S. (Oklahoma State University), M.T. (Southwestern State College), M.S. (Oklahoma State University); Assistant Professor of Occupational and Adult Education, 1971-73

Gerald G. Clements, B.A. (American University), M.A. (Yale University); Assistant Professor of Philosophy, 1965-70

Corydan Cochran, B.A. (Oklahoma City University), M.Ed. (University of Oklahoma); Special Instructor in Education, 1963; Instructor in Education, 1965; Assistant Professor of Special Education, 1968-69

Richard Edward Collier, B.S. (State Teachers College, New York), M.S. (Syracuse University), Ed.D. (Syracuse University); Assistant Professor of Education, 1956; Associate Professor of Education, 1959-61

Dorothy Colpitts, B.A. (Phillips University), M.S. (University of Illinois); Assistant Reference Librarian, 1962; Instructor in Library Science and Assistant Reference Librarian, 1965; Assistant Professor of Library Science and Assistant Reference Librarian, 1972-73

Don E. Combrink, B.S. (Oklahoma State University); Part-time Instructor in Industrial Arts Education, 1968; Instructor in Industrial Arts of Education, 1970-72

Martha W. Combs, B.A. (University of Florida), M.Ed. (University of Florida), Ed.D. (University of Florida); Assistant Professor of Curriculum and Instruction, 1983; Associate Professor of curriculum and Instruction, 1988-

Napoleon Conger, B.S. (Ohio University), L.L.D. (Cumberland University), M.A. (Columbia University), Ph.D. (Columbia University); Dean of the School of Education, 1936; Professor of Education and Dean of the School of Education, 1940; Research Professor Emeritus of Education and Dean Emeritus of the School of Education, 1948

Thaddeus McKelvey Cowan, B.A. (Centre College), M.A. (University of Connecticut), Ph.D. (University of Connecticut); Assistant Professor of Psychology, 1966; Associate Professor of Psychology, 1968-70

Ruth E. Coyner, B.A. (Central State Teachers College); Instructor in Education and Demonstrator in the Junior High School, 1927

John Ward Creswell, B.A. (Muskingum College), M.A. (University of Iowa), Ph.D. (University of Iowa); Assistant Professor of Educational Administration and Higher Education, 1974; Associate Professor of Educational Administration and Higher Education, 1978-78

Henry Allen Cross Jr., B.A. (Bethany-Peniel College), M.S. (University of Oklahoma), Ph.D. (Ohio State University); Assistant Professor of Psychology, 1961; Associate Professor of Psychology, 1962-64

Meredith W. Darlington, B.S. (University of Nebraska), M.A. (University of Nebraska), Ph.D. (University of Nebraska); Assistant Professor of Education, 1941; Military Leave, 1943; Associate Professor of Education, 1946-46

Michael Daugherty, B.S. (Oklahoma State University), M.S. (Oklahoma State University); Instructor, Occupational and Adult Education, 1988-

Allen Seymour Davis, B.A. (College of Emporia), M.A. (College of Emporia), D.D. (College of Emporia), Diploma (Princeton Theological Institute); Professor of Religious Education, 1922

Charles Robert Davis, B.S. (University of Oklahoma), M.Ed. (University of Oklahoma), Ph.D. (University of Oklahoma); Assistant Professor of Applied Behavioral Studies in Education, 1978; Associate Professor of Applied Behavioral Studies in Education, 1988-

Jerry G. Davis, B.A. (Central State University), M.Ed. (Central State University), Ph.D. (Ohio State University); Assistant Professor of Occupational and Adult Education, 1981-

Graydon Dawson, B.S. (Bethany Nazarene College), M.A. (Bethany Nazarene College), Ed.D. (Oklahoma State University); Assistant Professor of Curriculum and Instruction, 1977-78

Donald Denum, B.S. (University of Houston), M.A. (University of Texas), Ph.D. (University of Texas); Associate Professor of Education, 1965-71

Ernest Wayne Dewey, B.A. (University of Kansas), M.A. (University of Kansas), Ph.D. (University of Texas); Assistant Professor of Philosophy, 1954; Associate Professor of Philosophy, 1958-60

Gregory F. Dickey, B.A. (Southeast Missouri State College), B.S. (Southeast Missouri State College), M.Ed. (University of Missouri); Assistant Professor of Education, 1963-65

Marcia M. Dickman, B.S. (Purdue University), M.S. (Purdue University), Ph.D. (Purdue University); Assistant Professor of Applied Behavioral Studies, 1986-

Don Robert Dickson, B.S. (University of Utah), M.S. (University of Utah); Assistant Professor of Meteorology, 1955-56

John Milton Dillard, B.S. (Wilberforce University), Ed.M. (State University of New York), Ph.D. (State University of New York); Assistant Professor of Applied Behavioral Studies in Education, 1976; Associate Professor of Applied Behavioral Studies in Education, 1980-84

Judith E. Dobson, B.S. (University of Wisconsin), M.S. (University of Nebraska), Ph.D. (University of Wyoming); Assistant Professor of Education, 1971; Associate Professor of Applied Behavioral Studies in Education, 1973; Professor of Applied Behavioral Studies in Education, 1977-

Russell Lee Dobson, B.A. (Northeastern State College), M.T. (Northeastern State College), Ed.D. (University of Oklahoma); Assistant Professor of Education, 1967; Associate Professor of Education, 1969; Professor of Curriculum and Instruction, 1973-

J. Karl Doss, B.S. (East Central State College), M.S. (Oklahoma State University), Ed.D. (Oklahoma State University); Assistant Professor of Trade and Industrial Education, 1957; Assistant Professor of Education, & Associate Director of the Southwest Center for Safety Education and Research, 1961; Associate Professor of Education, Director of the Safety Center, and Director of Continuing Education, 1966-68

John E. Drevdahl, A.B. (University of Michigan), Ph.D. (University of Nebraska); Assistant Professor of Psychology, 1957-59

Carol Duckworth, B.A. (Oklahoma Baptist College), M.S.E. (Arkansas State University); Instructor, Occupational and Adult Education, 1988-

Cecil W. Dugger, B.S. (Texas A. and M. University), M.Ed. (Texas A. and M. University), Ed.D. (Oklahoma State University); Assistant Professor of Technical Education, 1965; Associate Professor of Technical Education, 1970; Associate Professor of Technical Education and Acting Director of the School of Occupational and Adult Education, 1980; Associate Professor of Technical Education, 1981-

Roy Dugger, B.S. (Texas A. and M. University), M.Ed. (Texas A. and M. University), Ed.D. (Oklahoma State University); Assistant Professor of Agricultural Education, 1955; Associate Professor of Agricultural Education, 1957; Associate Professor and Acting Head of Department of Technical Education and State Supervisor of Technical Training Services, 1958; Associate Professor and Acting Head of Department of Technical Education and State Supervisor of Technical Training Services, and Acting Director of Industrial Education, 1959; Associate Professor and Acting Head of Department of Technical Education and State Supervisor of Technical Training Services and State Supervisor of Trade and Industrial Education and Acting Director of Industrial Education, 1960-66

Sam Duker, B.A. (University of California), L.L.B. (Hastings College of Law, University of California), M.S. (Oklahoma A. and M. College); Instructor in Psychology, 1947; Assistant Professor of Psychology, 1948-49

George Washington Dunlary, B.S. (Eastern Iowa Normal College), B.A. (Eastern Iowa Normal College); Visitor of Schools, 1917; Associate Professor of Education and Visitor of Schools, 1919

Benjamin Cicero Dyess, B.S. (Oklahoma A. and M. College), M.A. (University of Colorado); Assistant Professor of Education, 1921; Associate Professor of Education, 1927; Associate Professor Emeritus of Education, 1947

Walter Hendricks Echols, B.S. (Columbia College, Texas), B.A. (Southeastern State Teacher's College), M.A. (University of Colorado); Instructor in Education, 1923; Assistant Professor of Education, 1924; Associate Professor of Education, 1927; Professor of Education, 1930; Professor Emeritus of Education, 1945

John Carl Egermeier, B.S. (Oklahoma State University), M.S. (Cornell University), Ed.D. (Oklahoma State University); Associate Professor of Education, 1964; Associate Professor of Education and Associate Director of the Research Foundation, 1967-70

Bill F. Elsom, B.S. (North Texas State University), M.Ed (North Texas State University), Ed.D. (North Texas State University); Associate Professor of Applied Behavioral Studies in Education and Director of the Bureau of Tests and Measurements, 1972; Professor of Applied Behavioral Studies in Education and Director of the Bureau of Tests and Measurements, 1976; Professor and Head of the Department of Applied Behavioral Studies in Education and Director of the Bureau of Tests and Measurements, 1978-86

Francis E. Everett, B.S. (Oklahoma State University), Ph.D. (University of New Mexico); Part-time Instructor, Oklahoma City Technical Institute, 1973; Assistant Professor of Psychology, 1978-81

Millard Spencer Everett, A.B. (William Jewell College), Ph.D. (University of Chicago); Professor of Philosophy and Humanities, 1953; Professor Emeritus of Philosophy and Humanities, 1963

Nathaniel H. Evers, B.S.Ed. (University of Wisconsin), M.S.Ed. (Northwestern University), Ph.D. (Northwestern University); Professor of Education and Associate Director of Teacher Education, 1961-63

William Price Ewens, B.S. (University of Missouri), M.Ed. (University of Missouri), Ed.D. (Stanford University); Professor of Education, 1959; Professor of Applied Behavioral Studies in Education, 1973; Professor Emeritus of Applied Behavioral Studies in Education, 1979

Nancy F. Fagley, B.A. (University of Utah), M.A. (University of Utah), Ph.D. (University of Utah); Assistant Professor of Applied Behavioral Studies in Education, 1987-88

Jesse Earl Farris, A.B. (University of Michigan), M.A. (University of Michigan); Instructor in Education, 1948-49

Betty Jean Feir-Walsh, B.A. (University of Texas), M.A. (Rollins College), Ph.D. (University of Okla.); Assistant Professor of Education, 1973-74

Elmer F. Ferneau, B.S. (Iowa State College), M.A. (Northwestern University), Ph.D. (University of Chicago); Associate Professor of Education, 1955-57

Deborah Feuquay, B.S. (University of Oklahoma), M.S. (Oklahoma State University), Ed.D. (Oklahoma State University); Visiting Assistant Professor of Applied Behavioral Studies in Education, 1980-81

Jeffrey P. Feuquay, B.S. (University of Oklahoma), M.S. (Oklahoma State University); Visiting Assistant Professor of Applied Behavioral Studies in Education, 1980-81

J. Conner Fitzgerald, B.S. (Central State College), M.S. (Oklahoma State University), Ed.D. (Oklahoma State University); Extension Specialist in Audio Visual Aids and Rural School Service, 1946; Director of the Audio Visual Center, 1950; Assistant Professor and Assistant Director of College Extension of Audio-Visual, 1954; Director of Continuing Education, 1956; Associate Professor of Education and Director of Continuing Education, 1958; Associate Professor of Education, 1963; Professor Emeritus of Education and Director Emeritus of Continuing Education and Associate, 1969

James Ford, B.S. (Henderson State College), M.S. (State College of Arkansas), M.A. (University of Arkansas), Ph.D. (Ohio State University); Assistant Professor of Curriculum and Instruction, 1972-74

Larry D. Foreman, B.S. (Northeastern Oklahoma State University), M.T. (Northeastern Oklahoma State University), Ed.D. (Oklahoma State University); Adjunct Assistant Professor, 1985-

Patrick Bernard Forsyth, B.A. (Marist College), M.A. (New York University), Ed.D. (Rutgers University); Assistant Professor of Educational Administration and Higher Education, 1977; Associate Professor of Educational Administration and Higher Education, 1981-83

Eli C. Foster, A.B. (Drury College), A.M. (Columbia University); Instructor in Secondary Education, 1941; Military leave, 1944; Assistant Professor of Education, 1947; Associate Professor of Education, 1950; Associate Professor of Education and Director of Education Student Personnel, 1952; Associate Professor Emeritus of Education, 1959

Thomas D. Franks, B.S. (Stephen F. Austin State College), M.Ed. (University of Houston), Ed.D. (University of Indiana); Assistant Professor of Education, 1961-63

James Edwin Frasier, A.B. (Colorado State College of Education), M.A. (University of Michigan), Ed.D. (Colorado State College of Education); Assistant Professor of Education, 1955; Associate Professor of Education, 1957-63

William Donald Frazier, B.A. (Phillips University), M.A. (Phillips University), Ed.D. (Oklahoma State University); Assistant Professor of Education, 1966; Associate Professor of Occupational and Adult Education, 1974-78

Franz Frederick, A.B. (Kansas State Teachers College), B.S. (Kansas State Teachers College), M.S. (Kansas State Teachers College), Ed.D. (Indiana University); Assistant Professor of Education, 1963-67

Joyce S. Friske, B.S. (Oklahoma State University), M.Ed. (University of Texas, Austin), Ph.D. (University of Texas, Austin); Assistant Professor of Curriculum and Instruction, 1983; Associate Professor of Curriculum and Instruction, 1988-

Donald Karl Fromme, B.M. (Boston University), Ph.D. (University of Iowa); Assistant Professor of Psychology, 1967; Associate Professor of Psychology, 1970; Professor of Psychology, 1976-

Edward Moses Frye, B.A. (University of Oklahoma), L.L.B. (Oklahoma City University), J.D. (Oklahoma City University); Assistant Professor of Educational Administration and Higher Education, 1976; Associate Professor of Educational Administration and Higher Education, 1982; Associate Professor Emeritus of Educational Administration and Higher Education, 1985

Benton Franklin Fuller Jr., A.B. (Southeastern State College), M.A. (Columbia University); Instructor of Education, 1940; Assistant Professor in Education, 1941; Military Leave, 1942

Dale R. Fuqua, B.A. (Eastern Illinois University), M.A. (Eastern Illinois University), Ph.D. (University of Indiana); Professor and Head of Applied Behavioral Studies in Education, 1987-

Rondal Ross Gamble, B.S. (Central State College), M.Ed. (Adams State College), Ph.D. (University of Oklahoma); Associate Professor of Education, 1967; Professor of Education, 1971; Professor of Applied Behavioral Studies in Education, 1973-

John Jacob Gardiner, B.A. (University of Florida), Ph.D. (University of Florida); Assistant Professor of Educational Administration and Higher Education, 1979; Associate Professor of Educational Administration and Higher Education, 1982; Professor of Educational Administration and Higher Education, 1987-

Roger Gingerich, Flight Instructor, 1981-82

Rickey L. Gladden, B.S. (Oklahoma State University); Flight Instructor, 1970; Chief Flight Instructor and Head of Aviation Education, 1974; Acting Coordinator, 1975-78

Roy Gladstone, B.S. (University of Illinois), M.S. (University of Illinois), Ph.D. (University of Illinois); Assistant Professor of Education, 1949; Assistant Professor of Educational Psychology, 1951; Associate Professor of Educational Psychology, 1954; Associate Professor and Acting Head of Educational Psychology and Acting Head, 1955; Professor of Educational Psychology, 1961; Professor Emeritus of Psychology, 1980

Mickey Glaunert, Flight Instructor, 1979; Instructor in Occupational and Adult Education, 1981-82

David Glenday, B.A. (New York State College for Teachers), M.A. (Teachers College, Columbia University), Ed.D. (Teachers College, Columbia University); Assistant Professor of Education, 1966; Associate Professor of Education, 1968-69

Vera R. Grant, B.A. (East Central State Teachers College), B.S. (East Central State Teachers College); Instructor in Education and Demonstrator in Primary, 1927

Vicki Green, B.A. (University of California, Berkeley), M.A. (University of California, Berkeley), Ph.D. (Colorado State University); Assistant Professor of Psychology, 1974; Associate Professor of Psychology, 1979-

William John Griffiths, A.B. (Dartmouth College), M.S. (Ohio State University), Ph.D. (University of Cincinnati); Professor and Head of Psychology, 1956-60

Stephen E. Grissom, B.S. (Missouri Southern State University), Ph.D. (Oklahoma State University); Visiting Assistant Professor of Applied Behavioral Studies in Education, 1979; Assistant Professor of Applied Behavioral Studies in Education, 1980-82

Levarl Merle Gustafson, B.A. (University of Illinois), M.A. (University of Illinois), Ph.D. (University of Illinois); Assistant Professor of Psychology, 1953; Associate Professor of Psychology, 1957-60

Philip E. Hale, Flight Instructor, 1969-75

Ruth Hammond, A.B. (Drury College), B.S. (University of Illinois); Assistant Professor of Library Science, 1948-57

Margaret T. Hampel, A.B. (University of Denver), M.A. (Teachers College, Columbia), Ed.D. (Teachers College, Columbia); Associate Professor of Education, 1946-53

John David Hampton, B.G.D. (University of Omaha), M.S. (Trinity University), Ph.D. (University of Texas); Assistant Professor of Education, 1967; Associate Professor of Education, 1979; Professor of Applied Behavioral Studies in Education, 1973; Professor Emeritus of Applied Behavioral Studies in Education, 1983

Harold D. Hantz, A.B. (University of Colorado), M.A. (University of Colorado), Ph.D. (Columbia University); Associate Professor of Philosophy, 1946; Associate Professor and Head of Philosophy, 1948-48

Larry Hapke, M.S. (Morningside College), M.A. (Bowling Green State University); Fight Instructor, 1973-75

William Eric Hardy, A.B. (Furman University), B.S. (Southwestern Louisiana Institute), M.S. (Massachusetts Institute of Technology); Assistant Professor, Institute of Technology, 1949; Assistant Professor of Meteorology, 1951; Associate Professor and Head of Meteorology, 1953-57

Arthur Ernest Harriman, A.B. (Bucknell University), Ph.D. (Cornell University); Professor and Head of Psychology, 1966; Research Professor of Psychology, 1967; Professor of Psychology, 1969-

Harold Ernest Harrington, B.S. (Oklahoma A. and M. College), Ph.D. (University of Texas); Instructor in Training High School, 1925; Assistant Professor of Physics, 1932; Associate Professor of Physics, 1938; Professor, Head, and Director of Research, 1947-68

Anne Marie Harvey, B.S. (Southern Connecticut State College), M.S. (Southern Connecticut State College), Ed.D. (Oklahoma State University); Instructor in Applied Behavioral Studies in Education, 1974-76

Vivian Sue Hawkins, B.S. (Central Missouri State College), M.Ed. (University of Missouri), Ed.D. (University of Missouri); Assistant Professor of Education, 1967; Associate Professor of Education, 1969-71

Larry Kilburn Haynes, B.S. (Oklahoma State University), M.S. (Texas A. and M. University), Ed.D. (Oklahoma State University); Adjunct Professor of Sociology, 1965; Associate Professor of Education and Assistant Dean of the College of Education, 1966-68

Howard William Heding, B.A. (University of Wisconsin), M.S. (University of Wisconsin), Ph.D. (University of Wisconsin); Assistant Professor of Education, 1956; Associate Professor of Education, 1957-59

Bob Helm, B.A. (Wichita State University), M.A. (Wichita State University), Ph.D. (State University of New York, Albany); Assistant Professor of Psychology, 1972; Associate Professor of Psychology, 1976-

A. Stephen Higgins, A.B. (Pennsylvania State University), A.M. (Teachers College, Columbia University), Ed.D. (Teachers College, Columbia University); Associate Professor of Education, 1968-72

William W. Hildreth Jr., B.S. (University of New Hampshire), M.S. (Massachusetts Institute of Technology); Instructor, 1951; Assistant Professor of Meteorology, 1953-54

Cary L. Hill, B.S. (Kansas State Teachers College), M.S. (Oklahoma State University); Instructor, 1939; Associate Professor of Industrial Arts Education, 1946; Associate Professor and Head of Industrial Arts Education, 1955; Associate Professor Emeritus and Head Emeritus of Industrial Arts Education, 1962

Walter Raymond Hill, B.A. (State University of Iowa), M.A. (State University of Iowa), Ph.D. (State University of Iowa); Associate Professor of Education, 1958; Associate Professor and Director of the Reading Clinic, 1958-59

Larry Hochhaus, B.S. (Iowa State University), M.A. (Iowa State University), Ph.D. (Iowa State University); Assistant Professor of Psychology, 1971; Associate Professor of Psychology, 1975-

Alvin Scollay Hock, B.S. (Oklahoma A. and M. College), M.S. (Oklahoma A. and M. College); Professor of Religious Education, 1929-49

Leslie Melvin Hohstadt, A.B. (Central State Teachers College), B.S. (Central State Teachers College), M.Ed. (University of Oklahoma); Instructor in Extension Education, 1937; Extension Teacher, 1940; Associate Professor and Director of Bureau of Visual Instruction, 1945; Associate Professor of Education, 1959-60

James Andrew Holley, B.A. (University of Colorado), M.A. (Columbia University), Ed.D. (Columbia University); Professor and Head of Business Education, 1940; Military Leave, 1942; Professor and Head of Business Education, 1945; Professor of Education, Dean of the School of Education, and Director of Summer Session, 1951; Dean of the School of Education, 1955; Professor Emeritus of Education and Dean Emeritus of the College of Education, 1964

Jack Alroy Holmes, A.B. (University of California), M.A. (University of California); Assistant Professor of Psychology, 1947-48

Mabel Davis Holt, B.S. (Oklahoma A. and M. College), A.M. (Teachers College, Columbia University); Assistant Professor of Secondary Education and Critic Teacher, 1924; Assistant Professor of History, 1931

Bruce D. Hoover, B.S. (Arkansas Technical University), M.S. (Oklahoma State University); Head of Aviation Education, 1978; Flight Instructor, 1978; Instructor, Administrator, 1981-87

Charles Oliver Hopkins, B.S. (Oklahoma State University), M.S. (Oklahoma State University), Ed.D. (Oklahoma State University); Assistant Professor of Occupational and Adult Education, 1969; Associate Professor of Occupational and Adult Education, 1975-78

Victor O. Hornbostel, B.S. (Kansas State Teachers College), M.S. (University of Wisconsin), Ph.D. (University of Wisconsin); Associate Professor of Education, 1964; Professor of Education, 1966-67

Wayne K. Hoy, B.S. (Lock Haven State College), M.Ed. (Pennsylvania State University), Ed.D. (Pennsylvania State University); Assistant Professor of Education, 1965; Associate Professor of Education, 1967-68

Anne Keller Hoyt, B.A. (University of Arkansas), M.Ed. (University of Arkansas), M.S.L.S. (Louisiana State University); Assistant Professor of Library Science, 1969; Associate Professor of Library Science, 1975; Associate Professor Emeritus of Library Science, 1984

William Hull, B.S. (Southwestern State College), M.Ed. (University of Oklahoma); Assistant Professor of Education, Summer of 1974

DeWitt Talmadge Hunt, B.S. (Valparaiso University), B.M.T. (Valparaiso University), M.A. (Ohio State University), Ph.D. (Ohio State University); Superintendent of Shops, 1917; Professor and Head of Shops, 1924; Professor and Head of Industrial Engineering, 1925; Professor and Head of Industrial Arts Education, 1931; Professor Emeritus of Industrial Arts Education, 1955

Richard E. Hyde, A.B. (University of West Virginia), A.M. (Columbia University), Ph.D. (University of Pittsburgh); Assistant Professor of Secondary Education, 1930

Adrienne Evans Hyle, B.A. (Kansas State University), M.A. (University of Kansas), Ph.D. (Kansas State University); Assistant Professor of Educational Administration and Higher Education, 1987-

Deborah L. Inman, B.A. (University of Florida), M.A. (Columbia University), Ed.D. (Columbia University); Assistant Professor of Educational Administration and Higher Education, 1983-84

Eula Oleta Jack, B.S. (Oklahoma A. and M. College); Instructor in Training High School, 1923

Waynne B. James, B.Engr.Ed. (Washington State University), M.S. (University of Tennessee), Ph.D. (University of Tennessee); Assistant Professor of Occupational and Adult Education, 1978; Associate Professor of Occupational and Adult Education, 1980-81

William Elbert Jaynes, B.S. (Ohio State University), M.A. (Ohio State University), Ph.D. (Ohio State University); Professor and Head of Psychology, 1967; Professor of Psychology, 1977-88

Monte Jestes, Flight Instructor, 1971-77

Mark E. Johnson, B.A. (University of California, Santa Barbara), M.A. (University of California, Santa Barbara), Ph.D. (University of California, Santa Barbara); Assistant Professor of Applied Behavioral Studies in Education, 1985-

Wilbur "Deke" Johnson, B.S. (Rocky Mountain College), M.Ed. (University of Montana), Ed.D. (Western Michigan University); Assistant Professor of Educational Administration and Higher Education, 1974; Associate Professor of Educational Administration and Higher Education, 1979-

Thomas D. Johnsten, B.S. (Kansas State Teachers College), M.S. (Fort Hays Kansas State College), Ed.D. (University of Nebraska); Associate Professor of Curriculum and Instruction, 1969; Professor of Curriculum and Instruction, 1973-

Helen Mary Jones, B.S. (University of Oklahoma), M.S. (University of Oklahoma); Special Instructor in Curriculum and Supervision, 1955; Associate Professor of Education, 1959; Associate Professor Emeritus of Education, 1965

Vera Jones, A.B. (Northeast State Teachers College), M.S. (Oklahoma A. and M. College), Special Certificate in Adult Education (Teachers College, Columbia University); Associate Professor of Education, 1936

Richard Philip Jungers, B.E. (LaCrosse State College), Ph.M. (University of Wisconsin), Ph.D. (University of Wisconsin); Assistant Professor of Education, 1957; Associate Professor of Education, 1959; Professor and Director of Education, 1962; Professor and Director of Field Studies and Extension Education, 1965; Professor Emeritus of Educational Administration and Higher Education and Director Emeritus of Extension, 1979

Robert B. Kamm, B.A. (University of Northern Iowa), M.A. (University of Minnesota), Ph.D. (University of Minnesota); Dean of the College of Arts and Sciences, 1958; Vice President for Academic Affairs, 1965; President of Oklahoma State University, 1966; President and Professor of Educational Psychology, 1970; University Professor and Past President, 1977; President Emeritus and University Professor Emeritus, 1988

Thomas Allan Karman, A.B. (Albion College), M.A. (Harvard University), Ph.D. (University of Toledo); Assistant Professor of Education, 1972; Associate Professor of Educational Administration and Higher Education, 1974; Associate Professor and Head of Educational Administration and Higher Education, 1976; Professor and Head of Educational Administration and Higher Education, 1978-

Delbert Karnes, B.S. (Central State University), M.S. (Central State University), Ed.D. (Oklahoma State University); Assistant Director of the Southwest Center for Safety and Instruction, College of Education, 1969; Associate Director of the Southwest Center for Safety, 1970; Assistant Professor of Curriculum and Instruction, 1972-77

Phillip Kenyon, Flight Instructor, 1974-75

Michael Kerr, B.A. (Eastern Washington University), M.S. (University of Kansas), Ph.D. (University of Kansas); Assistant Professor of Applied Behavioral Studies in Education, 1981-88

Charles Leonard Kezer, B.S. (Oklahoma A. and M. College), Life Diploma (Oklahoma Central Normal) A.B. (University of Kansas), M.A. (Iowa State University); Principal of the Secondary School and Supervisor of Practice Teaching, 1919; Professor of Secondary Education and Principal of the Secondary School, 1922; Professor of Secondary Education, 1924; Principal of the Training High School, 1927; Professor of Secondary Education, 1931; Professor of Secondary Education and Director of Certification, 1936; Professor Emeritus of Secondary Education and Director of Certification, 1944

Kenneth L. King, B.A. (Southwestern State College), M.Ed.. (University of Oklahoma), Ed.D. (University of Oklahoma); Associate Professor of Education, 1972; Associate Professor of Curriculum and Instruction, 1975; Professor of Curriculum and Instruction, 1976; Associate Director of Teacher Education, 1976; Associate Dean of the College of Education, 1984; Interim Dean of the College of Education, 1988; Dean of the College of Education and Director of Teacher Education, 1989-

Lloyd R. Kinnison, B.A. (University of Northern Colorado), M.A. (University of Northern Colorado), Ed.D. (University of Kansas); Associate Professor of Applied Behavioral Studies in Education, 1976-78

Clyde B. Knight, B.S. (East Central State College), M.S. (Oklahoma State University), Ed.D. (Oklahoma State University); Assistant Professor of Trade and Industrial Arts Education, 1966; Assistant Professor and Chief of Party, Thai/Oklahoma State University Team in Bangkok, Thailand, 1968; Associate Professor of Trade and Industrial Education, 1975-

Pamela L. Knox-Harbour, B.S. (College of Charleston), M.S. (Virginia Commonwealth University), Ph.D. (Virginia Commonwealth University); Assistant Professor of Applied Behavioral Studies in Education, 1987-89

John Randall Koetting, B.A. (LaSalette Major Seminary College), M.A. (St. Louis University), Ph.D. (University of Wisconsin, Madison); Assistant Professor of Curriculum and Instruction, 1979; Associate Professor of Curriculum and Instruction, 1982-

Deborah King Kundert, B.A. (State University of New York), M.S. (University of Wisconsin, Madison), Ph.D. (University of Wisconsin, Madison); Assistant Professor of Applied Behavioral Studies, 1981-86

Guy Annadale Lackey, B.A. (University of Oklahoma), M.A. (University of Chicago); Assistant Professor of Education, 1925; Associate Professor of Education, 1929; Professor of Education, 1951; Professor of Education and Chairman of Elementary Education, 1953; Professor Emeritus of Education, 1959

Marshall Lakin, B.S. (Central Missouri State College), M.S. (Central Missouri State College), CAA; Commercial Pilot with Single- and Multi-Engine and Instructor Rating Chief Flight Instructor in Aviation Education and Charter Pilot, 1950; Part-time Ground School Instructor in Aviation Education, 1953-54

Imogene L. Land, B.S.E (Arkansas State University), M.S.E (Arkansas State University), Ed.D. (Oklahoma State University); Assistant Professor of Applied Behavioral Studies in Education, 1977; Associate Professor of Applied Behavioral Studies in Education, 1983-

David D. Lane Jr., B.A. (St. Olaf College), Ph.D. (Florida State University); Assistant Professor of Applied Behavioral Studies in Education, 1983; Associate Professor of Applied Behavioral Studies in Education, 1987-

Tiner A. Lapsley, Flight Service Pilot, 1953; CAA Ground School Instructor, 1958; Head of Aviation Education and Flight Training, 1964-68

Charles Ernest Larsen, A.B. (Doane College), M.A. (University of Wyoming), Ed.D. (University of Wyoming); Temporary Assistant Professor of Education, 1963; Assistant Professor of Education, 1964; Associate Professor of Education, 1965-70

Roy W. Leaghty, B.S. (Oklahoma State University), M.S. (Oklahoma State University); Instructor of Industrial Arts Education, 1974-77

Marcus Lemon, B.S. (Oklahoma State University); Flight Instructor, 1981; Instructor of Occupational and Adult Education, 1982-83

Helen L. Lindsey, B.S. (Southern Illinois University), M.S. (Southern Illinois University), Ph.D. (Southern Illinois University); Assistant Professor of Applied Behavioral Studies in Education 1974-77

Evert Travis Little, B.S. (Panhandle A. and M. College), M.Ed. (University of Oklahoma), Ed.D. (Oklahoma A. and M. College); Instructor, 1949; Assistant Professor of Education, 1950; Assistant Professor of Educational Psychology, 1951; Director of Secondary Agricultural School (Ethiopia), 1954; Associate Professor of Educational Psychology, 1955-56

Wilson R. Little, A.B. (North Texas State Teachers College), M.Ed. (University of Texas), Ph.D. (University of Texas); Associate Professor of Education and Dean of the School of Education, 1948; Professor of Education, 1951-51

Helen Lloyd, B.A. (University of Oklahoma), M.L.S. (University of Oklahoma); Instructor of Library Science, 1963; Assistant Professor of Library Science, 1966-66

Wayne N. Lockwood Jr., B.S. (Purdue University), M.S. (Purdue University), Ph.D. (University of Illinois); Assistant Professor of Occupational and Adult Education, 1974-77

Idella Lohmann, B.A. (Oklahoma State University), M.A. (Oklahoma State University), Professional Diploma (University of Tulsa), Ed.D. (University of Tulsa); Associate Professor of Education, 1961; Professor of Education, 1966; Professor Emeritus of Curriculum and Instruction, 1975

Kathryn Marie Long, B.A. (College of Emporia), B.S. (Teachers College, Columbia University), M.A. (Columbia University); Assistant Professor of Education, 1925; Associate Professor of Education and Director of the Elementary Demonstration School, 1926; Associate Professor Emeritus of Education, 1947-60

Richard F. Loose, Commercial Pilot with Flight Instructor Rating; Flight Instructor in Aviation Education and Flight Training, 1955-57

Edmon Low, A.B. (East Central State College), B.S. in Library Science (University of Illinois), M.A. in Library Science (University of Michigan); Head Librarian, 1940; Librarian with Rank of Dean, 1946; Professor and Head of Library Science, 1959; Librarian Emeritus with Rank of Dean, 1967-73

Neil Robert Luebke, A.B. (Midland College), M.A. (Johns Hopkins University), Ph.D. (Johns Hopkins University); Assistant Professor of Philosophy, 1961; Associate Professor of Philosophy, 1971

James Joseph MacDonald, B.S. (University of Wisconsin), M.S. (University of Bridgeport); Assistant Professor of Education, 1959-63

Mark Kelly Macneil, B.A. (University of Oklahoma), M.S. (University of Oklahoma), Ph.D. (University of Oklahoma); Assistant Professor of Psychology, 1966; Associate Professor of Psychology, 1968; Associate Professor Emeritus of Psychology, 1968

Charles H. Mahone, B.A. (University of Oklahoma), M.S. (University of Oklahoma), M.A. (University of Michigan), Ph.D. (University of Michigan); Assistant Professor of Psychology, 1963; Associate Professor of Psychology, 1965-65

John Malcoyannis, Instructor in Applied Behavioral Studies in Education, 1981-81

Robert E. Mangum, B.S. (St. Louis University), M.S. (Indiana University), Ph.D. (University of Missouri); Assistant Professor and Coordinator of Educational Psychology, 1969; Associate Professor and Coordinator of Educational Psychology, 1971; Professor and Head of Applied Behavioral Studies in Education, 1975-75

Steven K. Marks, B.S.E. (Emporia State University), M.S. (ibid.), Ed.D. (Oklahoma State University); Visiting Assistant Professor of Curriculum and Instruction, 1980; Instructor, Aviation and Space Education, 1988

Virginia Lewis Marsden, B.S. (Central Missouri State College), M.A. (Colorado State College of Education); Assistant Professor of Education, 1953; Associate Professor of Education, 1966; Associate Professor Emeritus of Education, 1975

Willis Ware Marsden, B.S. (Central Missouri State College), M.A. (University of Missouri), Ed.D. (Colorado State College); Associate Professor of Education, 1953; Associate Professor of Education and Director of Student Teaching, 1954; Professor of Education, Director of Student Teaching, and Head of Department of Education, 1957; Professor of Education and Director of Teacher Education, 1963; Professor Emeritus of Teacher Education, 1972

Mavis Doughty Martin, B.A. (University of Oklahoma), Ed.M. (University of Oklahoma), Ph.D. (Iowa State University); Assistant Professor of Education, 1959-62

Sue Mason, B.S. (Oklahoma State University); Flight Instructor, 1973-76

Jerald L. Massey, Graduate of the Spartan Flight School; Flight Instructor in Aviation Education, 1953; Supervisor of Flight Training, 1954-56

Terry Matson, Flight Instructor, 1974-76

Jack Earl Mauney, B.S. (University of Florida), B.A. (University of Florida), M.A. (University of Florida); Assistant Professor of Psychology, 1950-52

Elizabeth Max, B.S. (Texas Woman's University), M.L.S. (North Texas State University), Ed.D. (Oklahoma State University); Assistant Professor of Curriculum and Instruction, 1970; Associate Professor of Curriculum and Instruction, 1978-

Thomas Calvin Mayberry, A.B. (Oklahoma State University), M.A. (Oklahoma State University), Ph.D. (University of Washington); Instructor, 1953; Associate Professor of Philosophy, 1957; Associate Professor and Head of Philosophy, 1961; Professor and Head of Philosophy, 1966-70

Fred McCarrell, B.S. (Oklahoma A. and M. College), M.S. (Oklahoma A. and M. College); Instructor of Education, 1917-18; Assistant Professor of Education, 1918-1922; Associate Professor of Education, 1922-1923

Virgie McCarrell, B.S.; Specialist in Primary Education, Summer, 1919

Thaine Delbert McCormick, B.S. (Oklahoma A. and M. College), M.S. (Oklahoma A. and M. College); Assistant Professor of Trade and Industrial Education, 1954-57

Mac McCrory, B.S. (Oklahoma State University), M.S. (Oklahoma State University), Ed.D. (Oklahoma State University); Flight Instructor, 1975; Assistant Chief Flight Instructor, 1976; Program Specialist, 1977

Frank Eugene McFarland, B.A. (Baylor University), M.A. (Columbia University), Ed.D. (Columbia University); Professor of Psychology and Dean of Student Affairs, 1961; Professor of Education, 1968; Professor of Applied Behavioral Studies in Education and Director of Student Services, 1973; Professor Emeritus of Applied Behavioral Studies in Education, 1984

Evangie McGlon, B.S. (Central State University), M.T. (Central State University), Ph.D. (University of Oklahoma); Assistant Professor of Applied Behavioral Studies in Education, 1978; Associate Professor of Applied Behavioral Studies in Education, 1984-

Michael E. McGuffee, Flight Instructor, 1975; Acting Chief Flight Instructor, 1981-81

Julia Louise McHale, A.B. (Syracuse University), Ph.D. (University of Minnesota); Associate Professor of Psychology, 1960; Professor of Psychology, 1963-85

Kenneth H. McKinley, B.A. (Tarkio College), M.S. (University of Iowa), Ph.D. (University of Iowa); Assistant Professor of Education, 1973; Associate Professor of Educational Administration and Higher Education, Director of Education Research and Projects, and Associate Director of Education Extension, 1976; Professor of Educational Administration, Director of Education Research and Projects, and Associate Director of Education Extension, 1982-

C. Warren McKinney, B.S. Ed. (Georgia Southern College), M.Ed. (Georgia Southwestern College), Ed.D. (University of Georgia); Assistant Professor of Curriculum and Instruction, 1987; Associate Professor of Curriculum and Instruction, 1988-

Joey McKinney, Instructor in Occupational and Adult Education, 1982-83

Darrell Meachum, Instructor of Occupational and Adult Education, 1982-83

Gladys Hulsey Means, M.S. (University of Alabama), M.A. (University of Alabama), Ph.D. (University of Alabama); Assistant Professor of Education, 1968-72

Robert Samuell Means, B.A. (University of Alabama), M.A. (University of Alabama), Ph.D. (University of Alabama); Assistant Professor of Education, 1968-72

Robert Meisner, B.S. (Oklahoma State University), M.S. (Oklahoma State University), Ed.D. (Oklahoma State University); Assistant Professor of Education, 1966; Associate Professor of Education, 1969

A. J Miller, Assistant Professor of Teacher Education, 1962-63

Donald R. Miller, A.B. (University of Missouri), A.M. (University of Missouri), Ed.D. (University of Missouri); Assistant Professor of Education, 1963; Assistant Professor of Education and Assistant Director of Education, 1965-65

Elizabeth C. Miller, B.Di. (Iowa State Teachers College), Ph.B. (University of Chicago); Assistant Professor of Education and Supervisor of Teacher Training, 1924; Assistant Professor of Education and Specialist in Primary Education, 1926

Melvin D. Miller, B.S. (Oregon State University), M.S. (Oregon State University), Ph.D. (Oregon State University); Professor and Director of Occupational and Adult Education, 1981-

Paul M. Miller, B.S. (Ohio State University), M.S. (Idaho State University), Ph.D. (University of Utah); Assistant Professor of Applied Behavioral Studies in Education, 1986-

Terence John Mills, B.S. (Western Illinois University), M.S. (Western Illinois University), Ed.D. (Indiana University); Assistant Professor of Education, 1970; Associate Professor of Curriculum and Instruction, 1973; Professor of Curriculum and Instruction, 1978-

Elizabeth Katherine Morehardt, Graduate (New England Conservatory); Instructor in Voice, 1920

Clayton A. Morgan, B.A. (Millsaps College), M.Ed. (University of Texas), Ed.D. (University of Texas); Associate Professor of Psychology, 1958; Professor of Psychology, 1967; Professor Emeritus of Psychology, 1984

J. Brown Morton, B.S. (Oklahoma State University), M.S. (Oklahoma State University), Ed.D. (Oklahoma State University); Assistant Professor of Occupational and Adult Education, 1971; Associate Professor of Occupational and Adult Education, 1978; Associate Professor Emeritus of Occupational and Adult Education, 1978

John Charles Muerman, A.B. (Washington State College), A.M. (George Washington University), Ph.D. (George Washington University); Professor of Rural Education, 1930; Professor of Rural and Visual Education, 1937; Professor Emeritus of Rural and Visual Education, 1944

Sharon Muir, B.A. (Graceland College), M.A. (University of Northern Iowa), Ph.D. (University of Nebraska); Assistant Professor of Curriculum and Instruction, 1978; Associate Professor of Curriculum and Instruction, 1981-86

John Mulhern, B.A. (Boston College), M.Ed. (State Teachers College, Bridgeport), Ph.D. (University of Wisconsin); Assistant Professor of Education, 1962-63

Leon Langley Munson, B.A. (University of Iowa), M.S. (Indiana University), Ed.D. (Indiana University); Assistant Professor of Education, 1966; Associate Professor of Education, 1969; Professor of Curriculum and Instruction, 1975-83

Philip J. Murphy, B.A. (City College of New York), M.A. (University of Maryland), Ph.D. (University of Maryland); Assistant Professor of Psychology, 1972; Associate Professor of Psychology, 1977-82

Donald Myers, B.A. (University of Nebraska), M.A. (University of Chicago), Ph.D. (University of Chicago); Professor and Head of Curriculum and Instruction, 1973-79

Robert S. Neu, A.S.; Instructor in Occupational and Adult Education, 1975-79

Dianna Lee Newman, B.A. (Nebraska Wesleyan University), M.A. (University of Nebraska), Ph.D. (University of Nebraska); Assistant Professor of Applied Behavioral Studies in Education, 1982-88

Donald Nimmer, B.S. (University of Northern Iowa), M.S. (University of South Dakota), Ed.D. (University of South Dakota); Visiting Assistant Professor of Applied Behavioral Studies in Education, 1977-79

Robert E. Noland, B.A. (Loyola University of Chicago), M.A. (Loyola University of Chicago), Ed.D. (Northern Illinois University); Assistant Professor of Occupational and Adult Education, 1986-

Audrey Eleanor Oaks, B.S. (State University of New York), M.S. (University of Wisconsin), Ed.D. (Oklahoma State University); Assistant Professor of Education, 1964; Associate Professor of Curriculum and Instruction, 1972-

Leonard A. Ostlund, B.A. (Colgate University), M.A. (Clark University), Ph.D. (University of Kansas); Assistant Professor of Psychology and School Examiner of the School of Arts and Sciences, 1953-56

John W. Otey, B.S. (Oklahoma State University), M.S. (Oklahoma State University), Ph.D. (University of Oklahoma); Assistant Professor of Applied Behavioral Studies in Education, 1976-78

John J. Outterson, B.S. (University of Florida), M.Ed. (University of Florida) Assistant Professor of Education, 1961-64

Era Bernice Owens, A.B. (Southeastern State College), M.A. (Teachers College, Columbia University); Assistant Professor of Education, 1950-52

Thomas S. Parish, B.A. (Northern Illinois University), M.A. (Illinois State University), Ph.D. (University of Illinois); Assistant Professor of Curriculum and Instruction, 1972-76

Herbert Patterson, A.B. (Wesleyan University), A.M. (Wesleyan University), A.M. (Yale University), Ph.D. (Yale University); Professor of Education, Dean of the School of Education, and Director of Summer School, 1919; Dean of Administration, 1937; Dean Emeritus of Administration, 1952

Robert Peace, B.S. (St. Louis University); Instructor of Meteorology, 1955-61

Joseph H. Pearl, A.B. (University of Michigan), Ph.D. (University of Michigan) Assistant Professor of Education, 1971; Associate Professor of Applied Behavioral Studies in Education, 1974

A. Clinton Pereboom, B.S. (University of California, Los Angeles), M.A. (University of California, Los Angeles), Ph.D. (University of California, Los Angeles); Assistant Professor of Psychology, 1955-56

David W. Perrin, B.A. (Davidson College), M.S. (Fort Hays State College), Ph.D. (University of Iowa); Assistant Professor of Applied Behavioral Studies in Education, 1975; Assistant Professor of Applied Behavioral Studies in Education and Assistant to the Vice President for University Relations, Development and Extension, 1979

Katye M. Perry, B.S. (Bishop College), M.Ed. (Southeastern Oklahoma State University), Ph.D. (Oklahoma State University); Lecturer in Applied Behavioral Studies in Education, 1979; Assistant Professor of Applied Behavioral Studies in Education, 1983; Associate Professor of Applied Behavioral Studies in Education, 1988-

Reginald Carman Perry, B.A. (Mt. Allison University), B.D. (University of Toronto), M.A. (University of Toronto), Ph.D. (University of Toronto), Assistant Professor of Philosophy, 1948-51

Bruce A. Petty, B.S. (Fort Hays State College), M.S. (Kansas State University), Ph.D. (Kansas State University); Assistant Professor of Curriculum and Instruction, 1978; Associate Professor of Curriculum and Instruction, 1982-

Warren Waverly Phelan, A.B. (Columbia University), A.M. (Columbia University), Ph.D. (George Washington University), L.L.D. (Oklahoma Baptist University); Professor of Education, 1931-35

Jack Phelps, B.S. (Panhandle A. and M. College), M.A. (Western State College, Colorado), Ed.D. (Oklahoma State University); Visiting Professor of Curriculum and Instruction, 1979-80

Donald Stephen Phillips, B.S. (Oklahoma State University), M.S. (Oklahoma State University), Ed.D. (Oklahoma State University); Instructor of Technical Education, 1964; Assistant Professor and Head of Technical Education, 1965; Associate Professor and Head of Technical Education, 1972; Professor and Head of Technical Education, 1972

James L. Phillips, B.A. (University of Arizona), M.A. (Southern Illinois University), Ph.D. (Southern Illinois University); Professor and Head of Psychology, 1977-

Harold Jackson Polk, B.A. (San Jose State College), M.A. (San Jose State College), Ed.D. (University of Missouri); Associate Professor and Head of Industrial Arts Education, 1969; Associate Professor of Industrial Arts Education, 1978; Associate Professor Emeritus of Industrial Arts Education, 1986

Nicholas Peter Pollis, B.A. (Johns Hopkins University), Ph.D. (University of Oklahoma); Assistant Professor of Psychology, 1963-68

Gene L. Post, B.A. (Bethany Nazarene College), M.Ed. (University of Oklahoma), Ed.D. (Oklahoma State University); Assistant Professor of Education, 1964; Professor of Curriculum and Instruction, 1973; Professor Emeritus of Curriculum and Instruction, 1986

Richard S. Prawat, B.A. (Michigan State University), Ph.D. (Michigan State University); Assistant Professor of Education, 1972; Associate Professor of Applied Behavioral Studies in Education, 1975-77

Gordon David Pred, A.B. (University of Miami), M.S. (Purdue University), Ph.D. (Purdue University); Associate Professor of Psychology, 1950-53

Edson David Price, B.S. (Phillips University), M.A. (University of Missouri); Instructor in Elementary Education, 1942

James Manuel Price, B.S. (University of Oklahoma), M.A. (University of Oklahoma), B.A. (University of Oklahoma), Ph.D. (University of Oklahoma); Visiting Assistant Professor of Psychology, 1977; Assistant Professor of Psychology, 1979-

Haskell Pruett, B.S. (George Peabody College for Teachers), M.S. (University of Oklahoma), M.A. (George Peabody College for Teachers), Ph.D. (George Peabody College for Teachers), additional study at Winona School of Photography; Special Instructor of Visual Education and Business Manager, 1936; Chairman of the Department of Audio-Visual Education and Photography, 1946; Professor of Education, 1950; Professor of Education and Head of Photography, 1955; Professor Emeritus of Education, 1962

Clarence Martin Pruitt, A.B. (Indiana University), M.A. (Indiana University), Ph.D. (Teachers College, Columbia University); Assistant Professor of Arts and Science Education, 1938; Associate Professor of Education and Physical Science, 1946; Assistant Professor of Education and Physical Science, 1950-51

John R. Purvis, B.A. (Western Washington State College), M.Ed. (Western Washington State College), Ph.D. (University of Texas); Assistant Professor of Education, 1971; Associate Professor of Education, 1974-78

Robert Thomas Radford, B.A. (Baylor University), M.A. (Baylor University), Ph.D. (University of Texas); Assistant Professor of Philosophy, 1963-82

William Walter Rambo, A.B. (Temple University), M.A. (Temple University), Ph.D. (Purdue University); Assistant Professor of Psychology, 1956; Associate Professor of Psychology, 1960; Professor of Psychology, 1966-

Richard Jimmy Rankin, A.B. (University of California), M.A. (University of California), Ph.D. (University of California); Assistant Professor of Psychology, 1961; Associate Professor of Psychology, 1963-66

Darrel D. Ray, B.A. (Northwestern State College), M.S. (Oklahoma State University), Ed.D. (Oklahoma State University); Associate Professor of Education, 1965; Professor of Curriculum and Instruction, 1970-

Joe L. Reed, Professor and Head of Trade and Industrial Education, 1959-61

Solomon Luther Reed, A.B. (Susquehanna University), A.M. (Susquehanna University), A.M. (Yale University), Ph.D. (Yale University); Assistant Professor of Education, 1920; Associate Professor of Education, 1921; Professor of Education, 1922; Professor of Education and Director of Educational Psychology, 1927; Professor of Education and Head of Psychology and Philosophy, 1937; Professor of Psychology and Head of Psychology and Philosophy, 1938; Professor and Head of Psychology and Philosophy, 1939; Professor and Head of Psychology, 1948; Professor Emeritus and Head Emeritus of Psychology, 1955

Nancy Reese, B.S. (M.S.C.W.), M.A. (Mississippi State University), Ph.D. (Mississippi State University); Instructor in Applied Behavioral Studies in Education, 1974; Assistant Professor of Applied Behavioral Studies in Education, 1975-78

Milton D. Rhoads, B.S. (Central Michigan University), M.S. (Michigan State University), Ed.D. (Michigan State University); Assistant Professor of Curriculum and Instruction, 1972; Associate Professor of Curriculum and Instruction, 1977-

Theodore D. Rice, A.B. (University of Denver), M.A. (University of Denver), Ph.D. (Northwestern University); Professor of Education, 1945

James Walls Richardson, B.A. (Indiana University), Ed.M. (Harvard University), Ph.D. (Columbia University); Professor of Education, 1949; Professor Emeritus of Education, 1960

Melvin Gillison Riggs, B.A. (Baker University), M.A. (University of Pennsylvania), Ph.D. (University of Pennsylvania); Associate Professor of Psychology and Philosophy, 1938; Military Leave, 1942; Professor of Psychology and Philosophy, 1948-49

J. Randy Roberts, Flight Instructor in Occupational and Adult Education, 1978-81

Tommy L. Roberts, B.A. (East Central State College), M.T. (East Central State College), Ed.D. (University of Oklahoma); Assistant Professor of Education, 1966-68

Donald Walter Robinson, A.B. (Carthage College), M.A. (Bradley University), Ph.D. (Bradley University); Professor of Psychology and Higher Education, Dean of the College of Education and Director of Teacher Education, 1972; Professor Emeritus of Educational Administration and Higher Education, Dean Emeritus of the College of Education, and Director Emeritus of Teacher Education, 1988

Edward Schouten Robinson, A.B. (Harvard University), A.M. (Harvard University), Ph.D. (Harvard University); Assistant Professor of Psychology and Philosophy, 1938; Military Leave, 1942; Assistant Professor of Psychology and Philosophy, 1945-46

Richard M. Robl, B.A. (St. Benedict's College), B.S. (University of Kansas), M.S. (University of Kansas), Ed.D. (Oklahoma State University); Instructor and Assistant to the Vice President for Academic Affairs, 1970; Assistant Professor of Education and Director of Educational Development, 1971; Associate Professor of Educational Administration and Higher Education and Director of Educational Development, 1975; Adjunct Associate Professor of Educational Administration and Higher Education and Director of Educational Development, 1977-78

Alma Lois Rodgers, B.A. (North Texas State Teachers College), M.S. (University of Oklahoma); Instructor in Education, 1929

Maurice W. Roney, B.S. (Oklahoma State University), M.S. (Oklahoma State University), Ed.D (University of Maryland); Instructor, School of Technology, 1940; Instructor of Electronics, School of Technology, 1946; Acting Director, School of Technology and Assistant Director of Imperial Ethiopian College, Ethiopia Project, 1953; Acting Director, School of Technology and Director of Industrial Education and Assistant Project Director, Pakistan Technical Education Program, 1955; Director of Industrial Education, 1956; Director of Division of Technical Education, U.S. Office of Education, 1960; Professor and Director of Industrial Education, 1963; Professor and Director of School of Occupational and Adult Education, 1966-69

Marie C. Roos, B.S. (St. Mary of the Woods College), M.S. (Indiana University), Ph.D. (Indiana University); Assistant Professor of Curriculum and Instruction, 1975-77

Ralph Ross, B.S. (Central State University), M.Ed. (Oklahoma State University), Ed.D. (Oklahoma State University); Adjunct Assistant Professor of Occupational and Adult Education, 1976; Assistant Professor of Occupational and Adult Education, 1978-79

Roscoe Rouse, B.A. (University of Oklahoma), M.A. (University of Oklahoma), M.A. (University of Michigan), Ph.D. (University of Michigan); Librarian with rank of Professor and Director of the Library Science Institute, 1967-87

George P. Rush, B.A. (Southeastern State College), M.A. (Texas Technical University); Assistant Professor of Education, 1968-72

Richard George Salmon, B.S. (University of Florida), M.Ed. (University of Florida), Ed.S. (University of Florida), Ed.D. (University of Florida); Assistant Professor of Education, 1970-72

Ray Sanders, B.S. (Oklahoma State University), M.S. (Oklahoma State University), Ed.D. (Oklahoma State University); Visiting Instructor, 1985; Assistant Professor, 1988-

Kenneth Douglas Sandvold, B.A. (Concordia College), M.A. (University of North Dakota), Ph.D. (University of Illinois); Associate Professor of Psychology, 1965; Professor of Psychology and Director of Clinical Psychology, 1973-

Walter Ernest Scharetzki, A.B. (Monmouth College), A.M. (University of Illinois), Ph.D. (Cornell University); Assistant Professor of Philosophy, 1948; Associate Professor of Philosophy, 1951-53

Millard Scherich, A.B. (Hastings College), Th.M. (Iliff School of Theology), Th.D. (Iliff School of Theology), M.A. (Yale University), Ph.D. (Yale University); Assistant Professor of Education, 1945; Associate Professor of Education, 1946; Professor and Chairman of Philosophy, 1948; Professor of Philosophy and Chair of Religious Education, 1954-61

Robert S. Schlottmann, B.A. (Louisiana State University), M.S. (Tulane University), Ph.D. (Louisiana State University); Assistant Professor of Psychology, 1970; Associate Professor of Psychology, 1974; Professor of Psychology, 1982-

Richard H. Schmidt, B.S. (Oklahoma A. and M. College), M.S. (Oklahoma A. and M. College); Instructor in Psychology, 1947; Part-time Instructor, 1949

Myrtle Cooper Schwarz, A.B. (Western Kentucky Teachers College), A.M. (Teachers College, Columbia University); Assistant Professor of Education, 1946; Associate Professor of Education, 1953; Associate Professor Emeritus of Education, 1966

Robert Westland Scofield, B.S. (Teachers College of Connecticut), M.A. (University of Chicago), Ph.D. (University of Chicago); Assistant Professor of Psychology, 1956; Associate Professor of Psychology, 1959; Professor and Head of Psychology, 1961; Professor of Psychology, 1965-66

Margaret M. Scott, B.A. (University of Northern Colorado), M.A. (New Mexico State University), Ph.D. (New Mexico State University); Assistant Professor of Curriculum and Instruction, 1987; Associate Professor of Curriculum and Instruction, 1988-

Walter Gaylord Scott, B.A. (Baylor University), B.D. (Southwest Baptist Theological Seminary), Th.M. (Southwest Baptist Theological Seminary), M.A. (Baylor University), Ph.D. (Johns Hopkins University); Assistant Professor of Philosophy, 1960; Associate Professor of Philosophy, 1970-

William Charles Scott, B.A. (Bethany College), M.A. (Texas Christian University), Ph.D. (Texas Christian University); Assistant Professor of Psychology, 1969; Associate Professor of Psychology, 1975; Professor of Psychology, 1982-

James Madison Seals, B.S. (Abilene Christian College), M.A. (Southwest Texas State College), Ph.D. (East Texas State University); Assistant Professor of Education, 1968; Associate Professor of Education, 1971; Professor of Applied Behavioral Studies in Education, 1975-

William E. Segall, B.A. (Yankton College), M.Ed. (University of Texas at El Paso), Ed.D. (University of Arkansas); Assistant Professor of Education,1969; Associate Professor of Education, 1971; Professor of Curriculum and Instruction, 1975-

Daniel Selakovich, A.B. (Western State College of Colorado), M.A. (Washington State University), Ed.D. (University of Colorado); Associate Professor of Education, 1963; Professor of Curriculum and Instruction, 1968-

Terry Shaw, B.S. (Oklahoma State University), M.A. (University of California), Ed.D. (Oklahoma State University); Visiting Assistant Professor of Curriculum and Instruction, 1978-79

Ronnie G. Sheppard, B.S. (Southeastern Oklahoma State University); Flight Instructor, 1976-79

Richard Sheppard, B.S. (Texas A. and M. University), M.S. (Oklahoma State University); Assistant Professor of Trade and Industrial Education, 1975-76

David Michael Shoemaker, A.B. (Indiana University), M.S. (Bowling Green State University), Ph.D. (University of Houston); Assistant Professor of Psychology, 1966-69

Noah Gayle Simmons, B.S. (Eastern Missouri State College), M.A. (Washington University, Missouri), Ed.D. (Washington University, Missouri); Associate Professor of Education, 1962-63

Ronald R. Simmons, B.S. (Panhandle State College), M.S. (Colorado State University), Ph.D. (Oklahoma State University); Flight Instructor, 1978-80

Harold W. Skinner, M.A. (East Central Oklahoma State University), Ed.D. (Oklahoma State University); Instructor, Coordinator, and Rehabilitation Counselor of Training Program, 1968; Visiting Assistant Professor of Psychology, 1978-79

Charles L. Smith, B.M. (Central Methodist College), M.A. (University of Colorado), M.A. (University of Northern Colorado), Ed.D. (University of Northern Colorado); Assistant Professor of Education, 1972; Associate Professor of Curriculum and Instruction, 1976; Associate Professor Emeritus of Curriculum and Instruction, 1986

Glenn Smith, A.B. (University of Oklahoma), M.S. (Oklahoma A. and M. College); Professor and Head of Trade and Industrial Education, 1938; Professor Emeritus and Head Emeritus of Trade and Industrial Education, 1959

H. Gene Smith, B.S. (Oklahoma State University), M.B.A. (Oklahoma State University), Ed.D. (Oklahoma State University); Adjunct Assistant Professor of Occupational and Adult Education, 1977; Assistant Professor of Occupational and Adult Education, 1978; Associate Professor of Occupational and Adult Education and Director of Occupational and Adult Education System Design and Computer Services, 1983-

Ida Townsend Smith, B.A. (Central State College), M.A. (Colorado State University), Ed.D. (Colorado State University); Assistant Professor of Education, 1948; Associate Professor of Education, 1952; Professor of Education, 1957; Professor Emeritus of Education, 1964

Jerome Smith, B.A. (New York University), M.A. (University of Connecticut), Ph.D. (University of Connecticut); Assistant Professor of Psychology, 1964-66

Thomas J. Smith, B.S. Ed. (East Central Oklahoma State University), M.S. (Oklahoma State University), Ed.D. (Oklahoma State University); Professor of Educational Administration and Higher Education and Director of Education Extension, 1979; Professor of Educational Administration and Higher Education, Director of Educational Extension, and Oklahoma State University Coordinator of the University Center at Tulsa, 1982; Professor Emeritus of Educational Administration and Higher Education, 1988

Brent M. Snow, B.S. (Brigham Young University), M.S. (Oklahoma State University), Ph.D. (University of Idaho); Assistant Professor of Psychology, 1979; Associate Professor of Psychology, 1983-

Roy E. Sommerfeld, B.S. (Western Michigan State College), M.A. (University of Michigan), Ph.D. (University of Michigan); Assistant Professor of Educational Psychology, 1952; Associate Professor of Educational Psychology, and Director of the College Reading Clinic, 1954-56

Helmer Ellsworth Sorenson, B.E. (Eau Clare State Teachers College), Ph.M. (University of Wisconsin), Ph.D. (University of Wisconsin); Associate Professor of Education, 1949; Professor of Education, 1951; Professor of Education and Associate Dean of the School of Education, 1953; Professor and Head of Educational Administration and Vice Dean of the School of Education, 1955; Professor of Education and Dean of the College of Education, 1964; Professor Emeritus of Education and Dean Emeritus of the College of Education, 1972

Harry B. Spencer, A.B. (Muskingum College), M.Ed. (University of Buffalo); Professor of Education, 1962-64

Robert Francis Stanners, B.S. (University of Wisconsin), Ph.D. (University of Iowa) Associate Professor of Psychology, 1966; Professor of Psychology, 1971-

Winifred Stayton, B.A. (Central State Teachers College); Instructor and Demonstration Teacher of Education, 1928

James Kenneth St. Clair, B.A. (North Texas State University), B.M. (North Texas State University), M.M.E. (North Texas State University), Ed.D. (University of Texas); Associate Professor of Education, 1964; Associate Professor and Head of Education, 1967; Professor of Education, 1968; Professor of Educational Administration and Higher Education, 1973-

James S. Stephenson, Flight Instructor, 1964-67

Amos Kenneth Stern, B.S. (Messiah College), M.Ed. (Shippensburg State College) Ed.D. (University of Oklahoma); Assistant Professor of Educational Administration and Higher Education, 1980; Associate Professor of Educational Administration and Higher Education, 1985-

William W. Stevenson, B.S. (Oklahoma State University), M.S. (Oklahoma State University), Ed.D. (Oklahoma State University); Assistant Professor of Education, 1967; Associate Professor of Occupational and Adult Education and Director of the Vocational Research Coordinating Unit, 1970-78

Barbara Stewart, B.S. (Purdue University), M.S. (Purdue University), Ph.D. (Purdue University); Assistant Professor of Psychology, 1970; Associate Professor of Psychology, 1974-77

Martin Strand, B.S. (Abilene Christian University), M.S. (Abilene Christian University), Ed.D. (East Texas State University); Assistant Professor of Occupational and Adult Education, 1979-81

Anna Stringfield, A.B. (East Central State College), M.S. (Oklahoma A&M College); Instructor in Elementary Education, and Head of Counselors in the Residence Hall for Women, 1939; Director of Counselors, 1940; Instructor in Elementary Education, Head of Counselors in the Residence Hall for Women and Assistant Dean of Women, 1948-56

Dorothy Strom, B.S. (State University of New York, Plattsburgh), M.S. (University of Wisconsin, Superior), Ph.D. (Ball State University); Assistant Professor in Applied Behavioral Studies in Education, 1988-

Eleroy Leonard Stromberg, A.B. (Nebraska Wesleyan University), M.A. (University of Oregon), Ph.D. (University of Minnesota); Assistant Professor of Psychology and Philosophy, 1937; Assistant Professor of Psychology and Philosophy and Assistant Dean of Men, 1940; Military Leave, 1942

Gerald T. Stubbs, Director of Public School Services, 1945; Professor of Education and Director of Extension and Public School Services, 1957; Professor of Education and Director of Extension in Education, 1957; Professor of Education, Director of Extension in Education, and Director of Teacher Placement Services, 1958; Professor of Education Emeritus, 1962

Harry West Sundwall, B.S. (Brigham Young University), Ph.D. (University of California); Assistant Professor of Psychology, 1946; Associate Professor of Psychology, 1948-49

John Earle Susky, B.A. (University of Florida), M.A. (University of Florida), Ed.D. (Oklahoma State University); Instructor, 1956; Associate Professor of Philosophy, 1961; Professor of Humanistic Studies, 1979-

Robert Edward Sweitzer, B.A. (Muskingum College), M.A. (Teachers College, Columbia University), Ph.D. (University of Chicago); Associate Professor of Education, 1960-65

Orrin Tatchio, B.A.; Charter Pilot and Flight Instructor, 1965; Head, Aviation Education and Flight Training, 1970-75

John Bruce Tate, B.S. (Oklahoma A. and M. College), M.S. (Oklahoma A. and M. College), Ed.D. (Texas A. and M. University); Assistant Professor of Industrial Arts Education, 1955; Associate Professor of Industrial Arts Education, 1971; Associate Professor Emeritus of Industrial Arts Education, 1986

Della Farmer Thomas, B.Ed. (Wisconsin State Teachers College), B.L.S. (University of Wisconsin); Assistant Professor of Library Science, 1957; Associate Professor of Library Science, 1966-69

William Thomas, B.A. (Central State University); Instructor in Applied Behavioral Studies in Education, 1980-81

Richard W. Tinnell, B.S. (Oklahoma State University), M.S. (Oklahoma State University), Ed.D. (Oklahoma State University); Instructor, 1968; Assistant Professor of Technical and Adult Education, 1970; Associate Professor of Technical and Adult Education, 1978; Associate Professor and Coordinator of Academic Services, 1981-83

Tommy J. Tomlinson, Flight Instructor, 1976-77

Philip H. Trenary, Flight Instructor, 1976; Instructor in Occupational and Adult Education, 1978-83

Vernon Troxel, B.S. (Illinois State Normal University), M.Ed. (University of Illinois), Ed.D. (University of Illinois); Assistant Professor of Education, 1963; Associate Professor of Education, 1965; Professor of Education, 1970; Professor of Curriculum and Instruction and Director of Teachers Corps, 1978-

Gwendolyn Y. Turner, B.A. (Arkansas State University), M.Ed (University of Arkansas), Ed.D. (University of Arkansas); Assistant Professor of Curriculum and Instruction, 1986; Associate Professor of Curriculum and Instruction, 1988-

Donald J. Tyrrell, B.A. (University of Connecticut), M.A. (University of Connecticut), Ph.D. (University of Connecticut); Assistant Professor of Psychology, 1965-67

Joseph Paschall Twyman, B.A. (University of Kansas City), M.A. (University of Kansas City), Ph.D. (University of Kansas City); Assistant Professor of Education, 1960; Associate Professor of Education, 1962-66

Clayton S. Valder, B.A. (Omaha University), Diploma (McCormick Theological Seminary); Professor of Religious Education, 1941; Chairman of Religious Education, 1948-51

James R. Vandegrift, Instructor in Occupational and Adult Education, 1981-82

Richard W. Vaughan, B.A. (University of Northern Iowa), M.A. (University of Northern Colorado), Ed.D. (University of Northern Colorado); Assistant Professor of Education, 1971-73

Eddie Velasquez, B.S. (University of New Mexico), Ed.D. (Oklahoma State University); Visiting Assistant Professor of Curriculum and Instruction, 1978-80

William R. Venable, A.B. (Sacred Heart Seminary), M.Ed. (Wayne State University), Ph.D. (University of Michigan); Associate Professor of Occupational and Adult Education, 1982-

Linda Vincent, B.S. (Nicholls State University), M.Ed. (Nicholls State University), Ed.S. (Oklahoma State University), Ed.D. (Oklahoma State University); Assistant Professor of Occupational and Adult Education, 1979-85

Edwin Vineyard, B.S. (Oklahoma State University), M.S. (Oklahoma State University), Ed.D. (Oklahoma State University); Associate Professor of Education, 1961; Professor of Education, 1965-65

Edward M. Vodicka, B.A. (Southern Methodist University), M.Ed. (Southern Methodist University), Ed.D. (University of Texas); Assistant Professor of Education, 1958-61

Edwin Ruthven Walker, A.B. (Southwestern University, Texas), B.D. (Vanderbilt University), Ph.D. (University of Chicago); Professor of Philosophy, Chairman of Humanities, Chairman of General Education, 1947-48

Gail P. Walker, B.S. (Jacksonville State University), M.A. (Jacksonville State University), Ph.D. (University of Alabama); Visiting Assistant Professor, 1976; Assistant Professor of Applied Behavioral Studies in Education, 1977-78

Lorrin F. Walker, B.S. (Oklahoma State University), M.S. (Oklahoma State University), Ed.D. (Oklahoma State University); Part-time Instructor, 1979; Visiting Assistant Professor of Applied Behavioral Studies in Education, 1980-82

Hoyt Elmer Walkup, Aircraft Structure Diploma (University of Wichita), Commercial Pilot Rating; Manager of Airport and Instructor in Aviation Education, 1947; Manger of Airport and Coordinator of Flight Instruction, 1952; Flight Examiner, 1964-83

Gaylen Wallace, B.A. (Central State College), M.S. (Oklahoma State University), Ed.D. (Oklahoma State University); Assistant Professor of Education, 1966-68

Morris S. Wallace, B.A. (North Texas State College), M.A. (North Texas State College), Ed.D. (Teachers College, Columbia University); Associate Professor of Education, 1949; Professor of Education, 1951-55

Paul George Warden, A.B. (Baldwin-Wallace College), M.A. (Kent State University), Ph.D. (Kent State University); Associate Professor of Applied Behavioral Studies in Education, 1973; Professor of Applied Behavioral Studies in Education, 1978-

Michael M. Warner, B.A. (Occidental College), M.A. (University of Kansas), Ph.D. (University of Kansas); Associate Professor of Applied Behavioral Studies in Education, 1982-

John E. Watkins, B.S. (Oklahoma A. and M. College), M.S. (Oklahoma A. and M. College), Graduate of the New York Institute of Photography; Instructor in Photography, 1949-56

Robert John Weber, B.S. (Arizona State University), Ph.D. (Princeton University); Associate Professor of Psychology, 1967; Professor of Psychology, 1973-

David Steven Webster, A.B. (Brandeis University), A.M. (University of Chicago), Ph.D. (University of California, Los Angeles); Assistant Professor of Educational Administration and Higher Education, 1987-

Robert Morgan Weiman, B.A. (Central College), M.A. (University of California); Assistant Professor of Philosophy, 1947-51

Elliot Alan Weiner, B.A. (Frostburg State College), M.S. (Purdue University), Ph.D. (Purdue University); Assistant Professor of Psychology, 1970; Associate Professor of Psychology, 1975-77

Elizabeth Jane Whitt, B.A. (Drake University), M.A. (Michigan State University), Ph.D. (Indiana University); Assistant Professor of Educational Administration and Higher Education, 1988-89

Robert C. Wicklein, B.S. (Western Kentucky University), M.S. (University of Alabama, Birmingham), Ed.D. (Virginia Polytechnic Institute and State University); Assistant Professor of Occupational And Adult Education, 1986-

Alan Wieder, B.S. (Ohio State University), M.S. (University of Cincinnati), Ph.D. (Ohio State University); Visiting Professor of Curriculum and Instruction, 1977-79

Kenneth Edward Wiggins, B.S. (Troy State College), M.S. (Auburn University), Ed.D. (Auburn University); Assistant Professor of Education, 1962; Associate Professor of Education, 1964; Professor of Education and Associate Director of the Research Foundation, 1969; Professor and Head of Aviation and Space Education, 1987-

Lloyd Lee Wiggins, B.S. (Oklahoma State University), M.S. (Oklahoma State University), Ed.D. (Oklahoma State University); Assistant Professor of Occupational and Adult Education, 1968; Associate Professor of Occupational and Adult Education, 1971; Professor of Occupational and Adult Education and Head of Career and Occupational Education, 1976

Margaret Wiggins, B.S. (Troy State College), M.S. (Oklahoma State University), Ed.D. (Oklahoma State University); Consultant, 1973; Visiting Assistant Professor of Curriculum and Instruction, 1977-78

Robert Wiley, B.S. (Trinity University), M.Ed. (Trinity University); Part-time Instructor, 1968; Instructor, 1969; Assistant Professor of Correspondence Study Education, 1970-72

Janet Barbara Wilkinson, B.A. (University of New Hampshire), M.S. (Purdue University), Ph.D. (Purdue University); Assistant Professor of Applied Behavioral Studies in Education, 1975; Associate Professor of Applied Behavioral Studies in Education, 1980-

Janice Williams, B.S. (Frostburg State University), M.P.A. (California State University, Chico), Ph.D. (University of California, Los Angeles); Assistant Professor of Applied Behavioral Studies in Education, 1988-

Norman E. Wilson, B.A. (Oklahoma State University), M.S. (University of Oklahoma), Ph.D. (University of Texas); Assistant Professor of Education, 1965-68

Durham Wong-Rieger, Assistant Professor of Psychology, 1982-83

Kun Kan Woo, A.B. (Central Political Institute, China), M.A. (Colorado State College of Education); Assistant Professor of Psychology, 1948-50

Richard A. Wood, B.A. (Phillips University), M.A. (University of Nebraska), Ph.D. (University of Nebraska); Assistant Professor of Philosophy, 1966-68

Judith P. Worell, B.A. (Queens College), M.A. (Ohio State University), Ph.D. (Ohio State University); Assistant Professor of Psychology, 1960; Research Associate, 1962-66

Leonard Worell, B.A. (Queens College), M.A. (Ohio State University), Ph.D. (Ohio State University); Assistant Professor of Psychology, 1959; Associate Professor of Psychology, 1961-66

David Yellin, B.A. (Gettysburg College), M.A. (New York University), Ph.D. (Arizona State University); Assistant Professor of Curriculum and Instruction, 1978; Associate Professor of Curriculum and Instruction, 1982; Professor of Curriculum and Instruction, 1988-

James Yowell Yelvington, B.A. (Florida State University), M.M. (Florida State University), Ph.D. (Florida State University); Assistant Professor of Educational Administration and Higher Education, 1973-78

Raymond James Young, B.S. (Kansas State Teachers College), M.S. (Kansas State Teachers College), Ed.D. (University of Colorado); Assistant Professor of Education, 1950-54

*Information for this list came from college catalogs. Faculty positions in departments no longer with the College of Education are indicated only for those years the departments were with the college.

Appendix 3

College of Education Scholarships

ORA A. HENDERSON MEMORIAL ENDOWMENT FUND

Born on November 23, 1889, at Linden, Texas, Ora A. Henderson moved with her family to the Chickasaw Nation, Indian Territory. She was the second oldest of twelve children. For four years, she attended a district school in Pottawatomie County, commuting the three miles by foot, horse, wagon, or buggy until the family moved to Cleveland County to be near better schools. Three years later, she passed the state eighth grade examination and the county teacher's examination. She received a third grade certificate and began teaching in rural schools.

When not teaching, she continued her education at East Central Normal in Ada. In 1920, she received a diploma and teacher's life certification from Central State Normal in Edmond. She also did work at Oklahoma A. and M. College in Stillwater.

She taught in Pottawatomie and Cleveland Counties and at Cushing, Eureka, Kaw City, and Porter before retiring in 1950. She lent what aid and encouragement she could to her siblings to keep them in school. Of the twelve, nine attended college, six graduated, and four received master's degrees. Miss Henderson had almost completed her master's degree when she had to drop out because of poor eyesight. During her teaching career, she was a member of the Oklahoma Education Association, the National Teachers Association, and, after retiring, the Oklahoma Retired Teachers Association. She was also active in the American Association of University Women.

The Ora A. Henderson Memorial Endowment was established in 1973 by eighteen of Miss Henderson's brothers, sisters, nieces, and nephews. It was the first endowed scholarship in the College of Education.

The scholarship is reserved for a person enrolled in the College of Education, and preference is given to Oklahoma students coming from a rural area or a small city. To date, it has been awarded to Nikki Jean Seay (1974-75); Patricia Lynn Stuever (1975-76); Ramma E. Scifres and Glenda S. Murnan (1976-77); Vonda Arlene Hamm, Latricia Kay Mason, and Sheryl Sue Baird (1977-78); Robin Gay Norgaard, Rebecca Ann Boshan, and Jeanine Richardson (1978-79); Verna Kay Kelly, Stephen R. Baker, and Sherril Marie Anderson (1979-80); Laura Stephens, Maribeth Burns, and Paula Fine (1980-81); Maureen E. Wiggins, Brad David Leverett, and Elizabeth Ann Hall (1981-82); Kim Musick, Lori Freeze, and Nancy Shepherd (1982-83); Becky S. Wolf, Susan G. Wagnon, and Mark A. Ramsey (1983-84); Sandy Southall, Sherry Rooker, and Robin Kerr (1984-85); Ann Hayes, Susan Johnson, and Leigh Ann Rahn (1985-86); Paul Allen, Paula Willyard, and Susan Johnson (1986-87); Krista Blackburn, Trenda Martin, and Melinda Patton (1987-88); and Lacrisha D. Earls, Stephanie J. Porter, and Alma Wilson (1988-89).

DANIEL C. AND MARY L. HERD MEMORIAL SCHOLARSHIP

Daniel Calvin "Dan" Herd was born in Lafayette County, Missouri, on September 19, 1875, of sturdy pioneer people. Five generations before, a John Heard (Herd) came to America and settled in Virginia. Succeeding generations moved west to Tennessee, then to Missouri. It was not unthinkable that John Francis Herd moved his family, including Dan, to Indian Territory in 1886. They lived near what is now Bartlesville; then it was Jake Bartle's Store on the banks of the Arkansas River. Later, the family moved to Pawnee County where they lived on a homestead. When the Cherokee Strip was opened to settlement in 1893, Dan moved to Woodward County and claimed 160 acres of land three miles west of Sharon, Oklahoma. He improved this homestead.

On August 12, 1908, he married Mary Luzelle "Lue" Loudermilk. Lue was born June 13, 1885, in Greenbriar County, West Virginia. Her family had been in America since before the American Revolution and had lived on the frontier. Early in 1908, she and her family moved to Woodward County, Oklahoma.

After her marriage to Dan, they lived on the homestead and in the town of Woodward. In 1920 they moved to a farm in the Tangier community. By this time, they had three daughters: Lola, Lottie, and Leone. The family had moved to Tangier so that the girls could take advantage of the local high school.

The main goal for the family always remained—an education for the children. The girls finished high school and went on to Oklahoma A. and M. College, now Oklahoma State University. There, Lola and Lottie received B.S. degrees and Lottie an M.S. degree. Lola received an M.S. from the University of Arkansas. Leone received her B.S. degree from Northwestern State in Alva.

Lola and Lottie endowed the Daniel C. and Mary L. Herd Scholarship Fund on August 18, 1975. It was a memorial to their parents, who though lacking in formal education were wise and farsighted in providing an education for their children. As in all pioneer living, funds for schooling did not come easy. The sisters appreciated the hard work that their parents put into providing for them, and they wanted this scholarship fund to be a lasting memorial to their perseverance and interest in education for all people.

The fund provides one or more annual scholarships which are awarded to full-time students who are enrolled in the College of Education and majoring in elementary education. Financial need and scholarship are given first consideration, and the recipients must possess high ideals and moral principles. Other qualities are leadership, diligent work habits, genuine interest in getting a college education, personality, and the ability to get along with others.

To date, awards have been made to Debbie J. Glover (1976-77); Cynthia K. Floyd (1977-78); Katharine A. Lambring (1978-79); Sharon J. McGranahan, Barbara K. McLaughlin, and Teresa Lynn Shaffer (1979-80); Debbie Frye and Candace C. Cochran (1980-81); Debra Ann Bradley and Carolyn S. Reilly (1981-82); Lisa Ross, Shelly Rodgers, and Debra Hinckley (1982-83); Deborah S. Ford and Aaron Hunter Jr. (1983-84); Susan Linderer and Robin Cary (1984-85); Luan West and Vicki Morris (1985-86); Leigh Gosney, Kelly Soergel, and Raegan Rethard (1986-87); Wanda Jane Edwards and Elizabeth Muller (1987-88); and Krista Blackburn and Shannon Adams (1988-89).

LOCKE, WRIGHT, FOSTER, AND CROSS SCHOLARSHIP

When asked to provide information about this scholarship, Wendell Locke responded:

"I assume most donors and endowers do so because they feel a need to repay society or some particular phase of it; a need to say 'thank you'; a desire to share good fortune; a hope of some recognition or some form of reward and a sense of doing something that will be 'eternal,' that is, something that says we passed this way.

"Most or all of those reasons probably applied to us in varying degrees when we established our scholarship. All four of us, (Wendell W. Locke, Robert Wright, Norman Foster, and Jim Cross), were OSU graduates and felt loyalty and pride toward our university. We had developed and still do feel a great deal of loyalty and pride toward educators and the field of education.

"The profession of education has always been good to us. We have specialized in school facilities since beginning our firm in October 1962. Educational projects have accounted for 75 percent to 85 percent of all our work every year. We have done over 400 educational projects in six states and one in Saudi Arabia. We have served as officers and committee members of national school planning organizations, have won national school design awards and been included in national exhibits and magazine articles. We are school architects!

"We respect and admire school people and the purposes and programs of education. Educators have always been loyal to us. Most of our best friends are educators. I've even been accused of being a frustrated educator. I took it as a compliment! We've always been extremely pleased to be associated with educators and education.

"Dr. Richard Jungers, although never a client, was one of those educators who became a personal friend. In conversation one day I mentioned how indebted we felt toward educators and school superintendents in particular. He mentioned the struggle most of them have getting through the final lap of their degree ladder and suggested we might want to show our appreciation by helping at that stage.

"And that's the way it was . . . !"

The Locke, Wright, Foster, and Cross Scholarship was established on November 24, 1975, and was the college's first endowed graduate scholarship. It is intended for a person who is enrolled in the doctoral program in educational administration and who aspires to a school superintendency. Preference is given to those whose most recent employment has been within the state of Oklahoma.

To date, it has been awarded to Edward H. Seifert III (1975-76); John H. Benson (1976-77); John M. Pursell (1977-78); Jo Pettigrew (1978-79); Mable E. Gaskins (1980-81); Marsha J. Edmonds (1981-82); Martha Albin (1982-83); Robert E. Green (1983-84); L. Sue Hoevelman (1984-85); Patrick Jenlink (1985-86); Jess Andrews (1986-87); Ed Huckeby and Anita McCune (1987-88); and J. Michael McClaran (1988-89).

JAMES R. VANDEGRIFT SCHOLARSHIP

James Richard Vandegrift was born in Shawnee on January 13, 1931, the son of J. Richard and Virginia (Soozi) Vandegrift. He graduated from Stillwater High School in 1939. He married Celia Saverline on August 30, 1952, while attending Oklahoma Agricultural and Mechanical College. He was awarded his bachelor's degree in 1953 and was commissioned as a second lieutenant in the United States Air Force.

During his military career, he became a command pilot. His last assignment was with the Strategic Air Command in Nebraska, although he did serve in Vietnam. While in the service, he received the Meritorious Service Medal with cluster, the Bronze Star with cluster, the Air Medal, and the Air Force Commendation Medal with cluster.

In 1976, he retired as a lieutenant colonel and returned to Stillwater. In 1979, he joined the faculty of the Department of Occupational and Adult Education where he served as the coach of the nationally known Flying Aggies from 1979-83, during which time his teams won the national championship twice. Flying was a great love in his life, and his students referred to him as the "Air Marshall."

The James R. Vandegrift Coach's Trophy and Award was established by his widow, Celia Vandegrift Reyburn, on October 17, 1974. It is granted to the team pilot who most possesses the qualities of leadership, integrity, and team pride; who is aware of safety; and who scored a high number of points in competitive events. His widow also donated his extensive library on flight to the Oklahoma State University library.

To date, awards have been made to Kevin Fergerson (1984); Phillip Martin (1985); Tom Mekin (1986); Rusty Zaloudek (1987); and Roger Miller (1988).

J. ANDREW HOLLEY MEMORIAL SCHOLARSHIP

Born in Yale, Mississippi, J. Andrew Holley moved to Stigler, Oklahoma, with his family in 1902. He earned his bachelor's degree in 1923 in economics and pre-law from the University of Colorado. He then studied administration and supervision of secondary education at Columbia University, from which he earned his master's degree and diploma as a high school principal in 1928. He was awarded his Ed.D. by Columbia in 1947.

He began his teaching career in rural Oklahoma and later moved to Luther. From 1926 until 1940, he served the State Department of Education as assistant state high school inspector, chief state high school inspector, and director of curriculum. In 1940, he joined Oklahoma A. and M. College as head of the Department of Business Education. Two years later he enlisted in the Navy. When the war ended, Holley returned to Stillwater, and in 1951 he was appointed dean of the School of Education.

In 1924, Holley married Moreta Burnett, who died in 1936 while Holley was with the State Department of Education. He married Edith Johnson in 1937. After retiring as dean in 1964, Holley worked at the National Council for the Accreditation of Teacher Education in Washington, D.C., until 1970, when he and Mrs. Holley returned to Stillwater. Dean Holley died on September 3, 1976.

The J. Andrew Holley Memorial Scholarship was established on October 17, 1978, by his widow, Edith N. Holley. It is awarded to a full-time graduate student who is dedicated to a career in teacher education.

To date, it has been awarded to Vicki Laughter McNeil and Diana M. Bedrick (1979-80); Margie Drumm Harrison and Donald Buskirk (1980-81); Alicia Gail Woods and Catherine Ann Wilkinson (1981-82); Norma Cole and Sally Boyle (1982-83); William L. Lemons and Patricia Marshall (1983-84); Donna Brown and Malcom Phelps (1984-85); Gordon Riffel and Pamela Cook (1985-86); Sandra Bird and Dennis Baker (1987-88); and Wanda M. Johnson (1988-89).

THE JOHN LESLIE LEHEW III SCHOLARSHIP

John LeHew III was born on January 9, 1930, in Guthrie, Oklahoma. He was graduated from Guthrie High School. Although he had a scholarship to attend the Julliard School of Music to study trumpet, he chose instead to attend the University of Oklahoma's School of Medicine. He served his internship in the U.S. Navy, and during this time he met Dottie Garber, a Navy flight nurse. They were married on August 3, 1956. Dr. LeHew served as flight surgeon for the Navy's precision flight unit "The Blue Angels" and also did research at the National Aeronautics and Space Administration for the first moon shot.

He returned to Guthrie to enter practice with his father, Dr. John LeHew Jr. His love for flying continued, and he shared many happy hours in the sky with his wife and two sons, Leslie IV and Jan. Dr. LeHew taught his son Leslie IV how to fly and to perform aerobatics. He leased two Decathalons to OSU for precision training.

A certified flight instructor, Dr. LeHew was a member of the Flying Physicians Association, senior medical examiner for the Federal Aviation Authority, and chief of staff at Logan County Memorial Hospital.

His professional affiliations included memberships in the Logan County Medical Association; the American Medical Association; the Oklahoma, California, and Arizona Medical Boards of Examiners; a Fellow of the American Academy of General Practice; and a Fellow of the American Society of Abdominal Surgeons. He was also a diplomate of the American Board of Family Practice, a member of the American Society of Clinical Hypnosis, and a member of the University of Oklahoma Century Council.

He died on May 19, 1976, following a very brief illness. He was loved and highly respected in the community by his patients, friends and co-workers.

Because of his generous nature and because he gave so much of himself to others, it seemed appropriate to his widow, Dorothy, that a scholarship be established in his name. The scholarship was created on February 9, 1979.

The John Leslie LeHew III Scholarship is awarded to a full-time senior who evidences a continuing interest in aviation education and who demonstrates superior academic performance and leadership capabilities.

To date, awards have been made to Cynthia Grace Otes (1979-80); Berry Runnels (1980-81); Elizabeth Hall (1981-82); Jerry Marti (1982-83); Lori Hawk (1983-84); Christopher Herden (1985-86); David Chapman (1986-87); Michael Anderson (1987-88); and Brian Eppler (1988-89).

MABLE MARIETTA MACY-OAKS AND PERCY W. OAKS SR., MEMORIAL ART SCHOLARSHIPS

Mable and Percy W. Oaks Sr., were born in 1900 and reared in western New York near Jamestown. They were married in 1921 and had five children. Their one son and four daughters were Percy Walter Jr., Muriel Anita, Audrey Eleanor, Beverly Adoree, and Barbara Elaine. The children attended schools in Jamestown, New York; Bradford, Pennsylvania; and Batavia, New York, where all of them graduated from high school.

Before she was married, Mrs. Oaks was a legal secretary in Jamestown. After moving to Batavia, she served for several years as the director of the Batavia chapter of the American Red Cross. She was also active in the Batavia Order of the Eastern Star and was an avid painter. Although she had limited formal training in art, she continually experimented with various techniques and supplemented her activities with reading to improve her skills in oil painting. Much of her life was devoted to being a homemaker, and she often said that she felt "children should never have to come home to an empty house."

Percy, Sr., was employed by the Niagara Mohawk Power Company and retired in 1963 after thirty-five years with the company. While in Batavia, he was active in the Masonic Lodge and became a Thirty-second Degree Mason prior to moving to Oklahoma. He continued active membership in the organization in Oklahoma City until his death in 1981. His other interests were in travel and reading. Over his lifetime, he gathered an impressive library and was especially interested in history.

From the early 1930s until just prior to the death of Mrs. Oaks in May of 1967, the family traveled extensively throughout the United States, Mexico, and Canada. Even after the children had grown up and left home, Mr. and Mrs. Oaks traveled for several months every year. What had originally been an interest in gathering "pretty stones" turned into a serious interest in geology. When they moved to Oklahoma, one of the main features in their new home in Del City was the large lapidary shop that was included in the house plan. Since all of their children had gravitated to the Tulsa and Oklahoma City areas over the years, it seemed only logical that Oklahoma be the place that they would select for their retirement home. After establishing a home in Del City, they purchased land and built a home in Colorado. It was their plan to spend the winter in Oklahoma and the summers in Colorado. However, during the spring of 1967, following a trip to Hawaii, Mrs. Oaks suddenly became ill and passed away in May.

The Mable Marietta Macy-Oaks Memorial Art Scholarship was established on February 14, 1980, by Audrey Eleanor Oaks, a professor at Oklahoma State University since 1964, as a memorial to her mother. The recipient of the scholarship is to be an undergraduate art education major in the College of Education who has maintained a high level of scholarship and has demonstrated a serious desire to become an art teacher either at the elementary or secondary level. The award is made in order to help defray additional expenses incurred during the final semester of student teaching.

Following a brief illness, Mr. Oaks passed away in January of 1981. The Percy W. Oaks Sr., Memorial Art Scholarship was established in 1982 by Dr. Oaks in memory of her father. The recipient of this award is to be a graduate student pursuing either a master's or a doctoral program in art education through the College of Education and is awarded to help defray the expenses of typing, printing, and binding of the thesis or dissertation.

To date, the Mable Marietta Macy-Oaks Memorial Art Scholarship has been awarded to Ann Lee (1978-79); Elizabeth Crismon (1979-80); Alicia Woods and Linda Newman (1980-81); Cindy Shero (1981-82); Karin Hartline and Christine Ward (1984-85); Brenda Green (1985-86); Rhonda Springer and Darren Means (1987-88); and Patricia M. Drummond (1988-89).

The Percy W. Oaks Sr., Memorial Art Scholarship has been awarded to Alicia Woods and Robie London (1982-83); and Leanna G. Dent and Sherly Hale (1988-89).

RAY E. BROWN MEMORIAL SCHOLARSHIP

Ray E. Brown, the son of Oklahoma pioneers, was born on the family homestead near Lamont on December 26, 1906. He attended the rural Flower Valley School during his grade school years. Later he attended high school in Lincoln, Nebraska, and at the University Preparatory School in Tonkawa, Oklahoma, from which he graduated.

Following his first year of college at Northwestern State College in Alva, he transferred to Oklahoma Agricultural and Mechanical College, now OSU. He received his bachelor of science degree in 1930 and returned a few years later to complete his master's degree.

He began his teaching career as an industrial arts instructor at Longfellow Junior High School in Enid. He held that position for forty years. He enjoyed his work and spent many hours working in the shop beyond the required time. By example, he taught his students to take pride in their abilities and to strive for excellence in craftsmanship.

For many years he was an instructor in the summer recreation program in Enid. When help was needed, he worked with the Boy Scouts for several years. For four summers he was a crafts instructor for boys at Cheley's Camp in Estes Park, Colorado.

Mr. Brown was a member of the First Baptist Church in Enid. He passed away on March 11, 1977. His survivors are his wife, Retta; one daughter, Donna J. Cartwright; and a grandson, Wes Cartwright.

The Ray E. Brown Memorial Scholarship was established in September 1984 by his widow. The scholarship is awarded to a student who has a strong academic record, outstanding ability, and financial need. The recipient must be enrolled full-time at OSU, and preference is given to a student majoring in industrial arts, now known as industrial technology education. If no appropriate student is found in industrial technical education, the scholarship may be awarded to a student majoring in one of the other applied sciences.

To date, the scholarship has been awarded to James Dean Bridges (1985-86); Brad Collins (1986-87); Roger E. Miller (1987-88); and Rodney Gene Humble (1988-89).

LEON L. MUNSON MEMORIAL SCHOLARSHIP

Leon Munson was born in Carthage, Illinois, on July 22, 1923. One year after graduating from Carthage High School, he was drafted into the Army for a three-year stint in World War II. Three months after he married Margaret Knowles on October 12, 1943, he was sent to the European theatre for nineteen months.

After military service, he attended Illinois College in Jacksonville, Illinois, and later transferred to the University of Iowa, where he earned his B.A. degree majoring in psychology and minoring in English and history. Although he worked forty hours a week for the last year and a half, he completed the degree in three years. He remained at Iowa for two years of English education, during which time he did his student teaching at University High.

In 1951, he began his teaching career at Grant Community High School in Ingleside, Illinois, where he taught junior and senior English classes. He soon found that teaching salaries were inadequate to support a young family and left the classroom for a variety of better-paying jobs. By 1958, the salary situation had improved somewhat, and Munson returned to teaching at Washington School in Harvey, Illinois, where he first taught seventh grade and later (after reorganization) junior high language arts.

While living in the Chicago area, he began taking night classes through Indiana University's extension program in East Chicago. The professors encouraged him to enroll at the main campus in Bloomington. He was then forty-one years old, but within two years he completed both his M.S. in secondary education with minors in English and counseling and guidance (September 1965) and sociology (September 1966). Because he had so many English hours, one of his graduate assistantships was with the English methods professor. He completed enough additional hours in English at Indiana to qualify to teach secondary English methods.

In the fall of 1966, Munson accepted an assistant professorship in the College of Education at Oklahoma State University and taught until his death on May 10, 1983. His primary job was teaching secondary language arts and supervising student teaching. He was promoted to full professor in 1975. After a year's sabbatical leave in 1978-79 to study secondary reading, he was asked to help some of the freshman athletes with reading and study skills. He was achieving such remarkable results with his classes of freshman football players that he decided to write a manual outlining his technique. He became ill before finishing this project, but his daughter hopes to complete the manual because of the success she has had with her speech/language students using his ideas.

While he was in Stillwater, few colleagues ever called him "Leon." He was "Champ" and is remembered for his humor, intelligence, positive attitude, and zest for living. The Leon L. Munson Memorial Scholarship was established on October 29, 1986, by his widow, Marge, but it was actually the idea of some of his former English methods students. An honor fund was started by them and his colleagues before he died of cancer. Their ideas, as well as monetary contributions, were instrumental in beginning this scholarship. The recipient must be a language arts major planning to teach English at the secondary level; a senior or post-graduate student certified to teach English and showing potential for academic excellence (especially in major area); and a well-rounded individual with a pleasing personality and a good sense of humor, the latter quite fitting because of "Champ's" personality. The cash award is given at the beginning of the student teaching experience to help with the many added expenses at that time.

As an aside, it should be noted that "Champ's" family was no Johnny-come-lately to America, for he was the eleventh generation descendant of Thomas Munson, who arrived in the New

World in 1637 and settled in New Haven, Connecticut. Two of Thomas' grandsons helped establish Yale College, which sits, in part, on Munson land.

To date, the scholarship has been awarded to Stacey Hendren (1986-87), Kimberly Ann Regier (1987-88), and Mark Malaby (1988-89).

ROBERT B. KAMM DISTINGUISHED GRADUATE FELLOWSHIP

The Robert B. Kamm Distinguished Graduate Fellowship was established in 1987 and is the largest endowed fund associated with the college to date. The campaign to raise the endowment was organized by John J. Gardiner and spearheaded by Melvin Jones, M. B. Seretean, Veldo Brewer, W. D. Finney, Armon Bost, Hans Helmerich, and Dail C. West.

Dr. Kamm was born on January 22, 1919, at West Union, Iowa, and was reared on a farm during the Great Depression. After completing his B.A. degree in 1940 at the University of Northern Iowa, he taught in the Belle Plaine, Iowa, public schools until 1942, at which time he joined the U.S. Navy. As luck would have it, he was sent to Stillwater, Oklahoma, for training in radar at Oklahoma A. and M. College. He and his wife, Maxine, fell in love with the people of Oklahoma, with Stillwater, and with the college.

At the conclusion of World War II, Dr. Kamm returned to the university classroom, earning his M.A. in 1946 and his Ph.D. two years later, taking both from the University of Minnesota. From 1948 to 1955, he served Drake University as dean of students, and from 1955 to 1958 he was dean of the basic division and of student affairs at Texas A. and M. University. In 1958, he and his family returned to Stillwater, where he served for seven years as the dean of the College of Arts and Sciences. After serving one year as vice president for academic affairs, he became president of Oklahoma State University on July 1, 1966, a position which he held until February 1977, when he resigned the presidency and assumed the title of university professor and past president.

Shortly after leaving the presidency, he was enticed to enter politics and carried on a spirited but unsuccessful campaign for a seat in the U.S. Senate. He then returned to OSU and was a highly successful, productive, and respected professor in the College of Education's graduate program in higher education. In addition to his professorial responsibilities, he agreed in 1982 to supervise OSU's Centennial Histories Series, and he continues with that project even after officially retiring on December 31, 1987.

While his impact on OSU was nothing short of impressive, for as dean, vice president for academic affairs, and president he caused the university to develop academic programs appropriate to the splendid physical plant begun by former president Henry Bennett, the same may be said for his work off campus. He was the American ambassador to UNESCO in 1976 and 1977, chaired the Board of World Neighbors, Inc., served on the United States commission that planned the observance of the twenty-fifth anniversary of the United Nations, chaired the Council of Presidents of the National Association of State Universities and Land-Grant Colleges, held several posts associated with the American Council on Education, served as president of the American College Personnel Association, and has been on the Board of Visitors of several universities.

In addition to his involvement on the national and international scene, his services in Stillwater and Oklahoma include far too many items to be noted here. In 1977 the Oklahoma Broadcasters Association named him "Oklahoman of the Year" in recognition of his services.

The Kamm Fellowship is awarded to graduate students pursuing degrees in higher education administration in the Department of Educational Administration and Higher Education.

To date, the fellowship has been awarded to Dale Barnett and Margaret Payne (1987-88) and Kristie Nix and Larry Rice (1988-89).

AMY L. WAGNER READING SCHOLARSHIP FUND

Amy Wagner graduated from Cement High School in May 1923. She attended Oklahoma College for Women in Chickasha, Oklahoma for two years.

She dropped out of college to teach at Anadarko and Cement. It was during her teaching that she realized the importance of reading. For one reason or another, many students get a poor start in reading. If this problem is not recognized and corrected in the first three grades, they usually get further behind, lose interest, and drop out of school in junior high. Mrs. Wagner taught a few months in Lawton, but had to resign due to the illness and death of her mother.

In August 1928, she married Elden Wagner in Cement. They moved to Edmond where he was a student at Central State Normal and a part-time teacher in the Edmond High School. He graduated in the spring of 1929, and Amy graduated in the summer of the same year. They moved to Hominy, where both taught for many years in the Mound Valley consolidated school, north of Hominy.

In 1965, a group of school administrators and concerned citizens realized that there was a need for help in remedial reading in the schools of Osage County. A reading specialist and eight remedial reading teachers were hired. Mrs. Wagner was one of the eight remedial teachers.

Her reading scholarship fund is being used to train teachers to help students who are having reading problems. The fund was established on February 22, 1988, and the recipient must be a junior, senior, or graduate student working toward a degree in elementary education in the primary grades and having a desire to emphasize reading. Financial need is considered. The initial award will be made for the 1989-90 year.

CLAYTON A. MORGAN EXCELLENCE AWARD

Clayton A. Morgan was born in Jones County, Mississippi, on March 16, 1917, and was raised on the family farm near Ellisville, Mississippi. After graduating from Jones County Agricultural High School, he attended Jones County Junior College and then completed his undergraduate education at Millsaps College in Jackson, Mississippi, where he earned a B.A. in English in 1940. During World War II he earned the rank of technical sergeant while serving in the U.S. Air Force from 1941-1945. He later attended the University of Texas at Austin where he earned his M.S. and Ed.D. in educational psychology, the terminal degree being awarded in 1953.

While completing his education, he was the assistant director of student activities for the Wesley Foundation at the University of Texas. From 1952 to 1958 he was a vocational rehabilitation counselor for the Texas Education Agency in Corpus Christi. In 1958, he joined Oklahoma State University as the coordinator of the Vocational Rehabilitation Counselor Training Program in the Department of Psychology. Both Dr. Morgan and the rehabilitation program stayed with the College of Education when the Department of Psychology was placed within the College of Arts and Sciences. Dr. Morgan retired as professor emeritus in 1984.

He is a member of numerous professional organizations, boards, advisory committees, editorial boards, executive committees, task forces, and study groups. He chaired the Elkins National Counselor-of-the-Year Awards Liaison Committee and the Dabelstein Memorial Lecture Committee of the National Rehabilitation Association, was a delegate to the 1976 White House Conference on Handicapped Individuals, and was president of the Corpus Christi Council for the Mentally Retarded. He has also regularly contributed materials to scholarly journals, yearbooks, and books and developed the National Clearinghouse of Rehabilitation Training Materials at Oklahoma State University.

He received a special commemorative medallion at the fiftieth anniversary celebration of the establishment of the State-Federal Vocational Rehabilitation Program, has lectured in distinguished lecture series, received a Presidential citation for distinguished rehabilitation service, was invited to present at the Helen Keller Centennial Congress, was selected as the College of Education's Outstanding Teacher of the Year, and was the recipient of the first distinguished Career Service Award given by the National Council on Rehabilitation Education. In June 1988, he was given the Distinguished Leader Award by the Creative Education Foundation for over twenty years of volunteer service.

Once the Clayton A. Morgan Excellence Award is fully funded, it will be used to recognize an outstanding individual who is committed to helping those with disabilities better help themselves. Such an individual is to be distinguished by proven excellence in the process of professional preparation and/or service.

LLOYD L. WIGGINS SCHOLARSHIP

Lloyd Lee Wiggins, the son of Isaac and Ruby Wiggins, was born in Ringwood, Oklahoma, on March 26, 1929. He was reared in the Ringwood and Fairview area and was graduated from Fairview High School in 1947. He took his undergraduate degree at Oklahoma A. and M. College in 1951. Upon graduation, he began his professional career as a vocational agricultural teacher in northwestern Oklahoma.

From 1956 until 1961, he was associated with Oklahoma State University's internationally known Ethiopian project as an agricultural instructor. He then returned to Stillwater to resume his professional education, earning both the M.S. and the Ed.D. While working on those advanced degrees, he was able to serve for two years as a Peace Corps director in Pakistan.

In 1968, he again returned to Stillwater as an assistant professor of occupational and adult education and was promoted to professor and head of the Department of Career and Occupational Education in 1976. In the early 1970s, Dr. Wiggins was the director of the university's nationally recognized Educational Professional Development Act (EPDA) project, which was designed to prepare individuals for leadership positions at the state and federal levels of vocational-technical education. Several people who graduated from the program later became directors of state vocational-technical education systems. At the time of his death on January 7, 1985, he was also serving as the college's director of the multimillion dollar, multi-year Jordan Project.

When fully endowed, the scholarship will be for a graduate student in occupational and adult education. Priority will be given to students preparing for leadership positions in state agencies.

Appendix 4

Distinguished Alumni of the College of Education

JAMES B. APPLEBERRY—DISTINGUISHED ALUMNUS AWARD, 1987

James B. Appleberry received his B.S. in education, his M.S. in education, and his Ed.S. from Central Missouri State College in 1960, 1963, and 1967 respectively. After additional study at the University of Kansas, he earned his Ed.D. from Oklahoma State University in school administration in 1969. Dr. Appleberry began his professional career after completing his bachelor's degree as a teacher at Knob Noster public school and was appointed principal of the elementary school after two years and principal of the junior high school the following year.

He joined the faculty at Oklahoma State University in 1968 and became head of the Department of Educational Administration and Higher Education in 1973. While departmental head, he participated in the American Council on Education Fellowship, with Archie R. Dykes, chancellor of the University of Kansas, serving as mentor. In 1977, Dr. Appleberry was appointed as the seventh president of Pittsburg State University in Kansas, and in 1983 he was appointed president of Northern Michigan University at Marquette.

Dr. Appleberry is a member of Kappa Delta Pi, Mace and Torch, Phi Sigma Phi, Kappa Mu Epsilon, and the Hall of Recognition of Central Missouri State.

Dr. Appleberry and his wife, Patricia, have two sons.

JAMES H. ARRINGTON—HALL OF FAME AWARD, 1961

James Arrington was born on May 23, 1904, the son of Wes and Laura Arrington, in Jethro, Arkansas. He, along with eight brothers and sisters, was reared on the family farm and then attended Arkansas Tech University at Russellville, Arkansas. At Tech he played halfback for the "Arkansas Wonder Boys." At the age of twenty-four, he moved to Oklahoma and began teaching school in Ripley. In 1930, he married Veneta Berry. The following year he earned a bachelor's degree from Oklahoma A. and M. College. While a student, he was a member of the Student Senate, beginning a life-long interest in politics, and was the business manager of the *Redskin*.

In 1936, he combined an interest in business with education by joining the board of Thomas N. Berry and Company. Later, he served as a director of the O'Frac Corporation and Stillwater

National Bank and was vice president of the Oklahoma Independent Petroleum Association in 1975.

He was an active participant in many organizations, including the Sons of the American Revolution, the Oklahoma Heritage Association, the Oklahoma Art Center, the Oklahoma State University's Presidents Club, the Oklahoma State University Foundation, and the Oklahoma State University Alumni Association, in addition to being named to the Oklahoma State University Hall of Fame.

In 1942, he was elected as Payne County's representative to the state capital, a position he held for ten years without ever facing an opponent for reelection. He was a delegate to the Democratic National Convention four times and was regularly courted to run for state and federal offices, which he declined.

Mr. Arrington died on March 8, 1979, at his home in Oklahoma City.

JAMES H. "JIMMIE" BAKER—HALL OF FAME AWARD, 1989

James H. Baker was graduated from Oklahoma State University with a bachelor's degree in education in 1947. His band, the Collegians, played at weekly jam sessions and at numerous fraternity, sorority, and victory dances. Selected as the outstanding drum major in the United States, Mr. Baker delighted audiences with his high-stepping style and entertaining half-time routines. After graduation from OSU, he headed for Hollywood and began his forty-year career with the American Broadcasting Company.

Mr. Baker received six Emmy Awards, two ACE Awards for cable programming, and two Angel Awards for religious programming. He has produced and directed television programs featuring entertainment luminaries, such as Gene Kelly, Debbie Reynolds, Steve Allen, Paul Newman, and Rosey Grier.

In addition to his professional accomplishments, Mr. Baker has helped raise millions of dollars for the establishment of the Mt. Sinai Hospital's Thalian Clinic for emotionally disturbed children, the Oklahoma Myasthenia Gravis Foundation, and the Santa Marta Hospital in east Los Angeles.

Mr. Baker is a member of the OSU Pi Kappa Alpha Hall of Fame, Who's Who in California, and the Oklahoma Journalism Hall of Fame. He is a life member of the OSU Alumni Association, a member of OSU's Centennial Advisory Commission, and Keymen, a prayer group of major network executives in California who are seeking to reduce television violence.

Mr. Baker resides in Beverly Hills, California. Henry Bellmon, governor of Oklahoma, has designated him as an honorary Oklahoma ambassador.

E. T. DUNLAP—HALL OF FAME AWARD, 1977; HENRY G. BENNETT DISTINGUISHED SERVICE AWARD, 1980

E. T. Dunlap served as chancellor of the Oklahoma State System of Higher Education, the executive officer of the Oklahoma State Regents for Higher Education from 1961 to 1981. He was the second person to hold that post since the creation of the state system in 1941.

Dr. Dunlap began his education career in Oklahoma at the age of nineteen as the teacher in a two-room school near his home town of Red Oak. After teaching for three years in the Latimer County schools, he was elected county superintendent of schools for that county and served for two years.

In 1942, he became a high school inspector for accreditation for the Oklahoma State Department of Education. He returned to Red Oak as superintendent of schools in 1945, a position he held for six years. He also was elected to the Oklahoma House of Representatives in 1946, chaired the Committee on Education, and was principal author of the education code which was signed into law in 1949.

From 1951 to 1961, he was president of Eastern Oklahoma State College at Wilburton, from which he resigned to become chancellor.

Dr. Dunlap attended Eastern Oklahoma State College, received his bachelor's degree (1940) from Southeastern Oklahoma State University, and his master's (1942) and doctoral (1956) degrees from Oklahoma State University. He has also done graduate work at the University of Chicago.

He is a member of the Wesley Methodist Church of Oklahoma City, is a Thirty-third Degree Mason, and holds the Silver Beaver Scout Award. He has been active in the Lions Club for many years and holds a lifetime membership in the Wilburton club.

Dr. Dunlap and his wife, Opal, live in Oklahoma City. They have a son.

ROBERT A. KURLAND—DISTINGUISHED ALUMNUS AWARD, 1985

A 1946 Oklahoma State University graduate of the School of Education, Robert A. Kurland was a star of the 1945 and 1946 National Collegiate Athletic Association champion basketball teams coached by Henry Iba. He remains to this day OSU's leading scorer and only three-time All-American in basketball. The seven-foot Kurland was a member of the 1948 and 1952 Olympic gold medal teams. He was inducted into the Basketball Hall of Fame, Springfield, Massachusetts, in 1961. In 1987, the Missouri native was inducted into the Oklahoma Sports Hall of Fame and the Missouri Athletic Hall of Fame.

Immediately upon graduation from OSU, Mr. Kurland began his career with Phillips Petroleum Company. He retired as general manager of Special Product Sales from Phillips after thirty-eight years with the company. Kurland served in various marketing positions in Denver, Wichita, Memphis, Atlanta, and finally Bartlesville, where he lives today. He has served as a member of the OSU Foundation Board of Governors, the OSU Centennial Advisory Commission, and is a member of the board of the Basketball Hall of Fame in Massachusetts.

Mr. Kurland and his wife, Barbara, are the parents of four children.

FRANK L. MORSANI—HALL OF FAME AWARD 1985

A 1957 graduate of the OSU College of Education, Frank Morsani completed requirements for two associate degrees in automotive technology, service management and diesel technology. Later that year, Mr. Morsani finished requirements for a bachelor's degree in trade and industrial education. He is chairman of the board and principal owner of AMS Holding, Inc., a holding company which owns and operates six automobile dealerships and associated businesses. Mr. Morsani has served as the chairman of the board for the U.S. Chamber of Commerce, an organization which has almost 200,000 members, and served as president of the Tampa Bay Baseball Group, an organization of private investors intent on bringing a professional baseball team to Tampa. He also serves on several boards of trade associations in Washington. He is a member of numerous other civic boards including those of the University of Tampa, Florida Automobile Dealers Association, and the Greater Tampa Chamber of Commerce.

Mr. Morsani and his wife, Carol, an OSU alumna, live in Tampa. They are the parents of two daughters.

LELA O'TOOLE—HALL OF FAME AWARD, 1971; HENRY G. BENNETT DISTINGUISHED SERVICE AWARD, 1979

After attending Oklahoma Baptist University and Southwestern State College at Weatherford, Lela O'Toole earned bachelor's degrees in education and in home economics education from Oklahoma Agricultural and Mechanical College in 1935 and 1939 respectively. She completed her master's at Oklahoma Agricultural and Mechanical College in 1941 and her Ph.D. from Ohio State University in 1949.

Starting her educational career as an elementary and secondary school teacher in 1929, she became Oklahoma's state supervisor of home economics education in 1940. She returned to Stillwater as professor of home economics education in 1949 and became dean of home economics in 1951, a position she held until 1975. She has served as a consultant-leader for home economics in Norway and Pakistan and was the home economics advisor to Houghton Mifflin Company.

Her list of organizations and affiliations include Omicron Nu, Phi Kappa Phi, Kappa Delta Pi, Pi Lambda Theta, Delta Kappa Gamma, Mortar Board, Oklahoma Education Association, Oklahoma Home Economics Association, American Home Economics Association, and the American Vocational Association.

ALLIE P. REYNOLDS—HALL OF FAME AWARD, 1958; HENRY G. BENNETT DISTINGUISHED SERVICE AWARD, 1988

After graduating from the College of Education in 1942, Allie P. Reynolds spent a few years in baseball's minor leagues before advancing to the major leagues and playing for the Cleveland Indians (1941-1946) and the New York Yankees (1947-1954). Oklahoma State University's baseball stadium was named after him in 1981.

Leaving a successful baseball career behind, in 1957 Mr. Reynolds became owner and president of Atlas Mud Company. He was also president of the American Association Triple A. Baseball (1969-1971) and chairman of Newark Drilling Fluids.

His public and civic activities have involved him with the Kiwanis Club, O.K. Kids Baseball (commissioner), Big Brothers (board of directors), state sports director (polio and mental health), United Fund (co-chairman), muscular dystrophy, Young Men's Christian Association, Baseball Commission, American Indian Hall of Fame (president), Center of the American Indian (president), and Oklahoma Football Foundation (board of directors). He is also a Thirty-second Degree Mason.

Mr. Reynolds and his late wife, Dale Earlene, had three children.

EARL HARVEY RICHERT—DISTINGUISHED ALUMNUS AWARD, 1978

A 1936 graduate of the School of Education, Earl Harvey Richert began his journalism career as a reporter for the *Oklahoma News* in Oklahoma City before quickly moving first to the re-writer desk of the *Tulsa Tribune* and then to the *Indianapolis Times*. In 1944, he joined the News and Scripps-Howard Alliance as a political reporter in Washington, D.C., where he covered Harry S. Truman's White House. In 1969, he became editor-in-chief of the Scripps-Howard Newspaper Alliance, which has a daily circulation well in excess of two million and serves cities in Birmingham, Denver, Cincinnati, Cleveland, Columbus, Pittsburgh, Memphis, and Ft. Wayne.

Mr. Richert is a member of the Washington Gridiron Club, the National Press Club, and Sigma Delta Chi Professional Journalism Fraternity. He and his wife, Margaret, are the parents of a son and two daughters.

MYRON RODERICK—HALL OF FAME AWARD, 1975

A 1956 graduate of the School of Education, Myron Roderick coached the championship-winning Oklahoma State University wrestling team for thirteen years, capturing seven National Collegiate Athletic Association championships and 140 dual meets while having only ten losses and seven draws. In 1958, at the age of twenty-three, Coach Roderick was the youngest of any sport to lead a team to the NCAA championship.

Mr. Roderick was national wrestling coach of the year in 1959, 1962, and 1966. He was inducted into the Helms Foundation Hall of Fame and was selected as the Man of the Year in Amateur Wrestling. He had Olympic gold medal proteges at Rome in 1960, at Tokyo in 1964, and at Mexico City in 1968. Mr. Roderick won three national collegiate championships as a wrestler himself.

He and his wife, Jo Ann, have a son and a daughter.

CAROLYN SAVAGE—DISTINGUISHED ALUMNUS AWARD, 1979; HALL OF FAME AWARD, 1981

Carolyn Savage holds a bachelor's degree in elementary education from Oklahoma State University's College of Education. She has served in leadership positions in many educational and civic organizations, including Kappa Alpha Theta (president), Oklahoma CowBelles (president), P.E.O. Sisterhood (Oklahoma executive board and state president), PTA (local chapter president), and the Board of Regents for the Oklahoma Agricultural and Mechanical Colleges. She is also a member of the First Christian Church of Hominy.

Mrs. Savage and her husband, U. G. "Butch," who is a cattleman in Osage County, have a son and a daughter.

SHERLEEN S. SISNEY—DISTINGUISHED ALUMNUS AWARD, 1986

Sherleen Sisney received a B.S. in education from Oklahoma State University in 1968 and an M.S. from the University of Louisville. She has taught at schools in Colorado and California and has been at Ballard High School of the Jefferson County Public Schools in Louisville, Kentucky, since 1971. In 1979-80 the Kentucky Education Association named her the state's outstanding teacher. In 1980, she received Kentucky Jaycees Outstanding Young Educator's Award. Mrs. Sisney was selected as National Teacher of the Year from among 140,000 nominees in 1984.

She is a member of the Junior League of Louisville and helped institute the "Schools and Business" project which brings business specialists into the classrooms and takes students out to see businesses. She also serves as a member of the Kentucky Council for Economic Education.

BERTHA FRANK TEAGUE—HALL OF FAME AWARD, 1987

Bertha Frank Teague graduated from Oklahoma Agricultural and Mechanical College's School of Education in 1932 and served as a teacher and girls' basketball coach for the Byng Public Schools until she retired in 1969. She amassed 1,157 wins and 115 losses for a 91 percent winning record. Included in her career were eight state championships, forty district titles, twenty-two regional titles, thirty-eight conference titles, five undefeated seasons, and *twenty-seven straight years* of undefeated conference play!

One of many highlights of her career was being the first woman inducted into the National Basketball Hall of Fame in 1985. In that year, she was also inducted into the Oklahoma Women's Hall of Fame. In 1971, she was the first woman inducted into the Oklahoma Athletic Hall of Fame.

Ms. Teague is a member of numerous business and civic organizations.

GLADYS E. WARREN—DISTINGUISHED ALUMNUS AWARD, 1977; HALL OF FAME AWARD, 1980

Gladys E. Warren is a graduate of the School of Education, as well as the Industrial College of Armed Forces. She did additional graduate work at William and Mary College and served as state auditor. She has been active in civic, educational, and cultural organizations for over forty years. In 1968, she was chosen as one of three "Top Women Doers" in the United States. Two years later, she was listed among the "Top Ten Women in Business."

In 1972, she was appointed chairman-director of the Oklahoma Bicentennial Commission and was elected chairman of the Southwest Region American Revolution Bicentennial Alliance for 1973-74.

P. MICHAEL ADKINS—OKLAHOMA TEACHER OF THE YEAR, 1988-1989

As an undergraduate, P. Michael Adkins was unsure whether to launch a career as a lawyer or a teacher and consequently majored in political science (pre-law). Completing that degree in 1972, he proceeded to a master's program in education, which he finished in 1974. He then began his teaching career with the Moore Public Schools. Mr. Adkins taught United States and Oklahoma history at Central Junior High School until 1982, when he transferred to Moore High School and replaced Oklahoma history with government. In 1988, he moved to West Moore High School and taught U.S. history and sociology.

About ten years ago, Mr. Adkins was casting about for a summer job and tried his hand as a gun fighter at Frontier City. When Central Junior High celebrated Heritage Day the next school year, Mr. Adkins was ready with full gun fighter garb—the roles of history teacher and period gun fighter merged. Over the years, he has developed several nineteenth century characters, and he always selects ordinary men since his students can more easily identify those with their own grandfathers or great-grandfathers who migrated west to settle the territory.

In 1983, Mr. Adkins was selected as the American History Teacher of the Year by the Malcom Hunter Chapter of the Daughters of the American Revolution. Two years later, he was chosen as one of five young educators in Oklahoma by the Oklahoma Jaycees. In 1988, he was recognized as the Oklahoma Teacher of the Year. Also, that year, the Daughters of Colonial Wars granted him the Historical Preservation Award as well as selecting him as their American History Teacher of the Year.

Mr. Adkins has won several awards for best actor and/or best costume in period competition. He and colleagues have built a scale model of a Victorian western mining town (Colorado circa 1880) which was displayed at the Kirkpatrick Center, the Oklahoma City Library, and was made a part of the Fourth of July display at the Sheraton Century Hotel.

He and his wife, June, are parents of two sons.

SHERRY MORGAN—OKLAHOMA TEACHER OF THE YEAR, 1979-1980

Sherry Morgan earned her bachelor of science degree in secondary education in 1970 and her master's degree in secondary education in 1976. She has also accumulated in excess of thirty hours from other universities. She teaches at Charles Page High School in Sand Springs, where she is responsible for college-bound English and creative writing.

Mrs. Morgan received the National Teacher's Medal from the Freedom Foundation and was selected as the 1979-1980 Oklahoma Teacher of the Year. She has served on the State Textbook Committee, Oklahoma Education Association Public Relations Committee, the National State Teachers of the Year as president and vice president, and as judge for the National Council of Teachers of English Writing Contest. She has also been published in national and state journals and has presented numerous workshops.

She and her husband, Wayne, are the parents of a son and a daughter.

NANCY O'DONNELL—OKLAHOMA TEACHER OF THE YEAR, 1982-1983

Nancy O'Donnell earned her bachelor of arts in education from Oklahoma Panhandle State University in 1963 and accepted a position as a secondary teacher with the Perry Public Schools. In 1965, she went to work for the Hollis Public Schools as a teacher of English as a second language, which involved her in migrant education for the next half dozen years. From 1972-75, she was an elementary education teacher for the Maysville Public Schools before returning to Perry as an elementary teacher and coordinator of economics education.

While based in Perry, she began work on her master's and later her doctorate, earned in 1980 and 1988 respectively. In 1982, she was selected as the Oklahoma Teacher of the Year, the Noble County Teacher of the Year, and the Perry Teacher of the Year, all in addition to winning first place in the state for creativity in economic education. The following year, she was first runner-up as the National Teacher of the Year. She also was recognized by receiving the Oklahoma Foundation for Excellent Teaching Award. To date, Dr. O'Donnell is the only person to receive both the Oklahoma Teacher of the Year and the Oklahoma Foundation for Excellent Teaching Award. In 1988, she was appointed as adjunct assistant professor in the Department of Curriculum and Instruction in Education and as assistant to the dean.

Appendix 5

Kappa Delta Pi*

1921

Clarice Aldridge
Clara Bateman
E. L. Bolin
A. Berne Briggs
Marion E. Franklin
R. Q. Goodwin
Mabel Goodwin
Hattie Hayman Graham
Glenna Kramer Hendrickson
C. L. Kezer
Jeanne Steele Larner
Fred McCarrell
Clarice Eldridge Melton
John Norris
Herbert Patterson
Soloman Reed
Alice B. Traver
Pauline Morris Wood

1922

G. A. Briggs
James R. Campbell
J. W. Cantwell
J. B. Eskridge
E. L. Franklin
Clara Billman Lemon
Ed McCarrel
Nettie J. McWhorter
Valera Moorman
Lena Moser Crosnor
Mary Schenk Patterson
Julia Petty
Leona Sieglinger

1923

H. G. Barchardt
W. H. Bishop

Mable Caldwell
Frances Campbell
Bee Chrystal
E. O. Davis
J. W. Day
Fannie B. Day
Ben. C. Dyess
H. G. Faust
Anna Foster
Elsie I. Graves
Murriel Guberlet
Brice E. Hammers
Marie Hatcher
A. S. Hiatt
J. R. Holmes
Mabel Holt
James Ralph Jewell
Edna Johnson
Hilton Ira Jones
Mrs. Ed McCarrel
Mrs. Fred McCarrel
Mrs. H. P. Patterson
Ruth Hudgens Remund
Lillian Shuster
Leona Sieglinger Spillman
L. W. Taylor
J. A. Tolman
Olive Means Whitely
Alice J. R. Williams
C. L. Williams
Opal Johnson Willman

1924

Cecelia Bouquot
Blanche Collins
A. S. Davis
Grace C. Fernandes
Joseph Nelson Hamilton
Paul L. Heilman
Susie Kolb
O. G. McAninch
Harry W. McKinney
Dorothy Miles
Bernice Moore
Lucille Hunt Pendell
Haskell Pruett
A. Blanche Reifshneider
Lillie May Spencer
Frances Stewart Smith
Maude Buck Ward
Maude Helene Ward
Clyde Whiteley

1925

Frances Badger
Carolyn Bagby
Anna Baty
James H. Caldwell
W. H. Echols
Eugenia Edwards
Eunice Edwards

Mary Floyd
Lauretta Graves
Mrs. D. R. Hamilton
Dorothy Harris
Blanche Hiatt
Gladys Holliday
B. H. Howell
DeWitt Hunt
Fred N. Joachim
Fern Kinney
Bradford Knapp
Zena R. Lindsey
Kathryn M. Long
Jenhee Robberson Lowery
Ethel Markwell
Helen Mathewson
Lucy Helen Meacham
Lester Medlock
Elizabeth Miller
Millard Moore
Alice Moyer
Betty Baldwin Murphy
F. J. Reynolds
Arthur L. Richards
Frances Shelton
Viola Shuster
Walter R. Smith
Theodora Stavely
Bernice Stevens
Louise Bradford Wainscott
Anabell Wooley
Avonell Woolley

1926

Pearl Alspaugh
Betty Baldwin
N. B. Benich
Hilda Billman
Mrs. W. H. Bishop
H. G. Borchardt
Lois Bowman
Louis Bradford
Eula B. Brown
Joe Bruner
Edward Burris
Crystal Burris
Joe Butler
Hazel Cady
E. C. Campbell
M. L. Carter
Marlin Chauncey
Carrie Childs
Elsie Clodfelter
Mrs. T. A. Crays
Guy Cross
Margaret Darlow
Mabel Davis
Chester Davis
Frank L. Davis
Mrs. Ben Day
V. E. Estes
Mary Floyd
Ruth K. Fowler

Ruth Fox
M. E. Franklin
Laura French
W. B. French
Marguerite Gaspar
Walter Goe
R. O. Goodwin
Mrs. Mabel Goodwin
Floy Hammack
Harold E. Harrington
Maude Hasey
B. H. Hewett
Dilla Hill
Cassie Hyde Hock
Eula O. Jack
Ava James
James Jewell
Carroll Joachim
Glenna Kramer
Zena Lindsey
A. Frank Martin
Cliffie S. Morgan
Mattie O. Morrison
Elsie D. Mosher
Grace Mossler
Frances Mysuka
Mattie O'Morrison
Grace Tucker Otto
Elizabeth Oursler
Julia Petty
Della Remington
Jurhee Robertson
Mary Schenk
Lillian Shuster
G. T. Sims
Lily May Spencer
Dorothy Swank
Elizabeth Oursler Taylor
L. W. Taylor
J. A. Tolman
Hilda Whitman
Clyde Whitsley
Thelma Zinn

1927

Elmer Brinker
Harry H. Brown
Lawrence J. Burris
Alva Mae Calavan
E. C. Campbell
Jesse F. Cardwell
Ruby Chambers
Elsie Dunbar
Mabel Fuchs
Grace Gaspar
Eula Mae Griffin
Nina Hill
Mabel D. Holt
Mabel Horning
Eunice King
Maude Klepzig
Louise Hutchins Kleagles
Guy A. Lackey

Lois McGinnis
Addie P. Payne
Bernice Reden Marple
Lela Smith
Ed Speairs
Gale G. Wallin
Esther H. Wood

1928

Christia Allender
Emil Brodell
B. B. Chapman
Wilma Fisher
Thena Felts Goble
Vera Grant
Helen Griffin
Beula C. Griggs
Katheryne Hall
Dorothy Bell Hiatt
Ardis Hill
Charles L. Holley
Virginia Lee Holt
Gladys Hudson
Clarence W. Hunnicutt
T. A. Kennedy
H. L. McAninch
Martha Ann McBride
Robert McDole
Oscar H. McMahan
Inez McSpadden
Ella Merry
William W. Morris
Herman A. Murphy
Pearl Siebert
Cleta Mae Sharp
Mattie Esterling Smith
T. A. Tripp
Stella Yeager Werrell

1929

Margaret Baldwin
H. G. Bennett
Ruth Coyner
C. P. Davis
H. Farrington
Corrine Hart
Raymond H. Hicks
Mrs. A. S. Hock
Eunice Rice Holt
Mable D. Holt
W. Lou Howe
Elsie Masher
E. S. McCabe
Alice M. Merrell
O. J. Merrill
Vena Moore
Bernice Riden
Pearl Scales
Thelma Shaeffer
Cleta Mae Sharp
Wade H. Shumate

Fannie Spencer
Winifred Stayton

1930

Conrad Caldwell
Wayne Stanley Fellows
Florence Fithian
Thelma Foster
Parthenia Gregory
M. J. Hale
Rey F. Heagy
H. E. Herrington
Matthew Hesser
Macie Kirk
Bert Lindsay
Mary Dollarhide Long
A. O. Martin
Florette McNeese
Ethel Goodfellow Morrow
Zola Nay
Lula Page
Nora Platt
Hugh Vance Posey
Margaret Redfield
Winifred Scott
Thelma Shaffer
Mildred Sitton
Winifred Stayton
Velma Vollmer
Gale Wallin
Mrs. Allie B. Wallis
Bessie A. Weedman

1931

Louis Armstrong
Mrs. Thomas L. Bessire
Mrs. Edna Bryan
Conrad Caldwell
R. G. Campbell
Verna Finley
Florence Fletcher
W. B. French
Mary Green
Elsie Hall
Mary E. Hatcher
Inex Hatfield
Wendell Hagood
Cassie Hock
Willie Lou Howe
Dr. R. E. Hyde
Vella Johnson
Macie Kirk
Emma Lauderdale
Gwendolyn Levers
Bert Lindsay
Mrs. Bert Lindsay
W. W. McCollom
Elva Means
Mrs. Artine B. Miller
J. C. Muerman
Laura Nay

Norma Page
J. O. Payne
Woodrow Pearcy
Pattie Propst
Ethel Reed
Ruth Rogers
Myrtle M. Rouch
H. A. Sampson
Jessie B. Searle
Florence Fletcher Sexton
Lela Smith
Nellie Frances Smith
Marie A. Stamper
Belle Stephens
Walter Stepp
L. G. Weaver
Helen Wheat
Fannie Yeager

1932

Verna Finley
Blanche Hall
Ralph J. Hall
T. F. Hames
John T. Hefley
C. C. Johnson
Violet Kesler
Helen S. Love
Ruth Mohr
J. Gordon Mott
Maud Owen
Eva Palmer
Vera Pullin
Letha M. Ritchey
J. Carydon Shaw
R. O. Tate
Paul R. Taylor
Editha Whiteley
Thurza Young
W. E. Young
Dean Yount

1933

Lauda Jo Brengle
Vitas R. Dries
Esther Gibson
E. H. Homberger
John C. Howard
Anna Hyde
Aileen James
R. B. Johnson
Suzi Kelly
Neva Kennon
Ernest Kiker
John H. Lawrence
Helen Levers
Eugene B. Lewis
Evelyn Lewis
Juanita McFetridge
Cecil Moore
Villa M. Morris

Harvey Mullinex
William H. Oliver
Ruth Hartford Patterson
Beverly Queal
Mary Jane Ragan
Ida Alice Ramsey
Gladys Roe
C. V. Smith
Ellis M. Stafford
Winnie Taylor
Beulah Timberlake
Mollie Utter
Myrtle Williams
Houston Wright
T. Marie Young
Lola Zoldske

1934

Arthur Ackenbom
Inez Andrews
Cecil O. Benson
Mary Elizabeth Echols
John E. Holcomb
Ruth Lucille Houston
Pansy Ingle Kidd
Lorene K. Malloy
H. Horace Mannahan
L. C. McCall
Patricia Mills
Odus Leolen Morgan
Martin B. Nelson
Seborn Julius Payne
E. D. Price
Mary Angie Robinson
Thelma Schmidt
Otto E. Shaw
Sam J. Stratton
Maida A. Young

1935

Merrell Clinkenbeard
Lois Coffin
Harley C. Collier
Olive E. Grisso
Ruth Elaine Harritt
Troy Johnson Hicks
Mrs. Vernon Johnson
Oletta Jones
Marvin Kay
Elizabeth McCully
Merrell Klinkenbeard McMurry
Mary Elizabeth Mershon
Sally Million
Pearl Lee Minson
Ethmer Morris
Lela O'Toole
Thelma Blanche Payton
Faye White Penrod
Irma Richards
Stephen Romine
Margariete E. Smith

Ruth Strong
Leon R. Vance
Margaret B. West

1936

Mary Elizabeth Brown
Geraldine Cox
Albert J. Holland
Vera Jones
Ellis F. Nantz
B. R. Nichols
Ammie Beatrice Pruett
Adaline Prunty
Ruth Lytle Sims
Jay Franklin Smith
Ruth Strong
James Sidney Swinney
Katharine Terry
Archie Carithers Thomas
Frank Van Alstine
Roberta Wald
Melvin Wharton
Kate Galt Zaneis

1937

Janice Drummond
John C. Fitzgerald
Earl J. Grant
Thelma King
Ethel Knox
Lester Lake
Doris Watson McWhorten
Abagail Murphy
Thomas Reynolds
Florence Severson
Claire C. Stafford
Marjorie Taylor
Nellie Wheeler
Robert J. Wheeler
Velma Bardley Wheeler
Elizabeth E. Wright

1938

Mable Collins
Leva Conner
Art Griffith
Viola Griffith
Raymond Homer
Eldon Jackson
Lenore Culp Jones
Charlene Lamons
Maxine Long
Sylvia McCubbins
Barbara Yirsa McFarland
Andy Murphy
Jim Ragland
Ona C. Raines
Margaret Reed

Ula Mavis Reid
Melvin S. Rigg
Arrie Robertson
LaCreta H. Robinson
James L. Shanks
Argus Smith
B. R. Stubbs
Carrie Summers
Ruth Tompkins
Glen M. Varnum
Lois Veith
Emmit Wheat
Charlton Wise
Shelby Wyatt

1939

Barbara Black
Louanna Boydstone
N. Conger
William R. Cowling
Nan Elizabeth Davis
Frances Dickey
Zona Edwards
Dorothy Jean Estill
Laurece Fletcher
Lola Mae Green
Edgar Harris
Virginia Harrison
Annette Herald
Margaret Hurt
Mary Evelyn Jackson
Dorine Kindschi
Darwin Kirkman
Martin Maehr
Mae Ellen Merriott
Minnie Mae Needham
Lloyd Power
Louis Edward Rampp
E. S. Robinson
LaCreta Robinson
Bette Schiefelbusch
William L. Shepherd
Mary Louise Stout
Eleroy L. Stromberg
Horace W. Threldkeld
Leon Tisdale
Cleo Triplett
Nellie Margaret Waite
Mrs. J. R. Walsh
George Woodmore
James H. Zant

1940

Maude Clobaugh
Kathleen Fawcett
McKee Fisk
Clifford Hacker
Earl Hamon
Ruth Henthorn
Nora Hinrichs
Amy E. Johnson
Marvin B. Johnson
Paul Kennerly

Bonnie D. Kirkpatrick
Arthur D. Kerr
Clara Kinzer
Austin Kuykendall
Edith Ricks Lindly
Ruth Longstreet
T. G. Napier
Alta Odom
Eva Smith
Roe L. Smith
Permilia Ann Stringfield
L. C. Thomas
Maurice Turner
Charles F. Vaught
Fern Wallis
Loyd Ray Watson

1941

Florence Barr
Wlyma Black
Helen Beauchamp
Bernice Brady
Louis Casey
Marie B. Chauncy
Marguerite Downing
Helen Lee Dunlap
Nancy Echols
Merle Estill
Josephine Farha
Walter L. Fields
Wanda Ford
Neta Madeline Fox
Bob Scott Griffin
Erskine Hogue
Florence Henthorne
Dorothy Grace Jones
Dannie Kaye
Helen Marie Luthi
Fred Martin
Mildred F. McCollough
Carol McReynolds
Ernestine Ida Miller
Elizabeth Josephine Morris
Floyd Newberry
Clarence R. Pruitt
Goldie A. Russell
Bertha Seifert
Vernadene Sloan
Earl Spangler
Jean Steitz
Margaret Thomas
Rose Mary Tompkins
Joe E. Tinker
Anna Mary Walker
Eugene Wallen
Irene Walsh
Olivia Young

1942

Beatrice Lee Barnum
Annabel Beck

Alice Brown
Laurie Demers
Marguerite Downey
Margaret Miller
Willie Schlingman
Laverne Wasson
Lucille McCullouch
Geneva Sherman
Mildred Tinius

1943

Margaret Baade
Ann Blair
Adeline Fox
Isabelle Griebel
Sara Hellewell
Norma Jensen
Myra McLain Lee
Mavis Saker
Mary Sowers
Gwendolyn Wilder

1944

Clara Irene Hotchkiss
Betty Karr
Eleanor McGlamery
Anne Orr
Louise Spears
Charlotte Whitford

1945

Geraldine Albrecht
Nellie Blakely
Margaret Booth
Martha Braniger
Carol Deen
Bonnie Emerson
Jean Humphreys
Betty Hurst
Pollyanna Maxwell
Melba Osborn
Marjeane Weaver Smith
Barbara Blanton Starr
Marjorie Grace Tallman

1946

Doris Andrews
D. Elder
E. Elledge
F. Ellis
G. Friedemann
M. Hatcher
Ruth Helen Huskinson
L. Ireland
V. Johnson
Vera Jones

M. Kirkland
W. Lackey
Marcelyn Matthews
G. McCowen
E. Price
Edward Robinson
Jean Starr
Roy Tompkins

1947

Margaret P. Bieverdorf
D. Evans
L. Franklin
Margaret Hampel
M. Imel
R. Jeske
June Brown Johnston
A. Joyce Northington
Mariam Ann Oliver
M. J. Pope
June Smith
L. Smith
Betty Lou Tabor
A. Traver
T. Troth
Ilse Wolf

1948

Lora Nell Bass
Bracie M. Fawcett
Mary Foster
Bernadine Harrison
Dolores M. Hopkins
Wanda Kirkpatrick
Esther Menefee
Lester W. Metheny
Esther Patterson
Lawrence Penny
Mildred Pruett

1949

Harold Adams
Mabel Ashby
E. J. Blalock
Mary Blalock
Rose Brock
Velma Brogden
Arnold Brown
Carolyn Burnett
Patricia Carpenter
Cathleen Chambers
Carolyn Cooper
L. E. Crouse
Atla Clay Davis
Donald Dean
Grant Dobson
Lloyd DuBois
Jean Eifert

Freda Everett
Annedella Fincher
Mary Garrison
Patsy von Gonten
Betty Jane Harsha
Betty Hay
Madeleine Helfrey
Evelyn Hirschman
Pat Holcomb
Bettye Horton
Martha Hubbard
Joy Hunter
Clara Jander
Frances Jones
Very Jones
Kenneth Keahey
Marjorie Kemp
H. D. Krouse
Carol Larkin
Wilson Little
Claude Lumly
William Lundy
Wilma Marler
Eugene May
Ruth McCollum
Ruth McCoy
Edward McCray
Dorothy Morrison
Betty Murray
Betty Nash
Mary E. Neumann
Wanda Norris
Joyce Ogden
Phyllis Perkins
F. A. Riedel
Marion Rogers
Melvern Rupp
Madeline Russell
Anna Lee Sanders
Florine Smith
Phyllis Jo Smith
Jacqueline Strickland
Edwin Vineyard
Mary Walker
John Watkins
David C. Winslow
Lois Woodson
Ro Jean Yadon

1950

Leona Abshier
Betty Atkins
Mary Ballard
Mary Barnett
Charlene Blanken
Jane Bogue
Barbara Brown
Barbara Copeland
Particia Cosgrove
Letha Crossman
Dorothy Denton
Ben Dillard
Norma Earthman

Tena Franklin
Elaine Garrett
Fern Greer
Irene Hardin
Helen Harry
Barbara Holcomb
Edith Johnson
Evelyn Jones
Luree Jones
Joan Kindell
Nora Laws
Alta Lee
C. B. Loomis
Virgilene Marshall
Lila McElwain
Jean Noble
Betty Rowland
Grace Siegenthaler
Patricia Stone
Carolyn Stroupe
Mary Swift
Dorothy Vandiver

1951

Anna Adams
Alma Bartlett
Neoma Bateson
Freda Bell
Betty Bell
Coe Case
Ruth Clinard
Betty Davis
Glen Dill
Cynthia Elliott
Ruth Falkenstein
Harry Fitzpatrick
Wauneva Flanagan
Valye Fundis
Joann Gaines
Veda Gingerich
Pat Hair
June Harvey
Rosemary Hatcher
Joan Hollis
Ada Humphreys
Beverly Hunt
Carrol Hurst
Joyce Hutchison
Mary Lou Jefferson
Stella Jelsma
Neva Johnson
Clara Jones
Herschel Jones
Peggy Julian
Joel Keeter
Billie Kubik
Mary Lamon
Virginia Lane
Willa Lucas
Edna Marlatt
May Martin
Mary Martin
A. O. Martin

Lucile McCarty
Julia McKeeman
Charles McLain
Ruth McMinn
Carolyn McPeek
Jacob Morgan
Floyd Moyer
Carol Ann Naeter
Janet Pember
Irene Phillips
Elizabeth Puryear
Golden Daye Reed
Dorris Ring
Virginia Rowley
Sybil Saunders
Loraine Serwin
B. L. Shepherd
Nancy Stump
Tommy Swyden
William Thornton
Mary Lou Tiller
Ruth Trindle
Wm. T. Voight
Marilynn Webb
Mary Whittenberg
Barbara Williams
Renen Williams
Claudine Willis
Suenell Wimer
Clifford Wright

1952

Mary Ann Adams
Phyllis Anderson
Mary Lou Armstrong
Barbara Berglund
Marilyn Curry
Arthur Denner
Norma Duncan
Madonna Huston
Camille Jagou
Jo Ann Lawrence
Marilynn Leard
Bernard Lefebure
Joy McMann
Francis Roomsburg
Sue Snell
Raymond Young

1953

Della Conrad
Merna Jo Hart
Johnie R. Hartgraves
Charles Heusel
Rufus Hicks
Jean Holley
Erma Kelle
EmilyDever Langley
Marcia Mauzy
Barbara Neff
Louisa Porter

Louise Rowe
Dorothy Schere
Josie Mae Stevens
Arless Moser White

1954

Marion Allen
Haroldine Amis
Flora Boyd
Larry Burdick
Virginia Caplinger
Ardyth Carson
Shirley Daniel
Violet Davison
Jeanne Duncan
Mercedes Estes
Merrilyn Flint
Joanne Goff
Nancy Goucher
Patti Hall
Mary Heavner
Bini Heise
Eric Hemphill
Mary Holland
Helen Holley
Ann Jernigan
Genevieve Lawrence
Ann Leighty
Maureen Matthews
Jacque McKenney
Donna Nichols
Carol Pemberton
Verl Pharis
Doris Pownell
Margaret Ramsey
Marjorie Shuman
Evelyn Smith
Betty Stratton
Mary Tanner
Peggy Taylor
Darlene Tillman
Jo Turner
Mary Venable
Nancy Wheeler
Arless White
Shirley Winans
Carolyne Wooldridge
Larry Wright
Joan Zaloudek

1955

Joan Atkerson
Ruth A. Carter
M. R. Chauncey
Irene Combes
Virginia Fite
Betty Green
Joann Haynes
Sue Marshall
Marleba Ramsey
Millard Scherich

Sue Tucker
Judy Vogt

1956

Tamara Balenko
Marlene Ciskowski
Beverly Collins
Betty Duncan
Myra Fretwell
Mary Gaddis
Phyllis Greene
Edwina Harrison
Mary Hemphill
Beryl Johnston
Patricia Kincaid
Yvonne King
Carolyn Lee
Ronald McKinzie
Y'Vaughan Ramsey
Nevaleen Schmitz
Dorothy Slaven
Billie Talley
Geraldine Washington
Mary Young

1957

Pat Clarke
Dolores Dolezal
Ava Fullerton
Nadine Hackler
Donna Hadwiger
Virginia Hall
Andrew Holley
Darla Milford
Carolyn Nickles
Carroll Noske
Wanna Preston
Sue Schrimsher
Dona Selby
Jane Stewart
Mabel Tarpey
Pat Taylor
Virginia Wyatt

1958

Gaylene Able
Joyce Barber
Lois Burlingame
Helen Caron
Joyce Hill
Barbara Murray
Mary Louise Odom
Verna Rinker
Mary Zell Sands
Janet Simpson
Joyce Stretter
Ramona Ware
Phyllis Wright

1959

Barbara Adams
Pat Anderson
Kay Baum
Barbara Boyd
Pat Bratcher
Cumi Faye Brewster
Joyce Bromley
Carlotta Calvert
Mary K. Carter
Judith Catharine
LaNese Craft
Dee Dickens
Shirley Ewing
Mary E. Faulkner
Jan French
Mary Ellen Gilmore
Nita Sue Hanna
Alberta Heiserman
Laural Hirschman
Emagene Jenkins
Janet Johnston
Susann Keely
Georgia Kerby
Kaye Keso
Karol King
Howard A. Kivett
Rose Marie Kubricht
Mona June Linden
Donna Paris
Ramona Rhodes
Jean E. Rickstrew
Betty Rooker
Sylvia Rutherford
Gene Scovel
Dee Spickelmier
Eddie Sutton
Patsy Sutton
Joylyn Teeters
Janet Wever
Yvonne Williamson
Gay Wion
Kathryn Wooster

1960

Johnye Barnes
Adelle Beathe
Eleanor Bristow
Edys Burris Cacy
Rosalind Cihak
Kathleen Crook
Jayne Curtis
Eldon Divine
Kay Enmeier
Suzanne Fenton
Pat Going
Geraldine Goodwin
Sandra Hadwiger
Lawanna Hardy
Jean Hood
Linda Lewis
Lola Faye Overton
Mary Louise Page

Billye Porter
Howard Potts
Suzanne Rucker
Linda Skidmore
Sandra Thomas
Ann Whitehead
Celia Wilson
Paula Wise

1961

Emily Bales
Ann Bernhardt
Frances Bolling
Peggy Cornels
Judy Dennis
Elsie Dickey
W. Price Ewens
Karyl A. Krohn
Jerry A. Lewis
Karen Ludwig
Susan Markley
Donna K. Miller
Margherita Neville
Nancy Nickles
Patricia Patton
Claudia Shannon
Sandy Springer
Carolyn S. Thomas
Mary F. Vanpool

1962

Elaine Allison
Anita Baldwin
Charles Brinker
Phyllis Bryant
Sandra Bussett
Corinne Carpenter
Ruth Gatz
Betsy Grinslade
Roberta Hairfield
Gloria Herring
Charlene Kendrick
Ware Marsden
Darrell Nelson
Jo Pender
Martha Peterman
Barbara Ramming
Sondra Self
Anita Stewart
Glenda Sutherland
Russell Walker
Frankie Worstell
Bettye Yahn

1963

Barbara Armstrong
Leah Barrier
Janice Beltz

Judy Edwards
Pat Ent
Grace Frederick
Jim Gatz
Ruthie Gatz
Carol Glover
Suzanne Harder
Ann Harriger
Ann James
Joyce Maxwell
Carleene McDaniel
Lyman McDonald
Nancy Page
Diva Resende
Ila Rimer
Karen Smith
Bennie Van Vacter

1964

Lynn Anderson
Carole Baker
Ruth Ann Baker
Sue Bondurant
Janice Buckles
William R. Buckles
Gladeen Burris
Linda L. Carnes
Mary Conley
Nancy Connor
Vivian Rae Crowder
Lajuana Dennis
Mary Francis
Patricia Graham
Becky Hart
Ellen Hesson
Barbara Houck
Glenda Howl
Phyllis Deanna King
Sandra Gayle Lemonnier
Mary Mann
Kaye Massey
Marcia Moberg
Laura Paynter
Mary Quinnette
Ruth Rogers
Mattie Ann Scheihing
Ruth Shafer
Archie Thomas
Elizabeth Webb
Lou Wheeler
Linda White
Mary Williams
Marilyn Wilson

1965

Linda Adams
Carolyn Baker
Roger Baumgartner
Karen Kay Black
Judy Bradbury

246

Kathy Butterfield
Janice Chandler
Nancy Collins
Jan Creveling
Karen Curtis
Cindy Davenport
Ann Davis
Kathryn Denny
Sherry Jo Domnick
Sara Downing
Patricia Diane Erbert
Janet Entwistle
Pat Graff
Nancy Hansens
Jill Harris
Vivian Mickle Hawkins
Kyla Hayes
Robert Hollrah
Ann Holmes
Susan Holmes
Patricia Huston
Robert G. Johnson
Bill Loughridge
Judith Ann Meyer
Lawrence Miller
Irene Mires
Sue Otis
Mary Nell Parrott
Sherry Junell Patterson
Mark Peterson
Barbara J. Polk
Terry Lynn Prater
Mary Rabbit
Ruth Rice
Donna Georgene Rowsey
Ann Alice Rumbaugh
Petrina Russo
Mary Jo Sartor
Susie Scarborough
Carolyn Stieferman
Shirley Swinney
Rebecca Tomlin
Patricia Ward
Gail Wood
Elizabeth Woods

1966

Trish Abernathy
Linda Allen
DeAnne Brewster
Carol Byrd
Connie Courtner
Evelyne Doty
Georgianna Drummond
Barbara Duncan
Carol Glahn
Judy Gurley
Judy Herring
Virginia Holt
Jo Ellen Johnson
Sharon McCan
Carolyn McCracken
Carol McCune

Kathy McGlasson
Sarah Mires
Ilene Moore
Mary Newbauer
Janet Piquet
James M. Seals
Jimmie Smith
Connie Staff
Susan Thomas
Linda Wallace
Jayne White
Ruth Wolf

1967

Karen Anderson
Pat Appleby
Dr. Jacob Blankenship
Karen Bone
Judy Brewer
Shirley Callicoat
Judith Crouch
Claire Danielson
Linda DeMoss
Janice Ellison
Jane Ernest
Claire Garnier
Alyson Hall
Brita Hedlund
Lexie Lassley
Jan Love
Wilma Ramming
Mary Rink
Susan Scheffel
Barbara Shell
Sandra Thompson
Diane Tucker

1968

Natalie C. Babcock
Ellen Barnes
Nancy Bradley
Betty Bullard
Myrna Campbell
Jana Cook
Linda Cook
Mary Lou Defratus
Marilyn Dettle
Ramona Duvall
Anna Evans
Billie Fairman
Judy Fears
Janetta Glenn
Hugh H. Guthrie
Pam Heath
Glenda Sue Howell
Norma Kepford
John Kusel
Sandra Lawrence
Shirley Mitchell
Carolyn Niebruegge
Suzanne Ohan

Judith Osborne
Carolyn Patillo
Merry Price
Marsha Rickey
Carol Scott
Charlene Seeback
Kathleen Simmons
DeAnn Stinchcomb
Connie C. Tate
Karen Thomas
Linda Via
Marion White
Sharon Williams

1969

Nancy Albritton
Joanne Alexander
Carol Andrews
Davida Barkley
Ann Belew
Nancy Bollmer
Marilyn Brady
Carol Brazil
Janice Cagle
Jane Carlile
Kay Carter
Pamela Coke
Connie Coonrad
Marilyn Ensch
Dee Ann Garrett
Linda Gillig
Linda Gooch
Sherry Hale
Cheryl Hicks
Kris Holmberg
Karen Huneke
Sharon Johnston
Eileen Kelle
Janet Loomis
Kay Maynard
Merrily Milburn
Jo Ann Myers
Janet Nichols
Martha Parker
Joyce Powers
Deloris Ramsey
Elizabeth Riddle
Kathy Risner
Linda Rose
Linda Smith
Juanita Squire
Carolyn Stephens
Martha Wheatley
Yukio Yokoyama
Paula Young
Carla Young

1970

Toni Adams
Barbara M. Batchelder
Gayle Bicket

Judith F. Bolar
Lynda Lorene Burrow
Royce G. Caldron
Sherry L. Ethridge
Linda Garner
Anne Garrett
Nancy Green
Charla Sue Gulick
Susan M. Howell
Linda L. Jump
Charlotte Ann Kramer
Jan Lale
Katherine Diane Larkey
Linda Sue Lavery
Linda J. Madison
Kathleen S. Mittelstet
Clarice Morris
Jeane Otsuki
Mary A. Parrott
Sandra Jean Partridge
Sherry Arlene Price
Marilyn Proctor
Vivian Reininger Rice
Gail J. Schwamb
Jana L. Scott
Nancy S. Skach
Linda J. Smith
Carolyn Stebbing
Shirley Jean Stout
Sheralyn L. Summers
Cynthia Ann Taylor
Marjorie L. Tytenicz
Dorothy Webb
Neal A. Willison
Rose Marie Yunker

1971

Carol B. Acuff
Katharine E. Alden
Deborah L. Ali
Kay E. Bales
Mary M. Bales
Carol L. Barnett
Kathy Hudson Berry
Mary E. Berryman
Susie Bevins
Catherine Bird
Shirley J. Blair
Kathy Bocox
Danny G. Bohlender
Connie W. Bone
Linda C. Bowling
Betty Ann Bradshaw
Linda Brandenburg
Mary J. Breedlove
Richard M. Brown
Kathleen B. Burdge
Cassandra R. Bynum
Peggy L. Carpenter
Carolyn R. Carter
Charles Edward Cheatham
Linda F. Chitwood
Dianna L. Cole

Judith S. Collins
Jeanne E. Croka
Dorlana J. Crowell
Kathleen E. Currie
Renee Ann Daugherty
Cynthia J. DeBord
Jorge G. De Mello
Juhree V. Dickey
Patricia C. Dollarhide
Jimmie Ann Duncan
Donna J. Emerson
Ruslyn L. Evans
Barbara Sue Fatheree
Charlotte S. Gales
Frederick H. Gesin
Betty S. Gerber
Marcia L. Goff
Janell S. Green
Judith A. Griffin
Barbara A. Hadley
M. Sue Haggard
Peggy A. Hamill
Gail E. Hanna
Janice M. Harris
Deborah A. Herrman
Elizabeth A. Hodges
Kim R. Hogan
Nelda S. Holder
Norma Carole Hornback
Cathy Hronopulos
Brenda J. Hutcheson
Sally R. Hughes
Pamela L. Huntley
Lou Ella Jackson
Jerri A. James
Patricia Gayle Johnson
Judy Kay Judkins
Nancy J. Jung
Carolyn R. Keithline
Lois J. Klinger
Pamela Sue Krittenbrink
Diane Kay Kreie
Rebecca LaBahn
Lelan Ray Lancaster
JoNelle Langdon
Roy W. Leaghty
Jeffrey J. Ledewitz
Cheryl L. Lee
Terri J. Manning
Carol Margaret Manson
Joanne M. Martin
Patricia Martin
Joan L. Mathewson
Catherine J. McClanahan
Julie A. Meyer
Mary Ann Miller
Carmen L. Mitchell
Janet Sue Modin
Nancy E. Murray
Nancy Ann G. Nelson
Nancy A. Paris
Janice F. Pellam
John J. Pennington
Connie B. Perry
Pamela L. Peschl
L. Allen Peterson

Kari A. Pitman
Mike R. Poston
Linda Sue Powers
Sharon L. Price
Paula K. Pritchett
Peggy S. Rennington
Karen G. Ridley
Sharon D. Ridley
Carol L. Rotzinger
Phyllis A. Sams
Pat Schmitz
Lorna A. Seaman
Jeannine Seeds
Elizabeth A. Semtner
Dixie A. Shaw
Rhonda Sue Shedrick
Joel B. Sherrer
Margaret J. Shimanek
Sandra K. Simons
Micki A. Sims
Cheryl K. Smith
E. Relleen Smith
Mary Margaret Smith
Carol A. Snethen
Judy Snodgrass
Cindy Spear
Gayle C. Spencer
Kathy J. Spess
Claudia A. Staerkel
Lee R. Tarrant Jr.
Phyllis A. Tarrant
Leta A. Testerman
Francis E. Thomas
Joyce E. Thomas
Coleen A. Trosper
Juanita J. Tweedy
Abbigail B. Vance
Annette W. Villines
Sharon M. Wade
Nancy C. Ward
Linda S. Wegener
John E. Wente
Judy C. Whitaker
Julia R. White
Linda A. Wilbanks
Sally G. Wilber
Sally Ann Wilcox
Carolyn A. Williams
Paula J. Wilson
Jeffrey A. Yellin
Cathy Jo Young
Mary Alice Wright

1972

Bonnie Sue Aldrich
Pegge L. Alciatore
Anita Kaye Allen
Anita Anderson
Darla K. Armstrong
Allyson Kay Arnold
Charlotte J. Back
Barbara Sue Bagwell
Nancy E. Bagwell

Christie Sue Ballard
Karen K. Barclay
Patricia J. Beall
Jan Bennett
Randy Bernard
Patricia A. Betty
Ardon H. Birdsong
Larry P. Blakley
Brenda Jo Bobo
Kay Merlene Bowers
Susan Brandt
Claudia Malone Burris
Debra Callihan
Janet Castle
Leah Frances Cloud
Mary Suzan Chambers
Rilla Cobb
Beverly Jo Couch
Mildred Ann Cummings
Peggy S. Cummings
Diane Darr
JoAnn Davis
Johnnie A. Davis
Marcia Kay Davis
Cara Ditto
Ellen Kathleen Dolan
Eunice Kathleen Driskel
Martha Joan Drus
Linda Louise Dungan
Sherri Durham
Sandra M. Dupire
Susan Denise Dyer
Teresa Early
Ada Louise Eason
Nellene Eldridge
David V. Elijah Jr.
Barbara Ann Endicott
Beth Ann Fenimore
Barbara Ann Fischer
Charlotte Fischer
Wanda J. Fite
Tina K. Flanagan
Gloria Flanagin
Mary Kay Friels
Jack I. Fryrear
Carolyn Sue Gang
Michele Ladean Garrett
Marilyn Sue Garrison
Patricia Ann Garrison
Julie Gater
Mary Jo Gerdes
Mary Irene Gettys
Phyllis Giacomo
Patricia Gayle Gilchrest
Jean Gillham
Peggy Glass
Mary Helen Glenn
Marsha Graham
Barbara Gray
Connie L. Greb
Inez Grider
Virginia Ann Guild
Rebecca Lou Gum
Jolene Hadley
Helen J. Hager
Jan Harris

Molly Maurine Harris
Gary Harrold
Charles E. Heerman
William E. Hodges
Janet Leigh Hoeltzel
Mark Huckby
Edna Huffman
Deborrah Huggins
Cleta C. Hulett
Linda K. Humphry
Janice Hutchins
Gail A. Jared
Janice Sue Jennings
Jan Adelle Jones
Jennifer L. Kamphaus
Catherine M. Kehe
Nancy Bettis Kirby
Deborah Sue Klinger
Bettie Jo Knight
Jane Anne Knoblock
Donna M. Kucera
Christine Marie Kunkel
Patricia Ann Lackey
Janice Landgraf
Mary V. Laurence
Donna M. Le
Susan Letzig
Barbara J. Lewis
Janet Llyn Listen
Marilyn K. Lockridge
Judy C. Love
Mary H. Mack
Kathy Lyn Mackey
Catherine M. Mader
Laneta Joy Mann
Judith K. Massey
Kathy Maxwell
Janis Lynn Mayberry
Cathy E. McCart
Kay McClain
Venus McCoy
Carol McGehee
Judith McGhay
Joanna L. McHugh
Cheryl Lynne McKay
Sheila Ann McKinney
Darla Milburn
Marilyn Claire Mitchell
Bobbie Jeanne Mollett
Franna Kay Moore
Teresa Ann Moore
Marsha Murphy
Martha Ruth Murphy
Jeannie Muzik
Nancy Sue Naurath
Patricia Ellen Neel
Janice L. Noller
Deborah O'Brien
Patsy Ruth Oliver
Ann Patterson
Frieda Pearce
Jack Lynn Perkins
Lynell Jean Petersen
Mary F. Podpechan
Judy Polson
Dannie W. Powell

Beth Renee Randall
Judy Kay Reed
Mary Jane Reedy
Katherine S. Riddle
Rachael E. Riddle
Clayton Wayne Rogers
Glenda Kay Rogers
Justina Jan Rohrer
Joy S. Roswell
Barbara Sauer
Linda J. Schafer
Catherine R. Scherler
Wayne Schmedt
E. M. Schmidt
Mary Schlegel
Jo Ann Seely
Nelda Shafer
Terry Dee Shriver
Diane Smith
Rhonda Smith
Susan Amner Smith
Janet Sorenson
Preston O. Stanley
Deborah Lou Swan
Sherry Jean Swearingen
Debra K. Teofel
Carolyn Sue Thomas
Deborah A. Thomson
Burton Duwayne Thurman
Jackie Sue Tolle
Sheryl Trout
Mary J. Tucker
Marvin Turney
Susan Lee Wagnon
Janice Kay Walters
Linda Jean Wegener
Tim J. Wells
Jane Weingartner
Susie Whitworth
Linda Diane Wickham
Susan Lee Willhour
Donna Kay Williams
Monetha June Williams
Shirley Ann Williams
Linda Diane Willoughby
Laura Chase Winters
Birda Carol Wirth
Anabele Witcher
Christine Yasik

1973

Liz Acton
Kathy Albright
Marsha Ann Alexander
Carol Allton
Sherry Amos
Candice Anderson
Carl R. Anderson
Kim B. Anderson
Larry Anderson
Cathy Arment
Carol Armour
Larry Gene Bain

Karen Jeanne Bachle
Anja Lee Baldwin
Hannah Banks
Linda Woodring Barnes
Janet Lee Bateman
Joyce E. Bates
Lee Ann Beaver
Vernon L. Beebe
Barbara Behrens
Jan Ellen Berry
David Beshear
Dwana Diane Biggs
Patricia Z. Bittle
Elizabeth Ann Black
Frances Blickenstaff
Kay Boman
Mary Louise Bomaros
Arthur Booth
Jane Morgan Bost
Cheryl Ann Bower
Janice Bradley
Burton Fred Brandt Jr.
Mary Katherine Brehm
Jeanie Brooks
Denise Brown
Christi Lan Brownback
Cynthia S. Brunqardt
Michaele Buell
Judith Alison Burdge
Cynthia A. Burnett
Guy Burnett Jr.
Peggy Ray Burrus
Joce C. Butler
Verlan M. Butler
James Callison
Nancy Carpenter
Cheri Catherine
Matthu Churchill
Constance Clayton
Mary Clement
Harold D. Codding
Sherry D. Coleman
Kathy Jean Copeland
Patrick O. Cox
Linda Kay Craig
Phyllis Crawford
Barbara Cunningham
Jan Ette Dahms
Susan J. Davett
Rhonda Davis
Mary Jo Dickinson
Mark Stanley Dobson
Susan Drehmer
Vicki Lynn Duncan
Jann Earley
Ralph Ellis
Margaret Jean Ellis
Rosalyn June Elms
Jeri Jo Elliott
Debra Enmeier
Karen Trese Ericksen
Linda Kay Evans
Kristie S. Evans
Ted Evicks
Chris Faulkner
Julia Franklin

Mia M. Feighther
Cynthia Fentem
Lynn Field
Becky Furgason
Jolene Galloway
Kathy Gamble
Deborah Kay Garrett
Elnora G. Gardner
Cindy Glenn
Rebecca J. Glenn
Marsha Grace
Larry Grantz
Janice Graves
Connie Dean Hack
Carol Haliburton
Kathryn Hallford
Levonia Hamilton
Debbie Hamlin
Patsy Ann Hardin
Anne Marilyn Hardy
Lisa Harms
Mary Lynn Harris
Benna Kay Hastings
Denice Kay Haworth
Debra Haynie
Rhonda A. Hays
Linda Heizer
Mary F. Heller
Brenda Janelle Helms
Patti Henneke
Carolyn Jane Hill
Linda Holden
Peggy Holman
Deborah J. Hughes
Helena Hutton
Paula Kay Ihle
Susie Inman
Cheryl Ann Jackson
M. Jan Jackson
Debra S. James
Mary M. Johnson
Marjory M. Jones
Peter Alan Kaufman
Deborah Kidd
Lee Ann Kilpatrick
Susan Kimbrough
Pamela Kindschi
Sondra Kraemer
Kathy Kraft
Roberta Krismer
Shirley LaDuke
Peter W. Lander
James Law
Lisa Lawrence
Stacy L. Lee
Alane LeGrand
Gaye Leslie
Paula Lewis
Linda Lilly
Patty Linn
Nancy Marie Jones London
Pamela Jean Magee
Marilyn Malcom
Janice M. Marsh
Sheri Ratliff Martens
Joe Martin

Stanley Gene Maseley
Erlene McAllister
Karen McCracken
Sheryl L. McCreight
Lelia L. McGuire
Marsha Kay McIntyre
Melissa McKee
Donna A. McMillin
Susan J. McPherson
Mary Elizabeth Mertens
Cynthia E. Miller
Linda Miller Rhonda Miller
Steven J. Miller
Don Mooneyham
Jane Eleanor Morgan
Joan Eileen Morgan
Pam Morgan
Karen T. Morris
Katherine F. Morris
Benjamin Mullinix
Anita M. Musshafen
Diana L. Newman
Glenna Gay Ott
Janice L. Overby
Joyce Uly Panos
Ronald G. Paquette
Merrye Angela Parker
Susan Annell Parks
Janet Patton
Melinda Paul
Nancy Talley Payne
Kathryn E. Pelton
Barbara L. Peterson
Carl R. Phelps
Nannette Pope
Carol Pottebaum
Linday Faye Pratt
Carol Proctor
Sherry Rader
Terry Rader
Tamara Rains
Julie K. Randel
Troy Reavis
William R. Richardson
Alisha Ann Richey
Teresa Ann Ripley
Donora G. Rippy
Rebecca Kaye Robertson
Sandra Rogers
Janet Rohde
Carole Russell
Kathy E. Savage
Cynthia Sawatzky
Orene Schurter
Deborah Sears
Emilie Shelton
Alice Jane Simmons
Allison Sinclair
Dale Sinclair
Susan Smallwood
Betty Shaha Spann
Rosemary Spradlin
Debbie Lynn Stark
Tom Steen
Evelyn Steichen
Pam Stewart

Elizabeth Ann Stout
Jacquilyn Sue Strain
Nancy Strickland
Karen L. Tarrant
Susan L. Taylor
Carol Jo Teel
Sue Lynn Teel
Becky Terbush
Teresa Thompson
Carl Tiemann
Carolyn Tiner
Patricia Tripp
Katherine Troutman
Steve Vester
Nora J. Vinson
Linda Wade
Donna Carole Ward
Connie Warren
Carol Washburn
Gary R. Winters
Merlin Witt
Samuel Joseph Wylie
Jeane W. Yates

1974

Anita Claire Anderson
Hannah Lourinda Banks
Mellanie La Baron
Glynden McCulloh Bode
Louise Bowers
Denise J. Carmichael Brown
Joyce Calvin Butler
Janet Lee Castle
Linda Faye Craft
Janet Cundiff
Deborah Jo Davis
Patricia Gail Gilchrist
Rebecca A. Furgason Gordon
Patricia Grummer
Guy Burnett Jr.
Martha Joan Krus
Susan Neff Letzing
Earlene Brimmer McAllister
Susan Ann McKee
Dianna Mendenhall
Darla Kay Milburn
Anita Marie Musspafen
Cynthia S. Norcom
Susan Annell Parks
Barbara Ann Patterson
Pamela Sue Pennington
Marinee G. Engel Perkins
Lynell Jean Petersen
Nyla Ptomey
Cheryl L. Wilco Schuermann
Rhonda S. Carpenter Smith
Ruth Arline Spurgeon
Sandra Kay Styve
Karen Louise Tarrant
Rebecca Ralene Turbush
Cynthia Ann Vanderventer
Cecilie Walker
Diana Wallace
Donna Carole Ward

Jeri Lynn Werneke
Deborah Kay Wright

1975

Susan C. Milliren Adams
Virginia Carol Allen
Cathy Anderson
Nancy L. Thompson Antle
Patricia Atkins
Paula Gene Bake
Deborah Balint
Mary L. Stone Barnosky
Catherine Ann Beck
Paula Jean Bembrook
Deborah Ann Benedicts
Pamela S. Pennington Benne
Nina Marie Billingsley
Rita Michele Brewer
D. Ann Bruton
William T. Bryant
Linda Buffa
Linda Lou Burnett
Brenda Kay Burrow
Jeanine Butcher
Deborah Lois Calame
Renae Louise Campbell
Nancy Leigh Cannon
Mary Janet Cannon
Christie Kaye Clayborn
Lana Adell Corr
Cheryl J. Cottrell
Bobbi L. Sexson Cowherd
Mercedier Cunningham
Connie Sue Czirr
Nancy Ann Delano
Margaret Anne Dow
Marilyn Jean Dupy
Norma Eaues
Debi Eddington
Linda C. Eisenhauer
Cheryl Ann Elias
Cynthia Lynn England
Norma Kathryn Fearnow
Jo Ellen Finimore
Jane Ellen Gertsen
Carol Anne Gibson
Kathryn Ann Goins
Susan Lynn Haley
Patti Hamm
Robyn Jon Harrison
Sue Hensley
Mary K. Hill
Janet Hofmann
Carol Ann Hoyle
Barbara Huber
Sheila D. Mears Hueste
Linda Johansen
Nancy L. Johnson
Janet Lee Johnson
Donald George Wentroth Jr.
Marilyn Jean Kennedy
Christine Marie Kessler
Janice Kilgore
Barbara Kirby

Linda Suzanne Lane
Vicki Laughter
Jody Johnson Long
Deborah Dawn Long
Elizabeth Ann Lucas
Mary Kevin Mahan
Barbara Cheryl Mainers
John P. Maley
Lu Ann Marshall
Judith Ann McMasters
Susan L. Blose Mongon
Linda Geraldine Morrissey
Brenda G. Morrissey
Barbara Morton
Rebecca Sue Morton
Stacey Ellen Mulholland
Patricia Ann Neely
Mellanie Ellen Nelson
Alberta Joan Nightengale
Kathryn Ann Nobles
Lynn S. Novak
Fred E. Oliver
Lynda Jean Oltmann
Lizbeth Kay Oyler
Donna Suzanne Phelps
Nancy Lynn Phillips
Becky Sue Pieratt
Paula Faye Plater
Laura Lynne Poole
Rebecca Lynn Prado
Kathryn Ann Prickett
Jo Ann Reynolds
Carol Riddle
Linda Sue Robertson
Pamela Katherine Rose
Carrie Rouk
Lanellda Frances Rufner
Pamela Joyce Scheidt
Ramona Ellis Scifres
Nikki Jean Seay
Patricia Claire Smith
Karen P. Snow
Cheryl Stevens
Cathy A. Strong
Darrell Wayne Swaim
Cindy June Taylor
Nancy Ruth Thomas
Beverly Jayne Tinsley
Stacey Joann Tomlinson
Katherine Margaret Trentham
Barbara Jan Underhill
Janet Walker
Robert Dale West
Jan Ellen Wilkerson
James Daniel Wiltsey
Karen Windmer
Melodie Ann Wingo
Mary Tamara Woodring
Cheryl Jane Wyatt

1976

Carol Abernathy
Kathy Lee Angel
Deborah Bacher

Sheryl Sue Baird
Ramona Lynn Barker
Teresa Lynn Barret
Betty Barton
Verna Lois Bateman
Vicky L. Beck
Ann Morris Bentley
Deborah E. Blackwell
Johnette Susan Bolene
Hope I. Boling
Pamela Marisa Bracy
Kristi Ann Bredel
Sandra Kay Brewer
Donna Bricker
Elizabeth Jayne Burns
Patti C. Buschner
Teresa A. Byrd
George Neal Campbell
Petra Carpenter
Melva Jo Whitson Carroll
Karen Lee Cartwright
Cynthia Patrick Cassiday
Christy Kay Clark
Karel Ann Clark
Sandra Clark
Karen Sue Coate
Sandra Lee Coker
Linda Marie Courtney
Glee Dale
Pamela Jo Davis
Dana Dayton
Louise DeVerges
Terease Summers Dewitt
Deborah Louise Drake
Suzanne Carol Durossette
Jimmy Dean Everett
Patricia Diane Evans
Helen Mary Eylar
Cheryl W. Ferguson
Susan E. John Ford
Kay Fry
Charlotte Ann Haugh Galloway
M. Elaine Gardner
Bernadine June Gates
Deborah Jean Glover
Christa Kay Goad
Janet Sue Goertz
Debbie Graybill
Linda Gayle Green
Joseph Nathan Greene III
Kim Jean Grunwald
Patricia Guillaume
Robin Lea Hadlock
Bernadette Delores Hague
Vonda Arlene Hamm
Sandra Yvonne Hardy
Anita Kay Harris
Jane Adele Hite
Patricia Henrick
Robin Ann Hessel
Bill Hindman
Scott Hininger
Genell Ann Hooper
Mark C. Howard
Steva Hromas
Evelynn Arleen James

Clifton Johnson
Deborah Kay Johnston
Janice Jones
Carla Jean Jordon
Cheryl Lea Kallenberger
Rose Marie Karleskint
Pauline Kelley
Wanda Diane Kienholz
Floyd Kirk
Melissa Ann Kirk
Susanna Koesler
Donna Kay Kruta
Ruby Lancaster
Susan Langford
Cindy Ledford
Lisa Love
Brenda Martin
Margaret Weiss Massie
Deborah Louise McDaniel
Teresa Ann McGuinness
Mary Meibergen
Janelle Meredity
Deborah Lynn Monroe
Holly Montgomery
Debra Lee Moreland
Lori Morrisey
Barbara Brents Morton
Deborah A. Fuller Moses
Deborah G. Lacy Musick
Ann Neely
Kathy Nelson
Jane Newton
Lu Ellen Norman
DeAnne Marie Nunnelee
Nancy Sue Osborn
Susan Denise Patterson
Billy Dean Pettitt
Victoria Jean Phillips
Vicky Ann Polk
Janet Porter
Virginia Sue Prather
Nancy R. Provine
Stacy Stierwalt Pugh
Cynthia Ann Pyles
Patrick Ray
Roger L. Reavis
Gregory Wayne Reed
Linda Richardson
Peggy Joyce Rieger
Kathryn Ann Roberts
Cindy Robertson
Martha Rupp
Maxine Anderson Rypkema
Sheila Kay Sams
Nancy Heinzer Sandstrum
Karen Schnaithman
Margaret Ann Schwenker
Barbara Jean Scott
Connie Self
Vicki Setser
Pamela Sue Shaffer
Lynette Sherman
Carol Jean Simmons
Jamie Marilyn Slade
James Charles Smith IV
Keith Smith

Richard Leon Stafford
Paula K. Barnes Starr
Margaret Ann Steel
Carol Steichen
Vicki Steinley
Vicki Sue Stevens
Charlotte Gayle Stewart
Kerry D. Abernathy Stewart
Jacqueline Ann Stone
Patti A. Stubbs
Patricia Sue Stuever
Jannie Sumpter
Marcia Lynn Taylor
Vincent Norman Terrill
Sandra Joyce Thomas
Jennifer Townsend
Karen Timmons Trivitt
Janet Lynn Turcott
Linda Kay Voelkers
James R. Wall
Nancy J. Walker
Nina Kathleen Walker
Sally Rebecca Walker
Sara Lee Walker
Susan Warmker
Valleri Kim Washburn
Jeree Luan Welch
Pamela Jo White
Susan White
Nita K. Whitmire
Debbie Williams
Nancy L. Willson
Diane Elizabeth Wilson
Gretchen I. Wilson
Emily Wonderly
Linda Diane Wright

1977

Craig P. Acuff
Junel Adams
Donna Alloway
Sheila Amason
Carolyn Anthis
Ronald G. Area
Jeanne Austin
Kathy Bain
Janet N. Baker
William D. Baker
Chapel Petty Barnes
Laurie J. Barr
Beth Batchelor
Joan Bell
Dale Bettes Jr.
Cathryn Kelley Bluethman
Rachel Bess
Blaine A. Billman
Cherilyn Blakemore
Jimmie Sue Blase
La Nora Bloom
Randall Bodenhamer
Rebecca A. Bostian
Julee Bounds
Jackie L. Boyle
Naola J. Bradley

Rita Brawdy
Brenda R. Bridenstine
Cynthia K. Brinkmeyer
Dianna Brintmall
Amy L. Brown
David B. Brown
David W. Brown
Richard S. Brown
Karen Burdick
Marilyn Burns
Ann M. Butler
Patsy Carpenter
Janice Carroll
Beverly D. Carter
Marilynn M. Chestnut
Ramona T. Clark
Sandra Clayborn
Pamela S. Collins
Nina R. Collins
Eleni Collins
Nancy L. Combest
Karla Combs
Nancy JoAnn Combs
Mary E. Conkling
Robert L. Conners
John Paul Cook
Diane E. Cooper
Richard Verne Coop
Steve Cowden
Nadine D. Cravello
Mary Sue Howard Craven
Patricia E. Cullins
Paul Czarniecki
Dixie Lee Dale
Laura F. Day
Marilyn D. Deal
Susan Deberry
David G. Delker
Terry Denzler
Nancy L. Dilbeck
Harrell Donaldson
Martha S. Dotson
Mary F. Duffe
Michael E. Duncan
Mary A. Eaton
Nancy Lee Eddleman
Barbie Edwards
Laurie Lin Erner
Brenda Sue Neer Evans
Diana Farmer
Loretta Fauchier
Jeffrey P. Feuguay
Karen Fisher
Cynthia K. Floyd
Joseph A. Ford
Cecilia Frey
Victoria Fullick
Michael Garrett
Doug Gentz
Shirley A. Gibbs
Robert Berry Gibson
Sara J. Glidewell
Deborah Gottschalk
Ronda Hadwiger
Meredith Ann Hames
Norma Harmon

Johnny Harp
Margaret Heisey
Kay Hellen
Janet Henderson
Sandra J. Henley
Tom Herrin
Mary Kay Herzfeld
Debra J. Hickey
Lisa A. Hoefler
Arthur F. Hoffman
Debra J. Holbrook
Rebecca J. Holt
Catherine Hostetter
Susan Houk
Angelic Huckleberry
Rhonda Ingham
Belinda K. Jackson
Constance D. Jackson
Mary F. Jackson
Karen Jacobs
Joanne M. Jamieson
Douglas Jech
Dana Rae Jencks
Sheldona Jennings
Elizabeth A. Johnson
Paul W. Jolly
Mary Anne Joslin
Karen B. Keck
Cari Jane Keith
Stanley S. Keller
Kim Bea Kennery
Jerelyn Kidd
Gayla Marie Kienholz
Sandina Robin Kinzie
Lisa Kirkpatrick
Dorthy Kizziar
Joyce Kleidon
Ronald Koehn
Gayla L. Kubecka
Katharine A. Lambring
Imogene L. Land
Virginia Lawrence
Ruth Ann Lenz
Kathleen J. Leithner
Margaret Lienhart
Martha A. Lindley
Walter J. Litwin
Llyn M. Lofgren
Kenneth L. Londot
Anne H. Loughridge
Ernest G. Lowden
Robert Lowrey
William K. Luster
Brenda K. Lynem
Viola L. Madrid
Ann Elaine Mann
Mary C. Mannering
Cindy Lee Marshall
Jimmy D. Mason
Latricia Kay White Mason
Marcia Kim Mathews
Ida Maxwell
Jeanne McClain
Tereasa McClure
Beverly M. McNew
Marinell McPherson

Yvonne K. Mears
Barbara A. Miller
Lori Suzanne Mills
Sarah Mitchell
Brenda Montgomery
James D. Moran III
Greg Y. Charles Mosier
Elizabeth Murphy
Dal Newberry
Lummy L. Newberry
Jean Newcomer
Priscilla J. Nichols
Maria T. Nievez
Nancy Lea Norman
Susan Norvell
Cynda Rae Overton
Tamara C. Overton
Janice Owsley
Lloyd E. Page
Susan Elizabeth Pansza
Mariana P. Parks
Julie B. Pate
Mary Payne
Robin Peden
Kim Pendleton
Ginger Perry
Kimi Sue Pranger
Debora A. Price
Judith Queen
Rebecca Raburn
Nancy Lee Reeves
Kathy Rhoades
Dana Lea Rice
Susan Richardson
Jana L. Ritz
Rhoda Rix
Patricia J. Roberson
Brenda P. Roberts
Sheri Diane Roberts
Alfred C. Robertson
Beverly Robertson
Edna Ladell Robinson
Ellen Rainwater Robison
Nancy Rogers
Vicki E. Rogers
Patricia Jo Rose
Janice Rowe
Linda Russell
Nancy Ruzicka
Mary R. Sampson
Janet Marie Saubert
Dena C. Scott
Janet Scott
Kay Scruggs
Cynthia Segress
Gwen E. Shaw
Jeanetta C. Shipp
Paula A. Shyrock
Anne Elizabeth Shull
Susan Marie Shull
Cheryl Dean Siever
Kimberlee Simon
Kathy L. Sims
Sandra Elaine Singleton
Julia Ann Slankard
Tom S. Smith

Barbara E. Snyder
Barbara Louise Sober
Barbara Ann Soerries
Virawan C. Sombutsiri
Pamela Ann Sparks
Susan Spillar
Melissa Stephenson
Mary Bernadette Stolfa
Keela Louise Stow
Mike Stroud
Tana L. Stubblefield
Kathy Sullivan
Kathie L. Swang
Iris E. Terre
Susan Thomas
Susan E. Thornberry
Nancy M. Tooker
Leigh Ann Travas
Emma R. Tusing
Debra Utsler
Diana L. Vest
Eddie T. Velasquez
Connie Jo Voigt
Laurie Walker
Jodine Ward
Fred R. Warford
Beverly Sue Watts
Julane Watts
Jessica Lee Wilkinson
Delise Ann Williams
Ellen Willims
Gene R. Wollenberg
Willa C. Wood
M. Catherine Woodrell
Suzanne Woodrou
Kathleen Woods
John H. Woodyard
Kerry Lynn Youngblood
Cruz D. Zambrano

1978

Jana Ackerman
Sue Allen
L. Carol Alexander
Rachel Anderson
Rhonda Angham
Margaret R. Armbruster
Deborah Asling
Sherri Babber
Stephen R. Baker
Larry L. Barker
Betty Jane Barnes
Brenda Kay Carr Barnes
Nita Barnes
Rhonda L. Barnes
William G. Barnett
Patricia Ann Barr
Michael J. Bayouth
Alvin Beadles
Valerie Beesley
Laura Bentley
Denise Johnson Binkley
Clarence Bones
Kristin Jane Bowers

Melinda C. Boyer
Laura S. Brodersen
Lois A. Brodersen
Lorene Brooks
Melia Brown
Wayne Brown
Edwina Jean Browning
Mike Bundy
Paula Butler
Ruth Carnagey
Cindy Carris
Marla Cavanaugh
Patricia Chaffino
Jana Chambless
Debra Chizmar
Michael Clagg
Sandy Clapp
George R. Clift
Stephanie Coates
Kent Collins
Bruce Cook
Melinda Copley
Sandra L. Cottom
Mary Saen Coyle
Mary Jo Crawford
Janice L. Creider
Margaret Crouse
Patricia Cullens
Karon Cunningham
Bob Cypert
Oanh Kim Dao
Debra Davis
Esther Davis
Jana Kay Davis
Janet Dixon
Jandra Dustina
Carolyn Eaton
Pam English
Charlotte Evans
Jayne Evans
Betsey Farbro
Victoria Fellick
Jaylene Ferda
Jana Ferguson
Henry Adams Finch
Sheila Foxworthy
Jacquetta Francis
Catherine Gandy
Melissa Garland
Sanda Garret
Fariborz Ghavidel
Sabrina Gregory
Kathy Gubas
Roxanne Hadwiger
Sally Haines
Linda Margaret Hanes
Ruth Ann Hardesty
Marianne Harding
Kay Harris
William Harwood
Elizabeth Hansen Hatcher
Kathy Lynn Henderson
Charles R. Hendon
Kay Henry
Kay Hillin
Carley Ann Horst

Ashley Hutchinson
Andy Inman
Kim Iverson
Kelly James
Karen Johnson
Paula Jones
Susan Leroyce Jones
Marlene Kauffman
Roberta Kelley
Jackie Kific
Mark Kirk
Leon S. Kot Jr.
Ginna L. Krietmeyer
Richard Kuerstow
Karen Lamport
Sherri Ledford
Meredith Legako
Charlotte Leven
Ellen MacKinnon
Elizabeth Marler
Kim Mathews
Roy Mathews
Greg McCorty
Kent McKinley
Terry J. Moody
Jim Moran
Maria Mottola
Tamara Moyer
Vicki Neck
Thomas Newton
Jonna Nordquist
Cynthia Opperude
Marion Paden
Cheryl Perring
Michael Phillips
Margaret Pickrell
Kimi Pranger
Regina L. Randall
Laurle Redefer
Jim T. Reese
Jeannine Richardson
Margaret Riggs
Cindy Ringeisen
Michael Thomas Rizor
Robin Roberts
Patricia Lynn Ross
Judith Rynders
Susan Sachau
Charyl T. Safley
Mary Elizabeth Sampson
Ray E. Sanders
Janet Sauzjers
Teresa Lynne Shaffer
James Simpson
Sharon Slater
John L. Smith
Lori Smith
Roger M. Smith
Betsy Snell
Donna Snider
Judy Snyder
Robert Louis Spinks
Curtis L. Stanford
Lisa Carol Stanley
Danette Stoops
Phyllis Anne Stratton

Billy Tom Strickland
Paul Stuart
Michael Sumner
Billie Taylor
Debbie Teeples
Annete Johnson Thomason
Kathy Ulmer
Marie Underwood
Sally Utley
Paula Waddill
Mary Ann Walker
Patricia Wayman
Dana Rae Jencks Weidner
Debra White
Delise Williams
Sherri Williams
Linda Jane Wilson
Ellen Wiltons
Jennifer Winborn
Tony Wisley
Carol Wood
Susan Woodruff
Tamara Jeanne Zoebel

1979

Denise M. Abrams
Debra S. Adams
Sherril Anderson
Ronda L. Andrews
Nancy Diane Ayres
Susan Marie Bailey
Teresa Leigh Baker
Phil Ball
Suzanne Biggs
Deloris Black
Sheryl Ann Blaser
Susan Boyd
Joan Juanita Breshears
Kim Brock
Becki S. Brown
Sandra Burson
Marrene Burton
Lillie Cary
Philip Caskey
Nancy Childress
Kathy Sue Clark
Marcia L. Cobb
Gail Cochenour
Lisa J. Courtney
Beverly B. Crawford
Donna E. Croy
Tracy Colene Culp
John M. Cummins
Deborah Damme
James Deals
Jill DeBerry
Cheryl L. DeMoss
Stacey A. Denzler
Robin Dodson
Jan Lee Drummond
Linda Wolf Dunn
Kathye Easley

Julie Elm
Linda Kay Elsom
Kimberly Elwell
Elsa Escobar
Sharon Evans
Steve Evans
Karen Marie Ferrero
Linda Ferrell
Cathy Anita Ford
Gail Ford
Linda J. Foster
Mary E. Freeman
Carol Fugate
Lesa J. Gadberry
Frances Gage
Kathy S. Gallagher
Marylee B. Golliver
Harold E. Goodman
Holly Greiner
Cheryl Anne Hannah
Janet Harrington
Maxwell J. Harrison
Perry Hassell
Jerry D. Hayes
Cynthia Lee Head
Evelyn L. Hearn
Connie L. Helfenbein
Julie A. Hellman
Clement R. Henderson
Melissa L. Heston
Michael Hignite
Joanne Hill
Lynda Jane Hill
Beverly Ann Hinkle
Teresa Jean Hockett
Teressa Jean Hulsey
Geraldine Ikerd
Martha J. Imel
Tamara K. Irwin
Rosa M. Jackson
Tamra Jackson
Verna Kay Kelly
Kristi Kretchmar
Kruetzer, Kristi
Lloyd B. Lacy
Jody Beth Lawson
Dale R. Lightfoot
Patricia B. Logan
Kellianne Lowrey
Diana L. Mackie
Nancy Maddux
Marilyn Martin
William B. McAllister
Barbara McLaughlin
Vicki Laughter McNeil
Lesa Means
Debra Medley
Catherine Ann Michaelis
Susan L. Moffatt
Jacqueline Molloy
Marcia Myers
Kay Neathery
Mary C. Noble
Julia B. Olvera
David K. Parrack
Charlene Parker

Elisabeth A. Patrick
Patricia Pazoureck
Patti Pearcy
Teresa Jo Phipps
Jane Pingleton
Kathryn Reeder
D'Ann Rexwinkle
Linda Rhoten
Mark Robertson
Tara Roderick
LaQuita E. Ruckman
Eydie Jo Russell
Michele Scheffe
Jana Seitsinger
Betty Selakovich
Cynthia S. Smith
Debra Sue Smith
Norma Smith
Tina Spavital
Carolyn Steinmetz
Rebecca Sykora
Rita Sue Taylor
Terri Louise Theis
Linda L. Thompson
Reese H. Todd
Sherri L. Troub
Peggy Dowman Turner
Judie Varnum
Shawna Walters
Jacqueline Wann
Jaye Michelle Warner
Gary Washington
Luanne Sewell Waters
Terri Jo Weir
Rhonda Wesson
Cathy White
Celeste White
Susan Rea Williams
Patricia A. Wilton
Katherine Yates Wright
Cheryl Zavodny

1980

Phillip Abernathy
Rinda Abernathy
Deborah Ellen Barton
Grace Berlin
Viola Kay Berry
Dana Janell Biggs
Kevin Biller
Sandra Bleer
Darla Bock
Judith Lynn Boyer
Debra Ann Bradley
Annette Louise Brorsen
Tamra Lynn Brown
Kathy Buchanan
Jennifer Bullock
Maribeth Burns
Julie Butler
Cindy Ann Caffey
Connie Campbell
Kayla Campbell

Nancy Carleton
Tami Clinton
Touri A. Clinton
Collette Cotter
Jan Best Courtwright
Mary Jane Criner
Veronica Cuellar
Kathy Daily
Daren Dale
Sherri Lynn Dean
Jana DeBoard
Stacey Dinzler
Melanie Dunn
Paula Lynn Fine
Cynthia Flannery
Debbie Sue Fry
Teresa Ann Fugate
Julie Gelmers
Carolyn Annette Griffith
Carolyn Haberland
Rhonda Hall
Lynette Harney
Linda Hart
Tressia Harvey
Rusty Haynes
Peggy Heath
Martha Herrman
Stephanie Hershberger
Joyce Meyer Hickman
Anita Marie Holley
Dena L. Holman
Sharon Beth Howard
Paula Huff
Teressa Hulsey
Lisa Lynn Hunsley
John Hurlburt
Beth Jackson
Rita Marie Jacobi
Carolyn Johnson
Lisa McClure Johnston
Tammie Sue Keeton
Kathy Elaine Kelley
Laura King
Kimberly Lamunyon
Terri Landeen
Lorraine LeMaster
Janelle Levalley
Denice Lynn Long
Donna Spencer Long
Janet K. Longan
Tamyra Mahoney
DeeAnn Mannering
Janice Martin
Deborah Mason
Janet McElwain
Joanne McEwene
Barbara McFadden
Terri McKee
Jonella Melton
Linda Diane Newman
Lori Lyn Niesen
Stacy Nolte
Susan Darlene Norwood
Joanne Olson
Glyndia Dell O'Neal
Judy Olvera

Christine Oppegard
Regina Charlene Orr
Donna S. Parmer
Denixe Paxton
Karen Peterson
Gary Pinkerton
George Renison
Mary Ann Rieger
Kathryn Ritchie
Joy Helen Russell
Christia Sodowsky
Lisa Diane Southall
Nary Stark
Laura Ann Stephens
Angela M. Stevens
Susan Merlyn Swinney
Linda Taylor
Kathleen Marie Themer
Lisa Tillman
Shelly Vassella
Susan Ward
Jane Ellen Watson
Carol Welch
Dolores Wickman
Catherine Wilkerson
Johelen Wilson
Kim Wilson
MaryJo Wilson
James Gerald Winnard
Susana Winney
Rose Ann Winters
Diane Wittrock
Alicia Gail Woods

1981

Carol Ahmad
Martha Albin
Becky Allgood
Cheryl Angelo
Joan Barrick
Cynthia Baucom
Carey Beatty
Luisa Biaggi
Darla Hill Black
Mona Boydston
Garry Bowyer
Steve Brannon
Cynthia Briggs
Amy Burkhalter Brown
Elizabeth Brown
Sheila Brown
Tracy Bruch
Beth Bullis
Kim Burkitt
Joan Burns
Yvonne Carmichael
Carol Clark
Brent Core
Katherine Lynn Corning
Cindy Corr
J. Alan Cunningham
Melanie Daniel
Kim Dargen

Lisa Dauphin
Susan Dodson
Mary Margaret Dolman
Ellen Dubois
Linda Farlow
David Leo Fischer
Lori Freeze
Charlotte Gilbert
Christi K. Gilbert
Deborah Gill
Karen Gilliam
Jack Gorczyca
Valerie Green
Cynthia Griffith
Darrell Gwartney
Laura Jean Gwinn
Melanie Gwinn
Elizabeth Hall
Susan Hanna
Patricia Haraughty
Bennette Harris
Carolyn R. Harris
Jawana Harris
Tracey Harris
Spirl Loy Hawkins
James Edward Helker
Sally Hill
Emily Hubber
Lori Hughes
Behrooz Jahanshahi
Patricia Jaynes
Jen Ann Jones
Carol Kackley
Rhonda Kammeyer
Vijit Kanungsukkasem
Patricia Karpuk
Catherine Kerr
Jana Lynn Kincaid
Nancy Kathryn Knight
Catherine Kohout
Susie Kramer
Melisa Ladd
Brenda Lyons
Ann Malcolm
Donna Maloy
Beverly Gail Mayes
Dan McCaghren
Sharon Lee McGrath
Deborah Kay McTaggart
Eleanor Meeker
Kay Moore
Steven Moran
Kerry Morford
Catherine Morgan
Terri Mullins
Kim Musick
Monica Neville
Kimberly Nickel
Robin Orendorff
Nilsa Ortiz
Dori Partain
Stephen Peterson
Gerry Pinkston
Bob Powell
Carolyn Reilly
Mary Reinhard

Nilda Reyes
Melissa Ann Rother
Denver Sasser
Lisa Scott
Helen Seely
Susan Shelton
Nancy Shepherd
Roberta Shipley
Nilavan Sinchanitas
Marlene Smith
Phyllis Sokolosky
Susan Sullivan
Ladonna Stebbins
Laura Stephens
Linda Taylor
Rosemary Thigan
Pam Tinney
Billie Tower
Jani Tripp
Deborah Ullom
Kathleen Walker
Margaret Wamptar
Sherry Weathers
Maxine Weber
Kim Westfahl-Jech
Debbie Whiteneck
Lori Whitfield
Kelly Willams
Sheila Wisherd

1982

Donna Lynn Bailey
Patricia Luann Barbree
Shan Rene Bennett
Mary Elizabeth Bledsoe
Kelly Ann Bohannan
Debra Ann Bradley
Katheryn S. Brown
Paige Allison Browne
Donita Clapp
Larry Erick Cockrell
Ann Crossley
Darrel Cunningham
Melanie Daniels
Gayla S. Davis
Colette Denney
Lisa Douphin
Philip H. Grant
Nancy Carol Guinn
Anne Hall
Georgia L. Hardt
Jacqueline Jane Harris
Danene Wilson Hartman
Cindy Cay Hein
Caroline Hershberger
Rhonda Kay Hill
Teresa Hillin Horner
Ann Hufnagel
Christine Hunt
Jenny Dean Jobe
Kathryn Diane Kelley
Kimberly Faye Kyle
Ellen Darline McGhee
R. Ann Nelson

Nancy Noack
Kelly Ann O'Brien
Zan Partain
Kani Lynne Rogers
Mendy L. Posey
Shelly Rogers
Carol Jean Rushton
Leslie Russell
Teresa K. Schumacher
Dana Lea Scott
Nancy Shepherd
Marie Snavely
Susan Sullivan
Susan Sundholm
Stephanie Swanson
Mary Thomas
Jani Tripp
Lois LaJean Webb
Meridith Llyn Wiley
Kathy Renee Williams
Kelly Williams
Margaret Teresa Wilson
Alice Alline Young

1983

Laurrie Avery
Beckie Black
Darrell Blackman
Nancy Blanchard
Gina Bolay
Melissa Brown
Barbara Brucken
Susan Buie
Marcy Bullis
Deborah Cassle
Bonnie Caudle
Lita Chase
Don Colston
Mrs. Don Colston
Marchelle Conway
Anna Maria Fialkowski
Joyce Stewart Fixico
Deborah Sue Ford
Lori Franke
Lee Ann Fuzzell
Donna Gilchrist
Sarah E. Givens
LeAnn Hamar
Kelly Rae Helm
Clara E. Hembree
Sylvia Herrod
Janet M. Higgins
Mary L. Huelskamp
Janice Hutson
Angie Ille
Lee Jackson
Shelley Johns
Lynette Peterson Johnson
Kenon Jones
Joan Junger
Gretchen Kahle
Patti Kelly
Phil Kennedy

Scott D. Kerucod
Roberta Kidd
Judy King
Vicki Lynn Kinman
Diane Lader
Kristina Lehr
Denise Ladusau
Michi Lockhart
Leslie Long
Wanda Long
Patricia Lukosius
Patricia Marshall
Kathryn McMath
Barbara Medley
Jimmy Meeks Jr
Laura Morris
Kay Ortmanns
Marsha Parrick
Janet McCoy Phillips
Michael Raines
Susan Reeves
Shelley Ann Rodgers
Chris Schroeder
Denice Schwoerke
Teresa Seifried
Brenda Sherwood
Carolyn Simpson
Karla Jones Skaggs
William Spafford
Margaret Stone
Cynthia Teehee
Kim VanAntwerp
Renee Walker
Bret Weimer
Maureen Wiggins
Mandy Wilson
Becky Wolf
Donette Hoover Yeilding

1984

Tina Hardgrove Ahern
Peggy Basler
Anne Blanchard
Donna Graham Brown
Toni Chrz
Jami Collier
Tanya Davis
Charles R. Davis
Lynette Fisher
Lila Leann Hamar
Beth Richetson Hancock
Julia Helander
Donna Hopper
Tambrey Johnson
Cheryl Kebo
Robyn King
Lynn Lewallen
Leslee Matheson
Diana Patterson
Kelli Schleicher
Susan Wagnon Shell
Susan L. Sunholm
Rhonda Swisher
Stan Trout

1985

Dale Barnett
Stacey Bond
John Britton
Janice Smith Burnett
Larry Burns
Georgeanne Fried
Harold R. Grimmett
Mike Haley
Derek Hallum
Cheryl Hastings
Lisa Hayden
Julie Hepner
Tina Homsey
Tammi Hood
Karen S. Hunter
Genee Jackson
Janele Dawn Johnson
Kathleen Kelly
Sheila Kay Lamb
Karen S. Lashley
Brenda Kay Layman
Louis Wyn Leftwich
Charlene L. Lingo
Rhonda E. Lyon
Tracy Martin
Megan M. Matthews
Jacqueline McGolden
Brenda Kay Miller
Elizabeth A. Muller
Stacie Norris
Kay Oltmanns
Andrea Parnell
Ann Patterson
Joyce Phillips
Anthony P. Piccinni
Lori Pruett
Teri Ridgers
Mary J. Rine
Lynetta Robinson
Martha Rohrbach
Tina M. Saddoris
Susan Cheryl Scharoun
Lois Faye Sharpton
James Sharpton
Loyet Sheafer
Susanne Shore
Brenda Silvers
Shari Stepken
Mary Stroemel
Harvey G. Taylor
Martha Tow
Luan Liberman West
Sheri Wills
Paulanita Willyard
Diane L. Wimberly
Melessa L. Wofford

1986

Rochelle Beatty
Beth Boggess
Lynne Bruce
Tina Dixon

Beverly Gafford
Lynn Greenly
Ann Hayes
Elizabeth Hayes
Quannah Hopper
Karen Johnson
Lynne Lanigan
Lori Lovelace
Susan McEachern
Vicki Morris
Shirley Parma
Donia Patterson
April Ranks
Teri Rodgers
Susan E. Russum
Cynthia Schultz
Leslie Sharpton
Tracy Virgen
Terri Ward

1987

Merilyn Ayers
Cy Boles
Kris Cable
Mary Cash
Jane Davis
Patricia Ferguson
Mildred Findley
Deborah Graham
Christina Hurd
Susan Kennedy
Kim Krehbiel
Carolyn Luthye
Cindy Ralph
Cynthia Sloggett
Kelly Soergel
Cynthia Sotesek
Gayle Stretch
Carol Trapp
Julia Wheeler
Raegan A. Rethard

1988

Linda Ammons
Stephanie Bayles

Sharmi Boyer
Karen Cowlishaw
Suzy Dart
Juanita L. Davis
Tiffany Dennis
Gail I. DeWeese
Verona Dow
Lacrisha D. Earls
Patric I. Fihley
Dana Flowers
Shirley Frederick
Kristye Garrett
Gayln Gray
Ann Renee Harris
Anne Henderson
Julie J. Horst
Mary Ann Kelly
Lane McFarland
Betty E. Morris
Kelli Provence
Sydney G. Ringer
Robert Schultz
Jane Schwartz
Kimberly Tommey
Thu-Hue Tran
Melissa Urban
Alma Wilson
Jean Wohlhuter

1989

Julie Altom
Gloria Bedwell
Krista Blackburn
Robin Carney
Jim Dees
Gayln Gray
Sherilyn Hock
Theresa Keleher
Wayla LaCaze
Rhonda Maynard
Nancy Miller
Anita Morgan
Betty Morris
Ronna Taylor
Ginna Wheeler

Kappa Delta Pi is an honorary society for education majors. The society originated at the University of Illinois in 1910. OSU's Nu chapter was established in 1921. Juniors and seniors must have a 3.30 overall grade point average and be fully admitted into the Teacher Education Program. In addition, juniors must have completed six hours of education course work, and seniors must have completed twelve hours of education course work. Graduate students must have been accepted to a career field in education and have a 3.70 overall grade point average.

*This list was compiled by using *Redskins*, Kappa Delta Pi records, and various College of Education publications.

Education Student Council*

1941

Ann Blair
Carol Colvin
Florence Ellen Conger
Lawrence Crable
Mary Cupp
George R. Darrow
Russell Drumright
Ann Orr
Earl Spangler
Rose Mary Tompkins

1942

Jane Blair
Ann Blair
Florence Ellen Conger
Lawrence Crable
Marguerite Downey
Frank Fuller, Advisor
LeRoy Guest
Max Godfrey
Jean Keith
Madalyn Lackey
Guy Lackey, Advisor
Ann Orr
Carol Ann Stringfield
Kathryn Tompkins

1943

Ann Blair
Jane Blair
Anna Belle Fowler
Madalyn Lackey
Olen Miller
Ann Orr
Emily Schwabe
Carol Ann Stringfield
Katherine Tompkins
Crystal Whorton

1952

Susie Askew
John Cunningham
Ann Davison
Marilynn Leard
Maureen Matthews
Joanne Pace
Trent Serini
Phillip Smith

1953

Nancy Adamson
Jenifer Brown
Jack Byron
Frances Cummins
Betty Duncan
Gene Howard
Marilyn Mack
Maureen Matthews
Jacque McKenney
Louise Noble
Mozelle Pitts
Joan Shackelford
Russell Smith
Clifford Todd
Shirley Winans

1954

Jack Byron, Advisor
Claire Escott
Nancy Goucher
Carol Jarvis
Maureen Matthews
Jacque McKenney
Doris Miller
Louise Noble
Mary Shaver
Loren Smith
Russell Smith
Eleanor Swalley
Darlene Tillman
Ellen Wilson
Shirley Winans
Larry Wright

1955

Jack Byrom
Betty Duncan
Joanne Goff
Maureen Matthews
Pat Parks
Mary L. Shaver
Nancy Sherrill
Darlene Tillman
Judy Wittmer
Larry Wright

1956

Jerry Billings
Jack Byron, Advisor
Betty Duncan

Myra Fretwell
Mary Gaddis
Carolyn Gee
Edwina Harrison
Martha Hunter
Ronald McKinzie
Pat Parks
Judy Rice
Janet Simpson
Billie Talley
Judy Wittmer

1957

Ruth Ahrberg
Barbara Autry
Jerry Billings
Helen Caron
Carolyn Gee
Mary Howard
Carroll Noske
Donna Paris
Sandra Price
Judy Rice
Janet Simpson
Janet Waters
Ronald Whorton

1958

Ruth Ahrberg
Marilyn Benson
Mary Helen Bogert
Helen Caron
Dr. Richard Collier
Mary Ellen Faulkner
Kay Blanch Hamra
Joyce M. Hill
Mary Ann Howard
Emagene Jenkins
Kaye Keso
Molly Mayfield
Donna Paris
Joyce Streeter Roark
Janet Simpson
Deanna Spickelmier
Janet Waters
Paula Wise
Yovene Yeaton

1959

Frances Arnold
Sandy Baldwin
Mary Helen Bogert
Richard Collier
Dee Dickens
Mary Ellen Faulkner
Janet Johnston
Richard Jungers, Advisor
Rose Marie Kubricht

Jerry Ann Lewis
Elizabeth Long
Karen Ludwig
Mary Ann Page
Claudia Shannon
Dee Spickelmier
Barbara Stanley
Franchelle Whiteside
Paula Wise

1960

Mary Binns
Mary Helen Bogert
Eldon Divine
Donald Drain
W. Price Ewens
Carol Sue Goucher
Robert Heusel
Richard P. Jungers, Advisor
Pat Kelley
Charlene Kendrick
Jerry Ann Lewis
Liz Long
Karen Ludwig
Sharon Muegge
Caroline Nixon
Sondra Self
Claudia Shannon
Jim Sloan
Sandy Springer
Martha Wallis
Franchelle Whiteside
Paula Wise
Bettye Kaye Yahn

1961

Ann Barnhardt
Pat Bomgardner
Kay Davies
W. Price Ewens
Patsy Farren
Jan Fleming
Melinda Harris
Charlene Kendrick
Jerry A. Lewis
Karen Ludwig
Jennie Miller
Darrell Nelson
Caroline Nixon
Sondra Self
Claudia Shannon
Anita Stewart
Brenda K. Turner
Martha Wallis
Bettye K. Yahn

1962

Betty Albin
Phyllis Bryant

Nelda Carter
Nancy Connor
Kay Davies
Roberta Hairfield
Melinda Harris
Judy Hunter
Bobbie Gale Jones
Charlene Kendrick
Patti McClain
Sondra Self
Anita Stewart
Walker Russell
Bettye Yahn

1963

Betty Albin
Barbara Armstrong
Gary Aston
Connie Beasley
Jancie Beltz
Nelda Carter
Pat Ent
W. Price Ewens
Barbara Gabriel
Pat Graff
Ann James
Nancy Johnson
Deanna King
Nancy Morehouse
Nancy Page
Jane Pool
Trudy Symes
Brenda Turner

1964

Connie Beasley
Judy Blackburn
Betty Cortwright
W. Price Ewens, Advisor
Mary Francis
Ellen Hesson
Ann Jeffrey
Nancy Johnson
Deanna King
Jan Lemaster
Anne McClaren
Larry McClendon
Sharon Olstad
Beverly Palecek
Jane Pool
Frances Reeder
Ruth Rice
Bobbie Rudolph
Trudy Symes
John Woods

1965

Karen Baxter
Judy Blackburn

Pat Graff
Wanda Gray
Jill Harris
Ann Jeffrey
Jo Johnson
Judy Jones
Ronald Lane
Sharon Olstad
Frances Reeder
Ruth Rice
Susie Scarborough
Shirley Swinney
Pat Ward
John Woods

1966

Dianne Baxter
Judy Blackburn
Connie Courtner
Beverly Cregg
Cindy Davenport
Georgianna Drummond
Michael Elliott
W. Price Ewens, Advisor
Ann File
Sharon Gafford
Janice Grant
Jill Harris
Jo Ellen Johnson
Susan Jones
Judy Jones
Sarah Mires
Janet Prater
Susie Scarborough
Susan Scheffel
Pat Tucker

1967

Pat Appleby
Nita Baxter
Beverly Cregg
W. Price Ewens, Advisor
Roxy Ganes
Ann Hallibuton
Pam Health
Judie Johnson
Judy Jones
Jan Love
Cindy Marsh
Cheryl Muehleisen
Barbara Pojezny
Nancy Samuelson
Sherri Sanders
Susan Scheffel
Sheralyn Summers
Pat Tucker
Pam Wilson

1968

Penny Ames
Pat Appleby

Oklahoma State University

267

Ellen Barnes
Beth Bledsoe
Lynn Case
Jackie Cunningham
Carol Dodds
Cathy Ebert
W. Price Ewens, Advisor
Ann Halliburton
Pam Heath
Judie Johnson
Carol Richert
Lynn Ridge
Sherri Sanders
Kathy Shipley
Mary Spicer
Pat Tucker
Vicki Von Tungeln
Pam Wilson
Susie Winters

1969

Ann Belew
Becky Brown
Susie Corgan
Cathy Ebert
W. Price Ewens, Advisor
Ovan Hallmak
Julie Johnson
Sandy Partridge
Carol Reichert
Lynn Ridge
Candyce Schaeffer
Vicki Shaw
Vicki VonTungeln
Susan Wilhour
Pam Wilson
Susie Winters

1970

Becky Brown
Royce Caldron
Ann Cummings
Cathy Ebert
W. Price Ewens, Advisor
Nancy Ferguson
Vivian Sue Hawkins, Advisor
Mike Howerton
Mary Jane Jeffries
Katy Martin
Ruth Ann Miller
Patsy Oliver
Sandy Partridge
Marilyn Proctor
Carol Richards
Candyce Shaefer
Kathy Shipley
Linda Skiller
Pat Vincent
Susan Willhour
Susie Winters

1971

Kay Arnold
Kay Bales
Pat Black
Betty Bradshaw
Ann Cummings
Kathleen Currie
Vicki Dominick
Nancy Furguson
Mike Howerton
Debbie Jump
Nancy Kirby
Mary McMains
Ruth Ann Miller
Pat Morgan
Paul Mullen
Patsy Oliver
Nan Paris
Ann Patterson
Suzie Penticuff
John Pennington
Ben Roekiek
Kathy Shipley
Linda Skinner
Annette Villines
Sam Wiley
Sally Wilker

1972

Kay Arnold
Kathleen Currie
Connie Geist
Ann Hardy
Janet Heath
Liz Hodges
Peggy Holloman
Jan Hutchens
Debi Jump
Janet Modin
Susan Moore
Pat Morgan
Patsy Oliver
Nan Paris
Ann Patterson
Al Peterson
Ben Roebuck
Kathy Shoemaker
Mike Stratton
Larry Wilkinson

1973

Nancy Aspenson
Barbie Bagwell
Jan Berry
Jeannie Brooks
Linda Buffa
Debbie Callahan
Janet Castle
Debbie Clure
Gerald Cole

Kathleen Currie
Dianne Darr
Ellen Dolan
Denise Downing
Debbie Edwards
Jo Ellen Fenimore
Lynette Frye
Carolyn Gang
Joe Gardner
Peggy Glass
Anne Hardy
Barbie Herzig
Peggy Holman
Jan Hutchens
Kathy Johns
Judi McGhay
Joyce Panos
Al Peterson
Jim Puckett
Charles Schultz
Mike Stratton
Pat Stuever
Betty Thomas
Jeri Werneke

1974

Barbie Bagwell
Paul Benbrook
Jan Berry
Linda Buffa
James Callison
Ray Chavez
Barbara Coble
Jim Corder
Dianne Darr
Kathleen Duffy
Jo Ellen Fenimore
Deborah Fuller
Carolyn Gang
Anne Hardy
Lee Ann Hatten
Peggy Holman
Janet Johnson
Judy Jordan
Martha Krus
Rodney Leird
Frank McFarland, Advisor
Nancy McGee
Judith McMasters
Debbie Moreland
Linda Morrissey
Lori Morrissey
Pam Powell
James Puckette
Charles Roberts
Becky Rodgers
Jo Ann Seely
Tom Steen
Pam Stewart
Steve Stinnett
Pat Stuever
Carole Suttie
Bekye Wampner
Jeri Werneke

Bobette Whitlock
Sue Wimberly
Debbie Wright
Nancy Wright

1975

Vicki Bain
Ray Chavez
Jim Corder
Kathleen Duffy
Charlene Faircloth
Vicki Finley
Joe Francis
Jane Gertsen
Cathy Grandstaff
Patty Guillaume
Nancy Heinzer
Bill Hindman
Janet Johnson
Jack Kilkenny
Rodney Leird
Frank McFarland, Advisor
Judith McMasters
Debbie Moreland
Linda Morrissey
Lori Morrissey
Debi Moses
Jerri Mosler
Lynn Novak
Jim Puckette
Richard Rains
Barbara Rambo
Barbara Sproull
Pam Stewart
Steve Stinnett
Cathy Strong
Pat Stuever
Marcia Taylor
Tim Van Eaton
Sue Wimberly

1976

Jeff Ahring
Vickie Boothe
Rebecca Bostian
Connie Czirr
Cindy England
Charlene Faircloth
Susan Ford
Joe Francis
Dody Frazee
Jane Gertsen
Debbie Glover
Patty Guillaume
Arlene Hamm
Nancy Heinzer
Bill Hindman
Patty Hollander
Mark Howard
Dana Jenks
Debbie Johnston

Carol Mason
Judith McMasters
Lori Morrissey
Debi Moses
Jerrilee Mosier
Debi Musick
Lynn Novak
Kim Pendleton
Vecky Rambo
Becky Rodgers
Ginger Roush
Dana Smith
Barbara Sproll
Kathy Strong
Pat Stuever
Sandy Thomas
Tom VanEaton
Vickie Varnell
Sue Wimberly
Cheryl Wyatt

Robin Norgaard
Cathy Ormond
Kim Pendleton
Barbara Rambo
Richard Rarick
Cindy Ridge
Becky Rodgers
Ginger Rousch
Nancy Sandstrum
Rick Schmigle
Angela Shinn
Melinda Shockey
Suzy Short
Dana Smith
Debbie Smith
Pat Steuver
Louise Sumpter
Sandy Thomas
Tom VanEaton
Sue Wimberly
Cheryl Wyatt
Nancy Wilson

1977

Jeff Ahring
Steve Ammentorp
Candy Block
Vickie Booth
Rebecca Bostian
Karen Burdick
Cheryl Cottrell
Connie Czirr
Kathleen Duffy
Suzanne Durossette
Sandy Edwards
Becky Elmore
Cindy England
Susan Ford
Ann Fowler
Dody Frazee
Joe Francis
Dodie Frazee
Jane Gertsen
Debbie Glover
Janet Goertz
Kris Goodman
Donna Graybill
Patty Guilliame
Arlene Hamm
Nancy Heinzer
Bill Hindman
Mark Howard
Kelly James
Dana Jencks
Janet Johnson
Deborah Johnston
Gina Lynn
Carol Mason
Frank McFarland, Advisor
Judith McMasters
Debbie Moreland
Jeri Mosier
Debi Moses
Tamara Moyer
Debi Musick

1978

Laura Bentley
Candy Block
Vickie Boothe
Rebecca Bostian
Karen Burdick
Maribeth Burns
Ann Butler
Marla Cavanaugh
Jana Chambless
Stephanie Coates
Mary Coyle
Janice Creider
Suzanne Durosette
Linda Foster
Dody Frazee
Mary Gibson
Debbie Glover
Janet Goertz
Suzy Goff
Patty Guillaume
Arlene Hamm
Jerry Hayes
Mark Howard
Mary Hughes
Kelly James
Debbie Johnston
Kay Kelly
Randy Kinnear
Kris Kunard
Gina Lynn
Katy McCaleb
Frank McFarland, Advisor
Robbie Mooney
Debbie Moreland
Tammy Moyer
Robin Norgaard
Cathy Ormond
Kim Pendleton
Bill Pettitt

Rick Rarick
Cindy Ridge
Tara Roderick
Nancy Sandstrum
Rick Schmigle
Angela Shinn
Melinda Shockey
Suzy Short
Debbie Smith
Carolyn Steinmetz
Laura Stephens
Melissa Stephenson
Sandy Thomas
Dana Weidner
Ann Worden
Suzanne Yokum

1979

Nancy Belie
Laura Bentley
Rebecca Bostian
Pamela Burkes
Maribeth Burns
Marla Cavanaugh
Jana Chambless
Stephanie Coates
Mary Coyle
Janice Creider
Stacey Denzler
Becky Dvorak
Nancy Eddleman
Juli Elm
Paula Fine
Will Frasier
Mary Gibson
Karen Gilliam
Jerry Hayes
Cindy Hopper
Mary Hughes
Kelly James
Kay Kelly
Kim Kelly
Susan Kirch
Gina Lynn
Katie McCaleb
Carol McDonald
Frank McFarland, Advisor
Brenda Moyer
Tammy Moyer
Lynette Peach
Bill Petitt
Tara Roderick
Angela Shinn
Debbie Smith
Lisa Southall
Lisa Stanley
Carolyn Steinmitz
Laura Stephens
Shelley Swope
Rose Ann Winters
Ann Worden
Suzanne Yokum

1980

Carey Beatty
Debbie Bradley
Beth Bullis
Pamela Burkes
Maribeth Burns
Stephanie Coates
Vicki Craft
Christy Creedon
Lisa Dauphin
Stacey Denzler
Becky Dvorak
Juli Elm
Paula Fine
Linda Foster
Mary Gibson
Karen Gilliam
Regina Goodwin
Kay Kelly
Kim Kelly
Susan Kirch
Nancy Knight
Danette Kuykendall
Lynette Lamer
Carol McDonald
Frank McFarland, Advisor
Kay McTaggart
Kathy Menke
Connie Miller
Brenda Moyer
Diane Perdue
Tara Roderick
Susan Schrag
Debbie Smith
Christia Sodowsky
Lisa Southall
Lisa Stanley
Carolyn Steinmetz
Laura Stephens
Stephanie Swanson
Shelly Swope
Rose Ann Winters

1981

Sherry Baker
Sharon Baustert
Carey Beatty
Kelly Bohannan
Debbie Bradley
Dyana Buckley
Beth Bullis
Pam Burkes
Maribeth Burns
Cynthia Butler
Bonnie Caudle
Bill Clark
Lynn Conzelman
Cindy Corr
Vicki Craft
Kim Dargen
Lisa Dauphin
Gayla Davis
Susan Dobson

Ellen DuBois
Paula Fine
Jane Gibson
Karen Gilliam
Barre Hendrix
Debbie Hinckley
Barry Hinson
Mary Huelskamp
Linda Johnson
Kim Kelly
Catherine Kerr
Susan Kirch
Carol McDonald
Frank McFarland, Advisor
Kay McTaggart
Kathy Menke
Brenda Moyer
Kim Musick
Monica Neville
Susan Patterson
Diane Perdue
Christie Plumer
Leslie Schroeder
Nancy Shephard
Lisa Southall
Laura Stephens
Renee Walker
Kim Westfahl
Becky Wolf

1982

Sherri Baker
Carey Beatty
Carolyn Beatty
Kelly Bohannan
Beth Bullis
Cindy Butler
Bonnie Caudle
Cindy Corr
Jeff Daffern
Kim Dargen
Lisa Dauphin-Ross
Gayla Davis
Susan Dobson
Ellen DuBois
Kellie Dugan
Jane Gibson
Karen Gilliam
Christine Haas
Leslie Haygood
Debbie Hinckley
Barbara Howell
Mary Huelscamp
Lori Hughs
Kim Jech
Kim Kelley
Catherine Kerr
Kimberly Kyle
Melanie Markwell
Frank McFarland, Advisor
Ellen McGhee
Kay McTaggart
Kathy Menke

Kim Musick
Monica Neville
Susan Patterson
Cindy Patterson
Christie Plumer
Lorrie Beth Powell
Leslie Russell
Nancy Shepherd
Sandy Southall
Stephanie Swanson
Renee Walker
Becky Wolf
Lisa Wood

1983

Katie Arp
Laurie Avery
Sherri Baker
Carolyn Beatty
Kelly Bohannan
Beth Bullis
Bonnie Caudle
Cindy Corr
Kim Dargen
Lori Downey
Lori Franke
Leslie Frazier
Christine Haas
Ellen Hall
Leslie Haygood
Shannon Highly
Debbie Hinkley
Robin Hogan
Teresa Horner
Lori Hughes
Ginger Jacobs
Robin Kerr
Kim Kirk
Kimberly Kyle
Allison Logan
Lisa Major
Beth McFall
Frank McFarland, Advisor
Ellen McGhee
Kim Musick
Monica Neville
Susan Patterson
cathy Payne
Michelle Phillips
Christie Plumer
Shelly Pulliam
Lisa Ross
Nancy Shepherd
Cindy Southall
Shea Thompson
Sheri Wakefield
Renee Walker
Kelly Williams
Becky Wolfe
Kim Wood

1984

Gerri Anderson
Katie Arp

Laurie Avery
Carolyn Beatty
Beth Boggess
Stacy Bond
Bonnie Caudle
Lori Downey
Amy Eischen
Lori Franke
Christine Haas
Ellen Hall
Ann Hayes
Shannon Highley
Robin Hogan
Meredith Houston
Ginger Jacob
Robin Kerr
Lynne Lanigan
Lisa Major
Beth McFall
Frank McFarland, Advisor
Sandy McNish
Pam Miller
Lisa Minjares
Vicki Morris
Susan Newman
Kathy Payne
Michelle Phillips
Susan Potts
Shelley Pulliam
Teri Rodgers
Sharese Smith
Rachel Smith
Sandy Southall
Bonnie Spence
Gayle Stretch
Susan Terry
Janna Thomason
Shea Thompson
Jana Tittle
LuAnna Urton
Renee Walker
Alyson Wey
Becky Wolf
Susan Wright

1985

Gerri Anderson
Katie Arp
Rachel Bail
Beth Boggess
Stacy Bond
Julie Brock
Natalie Burrie
Janet Coffey
Tina Dixon
Amy Eischen
Donna Eischen
Patty Ferguson
Julie Fisher
Georgianne Fried
Leigh Gosney
Debbie Graham
Diana Hauser

Ann Hayes
Debbie Henshaw
Shannon Highly
Robin Hogan
Ginger Jacob
Carolyn Keating
Cindy Kelly
Kenneth L. King, Advisor
Lynne Lanigan
Liz Little
Lori Lovelace
Tracy Martin
Chuck McKinney
Sandy McNish
Lisa Minjares
Jeanine Morris
Vicki Morris
Elizabeth Muller
Kelly Nash
Susan Newman
Staci Norris
Kristy Owens
Donia Patterson
Susan Potts
Kristy Provence
Terri Rodgers
Donald W. Seamans, Advisor
Sharese Smith
Kelly Soergel
Bonnie Spence
Susan Terry
Jana Thomason
Shea Thompson
Dala Tilley
Jana Tittle
Jana Vermillion
Tracy Virgen
Kristen Waugh
Alyson Wey
Susan Wright

1986

Gerri Anderson
Lisa Anderson
Melissa Archambo
Krista Blackburn
Patrick Dilly
Tina Dixon
Verona Dow
Kelly Drake
Donna Eischen
Patty Ferguson
Stacy Ford
Krista Friar
Georgianne Fried
Kristye Garrett
Susan Glazier
Leigh Gosney
Greg Graffman
Diana Hauser
Ann Hayes
Derek R. Holmes
Lisa Hunter
Carolyn Keating

Jerilyn Kisabeth
Lynne Lanigan
Christy Limes
Liz Little
Lori Lovelace
Kristin Mayes
Tracy Martin
Doreatha McHenry
Chuck McKinney
Mark Mitchell
Jeanine Morris
Vicki Morris
Elizabeth Muller
Kelly Nash
Susan Newman
Tawney Noon
Stacie Norris
Kristy Owens
Melinda Patton
Terri Price
Kristy Provence
Teri Rodgers
Donald W. Seamans, Advisor
Leslie Sharpton
Kelly Soergel
Bonnie Spence
Gayle Stretch
Deana Tansel
Jana Tittle
Jana Vermillion
Alyson Wey
Julie Wheeler
Paula Willyard
Brian Young
Kelly Young

1987

Shannon Adams
Paul M. Allen
Angie Anders
Gerri Anderson
Lisa Anderson
Kim Anthony
Missey Archambo
Krista Blackburn
Joy Brock
Cindy Brown
Jeanne Cheatwood
Verona Dow
Kelly Drake
Stacy Ford
Vicki Foster
Krista Friar
Kristye Garrett
Rhonda Harder
Tricia Hash
Diana Hauser
Jamie Henshaw
Derek Holmes
Jean Kelley
Pam LaFollette
Christy Limes
Marcella Moore

Elizabeth Muller
Kelly Nash
Melinda Patton
Beth Pearce
Terri Price
Kristy Provence
Susan Purvis
Linda Quay
Kimberly Regier
Lori Sawyer
Jane Schwartz
Donald W. Seamans, Advisor
Kelly Soergel
Laurie Steel
Jennifer Sumner
Dan Tanner
Angela Temples
Tammie Thompson
Staci Traverse
Jana Vermillion
Paula Willyard

1988

Shannon Adams
Lisa Anderson
Andrea Atchley
Carole Baker
Krista Blackburn
Cindy Brown
Susan Buck
Jeanne Cheatwood
Melinda Conner
Jennifer Ethridge
Kristen Evans
Stacey Ford
Vicki Foster
Kristye Garrett
Rhonda Harder
Diana Hauser
Kathryn Herber
D'andra Holley
Wendy Husby
Pam LaFollette
Libby Laing
Gary Layman
Christy Limes
Melissa McConnell
Jamie Miller
Donna Moore
Melinda Patton
Beth Pearce
Terri Price
Bill Priest
Kristy Provence
Susan Purvis
Kimberly Regier
Jacqueline Rule
Gaynell Schieber
Jane Schwartz
Donald W. Seamans, Advisor
Stephanie Shannon
Scott Spencer
Laurie Steel
Jennifer Sumner
Danny Tanner

Angela Temples
Tammie Thompson
Thu-Hue Tran
Staci Traverse
Teesha Upton
Katy Webb
Becky Whistler
Alina Wilson

1989

Kim Anthony
Andrea Atchley
Cindy Brown
Susan Buck
Carri Bush
Randy Butler
Suzann Casey
Jeanne Cheatwood
Emile Coffey
Melinda Conner
Christa Doudican
Jennifer Ethridge
Kristin Evans
Vicki Foster
Shelly Franks
Stacey Freeny
Kristye Garrett
Greg Graffman
Rhonda Harder
Susan Hillier

Sherilyn Hock
Wendy Husby
Pam LaFollette
Libby Laing
Gary Layman
Christy Limes
Ginger Lister
Gail Martin
Melissa McConnell
Jamie Miller
Donna Moore
Beth Pearce
Laurie Polhemus
Marla Robinson
Jacqueline Rule
Jane Schwartz
Donald W. Seamans, Advisor
Scott Spencer
Laurie Steel
Dan Tanner
Angela Temples
Tammie Thompson
Thu-Han Tran
Marill Waters
Katy Webb
Noelle Williams
Seth Williams
Stephanie Williams
Alina Wilson
Julie Wilson

Education Student Council is the unit of student government for the College of Education. In 1940, Dean Napoleon Conger moved to initiate the council, but it faded by the mid-1940s. The organization was reborn in 1951. It is made up of designated class representatives, a representative from each of the special interest clubs in the college, and the student who represents the College of Education in the Student Senate of the OSU Student Government Association. Applicants for class representatives must have a minimum 2.50 grade point average and are selected through an application and interview process.

*This list was compiled by using *Redskins* and various College of Education publications.

Bibliography

COLLECTIONS

Oklahoma State University, Edmon Low Library, Special Collections, Stillwater, Oklahoma:

Board of Regents for the Oklahoma Agricultural and Mechanical Colleges Minutes.

College of Education History Collection.

N. Conger Collection.

Record Book Committee, compiler. "Selections from the Record Book of the Oklahoma Agricultural and Mechanical College, 1891-1941. Compiled on the Occasion of the Fiftieth Anniversary of the Founding of the College." Vols. 1-2.

AUTHOR INTERVIEWS

Oklahoma State University, Edmon Low Library, Special Collections, Stillwater, Oklahoma:

Centennial Histories Oral Interview Collection:

Basore, Bennett, December 1987.

Brobst, Harry, 31 July 1986.

Dunlap, E. T., 30 May 1986.

Gaines, Paul, 4 December 1987.

Girod, Raymond, 7 July 1986.

Jungers, Richard, 3 July 1986.

Lowe, Florence Ellen Conger; Katherine Tompkins McCollom; Rose Mary Tompkins Duncan; and Dorothea Hodges, 14 April 1987.

Orlowski, Marjorie; Gladys Skinner; Benn Palmer; and Bill Hindman, 1 July 1986.

Robinson, Donald W., 14 January 1988.

Skinner, Gladys, 1 July 1987.

Sorenson, Helmer, 25 June 1986.

Tate, John B., 22 March 1986.

Wiggins, Kenneth, 8 December 1987.

Babb, Russell, 6 March 1989, Stillwater, OK.
Dugger, Cecil, 14 June 1989, Stillwater, OK.
Thomas, Della, 15 June 1989, Stillwater, OK.

NEWSPAPERS

Oklahoma A. and M. College *New Education*, 1909-1911.

Oklahoma City *Daily Oklahoman*, 1939, 1961, 1969.

Oklahoma State University Student Newspaper:

    Orange and Black, 1908-1924.

    O'Collegian, 1924-1927.

    Daily O'Collegian, 1927-1987.

Stillwater NewsPress, 1963-1981.

ARTICLES

Adams, H. P. "War Training Programs at A. and M." *Oklahoma A. and M. College Magazine*, vol. 17, no. 8 (May 1945), p. 5.

"Campus Briefs." *Oklahoma State Alumnus Magazine*, vol. 6, no. 2 (January 1965), p. 30.

"Campus Compendia—Education Dean Steps Down." *Oklahoma State Alumnus Magazine*, vol. 13, no. 1 (January 1972), p. 12.

Chapman, B. B. "Photographs for Posterity." *Oklahoma A. and M. College Magazine*, vol. 22, no. 8 (April 1951), p. 12.

"Children's Literature as a Bookman's Holiday." *Library Scene*, vol. 3, no. 1 (March 1974), pp. 14-18.

"College Has Greatest Growth Under Cantwell." *A. and M. Boomer*, vol. 1, no. 7 (21 April 1921), p. 9.

Conger, N. "A. and M. Accepts Rural Challenge." *Oklahoma A. and M. College Magazine*, vol. 8, no. 5 (February 1937), pp. 3-9.

Conger, N. "The Teacher Shortage." *Oklahoma A. and M. College Magazine*, vol. 18, no. 5 (February 1946), p. 3.

"Continued Learning, Public Education, In-Service Stressed." *Oklahoma State University Outreach*, vol. 15, no. 4 (April 1974), p. 32.

"Dean Holley Retires: Has New Position." *Oklahoma State Alumnus Magazine*, vol. 5, no. 7 (July 1964), p. 18.

"Education." *Oklahoma State University Outreach*, vol. 53, no. 2 (Winter 1981), p. 10.

"Education Counseling Clinic." *Oklahoma State University Magazine*, vol. 1, no. 3 (September 1957), p. 8.

"Education Graduates Employed." *Oklahoma A. and M. College Magazine*, vol. 7, no. 5 (February 1936), p. 6.

"Eyes, Ears, Wheels and Wings." *Oklahoma A. and M. College Magazine*, vol. 26, no. 1 (September 1954), pp. 10-13.

"Faculty Changes." *Oklahoma A. and M. College Magazine*, vol. 8, no. 1 (October 1936), p. 10.

"Faculty News." *Oklahoma A. and M. College Magazine*, vol. 3, no. 1 (October 1931), p. 4.

Hagood, Wendell. "The Graduate College Grows." *Oklahoma A. and M. College Magazine*, vol. 1, no. 7 (March 1930), p. 11.

Hart, Gordon. "Summer Clinics Benefit Freshmen." *Oklahoma State University Magazine*, vol. 3, no. 2 (August 1959), p. 4.

"Hitler's Oak Tree." *Oklahoma State University Outreach*, vol. 19, no. 2 (March-April 1978), p. 23.

Holley, Andrew. "Critical Issues in Education." *Oklahoma A. and M. College Magazine*, vol. 24, no. 2 (October 1952), p. 5.

Holley, Andrew. "Obtaining and Retaining Competent Teachers." *Oklahoma State University Magazine*, vol. 2, no. 10 (April 1959), pp. 18-19.

Holley, Andrew. "Teacher Shortage Looms High on Education Horizon." *Oklahoma A. and M. College Magazine*, vol. 27, no. 6 (February 1956), pp. 16-17.

Holter, George L. "When the School Was Young." *Oklahoma A. and M. College Magazine*, vol. 1, no. 3 (November 1929), p. 12.

"In-Service Education at A. and M." *Oklahoma A. and M. College Magazine*, vol. 16, no. 7 (February 1944), p. 13.

"Last of First Class Visits Campus." *Oklahoma State Alumnus Magazine*, vol. 11, no. 6 (June-July 1970), p. 21.

"Last of the First A. and M. Faculty." *Oklahoma A. and M. College Magazine*, vol. 21, no. 4 (December 1949), p. 11.

"Loyal Alumnus Dead; His Reports Gave Account of A. and M. Opening." *Oklahoma A. and M. College Magazine*, vol. 21, no. 8 (April 1950), p. 22.

Luebke, Phyllis. "Schedule a Skylab Mission." *Oklahoma State University Outreach*, vol. 14, no. 8 (November 1973), pp. 12-13.

"NASA Space Science Education." *Oklahoma State Alumnus Magazine*, vol. 10, no. 8 (November 1969), p. 7.

"New Dean of Education." *Oklahoma State Alumnus Magazine*, vol. 13, no. 8 (November 1972), p. 20.

"New Department Serves Schools." *Oklahoma A. and M. College Magazine*, vol. 18, no. 5 (February 1946), p. 4.

"News About the Faculty." *Oklahoma A. and M. College Magazine*, vol. 12, no. 6 (March 1941), p. 7.

"1933 Class Largest in History." *Oklahoma A. and M. College Magazine*, vol. 5, no. 2 (November 1933), p. 4.

"100 Year-Old Former Student Dies." *Oklahoma State University Outreach*, vol. 16, no. 3 (March 1975), p. 31.

Ray, Jack. "Is A. and M. Tradition Bound?" *Oklahoma A. and M. College Magazine*, vol. 10, no. 8 (May 1939), p. 3.

"Reinstate Secondary Schools; Enterprise Ticket Compulsory." *A. and M. Boomer*, vol. 1, no. 9 (July-August 1921), p. 4.

"Restoring Our Human Resources." *Oklahoma State University Magazine*, vol. 3, no. 5 (November 1959), p. 4.

"School and Faculty News." *Oklahoma A. and M. College Magazine*, vol. 3, no. 3 (December 1931), p. 9.

"Staff and Faculty Changes." *Oklahoma A. and M. College Magazine*, vol. 7, no. 1 (October 1935), p. 3.

"The Stairway to Knowledge." *Oklahoma A. and M. College Magazine*, vol. 25, no. 9 (May 1954), p. 11.

Stone, Walker. "Memorable Times." *Oklahoma State University Magazine*, vol. 2, no. 4 (October 1958), p. 30.

Stromberg, E. L. "Progress in Education." *Oklahoma A. and M. College Magazine*, vol. 9, no. 5 (February 1938), p. 3.

"Student Industries Are Enlarged." *Oklahoma A. and M. College Magazine*, vol. 1, no. 10 (Summer 1930), p. 7.

"Summer Session Attractions." *Oklahoma A. and M. College Magazine*, vol. 6, no. 8 (May 1935), p. 6.

"Telling 'How's' and 'Why's' of NASA." *Oklahoma State Alumnus Magazine*, vol. 11, no. 1 (June 1970), p. 16.

Wardsock, Robert E. "A Small Grey Man." *Oklahoma A. and M. College Magazine*, vol. 9, no. 8 (May 1938), p. 12.

"What Can Be Done About Dropouts." *Oklahoma State Alumnus Magazine*, vol. 5, no. 3 (March 1964), pp. 10-11.

Wise, Geneva Holcomb. "Do You Remember When . . . ?" *Oklahoma A. and M. College Magazine*, vol. 27, no. 9 (May 1956), p. 13.

"Y-Hut Closes Doors." *Oklahoma State Alumnus Magazine*, vol. 10, no. 3 (March 1969), p. 28.

"Your Credit Is Safe With Him!" *Oklahoma A. and M. College Magazine*, vol. 19, no. 2 (November 1947), pp. 10-11.

BOOKS

Bulletin—Revision of Catalog Issue for 1946-47.

General Statutes of Oklahoma—1908. A Compilation of all the Laws of a General Nature Including the Session Laws of 1907. Kansas City, MO: Pipes-Reed Book Company, 1908.

Gill, Jerry Leon. *The Great Adventure: Oklahoma State University and International Education.* Stillwater: Oklahoma State University, 1978.

Martin, Robert A., compiler. *Statutes of Oklahoma, 1890.* Guthrie, OK: State Capital Printing Company, 1891.

Oklahoma A. and M. College Catalog, 1891-1957.

Oklahoma A. and M. College Summer Bulletin, 1919.

Redskin. Oklahoma State University Yearbook, 1910-1987.

Rulon, Philip Reed. *Oklahoma State University—Since 1890.* Stillwater: Oklahoma State University Press, 1975.

Scott, Angelo C. *The Story of an Administration of the Oklahoma Agricultural and Mechanical College.* [Stillwater: Oklahoma Agricultural and Mechanical College, 1942].

Index

A

Abbott, William: 169.
Academic Bowl: 188.
Accounting: 119.
Ackenbom, Arthur: 49.
Adkins, Michael: 182, 192.
Administrative Organization: 116.
Administrator for Veteran's Affairs: 91.
Admissions Standards: 94.
Adrian, William B.: 168, 170.
Adult and Continuing Education: 75, 151.
Age of Aquarius: 111.
Age of Schoolmen: 157.
"Aggie Baggie": 91.
Agnew, Jeanne: 185.
Agricultural Education: 22, 96, 101, 113, 135, 167. *See also* Department of Agricultural Education.
Agricultural Experiment Station: 22, 61, 163.
Agriculture: 7, 11, 12, 16, 19, 21, 24, 26, 27, 51, 58, 60, 77, 84, 119, 139, 164.
Aichele, Douglas B.: 161, 179, 184, 185, 196.
Air Crew: 86.
Air Force: 86.
Air Force Aerospace Research Pilot School: 173.
Airport: 147, 176, 177.
Alabama: 133.
Alexander, Archibald: 172.
Allie P. Reynolds Stadium: 4.
All-university College: 94, 97.

Alumni Association: 192. *See also* Former Students Association.
American Association for the Advancement of Science: 53, 128.
American Association of Colleges for Teacher Education (AACTE): 129, 171.
American County Life Association: 78.
American Indian Education Personnel Development: 178.
Amis, Nancy: 128.
Ancient and Beneficent Order of the Red Red Rose: 49.
Andrews, Inez McSpadden: 49.
Angerer, C. L.: 114.
Apollo VII, XI, XIV: 174.
Appleberry, James B: 161, 163.
Aptitude Measures: 98.
Arkansas: 98, 189.
Army Aircrew, 85.
Army Specialized Training of Engineers: 85.
Army Specialized Training Unit (ASTU): 86.
Art Education: 58, 115, 120, 122.
Art Education Center: 147.
Asian Development Bank: 170.
Askew, Susie: 112.
Associate Dean: 196.
Association of Childhood Education International: 111, 112.
Astronomy: 121.
Attorney General: 123.
Audio-Visual Center: 100.
August Intersession: 52.

Austria: 128.
Aviation Education: 135, 161, 175, 176, 177, 182.

B

Babb, Russell: 175, 176.
Baby-boom: 111.
Bachelor of Science: 12.
Bachelor of University Studies: 94.
Baird, R. O.: 61.
Baker, J. N.: 126.
Baker, Nelda: 112.
Baker, William R.: 53.
Bangladesh: 129.
Barker, Robert: 6, 7.
Barnett, Dale: 171.
Bartlett Center for the Studio Arts: 26, 37, 50.
Bauer, Carolyn: 128.
Bayless, John R.: 169.
Becker, Carl: 3.
Bell, Terrell: 183, 184.
Bellmon, Henry: 128.
Bengston, L. H.: 137.
Bennett Complex: 4.
Bennett, Henry G.: 37, 45, 54, 55, 56, 57, 58, 63, 64, 67, 69, 72, 77, 79, 82, 84, 94, 98, 109, 123, 126, 148, 149, 175, 176.
Berdie, Ralph: 125.
Bermuda Shorts: 154.
Big Eight Athletic Conference: 3.
Biology Building. *See* Williams Hall.
Birk, Herbie: 114.
Bizzell, W. B.: 56, 58.
Black Kettle National Grassland: 195.
Black, Wylma: 83.
Block System: 80.
Board of Regents: 7, 10, 23, 24.
Boger, Lawrence L.: 171, 175, 183, 193.
Boggs, James H.: 162, 169.
Bolay, Mignon: 192.
Bookout, Jon: 168.
Boomers: 5.
Borneo: 113.
Borow, Henry: 125.
Bost, Jessie Thatcher: 13, 14.
Bowers, John H.: 20, 27, 31, 32, 33, 34, 35, 36, 37, 38, 40, 43, 47, 52, 61, 65, 107, 161, 196, 197.
Boy's Dormitory: 25.
Bradley University: 159.
Brann, Ralph: 137, 163.
Brannon, Luther H.: 114.
Brazil: 167, 168.
Brazilian Ministry of Education: 170.
Briggs, Lloyd D.: 146, 161, 162, 163, 166, 167, 170.

Briles, Charles W.: 31, 44.
British Ministry of Aviation: 173.
Brobst, Harry K.: 63, 95, 96, 97, 98, 124, 126, 129, 137, 144.
Brodell, A. C.: 48.
Broom Factory: 55.
Brown, Donald: 178.
Brown, Robert: 163.
Brown vs. The Topeka Board of Education: 124.
Bulger, Mac: 112.
Bull, Kay: 178.
Bureau of Applied Social Research: 165.
Bureau of Indian Affairs: 178.
Bureau of Schools Office: 178.
Bureau of Tests and Measurements: 51, 95, 97, 98, 115, 124, 126. *See also* University Testing and Evaluation Service.
Burrell, Paul: 176.
Business education: 96, 130, 135, 139. *See also* Department of Business Education. *See also* Department of Business Education and Administrative Services.
Byrom, Jack: 111, 112.

C

Cacy, King: 126.
Caldwell, Dorothy: 49.
California: 64.
California State University at Chico: 174.
Cameron, E. D.: 21.
Campbell, James R.: 53.
Campbell, John R.: 193, 196.
Campbell, N. Jo: 161, 162, 184, 192.
Campbell, O. K.: 83.
Campbell, Raymond G.: 55.
Campus Corner: 4.
Cantwell, J. W.: 35, 45, 49, 50.
Car Washers Association: 55.
Carabobo University: 170, 171.
Card, Ceila: 192.
Career Assistance and Learning Laboratory (CALL Center): 94.
Caribbean: 172.
Carlsbad Caverns: 79.
Carlyle, W. L.: 37.
Carnegie Foundation: 119.
Carnegie Reports: 194.
Carthage College: 159.
Caskey, Phil: 179.
Castellucix, Richard L.: 169.
Causey, J. P.: 122.
Central State College. *See* Central State University.
Central State University: 29, 179, 185, 189.

Ceramics Plant: 55.
Certificate: 21, 60, 62, 71, 89, 93.
Certification (certified): 15, 30, 115, 180, 186.
Chair of Agriculture for Schools: 22.
Chair of Pedagogy: 32.
Challenger: 174.
Chapel: 36.
Chapman, B. B.: 117.
Chapman, Pete: 137, 161.
Chauncey, Marlin Ray: 53, 70, 76, 83, 96, 102, 117.
Cheek, Helen: 179.
Chemistry Building: 24, 45, 46.
Children's Literature: 182.
China: 113.
Choike, James: 179.
Chrystal, Bee: 53.
Cimarron Turnpike: 189.
Civil Rights Movement: 152.
Civil War: 4.
Clark, Edward F.: 7.
Class Colors: 27.
Classroom Building: 28, 109, 112, 123, 142, 147, 166.
"Classroom Integration of Telecommunications: Focus Bulletin Boards, Electronic Model and Data Bases": 184.
Clinical Psychology: 178.
Coed Prom: 102.
Cole, Norma: 192.
College Auditorium: 82, 110.
College Barn: 24.
College Book Store: 102.
College Cafeteria: 55.
College Constituency Groups: 192.
College Courts: 86.
College Extension: 103.
College Farms: 55.
College of Agriculture: 8, 29, 35, 36, 38, 39, 40, 76, 82.
College of Arts and Sciences: 8, 19, 24, 27, 32, 34, 35, 38, 49, 51, 70, 77, 118, 119, 136, 138, 159, 178, 191, 194, 195.
College of Business Administration: 8, 47, 51, 84, 109, 119.
College of Business Administration Building: 147.
College of Education: 8, 15. *See also* School of Education.
College of Education Alumni Association: 192.
College of Education Alumni Association Scholarship, 182, 193.
College of Engineering, Architecture, and Technology: 8, 13, 35, 51, 77, 82, 84, 121, 139, 146, 167, 177.

College of Home Economics: 8, 26, 36, 38, 84, 119, 135, 139, 152, 167.
College of Veterinary Medicine: 8, 45.
College Teaching: 118.
Columbia Fellow: 108.
Columbia University: 67, 70, 108, 121, 165.
Colvin, Carol: 83.
Combs, Arthur: 125.
Commission on Education: 128.
Commission on Secondary Schools: 109.
Commissioner of Education: 102.
Committee on Cooperation in Research: 109.
Committee on High School and College Relations: 109.
Common Schools: 10, 12, 14, 16, 19, 20, 21, 22, 29.
Competency Testing: 184.
Conger, Florence Ellen. *See* Florence Ellen Conger Lowe.
Conger, Napoleon: 63, 67, 68, 69, 70, 73, 74, 75, 77, 78, 81, 82, 83, 84, 89, 90, 91, 93, 94, 95, 96, 98, 99, 100, 102, 103, 107, 109, 119, 123, 133, 140, 156, 186, 197.
Congregational Church: 8.
Connecticut: 43.
Connell, J. H.: 22, 24, 27, 28, 29.
Consolidation: 34, 60.
"Contemporary Issues in the Profession of Teaching": 184.
"Continuing Education/Multiple Option Renewal Experience" (CE/MORE): 181.
Conway, Russell: 192.
Cooperating Teachers: 154.
Cooperative Extension: 77.
Coordinators: 71.
Coptic Christian Church: 113.
Cordell Hall: 86, 147.
Cornell, Ezra: 11.
Cornell University: 3, 11.
Council: 6.
Council of Chief State School Officers: 174.
Council on Teacher Education: 125, 139, 140, 155.
Counseling and Guidance: 51, 75, 115, 124, 152, 178.
County Superintendent: 30.
Cowley, Suzanne: 179.
Creative Programming Award: 184.
Cruce, Lee: 29.
Cumberland University: 67.
Cundiff, Janet: 192.
Curriculum Examination: 187.
Curriculum Materials Laboratory: 127.
Cushing Public Schools: 80.

D

Dairy Building: 24.
Dakota Wesleyan University: 43.
Danforth Foundation: 75, 76, 119.
Daniels, Arthur: 7.
Darlington, Meredith: 77, 83.
Darnell, Lewis J.: 7.
Davidson, Ann: 112.
Davis, Allen S.: 53, 70.
Dawson, Howard: 122, 124.
Dean of Administration: 44, 63, 64, 91.
Dean of Men: 101.
Dean of Women: 100, 101.
Dean's Grant: 178.
Dearinger, Kathy M.: 192.
Defense Training Courses: 85.
Demobilization: 91.
Democratic Party: 6, 7, 23.
Demonstration Programs: 39.
Demonstration School: 51, 71.
Demonstration Trains: 76.
DeMumbrun, H. C.: 48.
Denney, Earl Charles: 96.
Department of Agricultural Education: 77.
  See also Agricultural Education.
Department of Applied Behavioral Studies
  (ABSED): 126, 161, 163, 180, 183, 184.
Department of Audio-Visual Aids and
  Photography: 101.
Department of Aviation and Space
  Education: 175, 176.
Department of Business Education: 109.
  See also Department of Business
  Education and Administrative Services.
  See also Business Education.
Department of Business Education and
  Administrative Services: 167. *See also*
  Business Education. *See also*
  Department of Business Education.
Department of Chemistry: 51, 179.
Department of Curriculum and Instruction
  (CIED): 161, 163, 177, 179, 181, 180,
  184, 185, 188, 195.
Department of Education: 27, 71, 81, 135,
  156, 160.
Department of Educational Administration
  and Higher Education (EAHED): 161,
  163, 168, 169, 184.
Department of Entomology: 8, 27.
Department of Family Relations and Child
  Development: 165.
Department of History: 8.
Department of Industrial Engineering: 13.
Department of Mathematics: 121.
Department of Pedagogy: 29.
Department of Philosophy: 136.
Department of Physics: 120.

Department of Psychology: 97, 126, 138,
  160.
Department of Public School Service: 79,
  95, 148, 157.
Department of Shops: 13.
Department of Sociology: 178.
Department of Vocational and Technical
  Education for Oklahoma: 169.
Desegregation: 123.
Development, Implementation, and
  Research for Educating Competent
  Teachers (DIRECT): 179.
Dewey, Ernest: 129.
Diamond, A. H.: 121.
Dinning, James S.: 97.
Director of Council on Teacher Education:
  148.
Director of Counseling Services: 152.
Director of Extension: 148, 191.
Director of International Programs: 169.
Director of Public School Service: 45, 98,
  114, 139, 147.
Director of School Transportation: 102.
Director of Student Teaching: 81.
Director of Teacher Certification: 139, 147.
Director of Teacher Education: 125, 139,
  147, 155, 160, 187.
Director of Teacher Training: 69, 73.
District Agricultural Schools: 47.
Division of College Extension: 77.
Division of Commerce. *See* College of
  Business Administration.
Division of Continuing Education: 128,
  141.
Division of Domestic Science and Arts.
  See College of Home Economics.
Division of Vocational Education: 166.
Dobson, Russell: 178.
Doctor of Arts Degree: 119.
Doctor of Education (Ed.D.): 96, 118, 119.
Doctor of Philosophy (Ph.D.): 97, 117,
  118, 119, 137.
Downey, Lori A.: 192.
Downing, Carl: 179.
Drake, Fred P.: 56.
Draper, Dan: 190.
Driver's Education: 141, 142.
Dugger, Cecil W.: 169, 172.
Duncan, Rose Mary Tompkins: 84, 94.
Dunlap, E. T.: 128, 150.
Dunlap, James D.: 56.
Dust Bowl: 43, 54.
Dyess, Benjamin C.: 53, 83, 97.

E

East Central University: 31, 185.
East Central State Normal. *See* East
  Central University.

284   Centennial Histories Series

East Pakistan. *See* Bangladesh.
Eau Claire State Teachers College: 133.
Echols, Walter H.: 53, 60, 83.
Edmison, Marvin T.: 138, 165.
Edmon Low Library: 9, 109, 147.
Education Day: 82, 84.
Education Extension: 190.
Education Society: 47, 49.
Education Student Council: 83, 84, 111, 113, 182.
Education Week: 112.
Educational Administration: 39, 59, 70, 99, 101, 102, 134, 135.
Educational Extension: 77, 100.
Educational Extension and Public School Service: 103, 147.
"Educational Microcomputer Software: Identification, Evaluation and Integration": 184.
Educational Philosophy: 39.
Educational Professional Development Act (EPDA): 166.
Educational Psychology: 39, 71, 137.
Educational Resources Information Center/Clearinghouse on Retrieval of Information and Evaluation on Reading (ERIC/CRIER): 145.
Educational Society: 37, 48.
Educational Student Services: 196.
Educational Tours: 79, 80.
Edwards Air Force Base: 173.
Egermeier, John C.: 165.
Egypt: 129, 172.
Eighth Naval District: 109.
Eisenhower, Dwight D.: 111.
Elementary Demonstration School: 76.
Elementary Education: 58, 60, 70, 71, 72, 86, 120, 128, 180.
Ellison, Jane: 123.
Elsom, Bill F.: 161, 163.
Emmert, Diana: 179.
Emotionally Maladjusted: 98.
Empire Test Pilot's School: 173.
Engineering: 8, 24, 57, 58, 97, 164.
Engineering and Trade and Industrial Education: 96.
Engineering Building, 1902: 15, 20, 24, 40, 45, 46, 72, 110, 146.
Engineering Building, 1912: 37, 120. *See also* Gundersen Hall.
Engineering Week: 82.
England: 173.
English and History Building. *See* Engineering Building, 1902.
English Language Institute: 167, 168.
Enrollment: 12, 17, 30, 50, 52, 93, 116, 117, 130.
Entrance Examination: 25.

Entry Year Assistance Committee (EYAC): 186.
Equalization: 33.
Eskridge, James B.: 50, 76.
Ethiopia: 113, 168.
Ethiopian College of Agriculture: 114.
Ethridge, Walter: 111.
Eubanks, Dwaine: 179.
Evans, Charles: 29.
Everett, M. S.: 129.
Ewens, W. Price: 137, 160.
Ewing, Amos: 7.
Executive Committee: 109.
Extension: 22, 31, 58, 76, 78, 100, 140, 181, 197, 198.

F

Federal Government: 4, 23, 92.
Federal Manpower Development and Training Act: 164.
Federal Technical School: 167.
Federal University of Rio Grande Do Sul: 168.
Fee: 25, 32, 52, 92, 93.
Field Service: 114.
Fire Service: 4.
Fisher, Leslie: 185.
Fitzgerald, J. Conner: 79, 80, 100, 128, 140, 141.
Five Civilized Tribes: 4.
Flight Service: 175, 176, 177.
Florida: 64, 99, 174.
Floyd, Henry W.: 123.
Flying Aggies: 176.
Ford Foundation: 129, 164, 167, 170.
Ford, Marilyn: 162.
Foreman, Larry: 178.
Former Students Association: 45, 89. *See* Alumni Association.
Foster, Eli C.: 83, 112, 129.
Foundation: 4.
4-H Club: 115.
4-H Club and Student Activity Building. *See* Gallagher-Iba Arena.
4-H Club Round-up: 72.
Fourth Naval District: 109.
France: 35.
Freshman Orientation: 112.
Freshman Programs and Services: 94.
Fresno State College: 97.
Friske, Joyce: 184.
Fuller, Frank: 77, 83.
Fundacion Gran Mariscal de Ayacucho (GMA): 170.
Funk, Mary Wallace "Wally": 176.
Fuqua, Dale R.: 161, 196.
Future Teachers of America: 111, 112.

G

Gaines, Paul: 144.
Gallagher-Iba Arena: 4, 72.
Gamble, Rondal: 145.
Gardiner Hall. *See* Bartlett Center for the Studio Arts.
Gardiner, John: 171.
General Education Board Scholarship: 108.
Geology: 8, 57, 58.
George Peabody College for Teachers: 101, 102.
Germany: 69.
G.I. Bill: 91, 92, 93.
Ginn and Company: 72, 73.
Girod, Raymond: 64.
Gladden, Ricky: 177.
Gladstone, Roy: 129, 137.
Golden Anniversary: 117.
Gordon, Marc: 114.
Graduate College: 4, 63, 96, 119, 139, 178.
Graduate Education: 61, 62, 149, 150.
Graduate School. *See* Graduate College.
Graff, Pat: 192.
Grafman, Greg: 182.
Great Depression: 45, 53, 54, 56, 57, 58, 61, 67, 68, 72, 74, 84, 92, 96, 175.
Great Lakes: 159.
Great Society: 117.
Greece: 128.
Gregg, Russell T.: 124.
Gries, George: 159.
Griffiths, William J.: 137.
Griggs, O. C.: 48.
Gundersen, Carl: 61, 120, 121.
Gundersen Hall: 15, 37, 82, 86, 110, 120, 121, 146, 147, 166. *See also* Engineering Building, 1912.
Gundersen South. *See* Engineering Building, 1902.
Gustavus Adolphus College: 46.
Guthrie, Al: 175.
Gymnasium: 24, 46.

H

Hammond, Ruth: 126.
Hampel, Margaret: 97.
Handicapped: 163, 178.
Hanner Hall: 86, 126.
Hansen, Leasa: 192.
Hardy, William: 129.
Harnden, E. E.: 48.
Harper, Ford C.: 59.
Harriman, Arthur E.: 137, 138.
Harrington, H. E.: 53.
Harris, Fred: 146.
Hart, Susan L.: 192.

Hartung, Maurice: 126.
Harvard University: 178.
Haynes, John: 154.
Haynes, Vivian: 125.
Heartsill, Gary: 176.
Heath, Georgianne: 192.
Helton, Robert: 173.
Henderson, Seth W.: 144.
Hennigh, F. R.: 48.
Herring, Amanda: 125.
Hickam, A. R.: 72.
Higher Education: 58, 118, 171.
Hill, Cary L.: 117, 146.
Hill, Walter: 141.
Hillside Consolidated School: 79, 80.
Hindman, Bill D.: 192.
Hitler, Adolph: 86.
Hodge, Oliver: 128.
Hodges, William: 192.
Hoggard, Paul: 31, 32.
Holcomb, John E.: 55.
Holley, G. A.: 107.
Holley, J. Andrew: 107, 109, 111, 113, 114, 115, 116, 119, 120, 121, 122, 128, 129, 130, 133, 135, 137, 138, 139, 146, 156, 157, 163, 177, 186, 187, 193, 197.
Holley, J. T.: 107.
Holmes Group: 187, 189, 194.
Holt, Mabel Davis: 53, 55.
Holy Roman Empire: 136.
Home Economics: 8, 21, 24, 36, 51, 57, 58, 77, 119, 123, 129.
Homecoming: 112.
Homesteaders: 5.
Hong Kong: 129.
Honors and Awards Banquet: 113, 173, 174, 193.
Hoover, Bruce: 177.
Hornbostel, Victor O.: 164.
Horticulture: 8, 21.
House Bill 161: 93.
House Bill 1706: 186, 187.
House of Representatives: 6.
Houston, Mamie G.: 15.
Hoyt, Anne: 128.
Human Resource Development: 162.
Humanities: 71.
Hunt, DeWitt: 13.
Hunt, Margaret: 143.
Hunter, Ella E.: 10, 11.
Husby, Wendy: 182.
Hyde, Richard E.: 80.
Hyle, Adrienne E.: 184.

I

IBM Grading Machine: 95.
Illinois: 159.
Illinois Wesleyan University: 27.

Imperial College: 114.
Indian Education: 51, 178, 179.
Indian Education Office: 178.
Indian Territory: 4.
Indiana Institute of Technology: 159.
"Individual Analysis Blank": 51.
Indonesia: 171.
Industrial Arts: 8, 101, 146, 161.
Industrial Arts Building: 146, 147.
Industrial Arts Education: 117, 135.
Industrial Arts Education and Engineering
  Workshops: 146.
In-service: 77, 78, 93, 100, 115, 177, 194.
Institute for Education and Teacher
  Training: 171.
Institute for Post-graduate Studies: 170.
Integration: 123, 124.
Interim Session: 86.
Interstate 35: 86.
Iowa State College: 15.
Ireland, Joseph C.: 69.
Italy: 69.
Ivy League: 94.

J

Jack, Eula Oleta: 53.
Jackson, Ralph: 142.
Jackson, Velma: 142.
Jamaica: 171.
Java: 113.
Jaynes, William E.: 138, 160.
Jefferson Grade School: 52.
Jeffords, T. M.: 29, 30.
Jimma Agricultural Technical School: 114.
Jobe, John: 185.
Johnson, Lyndon: 117.
Johnson Space Center: 172, 173, 174.
Johnson, Wilbur "Deke": 170.
Johnson-O'Mally Program: 178.
Jones, H. I.: 51.
Jones, Jim: 192.
Jones, Larry D.: 170.
Jones, Vera: 82, 83, 89, 97.
Jordan: 166, 169, 170.
Jungers, Edna: 192.
Jungers, Richard: 134, 147, 149, 163,
  166, 191.

K

Kamm, Robert B.: 159, 160, 168, 169,
  170, 171, 175.
Kamm, Robert B. Fellowships in Higher
  Education Administration: 171.
Kansas: 51, 189.
Kansas State Normal School. See
  Pittsburg State University.

Kansas State University: 184, 195.
Kappa Delta: 102.
Kappa Delta Pi: 48, 49, 111, 112.
Karman, Thomas A.: 161, 169, 192, 196.
Kendall College: 29.
Kennedy, Edward: 184.
Kent State University: 144.
Kentucky: 29, 68, 109.
Kerr, Robert S.: 69.
Keystone Telebinocular: 75.
Kezer, Charles L.: 15, 46, 49, 72, 74, 80,
  83.
King, Kenneth L.: 186, 194, 195, 196.
Kinnamon, Lynn: 192.
Knapp, Bradford: 47, 50, 54.
Knight, Clyde B.: 151, 168, 170.
Korean Conflict: 173.

L

Lackey, Guy A.: 49, 53, 60, 70, 81, 82,
  83, 89, 96, 97, 129.
Lafevre, Bernard: 112.
LaGrange College: 121.
Laird, Marilyn: 112.
Lake Carl Blackwell: 177.
Land-grant Mission: 20.
Land, Imogene: 178.
Land Runs: 5.
Lane, David S.: 184.
Lane, I. P.: 7.
Langston University: 123, 190.
Lapsey, Tiner: 137, 176.
Larsen, Charles E.: 152.
Leveridge, Karen: 184.
Lewis, Frank: 86.
Lewis, L. L.: 20.
Library: 24, 46, 110, 112, 123, 127.
Library Annex. See Engineering Building,
  1902.
Library Committee: 154.
Library Education: 127, 135.
Library Science: 126, 182.
License: 186.
Life Certificate: 60.
Lindly, Edith Ricks: 97.
Lip Reading Course: 143.
Little, Evert T.: 112, 114.
Little, Wilson: 98, 99, 103, 133.
"Loans for the Improvement of Vocational
  Education" (LIVE): 168.
Lohmann, Idella: 161.
Long, Kathryn: 49, 51, 53, 71, 76, 83.
Loomis, Robert: 114.
Louisiana: 109, 122, 188, 189.
Low, Edmon: 126, 154.
Lowe, Florence Ellen Conger: 63, 83, 94,
  95.

M

Magruder, Alexander C.: 7.
Mainstreamed: 178.
Maneval, Joan: 111.
Mangum, Robert E.: 161, 163.
Mann, Horace: 14.
Marland Mansion: 193.
Maroney, Samuel A.: 40, 46.
Married Student Housing: 4.
Marsden, Virginia: 125, 129.
Marsden, Ware: 81, 125, 127, 140, 151, 155.
Martin, A. O.: 45, 62, 89.
Martin, Gertrude Diem: 13, 14.
Massachusetts: 14, 43, 184.
Master of Art (M.A.): 63.
Master of Science (M.S.): 62, 63.
Mathematics: 7, 8, 12, 60, 86, 120, 125, 173, 179, 185.
Max, Elizabeth: 128.
Mayberry, Tom: 137.
M.B.A. Program: 190, 191.
McAuliffe, Christa: 174.
McCarrel, Fred: 40, 46.
McDonald, Michael: 35.
McElroy, Arlene: 111.
McElroy, Clarence: 59.
McFarland, Frank: 163.
McIntosh, Daniel C.: 63, 96.
McIntyre, J. C.: 48.
McKay, M. B.: 48.
McKinley, Kenneth: 162, 163, 166, 169, 178, 185, 186, 196.
McLaurin, George Washington: 123, 124.
McNeeley, Simon: 122.
Media Center: 147.
Meritt, Mary: 192, 193.
Meteorology: 115, 135.
Michaels, Ruth: 37.
Michigan Agricultural College: 121.
Michigan State University: 171.
Midlands Consortium Star Schools Project: 184.
Miller, Dean: 111.
Miller, Elizabeth C.: 53.
Miller, Melvin D.: 162, 196.
Mills, Terence: 179.
Ministry of Youth and Community Development: 172.
Minorities: 177, 178.
Mississippi: 38, 107, 189.
Missouri: 10, 107, 189.
Missouri School Board Association: 184.
Missouri State Department of Education: 184.
Mobile Space-age Education Demonstration Program: 172.
Monroney, A. S. "Mike": 146.

Moore, Allen J.: 48.
Moran Jr., William: 114.
Morgan, Barbara: 174, 175.
Morgan, Clayton A.: 143, 144.
Morgan, Sherry: 192.
Morrill Hall: 20, 23, 24, 25, 37, 39, 45, 47, 50, 64, 72, 97, 98, 102, 109, 120.
Morrow, George E.: 23.
Mosier, Jerrilee: 192.
Mott, Gordon: 49.
Muerman, J. C.: 60, 78, 83, 113.
Multicultural Education: 162, 178.
Murdaugh, Edmond D.: 23.
Murphy, Lloyd: 123.
Murray Hall: 59, 86, 147.
Murray, William H. "Alfalfa Bill": 56, 57, 58.
Murry, Jim: 111.
Music: 58.
Myers, Donald: 161, 163.

N

National Academic Championship: 188.
National Aeronautics and Space Administration (NASA): 172, 174, 175, 182, 194.
National Association and Councils of Business Colleges of the United States and Canada: 130.
National Association of State Universities and Land-Grant Colleges: 141.
National Board for Certification: 194.
National Conference of Professors of Educational Administration: 124.
National Continuing Education Association: 184.
National Council for the Accreditation of Teacher Education (NCATE): 130, 139, 140, 162.
National Defense Education Act (NDEA): 124, 125.
National Education Association (NEA): 152.
National Education Association's Department of Rural Services: 122.
National Education Association's educational policies commission: 54.
National Institutes of Health: 159.
National Intercollegiate Flying Association: 176.
National Safety Council: 141.
National Science Foundation: 124, 179, 180.
Naval Reserves: 109.
Naziism: 86.
Neal, James C.: 7.
Nebraska: 51.
Nemecek, Glen: 176.

New Mexico: 79, 189.
New York: 121.
New York Medical Center: 121.
New York University: 144.
Newton, Edna: 48.
Nixon, Richard M.: 154.
Normal School: 14, 22, 32, 57.
North Central Association (NCA): 77, 109, 129, 130, 159, 160.
North Dakota: 161.
North Murray Hall: 86, 126, 147.
Northeastern Oklahoma Junior College: 55.
Northeastern Oklahoma State University: 56, 190.
Northeastern State Teachers College. *See* Northeastern Oklahoma State University.
Northern Michigan University: 161.
Northern Oklahoma College: 22.
Northup, Frank D.: 8.
Northwestern State Teachers College: 56.
Norway: 121.

O

Oakland Normal Institute: 107.
O'Donnell, Nancy: 184, 192, 193.
Office of Economic Opportunity: 165.
Office of Educational Extension: 148, 166.
Office of Education Research and Projects: 162, 166, 167, 181.
Office of Extension: 149.
Ohio: 68.
Ohio Wesleyan University: 27.
Oines, Ronald: 173.
Oklahoma Academy of Science: 53, 54.
Oklahoma Association for Colleges of Teacher Education (OACTE): 195.
Oklahoma Central Normal: 15.
Oklahoma City: 3, 6, 23, 24, 67, 69, 86, 98, 143, 189.
Oklahoma City Community College: 189.
Oklahoma City School System: 126, 143, 164, 191.
Oklahoma City University: 189.
Oklahoma Coalition for Public Education: 184.
Oklahoma Constitution: 19, 21, 58.
Oklahoma Curriculum Improvement Commission: 115.
Oklahoma Department of Public Safety: 141.
Oklahoma Education Association (OEA): 53, 152.
Oklahoma Employment Security Commission: 164.
Oklahoma Historical Society: 25.
Oklahoma Institute of Technology. *See* College of Engineering, Architecture and Technology.

Oklahoma Legislature: 9, 21, 32, 47, 56, 93, 152, 186, 187.
Oklahoma Service for the Blind: 142.
Oklahoma State Board of Agriculture: 7, 21, 55, 57, 121.
Oklahoma State Chamber of Commerce: 59.
Oklahoma State Department of Education: 184.
Oklahoma State Regents for Higher Education: 88, 93, 123, 145, 147, 149, 181, 184, 187, 189, 190, 191.
Oklahoma State School for Dependent or Orphan Children: 35.
Oklahoma State Tech Rehabilitation Center: 143.
Oklahoma State University Board of Regents: 123, 193, 195.
Oklahoma State University Technical Institute: 146, 167.
Oklahoma Territorial Capital: 5, 6, 7.
Oklahoma Territory: 5.
Old Central: 9, 10, 24, 25, 27, 45, 46, 98, 121, 126, 163.
Olympics: 86.
Oral Roberts University: 189.
Oregon: 15.
Organic Act: 5.
Organization of Petroleum Exporting Countries (OPEC): 189.
Orloski, Marjorie: 72.
Oscar Rose Junior College. *See* Rose State College.
Oschman, Hattie I.: 15.
Outreach: 20, 191.

P

Pakistan: 129.
Panhandle: 3, 5.
Parrack, Rebecca Ann: 193.
Party Pic: 102.
Pathology: 57.
Patterson, Herbert: 43, 44, 45, 46, 47, 48, 49, 51, 52, 53, 54, 55, 56, 58, 61, 63, 64, 69, 80, 91, 107, 123, 160, 163, 182, 186, 193.
Patterson, Reverend and Mrs. John Nelson: 43.
Patterson, Ruth: 49.
Payne County Misdemeanant Program: 141.
Payne, Karel: 193.
Payne, Margaret: 171.
Pearl Harbor: 84.
Peck's: 88.
Pedagogy: 27, 32, 34.
Penitentiary: 5.
Pennsylvania: 43.

Pennsylvania State University: 178.
People's Party Alliance (Populists): 6, 7.
Pepsodent Company: 73.
Perkins, L. N.: 82.
Perry, Katye: 183, 184.
Perry School System: 193.
Phelan, W. V.: 113.
Phi Beta Kappa: 43.
Phi Delta Kappa: 124.
Phi Kappa Phi: 53.
Philippines: 113.
Philips, James: 138.
Phillips, Don: 161, 163.
Philosophy: 7, 8, 60, 70, 71, 98, 100, 135.
Photography: 100, 101, 102, 115, 135.
Physical Education and Athletic Programs: 122.
Physical Plant: 4.
Physical Sciences Building: 147.
Physically and Acoustically Handicapped: 97, 145.
Physics: 86.
Piedmont College: 64.
Pittsburg State University: 40, 161.
Placement Bureau: 4, 44, 45, 89, 93, 157.
Plains Indian tribes: 4.
Pogue, William R.: 173.
Point Four: 113.
Polk, Harold: 161.
Posey, H. Vance: 91.
Post Graduate Committee: 61.
Poultry Building: 147.
Power Plant: 24.
Powers, Linda: 193.
Practice Teaching: 15, 46, 52, 60, 140.
Pre-law Education: 57, 58.
Pre-medical Education: 57, 58.
Preparation of Teachers: 26, 32, 135, 139.
Preparatory Department. See Preparatory School.
Preparatory School: 7, 10, 11, 12, 13, 14, 15, 16, 28, 40, 46, 49, 50, 51, 74, 80, 197.
"Preparing Teachers to Serve Mildly Handicapped Students in Rural School Districts: A Unified Regular-Special Education Pre-Service Curriculum": 180.
Pre-pharmacy: 58.
Pre-service Instruction: 93, 114, 179, 181.
Primary Room: 32.
Professional Development: 186.
Professional Service: 100.
Professional Standard Boards: 195.
Professional Subjects: 32.
Professor of Agriculture for Schools: 30.
Professor of Pedagogy: 25, 26, 27.
Pruett, Haskell: 83, 101.

Pruitt, Clarence M.: 83.
Psychological Corporation: 98.
Psychological Testing: 152.
Psychology: 60, 70, 71, 98, 100, 115, 135.
Public Broadcasting System: 174.
Public Information Building: 147.
Public Law 94-142: 145, 178.
Public Schools: 16, 21, 22.

Q

Qualifying Examination: 119.
Queal, Beverly: 49.

R

Raburn, Randall: 193.
Ramsey, W. B.: 129.
Randels, Mildren: 56.
Ray, Darrel: 145, 178, 179.
RCA: 171.
Reading: 115, 141.
Reading Clinic: 120.
Reading Resource Center: 145.
Reagan, Ronald: 174, 184.
Record Book: 117.
Reed, Joe: 146.
Reed, Solomon L.: 46, 49, 53, 63, 70, 71, 81, 96.
Regional Institutions' Graduate Programs: 150.
Registrar and Director of Admissions: 64.
Rehabilitation Counseling: 143.
Rehabilitation Service Administration: 144, 145.
Religious Education: 60, 70, 71, 100, 101.
Republican Party: 5, 6, 7, 23.
Research: 100, 120, 138, 163, 197, 198.
Research Foundation: 138, 163, 164, 165, 166, 172, 173, 181.
Research Professor of Psychology: 138.
Reserve Officer Training Corps: 35, 85, 154.
Residence Halls: 152.
Rethard, Raegan: 179.
Reynolds, Jim: 95.
Reynolds Stadium. See Allie P. Reynolds Stadium.
Richardson, James: 117, 118.
Rigg, Melvin C.: 82, 83.
Roaring Twenties: 43, 53.
Roberts, C. H.: 48.
Robinson, Donald W.: 138, 159, 160, 163, 166, 170, 171, 172, 174, 178, 185, 186, 187, 189, 190, 193, 196, 198.
Rodgers, Becky: 192.
Roney, Maurice W.: 137, 146, 168.
Rose State College: 189.
Rouk, Hugh: 144.

Rouse, Roscoe: 154.
Route 33: 86.
Route 51: 86.
Rowley, George A.: 192, 193.
Rucker, Glenn: 176.
Rural Education: 33, 35, 36, 74.
Rural Schools: 60, 70.
Russia: 69.
Ruter, John W.: 56.

S

St. Clair, Kenneth: 134, 137, 169.
Saint Patrick's Day: 82.
Salary: 45, 52, 55, 59, 61, 93, 115, 116, 151, 186.
San Francisco State University: 144.
Sanborn, C. E.: 27.
Sapulpa Public Schools: 177.
Satellite: 183, 184, 185, 194.
Scandinavia: 128.
Scanell, Dale: 170.
Scherich, Millard: 129, 136.
Scholastic Aptitude Test: 111.
School administration: 96, 178.
School Dropouts: 164.
School Finance: 102.
School Health: 122.
School House Planning: 102.
School of Agriculture. See College of Agriculture.
"School of Athletes": 94.
School of Commerce. See College of Business Administration
School of Correspondence Study: 47, 77.
School of Domestic Science. See College of Home Economics
School of Education: 13, 14, 19, 20, 31, 34, 35, 36, 37, 38, 39, 40, 43, 44, 48, 49, 50, 51, 52, 54, 56, 58, 64, 67, 71, 84. See also College of Education.
School of Engineering. See College of Engineering, Architecture and Technology.
School of Home Economics. See College of Home Economics.
School of Industrial and Adult Education: 160.
School of Industrial Education: 146, 151, 161, 168.
School of Occupational and Adult Education (OAED): 135, 151, 161, 166, 167, 168, 177, 188.
School of Science and Literature. See College of Arts and Sciences.
School Surveys: 79, 163.
Schwartz, Myrtle: 112, 129.
Science Education: 7, 8, 11, 12, 57, 60, 124, 179.

Science Education Center: 147.
Science Teaching Center: 172.
Scofield, Robert: 137.
Scott, Angelo C.: 20, 23, 24.
Scott, Thomas: 37.
Scott, Walter: 137.
Scroggs, Schiller: 69, 118.
Secondary Education: 15, 32, 52, 60, 70, 71, 72, 179.
Secondary School. See Preparatory School.
Secretary of Education: 194.
Security Force: 4.
Segall, William: 188.
Segregation: 31, 124.
Selakovich, Daniel: 180.
Senior Career Day: 112.
September Experience: 128.
Seretean Center for the Performing Arts: 82, 156.
Shallenberger, G. D.: 48.
Shedrick, Bernice: 192, 193.
Shop Building: 24.
Short Course: 86.
Sigma Chi: 86.
Sigma Phi Epsilon: 102.
Simmons, Carol: 193.
Simonson, Joe: 114.
Sisney, Sherleen: 180.
Size of Faculty: 135.
Skinner, Linda: 193.
Sloan, Jimmy R.: 169.
Smith, Glenn: 146.
Smith, I. T.: 129.
Smith, Thomas J.: 191, 192, 193.
Smith-Hughes Act: 39.
Snell, Sue: 112.
Social Science: 60.
Sorenson, Helmer: 117, 118, 119, 129, 133, 134, 135, 136, 137, 138, 139, 146, 147, 150, 154, 155, 156, 157, 159, 160, 163, 169, 186, 193, 197.
South America: 95.
South Carolina: 38.
South Dakota: 43, 46.
South Oklahoma City Junior College: 189.
Southeastern Normal School: 68.
Southern Illinois University: 159.
Southern Regional Educational Board (SREB): 195.
Southern Regional Holmes Group Board: 195.
Southwest Center for Safety Education and Research: 141, 142.
Southwestern Oklahoma State University: 185, 195.
Soviet Union: 124.
Space Education: 177.

Space Science Education Project (SSEP): 172.
Spain: 128.
Spalburg, R. L.: 51.
Special Committee on Traffic Safety Research and Education: 141.
Special Education: 145, 163, 178, 180, 181.
Sputnik: 124, 172.
Staff Development: 185.
Stallard, Sandina: 193.
Standards for Admission: 116.
Standards for Certification: 61.
Stanford University: 121.
Star Schools: 184.
STAR Troops: 85.
Star Wars: 184.
State Attorney General: 32.
State Board of Education: 35.
State Board of Vocational Education: 164.
State Budget: 56.
State Certificate: 36.
State Department of Education: 21, 63, 84, 89, 102, 108, 109, 140, 187.
State Department of Vocational-Technical Education: 146, 172.
State High School Certificate: 60.
State Rural School Supervisor: 102.
State Superintendent of Public Instruction: 185, 194.
State System of Higher Education: 189.
State Teachers Colleges: 58.
Steed, Tom: 146.
Steele, George: 7.
Stephens, Grace: 111.
Stewart, L. F.: 30, 31.
Stillwater Chamber of Commerce: 113.
Stillwater Creek: 5.
Stillwater Gazette: 8.
Stillwater Public Schools: 13, 48, 80, 141, 179.
Stillwater Restaurant Association: 91.
Stillwater School Board: 52.
Stone, Walker: 121.
Stout, Julia: 59, 100.
Strategic Defense Initiative: 184.
"Streamline Schoolmarm": 82.
Stringfield, Anna: 83.
The Strip: 4.
Stroemel, Mary: 193.
Stromberg, Eleroy L.: 83, 95, 97, 103.
Stubbs, Gerald T.: 45, 77, 79, 98, 102, 134, 139, 140, 147, 148.
Student Assessment Programs: 183.
Student Council: 84.
Student-credit-hours: 138.
Student Employment Program: 55.
Student Organization Committee: 111.

Student Senate: 112.
Student Services Building: 147.
Student Teaching: 46, 80, 81, 115, 116, 128, 154.
Student Union: 28, 102, 109, 110, 112, 123.
Student Union Cafeteria: 150.
Sub-Collegiate Division. *See* Preparatory School
Sub-freshman Department. *See* Preparatory School.
Sue Bennett College: 68.
Sumatra: 171.
Summer Enrollments: 51.
Summer Institute: 30, 31, 124.
Summer Lecture Series: 31, 32.
Summer Normal Schools: 22, 31.
Summer Program: 35, 75, 123.
Summer Session: 28, 29, 37, 51, 52, 56, 58, 63, 74, 86, 88, 122, 124.
Sunday School: 71.
Superintendent of the United States Indian Field Service in the Midwest: 51.
Swan, Oliver J.: 96.
Swearingen, Eugene: 146.
Swim's: 49, 88.

T

Taft, William Howard: 113.
Tanner, Danny R.: 182, 193.
Tatchio, Orrin: 161, 177.
Tate, John: 117.
Taylor, Frank: 193.
Teacher Certificate Examination: 30.
Teacher Corps: 177.
Teacher Education: 14, 27, 48, 78, 99, 119, 129, 130, 139, 154, 155, 162, 167, 177, 178, 196.
Teacher in Space: 174, 175.
Teacher Placement: 56.
Teacher Preparation Programs: 155.
Teacher Shortage: 151.
Teachers' Correspondence Course in Agriculture: 19, 20.
Teachers' Institutions: 22, 30.
Teachers' Normal and Business Training: 24, 26.
Teachers' Normal Course: 153.
Teachers' Normal Division: 37.
Teachers of Exceptional Children: 145.
Teachers of the Year: 180, 184, 193.
Teaching Load: 58.
Technical Education: 135, 146, 161.
Technology Festival: 188.
Telecommunications: 183, 194.
Teleconference: 183, 184, 185.
Television: 54.
Tennessee: 53, 64.

Texaco: 188.
Texas: 72, 189, 195.
Texas Panhandle: 195.
Texas Tech University: 56.
Thailand: 168, 170.
Thatcher Hall: 13, 86.
Theta Pond: 28.
Thewes Vocational Teacher Training
School: 168.
Thomas, Della Farmer: 126, 127, 128,
137, 182.
Thompson, Harry E.: 10, 11, 12, 14.
Tiger Tavern: 55.
Tinnell, Richard W.: 168.
Title IV:, 178.
Tompkins, Rose Mary. *See* Rose Mary
Tompkins Duncan.
Tompkins, Roy R.: 69, 77, 140.
Trade and Industrial Arts Education: 146.
Trade and Industrial Education: 135, 146,
161, 168.
Trainable and the Educable Mentally
Handicapped: 145.
Training High School: 50.
Tran, Thu-Hue: 182.
Trendle, Ruth: 112.
Trinity Methodist Church: 50.
Troxel, Vernon: 177.
Tug-of-war: 28.
Tuition: 26, 92, 154.
Tulsa: 3, 29, 54, 81, 86, 87, 96, 154, 189,
190, 192.
Tulsa Classroom Teachers Association's
(TCTA): 154.
Tulsa Junior College: 189.
Tulsa Public Schools: 96, 184.
Tulsa State University: 190.
Tulsa Tribune: 154.
Turner, Dick: 114.
Tuttle, Francis C.: 169.
Twyman, J. Paschal: 128, 164.

U

Unassigned Lands: 5.
United Arab Republic: 129.
United Nations Educational, Scientific, and
Cultural Organization (UNESCO): 171.
United States Agency for International
Development (USAID): 168, 170, 172.
United States Air Force Academy: 173.
United States Air Force Thunderbirds:
173.
United States Bureau of Education: 102.
United States Congress: 20, 184.
United States Department of Education:
177, 178, 180, 194.
United States Department of State: 129.
United States Navy: 85, 86.

United States Office of Education: 122,
124, 145, 146, 159, 166.
United States Office of Special Education:
178.
United States Office of Vocational
Rehabilitation: 143.
United States Secretary of Education: 183.
United States Senate: 141.
United States Supreme Court: 124.
University Center at Tulsa (UCT): 3, 190,
191.
University Extension: 157.
University of Alabama at Birmingham:
184.
University of Arkansas: 102.
University of California at Berkeley: 63.
University of California at Los Angeles: 63,
178.
University of Chicago: 27, 126.
University of Chung Chou: 113.
University of Colorado: 108.
University of Florida: 125.
University of Illinois: 49, 193.
University of Kansas: 15, 161, 170, 184.
University of Louisville: 109.
University of Michigan: 97.
University of Minnesota: 94, 125, 178.
University of Mississippi: 184.
University of Missouri-St. Louis: 193.
University of Nebraska: 77.
University of Nebraska-Lincoln: 156.
University of Nebraska-Omaha: 161.
University of Northern Iowa: 133.
University of Ohio: 67.
University of Oklahoma: 22, 35, 56, 58,
101, 113, 123, 149, 150, 185, 189, 190,
195.
University of Southern California: 55.
University of Texas at Austin: 98.
University of Tulsa: 29, 125, 164, 189.
University of West Virginia: 27.
University of Wisconsin: 124.
University of Wisconsin-Madison: 133.
University Testing and Evaluation Service:
162. *See also* Bureau of Tests and
Measurements.
USDA Building: 147.
Utah: 183, 184.

V

Van Bebber, Jack: 56.
Vandegrift, James: 177.
Venezuela: 95, 170.
Vermilion, Jana: 193.
Vest, Neal I.: 169.
Veteran's Administration: 98.
Veteran's Village: 90, 91.

Vice President for Academic Affairs and
Research: 139, 162, 169.
Vice President for Development: 146.
Victory Halls: 85.
Vietnam War: 152.
Visual Education: 78, 101.
Vocational Building: 46.
Vocational Education: 39, 96, 151, 168.
Vocational Rehabilitation: 142, 143, 144.
Vocational Rehabilitation Clearinghouse:
144.
Vodicka, Edward: 125.

W

Walkup, Arlene: 176.
Walkup, Hoyt: 176, 177.
Wall Street: 54.
Wall Street Crash: 43.
Wallace, Morris: 102, 134.
Warner, Michael: 180.
Washington, DC: 4, 23, 35, 93, 102, 122,
124, 130, 159, 160, 162.
WAVES. See Women Appointed for
Voluntary Emergency Service.
Weekend Workshops: 181.
Weimer, Mary Ann: 111.
Welch, Martha Shirley: 82.
Wesleyan University: 43.
West Pakistan. See Pakistan.
Western Electric 4B Audiometer: 75.
Whitehurst Hall: 46, 47, 64, 72, 87.
Wiggins, Kenneth: 172, 173, 174, 175,
176, 177, 196.
Wiggins, Lloyd: 114, 163, 166, 169.
Wilbur, Philip: 121.
Wilkinson, John W.: 21, 27.
Willard Hall: 76, 86.
Willham, Oliver S.: 117, 129, 130, 135,
141, 147, 148, 175.
Williams, Benjamin Franklin: 24.

Williams, George: 111.
Williams Hall: 24, 82, 156.
Willow Pond: 28.
Wilson, C. E.: 48, 54.
Wilson, Jimmy V.: 169.
Wimberly, John: 7.
Wimer, Sue-Nell: 112.
Wisconsin: 133.
Witt, Henry V.: 56.
Women Appointed for Voluntary
Emergency Service: 85, 86, 87.
Women's Building. See Bartlett Center for
the Studio Arts.
World Bank: 162, 168, 169, 170, 194.
World War I: 13, 20, 35, 43, 46, 50, 51.
World War II: 35, 53, 54, 57, 64, 68, 71,
78, 80, 83, 84, 85, 88, 89, 91, 92, 96,
109, 115, 137, 175, 176.
Wrap Around Conference: 183.
Wright, W. N.: 48.

Y

Yale University: 43, 77, 94.
Yale University School Mathematics Study
Group: 125.
Yellin, David: 180.
Y-Hut: 142, 143.
Yost Lake: 82.
Young Men's Christian Association: 55,
101.
Young, Raymond: 112.
Young Women's Christian Association:
101.
Youngstown State University: 159, 166.
Yugoslavia: 128.

Z

Zant, James H.: 69.
Zenke, Larry: 184.
Zoology: 97, 119.

A History of the
Oklahoma State University
College of Education

is a specially designed volume of the Centennial Histories Series.

The text was composed on a personal computer, transmitted by telecommunications to the OSU mainframe computer, and typeset by a computerized typesetting system. Three typefaces were used in the composition. The text is composed in 10 point Melliza with 2 points extra leading added for legibility. Chapter headings are 24 point Omega. All supplemental information contained in the endnotes, charts, picture captions, appendices, bibliography, and index are set in either 8 or 9 point Triumvirate Lite.

The book is printed on a high-quality, coated paper to ensure faithful reproduction of historical photographs and documents. Smyth-sewn and bound with a durable coated nonwoven cover material, the cover has been screen-printed with flat black ink.

The Centennial Histories Committee expresses sincere appreciation to the progressive men and women of the past and present who created and recorded the dynamic, moving history of Oklahoma State University, the story of a land-grant university fulfilling its mission to teach, to research, and to extend itself to the community and the world.